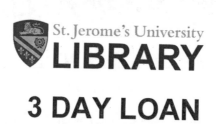

A DICTIONARY OF
ENGLISH MANUSCRIPT TERMINOLOGY
1450–2000

A DICTIONARY OF
ENGLISH
MANUSCRIPT
TERMINOLOGY

1450–2000

PETER BEAL

OXFORD

UNIVERSITY PRESS

OXFORD
UNIVERSITY PRESS

Great Clarendon Street, Oxford OX2 6DP

Oxford University Press is a department of the University of Oxford.
It furthers the University's objective of excellence in research, scholarship,
and education by publishing worldwide in

Oxford New York

Auckland Cape Town Dar es Salaam Hong Kong Karachi
Kuala Lumpur Madrid Melbourne Mexico City Nairobi
New Delhi Shanghai Taipei Toronto

With offices in

Argentina Austria Brazil Chile Czech Republic France Greece
Guatemala Hungary Italy Japan Poland Portugal Singapore
South Korea Switzerland Thailand Turkey Ukraine Vietnam

Oxford is a registered trade mark of Oxford University Press
in the UK and in certain other countries

Published in the United States
by Oxford University Press Inc., New York

© Peter Beal 2008

The moral rights of the author have been asserted
Database right Oxford University Press (maker)

First published 2008

British Library Cataloguing in Publication Data
Data available

Library of Congress Cataloging in Publication Data
Data available

Typeset by SPI Publisher Services, Pondicherry, India
Printed in Great Britain
on acid-free paper by
Biddles Litho

ISBN 978–0–19–926544–2

1 3 5 7 9 10 8 6 4 2

To Grace Ioppolo

Contents

Preface

This dictionary was originally inspired by John Carter's *ABC for Book Collectors* (first published in 1952). What he had done for books it seemed reasonable to do for manuscripts. Not, however, that the audience would be the same, for it is not necessarily collectors who handle manuscripts most. Almost everyone has been using, writing, annotating, or signing documents of one kind or another, whether letters, shopping lists, or tax forms, for most of their lives. Those with special interests in the field, who produce or handle them almost every day, range from writers and amateur genealogists to academics, archivists, historians, lawyers, postal workers, accountants, and, in effect, a host of others engaged in professions where documentation is their principal focus of attention. In the absence of a clear guide to such matters, it therefore seemed time to make a serious attempt to establish the language and vocabulary involved in the field of manuscripts and related subjects.

So what terms to include, what to exclude, and where to draw the line? In fact, as this dictionary evolved from an estimated 250 entries into 1,500 or more (counting 600 cross-references), and as brief definitions grew longer, and as the boundaries of John Carter's book were abandoned, it became clear that the main principle of selection operating here was my own interests and knowledge, which are now offered to the reader for what they are worth. The scope of this work is consequently as follows.

The date 1450 is taken as my starting point as approximating to the invention of moveable type which ushered in the age of printing. I therefore exclude most terms relating to medieval manuscripts, which is a specialist field I leave to medievalists, while nevertheless including terms for some common types of manuscript that survived longer than 1450. I also eschew discussion of the detailed features of different scripts flourishing before or after 1450, since this, too, is a subject in its own right, best left to palaeographers, who are able to describe and illustrate the features of these scripts elsewhere at much greater length and more expertly than I can. As for extending coverage to 2000,

I frankly admit to a special interest in the early modern period (16th–17th century), which the majority of the entries here makes perfectly obvious. Effectively I go up to the present, however, in so far as most earlier terms have continued to be used one way or another, or else remain of relevance to scholars and researchers in general, and in so far as they relate to writing matters and technologies in the pre-electronic era. In other words, I go as far as including 'typewriters', but (barring a few passing references) exclude the technical vocabulary generated by the age of computers (not excepting the ubiquitous 'hypertext'), which, too, is a subject in itself.

As for the term 'English' in my title, this is deliberately ambiguous. I deal with English terminology and also with terminology relating to English manuscripts or manuscripts in England and the English-speaking world. Nevertheless I take the liberty of very occasionally venturing overseas to non-English-speaking countries to mention other subjects that seem to me to be relevant in some respect, if only by way of contrast or comparison (such as 'amatl' in relation to paper, 'portolan' as a continental type of map, or the medieval 'pecia system' vis-à-vis English systems of scribal production).

So what terminology relates to manuscripts? I have attempted to encompass here a substantial number of types of document and related matters, including:

- manuscripts usually categorized by their physical form or by the nature of their contents or function they perform (codicil, glebe terrier, letters patent, psalter);
- physical materials associated with manuscripts (paper, ink, vellum);
- other physical features, such as size, textual layout, decoration, and seals (duodecimo, cross-hatching, historiated, Great Seal);
- condition of manuscripts (cockling, damp-staining, oxidation);
- writing instruments and appurtenances (pen, pencil, inkwell, penknife);
- writing surfaces (bureau, desk, writing box);
- manuscript containers (cabinet, dispatch box, solander box);
- writers and other functionaries responsible for document production (notary, scribe, scrivener);
- notable custodians and repositories of manuscripts (Master of the Rolls, British Library, Public Record Office);
- scripts and handwriting (secretary, italic, calligraphy);
- lettering and palaeographical features (ascender, duct, flourish);
- postal features (address, Bishop mark, gallows letter);
- editing or printing of manuscripts (collation, eclectic, emendation, lemma);

- other miscellaneous terms used in descriptions of manuscripts relating to such subjects as:

  –academic (matriculation register, supplicat);

  –accountancy and finance (cheque, invoice, ledger, waste book);

  –authorship (anonymous, ascription, *ignoto*);

  –cartography (portolan, rhumb-line, wind-rose);

  –dating (*circa*, contemporary, Old style, New style);

  –drama and literature (foul papers, promptbook, miscellany);

  –ecclesiastical (bull, missal, dimissorials);

  –ephemera (postcard, scrapbook, scripophily);

  –heraldry (coat of arms, emblazon, trick);

  –law (barrister, bond, courts of law, indenture);

  –maritime (log, order of battle, scrimshaw);

  –military (commission, return);

  –Public Records and State Papers (Close Rolls, Patent Rolls);

  –and other occasional subjects.

I have, on the other hand, excluded most of the many literary genres occasionally represented in manuscripts (acrostic, ballad, *carmen figuratum*, epigram), as well as the technical vocabulary of professional archivists (e.g. de-accession, declassification, disposition, screening), of which there are various currently available glossaries. As for the subject of bibliography, I inevitably overlap with Carter on various occasions (binding, colophon, hinges, title-page), but exclude his terminology that relates purely to printed books.

Clearly the types of manuscript included here could be extended by the hundred—as far as all those encompassed by the Dewey library classification system—if all are defined by their contents and subject matter (ranging from anatomy and erotica to witchcraft and zoology). By contrast, I have confined myself to just a few manuscripts defined by interesting subject (alchemical, Hermetic, Masonic, navigational, etc.) which tend to crop up from time to time in my own experience.

While no doubt arguments about what should or should not be included here could be extended indefinitely, and some of my definitions mulled over as well, I hope that a wide range of readers will find my selection and treatment useful and informative. I can, of course, explain only what I know, not what I do not know (such as when and where many of the terms originated). In this context, Ludwig Wittgenstein's famous observation comes to mind: 'The limits of my language mean the limits of my world.' In the interests of clarity and readability, I have also decided not to clutter up the text with innumerable footnotes and source references.

I hope, above all, that this dictionary will stimulate more general interest in a field of human activity that those closely engaged in its study find endlessly fascinating.

Illustrations

In an ideal world, every term in this dictionary would be illustrated. As it is, I am enormously indebted for the large number of illustrations included here to Sotheby's, London (which retains copyright in all its own photographs of items sold there at auction). All the illustrations are supplied and reproduced by kind permission of Sotheby's except for Illus. 61 ('plot'), which is reproduced by kind permission of the Governors of Dulwich College. In addition, the painting shown on the dust-jacket and frontispiece is reproduced by kind permission of the Royal Museum of Fine Arts, Brussels.

It is true that many of the common, but relatively humdrum types of document represented in the dictionary are not shown. The illustrations here tend to highlight royal, famous, or dramatic subjects more than what a fair representation of the field in general would permit (more people in history have dealt with conveyances than have received Royal Letters Patent). Nevertheless, it is hoped that the selection of illustrations will be thought justified by their intrinsic interest and by the number of terms that they do exemplify. Because the manuscripts illustrated are now so widely dispersed, their present locations cannot generally be cited.

Acknowledgements

Although I cannot possibly do justice to all the people who have made useful comments and suggestions relating to this dictionary over recent years, I owe special thanks to the following for their patience in reading substantial parts of this work in draft, and occasionally for saving me from egregious errors (those that remain are, of course, my own): Sir John Baker, Susan Cerasano, A. I. Doyle, Ralph Hanna, Grace Ioppolo, Elisabeth Leedham-Green, Harold Love, Steven May, Alan Nelson, and Henry Woudhuysen. For their helpful comments on particular definitions in their fields, I am also much obliged to Simon Adams, Sydney Anglo, Nicholas Bell, James Binns, David Cooper, Christopher de Hamel, Tony Edwards, Stephen Humphrey, Randall McLeod, Tessa Milne, Nigel Ramsay, Pamela Robinson, Rod Suddaby, Brian Vickers, and Heather Wolfe. If I have omitted to mention the names of others who have said something to me about terminology at one time or another, I crave their magnanimous forgiveness.

Peter Beal
May 2007

List of Illustrations

Dust-jacket and endpapers: Pieter Brueghel the Younger's *De Boerenadvocaat* ('The Country Lawyer') showing a provincial lawyer's office in the Netherlands *c*.1620 (Royal Museum of Fine Arts, Brussels).

The dust-jacket and endpapers reproduce a painting by Pieter Brueghel the Younger, De Boerenadvocaat *('The Country Lawyer'), now in the Royal Museum of Fine Arts in Brussels. It shows a provincial lawyer's office in the Netherlands c.1620, apparently run by two people: the hard-pressed, but self-assured country lawyer behind the desk on the right, quill behind his ear, and his industrious clerk behind a desk to the left next to the entrance, writing with a quill on a tablet, his inkwell before him as well as a bowl of sand or pounce. The lawyer is seated at a desk with a bowl of sand, an hourglass, and an open bag of coins before him, a printed calendar or almanac on the wall behind him. He is being importuned by a queue of nine, generally apprehensive-looking rustic clients, some of them holding or reaching for goods (eggs or mushrooms, poultry, grapes) with which to pay him in lieu of money.*

Bundles of manuscripts, generally tied up with cords or thongs, some of the documents detached or torn to pieces, are everywhere. They are piled up on shelves and on the counters; they are hanging in cloth or canvas pouches, bearing attached labels, from pegs or rows of pegs on the walls; and they are strewn about chaotically on the floor. Some tightly folded separate documents are filed by being stuck behind belts or straps on the open window shutter near the lawyer, behind wooden canes running along the wall beneath the window, between the wooden slats in the open shutter above the clerk, behind belts across the window to his side, and also between curious bamboo-like sticks sprouting hair against the wall behind him. A few open documents are even used as windows (as was also common in printing shops).

A

ABBREVIATION

An extremely common feature in medieval manuscripts, and to a lesser, but still significant, extent in early modern writing, an abbreviation (the word derived from the Latin *abbreviatio*) occurs when a word is written in shortened, or contracted, form, to save the labour of writing it in full. This was generally done by scribes in accordance with conventional or recognized usage of the period, depending on the script used (Gothic, for instance, was marked by the use of more abbreviations than Carolingian minuscule). By the sixteenth century, however, the use of abbreviations was somewhat freer than the fairly rigid and exact system of superscript signs denoting specific letters or groups of letters, especially in Latin texts, that had prevailed earlier. Many abbreviations that had become obsolete in normal writing by the end of the seventeenth century (and cannot be properly rendered in printing or digital fonts today) were, nevertheless, still used for some decades by law clerks for certain kinds of formal documents.

Words could be abbreviated by scribes in different ways. One way, examples of which are still in use today, was simply to omit some of the letters in a word: e.g. 'la' for 'lady', 'sd' for 'said', 'svice' for 'service', 'appurtennes' for 'appurtenances', 'dd' for 'delivered'. The plural was sometimes indicated by the doubling of a consonant: thus 'Lopp' for 'Lordships', 'Wopp' for 'Worships', as well as the still used 'pp.' for 'pages' and 'ff.' for 'folios' (i.e. leaves). One or more of the remaining letters might be written in superscript to signal that the word was a contraction: e.g. 'M^r' for 'Master' or 'Mister', 'S^r' for 'Sir', 'S^t' for 'Saint', 'Matie' for 'Majestie', 'l^p' for 'lordship', 'p^{s}vation' for 'preservation', 'w^h' for 'which', and 'wth' for 'with'. The superscript *r* is especially common: e.g. 'eu^{r}y' for 'every', 'o^r' for 'our', and 'p^{r}sent' for 'present'. Other superscript letters include *t*, such as in 'iudgm^t' for 'judgment', and *c* to expand the ampersand in '&^{c}' denoting 'etc.' (*et cetera*). The abbreviations for currency, often rendered in superscript, are also common: i.e. £ or *li* (= Latin *libri*) for pounds, *s* (= Latin *solidi*) for shillings and *d* (=Latin *denarii*) for pence (*see* Illus. 2, 25, and 26). An abbreviation whereby a word is represented by the first letter or two, followed by a full stop or other punctuation (e.g. 'lo.' for 'lord') is technically a 'suspension'. An abbreviation comprising the first and last letters of a word, with the intervening letters omitted (e.g. 'lp' for lordship) is technically a 'contraction'.

Another method of denoting a contraction was to write a macron or tilde over certain letters or groups of letters: such as, 'attēd' for 'attend', 'cō' for 'come', 'comission' for 'commission', 'thē' for 'them' 'vpō' for 'upon', 'observa-cōns' for 'observacions', and 'lrēs' (from the Latin abbreviation *lra* for *litteræ*) for 'lettres' (letters), although in hurried writing the macron in such words might well be omitted (*see* Illus. 1 for a prolific use of macrons). Yet another method was to modify the forms of certain letters so that they became symbols representing different lettering: for instance, the down-turned and extended terminal *e* (℮), meaning *es* (as in 'faceͺ' for 'faces'), or the *p* with various forms of transected or looped descender meaning respectively 'par', 'per', 'pre', 'prae', or 'pro' (as in words such as 'pliament' for 'parliament', 'pish' for 'parish', 'psons' for 'persons', and 'pclamation' for 'proclamation'). What by the sixteenth century looks like a *y* can also commonly represent *th*, being a degenerated form of the Old English thorn, þ. Thus 'yᵉ' denotes 'the', 'yᵐ' 'them', and 'yᵗ' 'that', while 'yʳ', which could mean 'your' (more commonly written as 'yoʳ'), might also be construed as 'their' if the *y* represented the thorn. It is no less common to find the use of a flourish to denote merely the fact that a contraction of some sort has taken place: for example, the letters *ll* were often transected by a swung dash, but when in the name 'Will' (making the word look like 'Witt') it would denote the whole name, 'William' (as in the signature of the dramatist William Congreve, for instance).

In modern transcriptions of text containing such abbreviations, different conventions may be used. The options include producing a completely

ILLUS. 1. *An autograph letter signed by Lord Burghley, to the Earl of Essex, 21 May 1597, in Burghley's characteristic cursive italic hand, with a proliferation of abbreviations chiefly marked by the use of macrons and superscript letters. The first few lines (with expansions of abbreviations shown here in brackets) read:*

My Lord I am lame in my bed and yet occupied wᵗ [with] mañy other matters and specially, wᵗ the sondry gredy offers of sōdry Mʳch. [Merchants] to be dealors for appellyḡ [apparelling] of yʳ sold. [soldiers] in yᵉ low Coñtr. [Countries] wherof I wish yʳ [your] appell [apparell] for yᵐ yᵗ [them that] shall cōe frō [come from] yᵉ low coñtryes might be here made redy to be delyvered at ther arryuall, but wᶜ [which] of these Gredy Mʳch: shall do it I know not as yet. . . .

13

My Lord I am lame in my bed, and yet occupied
wth maine other matters, and specially wth the
soudyne greedy offers of sundry Mrch. to be dealers
for appellyng of oz salt in ye low Cuntr. wherof
I wish yt appell for, yt yt shall coe for ye low
cuntreys might be heere made redy to be
delivered at their arryvall, bntw of these
greedy Mrch. shall lett it, I know not as yet

befor your frankd ca wth your lve, Js walt ralegh
had my bill for 3000/.
and if I shall yeld now the half of a oth 3000
wch is 1500/ I rest by my warrat fare
comanded pay it to Js walt: and to no other
as peell of ye xxvij 20

for wt purpose Js walt raleyh is to gyve las
bill wth a declaratio of ye expeditor
I can not for sayne wryt any more, but I
wish you ye fortunated of your noble desyres
one difficile pulchru 21. May
                              Yours L at om
                                  W Bingley

diplomatic transcription in which the abbreviations are reproduced exactly as they appear in the original; or producing an edited transcription in which all abbreviations are silently expanded in full (thus 'pliam^{t'}' is simply rendered as 'parliament'); or, alternatively, expanding abbreviations, but signalling that this has been done by enclosing the expansions in square or angle brackets (thus 'p[ar]liam[en]t' or 'p<ar>liam<en>t') or else printing them in italic ('*parliament*'). The mode adopted will depend on the function and intended readership of the transcription and on what is considered to be the least awkward in the circumstances.

ABECEDARIUM

Derived from 'ABC', the term 'abecedarium' (plural: abecedaria), sometimes italicized as *abecedarium* or rendered as 'abecedary', means a tablet or book containing the alphabet. Before the invention of printing, manuscript abecedaria were primers used for teaching children the alphabet and elementary rules of spelling and grammar. Their use became more widespread when printed versions appeared. The term could also be used figuratively for certain kinds of discourse, such as Sir Francis Bacon's philosophical treatise *Abecedarium novum naturae*, in which a subject was, as it were, surveyed from A to Z.

ABRIDGEMENT

An abridgement is a shortened or condensed version of a text. Abridgements were made in manuscript and later in printed form for various reasons, but chiefly in order to make a lengthy work more readable or have fresh currency by cutting out tedious or no longer relevant passages. Examples of early modern manuscript abridgements include at least two known condensed versions of Sir Walter Ralegh's ambitious *History of the World* (1614).

In a legal context, since the fifteenth century, an abridgement was a fairly comprehensive summary of a case, statute, proposition of law, or notable pleading, generally extrapolated from Year Books. Series of such abridgements were usually arranged for future reference in systematic and alphabetically arranged compendia rather like commonplace books. These compendia began to be printed from *c.*1490 onwards, after which the production of manuscript versions declined rapidly.

ABSTRACT

An abstract is a brief summary, epitome, or precis of a work, text, or document. Abstracts are often found, for instance, among legal papers— such as an abstract of title, in which is listed in chronological order all the documentary evidence for a person's entitlement to, or rights to possession of, particular property. State papers also contain abstracts, in which complicated administrative or political issues, procedures, or discourses are summarized for easier assimilating and understanding. These are usually produced by secretaries for the use of their superiors.

ACCENT

Accents in writing are marks (technically diacritical marks) qualifying certain letters to indicate particular meanings, sound values, or stresses on particular syllables. They are more common in continental languages such as French, Italian, Spanish, or German than in English: e.g., those in such words as *été* (acute accents), *aperçu* (cedilla), *être* (circumflex), *omertà* (grave accent), *mañana* (tilde), and *über* (umlaut). In early modern continental manuscripts the accents on letters are often omitted; in English manuscripts, especially when scribes are dealing with unfamiliar foreign words, they are almost invariably omitted.

ACCIDENTALS

See INCIDENTALS.

ACCORD

See TREATY.

ACCOUNTS

Accounts are financial documents detailing expenditure and income, often drawn up systematically in columns, with appropriate calculations. An account book is a book or ledger in which such accounts, or details of other financial dealings, are entered. It may be the product of an individual keeping a private account of personal income and expenditure (*see* Illus. 2); or of a professional involved in money transactions, such as a merchant, banker, scrivener, or one of their clerks; or of an auditor, in government, legal, ecclesiastical, or other administrative or business circles (*see* Illus. 58); or else of a steward for a great household or estate. Numerous manuscripts of this kind, from medieval times onwards, survive in both public and family archives in local estate and record offices.

Among the various types of accounts commonly encountered are bailiffs' accounts (of a manorial lord's manager), bridgewardens' accounts (of rents collected for the upkeep of bridges), receivers' accounts (of an officer of the court appointed to look after property), Treasury accounts (of government revenue and expenditure), and scriveners' and moneylenders' accounts

the mony wch I recieued of y^r Lo: att wittsontid
& 16 10 more wch I recckned nott for
before

Imprimis sentt my neeces barett of a token 2 ——————— 2 - 6
Item payed hubertt for bringeinge downe my hatt — 12
Item for wiare to make dressinges 2 —————————— 12
Item for 3 quiaer of papar 2 ——————————————— 12
Item for on wax candle 2 ———————————————— 6
Item for a coller 2 —————————————————————— 16
Item payed hubertt for caringe a payer of bodis to
for M^ris docter Ashworth 2 ———————————————— 6
Item for ter: sentt to London by the past att maydston 6
Item for on thousan of pines 2 ——————————— 18
Item for carnation taffaty 2 ————————————— 3 - 3
Item giuen to S^r francis fanes cocheman 2 —— 12
Item giuen to a poore woman 2 ——————————— 6
Item for on o_ of threed 2 ——————————————— 1 - 8
Item Last att playe in all, of this mony 2 ——— 3 0 4

                        Some is 19 = 11
the 10 wch I recieued of my brother Richard from y Lo: ^x 10
Imprimis for 12 yarces of whitt callycoe att 6 the yard
  to make my gowne 2 ——————————————————— 3 - 6
Item for on elle of sersnett to Line y bodis & sleeues
of itt 2 ———————————————————————————— 6
Item for 2 dozen sillke buttons 2 ———————— 11 - 6
Item for gallowne Lacis to Lacis y semes of itt 2 — 3 - 6
Item for wallbon 2 ———————————————————— 8
Item for stiffe canuis 2 ———————————————— 4

(including records of notable seventeenth-century figures such as Robert Abbot and Sir Robert Clayton). Other surviving accounts include those, sometimes drawn up on rolls, for medieval monastic almoners or sacristans; for mercantile adventures (such as Sir Thomas Myddelton's recording in 1593 expenditure of £16,708 and receipts of £17,275 for a voyage by Sir Walter Ralegh); for business enterprises (such as Philip Henslowe's so-called 'Diary' recording his financial dealings with playwrights and acting companies in 1593–1609); and for a variety of lucrative political offices (such as the 1617–20 account books of the Commissioner for the Licensing of Inns, Sir Giles Mompesson, who would be prosecuted in 1621 for his abuse of his monopoly). For some other types of accounts, *see* CHURCHWARDENS' ACCOUNTS, ESTABLISHMENT BOOK, HOUSEHOLD ACCOUNTS, ORDNANCE BOOK, RENTALS, and ROYAL HOUSEHOLD ACCOUNTS.

In legal parlance, from the early seventeenth century onwards, an account could also be a writ or action against a person such as a bailiff or receiver who refused to render a proper record of monies for which he was responsible.

Many formal and official accounts in the early modern period, such as Chancery and Exchequer accounts, retained the use of Roman rather than Arabic numerology. Thus, as is seen for instance in Illus. 25 and 26, sums are reckoned in terms of M ($= 1,000$), D ($= 500$), C ($= 100$), l ($= 50$), X ($= 10$), v ($= 5$), and i or (if in the final position) j ($= 1$), with combinations such as v^c ($= 5 \times 100 = 500$) and vi.C ($= 6 \times 100 = 600$), as well as occasional forms such as iv^{xx} ($= 4 \times 20 = 80$) or m ~/xiij ($= 13,000$).

ACHIEVEMENT

In heraldry, an achievement is a pictorial representation of a family's complete insignia or armorial devices, including their coat of arms, crest, and motto, together with supporters (for nobility) or other related features. Such representations may appear in various kinds of heraldic manuscripts and sometimes as frontispieces to grand or ostentatious volumes presented to, or commissioned by, particular noblemen.

ACQUITTANCE

An acquittance is a document normally written to acknowledge that records have been audited and found to be in order. If an individual or institution

ILLUS. 2 *A page in the account book of Margaret Spencer (1597–1613), written in a roman hand with semi-phonetic spelling, her* rs *bearing foot-serifs, showing her expenditure in shillings (s) and pence (d) on miscellaneous items in the early 1610s by the teenaged and short-lived daughter of the first Baron Spencer.*

gave an agent a sum of money, at the end of an accounting year he would be expected to produce a record of money he had disbursed and to return any money not disbursed. An acquittance formally testified to the correctness of the accounts and released the agent from any fiduciary obligation.

ACTA CURIÆ

Acta Curiæ (the Latin meaning 'acts of court'), sometimes known as Registers of the Chancellor's (or Vice-Chancellor's) Court, are records of the proceedings in ecclesiastical courts, and in quasi-ecclesiastical courts, notably those in the universities. These courts were often used by townspeople, classified as college servants, to settle disputes over debts and the like. The records often survive both in rough drafts, partly made out in advance and indicating the cases which the court expected to hear, and in fair copies, recording the actual business. Those at the University of Cambridge, for the Vice-Chancellor's Court, date from 1549 to 1883.

ADDRESS

An address may be a formal speech delivered to an audience (the Gettysburg Address of Abraham Lincoln on 19 November 1863, for instance). It is also, most commonly, an inscription on the verso of a letter, or on its outer wrapper, or, since the eighteenth century, on an envelope (*see* Illus. 24), giving information as to the person to whom, and place where, it should be delivered. In the early modern period, addresses were written on the outer (otherwise blank) leaf of the letter, most commonly the fourth page of a bifolium, before folding and sealing in the form of a small oblong packet so that the address was left exposed. This exposed segment may be called the 'address panel'. If the address is written on a blank leaf (when both the third and fourth pages of a bifolium are left otherwise blank), it may be referred to as an 'address' leaf (*see* Illus. 3). If the letter is enclosed in a separate sheet bearing the address, this is an 'address wrapper'.

The wording of the address in the early modern period would depend upon the circumstances of delivery. Thus a name only might be sufficient if it were delivered personally by a servant of the writer, with perhaps the addition of the name of the town or village if delivered by some other courier. More details of house and location, including sometimes the collection agent, such

ILLUS. 3 *The address leaf of a letter by Queen Elizabeth to the commander of her army in the Netherlands, Lord Willoughby De Eresby, 30 March 1588, with address panel in a scribe's secretary hand, a papered Signet Seal, dispatch slits, and endorsements in two other contemporary hands made after receipt.*

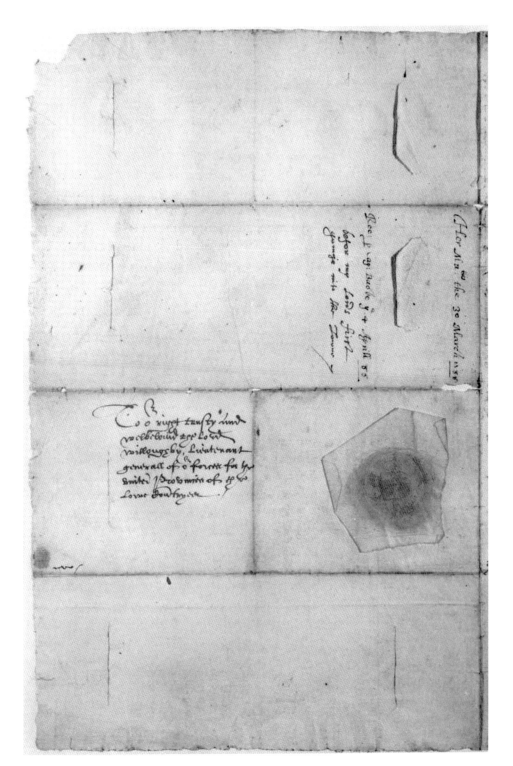

Her Ma:ᵗⁱᵉ the 30 March 1589

Recᵈ p̃ ag: Burle y 4 Aprill 89
before my Lords First
George wᵗʰ the Lᵉ̃ Tⁿⁿⁿ

R
To o right trusty and
welbeloued the Lord
willoughby, Liuetenant
generall of o forces for the
United Prouinces of the
Lowe Countryes

9

as an inn or scrivener's shop, would be added if necessary: e.g. 'To Mr Morris at the Flyeinge horse neare the Old Exchainge London'. The wording would often incorporate elements of a salutation, with formal respect shown for the addressee's titles or social status: e.g. 'ffor [i.e. For] the right Worshipfull Sr Robert Clayton at his house in Old Jury these present'. If sent through the official postal service, the address would also bear postal marks.

ADDRESSEE

An addressee is the person to whom a letter is addressed. Addressees or recipients of letters have often contributed to their history by docketing or endorsing them, recording, perhaps, who the writer was, or when the letter was received, or even what the letter is about. Such docketing was usually made for filing purposes, so that folded letters stored in bundles, for instance, could readily be identified without having to reopen and reread each one.

ADMINISTRATION

See LETTERS OF ADMINISTRATION.

ADVERSARIA

Adversaria, or in its Latinized form *adversaria*, is a term applied to a merchant's waste book and hence to any kind of memorandum book or notebook, large or small, in which unassimilated matter is recorded or roughly entered just as occasion arises, without any conscious or formal arrangement.

The term, meaning in Latin 'writings turned towards one', was originally applied to Roman writings in which the text was written on one side of a diptych (a two-leaved hinged tablet) with notes facing on the opposite side. Thence it was extended, particularly by humanist scholars, to mean also a collection of textual notes or commentaries.

ADVOWSON

An advowson is the patronage of an ecclesiastical office, or of a religious house, and consequent right of presentation to a benefice or living. The term is therefore used to denote a document making or recording the investment or exercising of this privilege.

AEROGRAMME

An aerogramme is a type of lightweight printed stationery manufactured specifically for use as a letter sent by air. Aerogrammes are also sometimes known as 'air letter sheets', the first of which were issued in 1923. A type of stationery used in Thailand in 1932 was called 'Air-o-Gram', after which different types of aerogramme, some incorporating a postage stamp, were developed throughout the world.

AFFIDAVIT

An affidavit (the Latin meaning 'he has pledged his faith' or 'he has stated on oath') is a legally binding written statement or official deposition, usually signed by the deponent, the truth of which is affirmed on oath before an appropriate authority such as a public notary. It may be used as evidence in court as a substitute for personal oral testimony.

ALBUM

In Roman times, an album (the Latin word means 'white') was a white tablet on which the public notices of a praetor (magistrate) were recorded. The term came to mean a book of originally blank leaves in which miscellaneous materials are entered, or intended to be entered, whether by direct application on the pages, such as signatures, inscriptions, or drawings, or else by the insertion or affixing of separate pieces of paper or card, such as letters, photographs, postage stamps, visiting cards, or other paper souvenirs (*see* AUTOGRAPH ALBUM, SCRAPBOOK, and STAMP ALBUM). Although it is possible to find other kinds of blank books, they would not generally be called 'albums' if they were evidently intended for other uses, such as account books or commonplace books. Albums date from the sixteenth century. *See* LIBER AMICORUM.

ALCHEMICAL MANUSCRIPT

Alchemy is the pseudo-science relating to the transmutation of base metals into silver or gold and to the quest for the Philosopher's Stone, which supposedly enables such a process to take place. It is a pursuit that dates back to ancient Egypt and is linked to a complex of Hermetic and occult cosmological belief systems. Via the Greeks and Arabs, alchemical practice became rooted in Europe in the twelfth century. Although to some extent driven underground after its condemnation by Pope John XXII in 1317, it flourished as a controversial, but dynamic and widely accepted scientific pursuit and philosophy. It had great influence on intellectual thinking and investigation until well into the seventeenth century, before the scientific rationalism of Robert Boyle, Isaac Newton, and their contemporaries saw its virtual demise (although even Newton gave alchemy serious consideration).

ILLUS. 4 *Part of a pictorial alchemical scroll on vellum, 12½ feet (c.3.81 metres) long, produced in 1624 by one Leonard Smethley, representing symbolically the mysteries of the process of distillation for making gold or silver, being a copy of a scroll first produced in the 1470s by the Yorkshire alchemist George Ripley.*

Among other things, a result of this philosophy or pursuit was a large output of alchemical manuscripts from medieval times onwards. These take the form of treatises on the subject, often set out with diagrams and illustrations depicting the mysterious processes of distillation and transmutation (through the White Stone, Red Stone, and Elixir Vitae), as well as large, coloured, pictorial scrolls (upwards of 12 feet or 3.65 metres long), alchemical notebooks, compilations, and the like. These manuscripts are invariably written and illustrated with their own special coded terminology and rich, complex, and often ambiguous symbolism: thus a wingless dragon represents the male agent sulphur, a winged dragon is the female agent quicksilver, their union and the dragon's blood represent the magical mercurial water that dissolves metals, and so on (*see* Illus. 4 and 75). The very secrecy, deliberate obscurity, and aims of this cult, as well as the potential power that might result from their successful application, made such manuscripts highly desirable in their own time, as well as to collectors today (such as the novelist Umberto Eco), and it is not surprising that so many alchemical works were published by early printers to meet a ready market.

ALIENATION

See LICENCE OF ALIENATION.

ALLEGATION

See MARRIAGE ALLEGATION.

ALMANAC

Deriving from the Spanish-Arabic *al manakh* ('calendar'), the term 'almanac' means a type of calendar showing the days, weeks, and months of the year. It usually also contains information such as the recording of religious festivals and feast days, meteorological forecasts, expected seasonal activities for farmers to take note of, sets of prayers, tables of weights and measures, and, especially, astronomical phenomena and related astrological inferences and predictions, such as the influence on human events of particular planetary conjunctions, eclipses, etc. The use of almanacs in this wider sense, particularly with their astrological dimension, dates from about the thirteenth century, although cruder types of almanac, known as 'clog almanacs', in which days of the year were represented by notches cut in blocks of wood, date from much earlier. The latter type of almanac persisted until the seventeenth century, developing into carved wooden, brass, or horn sticks, bearing information about lunar cycles and church festivals, and were usually small enough to be carried in the pocket or hung up near fireplaces.

Manuscript almanacs, by contrast, could be very elaborate, being, for instance, volumes of vellum leaves, neatly written and decorated in different coloured inks, with tables and solar diagrams. The first printed almanac, produced by Gutenberg, dates from as early as 1448, the first English one, a translation imported from Flanders, appearing in 1493, after which period they became extremely popular throughout Europe. In the sixteenth and seventeenth centuries in England, especially during the political and religious controversies from about 1640 to 1700, almanacs produced by Richard Allestree, John Gadbury, William Lilly, Thomas Gallen, and others were probably the most widely produced and distributed type of printed book after the Bible.

They could take various forms, including large printed wall charts similar (but for the astrological features) to calendars, as well as sometimes illustrated bound volumes, but a common feature of the bound volumes was their incorporation of blank pages or spaces for owners' personal entries to be made by hand. Surviving examples of such almanacs annotated by early owners include those owned by John Evelyn, which inspired or supplemented the systematic writing of his massive diary for 1620–1706. Various printed almanacs also incorporated blank leaves specially treated or coated so that they could be used for making erasable notes, thus performing virtually the same function as table books, from which, indeed, they are sometimes indistinguishable.

AMANUENSIS

Strictly speaking, an amanuensis (plural: amanuenses) is a person who writes or copies text from someone's dictation. Nevertheless, the term is often used more loosely to denote simply a personal secretary or someone who copies text under supervision.

AMATL

Amatl is a type of writing material, quite distinct from the paper, parchment, or papyrus (made from papyrus plants) used in Europe, and is apparently peculiar to the region of Mexico as produced by the Mayans and Aztecs (or Mexica, as the latter were originally known). It comprises sheets made of crushed bark and leaves treated with lime paste. The great sixteenth-century Mesoamerican pictorial and Nahuatl codices, many in the form of screenfolds or long sheets folded accordion-style, are made of this material.

AMERCEMENT

In courts from the Middle Ages onwards, amercement, or amerciament, was a form of punishment for an offender who had placed himself at the mercy of the court. It consisted of an arbitrary fine: that is, one imposed at the discretion of the court or feudal lord, rather than a fixed fine, and was made usually in accordance with the offender's means to pay. Offenders so dealt with were amerced. Amercement could also on occasion be levied by superior courts on towns or counties. Hence, an amercement may also be a written record of such a judgment or its enactment.

AMPERSAND

The ampersand is a symbol for the word 'and', namely '&' or variants thereof; the word derives from a corruption of the Latin *et per se* ('and by itself'). This symbol is a monogram derived from a scribal ligature for the word *et* ('and') alone. Written forms of it vary so widely that it is often the single feature most useful to examine first when looking for writers' handwriting idiosyncrasies, or when comparing two examples of writing to check whether they are in the same hand.

ANALECTA

Described in 1623 as 'crumbs which fall from the table', *analecta* (in the Latin form of the word) or analects are literary gleanings: hence, a collection of scraps or extracts from various writings. The term *analecta* was also, however, used by the Yorkshire antiquary Charles Fairfax (1597–1673) to describe his large, elaborate, and illustrated manuscript compilation of family history called *Analecta Fairfaxiana* (now in the Brotherton Collection, University of Leeds, MSS Yks 1–3: *see* Illus. 5). This use would seem to be a deliberate fusion of *analecta* in its original sense with the term 'annals', meaning a narrative of historical events year by year, and was perhaps adopted by Fairfax because the form taken by his compilation combines elements of both meanings.

ANATHEMA

Originally meaning 'an offering to the gods', the Greek term 'anathema' (plural: anathemata) came in various contexts to have more malevolent connotations. In medieval books, most notably in monastic libraries, an anathema was a curse or imprecation written into the book, usually by a librarian, calling down sorrows upon the head of anyone who stole it (as frequently happened, even in chained libraries). Some scribes also included anathemata in their colophons against unauthorized copyists into whose hands the manuscript might fall. Anathemata seem to have lost whatever force they ever had and to have ceased being written with the coming of printed books, when books became both cheaper and more common.

ILLUS. 5 *A page of the* Analecta Fairfaxiana *compiled by the antiquary Charles Fairfax, c.1660–3, including some of the family coats of arms drawn in trick.*

ANGLICANA

See COURT HAND

ANNOTATION

An annotation is a written note added to, or inserted in, a manuscript or printed text, usually in the margin, sometimes interlineally, by way of expansion, comment, gloss, or explanation. *See also* MARGINALIA and SIDE-NOTE, and Illus. 6 and 49.

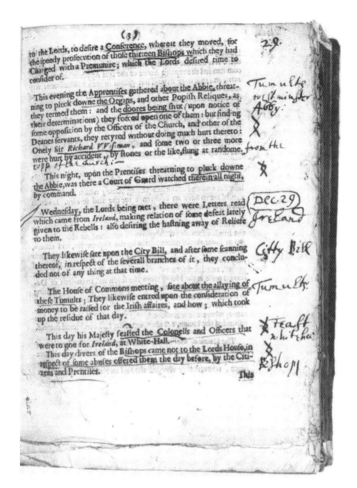

ILLUS. 6 *A page in a printed parliamentary diurnal of the 1640s with extensive marginal annotations or marginalia, including (near the gutter) a type of pointing hand or manicule, written in the hand of the historian John Rushworth, secretary to the Parliamentary general Lord Fairfax.*

ANONYMOUS

A huge number of literary works, both printed and manuscript, may be classified as 'anonymous' (the term often abbreviated to 'anon.')—from the Greek *an* ('without') *onyma* ('name')—meaning of unknown, undeclared, or unacknowledged authorship. Such anonymity may arise either because the work in question was deliberately published or circulated without indication of authorship; or because, as with jokes, ballads, and nursery rhymes, authorship was never a matter of real concern in its original transmission; or else because its authorship, perhaps known to certain people party to its original circulation, was simply forgotten in the course of time. While some anonymously published books, whose authors can now be established, might be classified by bibliographers and book-dealers in catalogue entries as 'anonymous', with the name of the author supplied in square brackets (e.g. Anon. [George Puttenham], *The Arte of English Poesie*), entries specifying 'anonymous' for early modern manuscript works, where anonymity abounds, usually mean that the authorship really is unknown. Compilers of seventeenth-century verse miscellanies occasionally subscribe the Latin word *ignoto* ('by one unknown') to poems whose authorship they do not know. Otherwise, the absence of ascriptions or attributions in such miscellanies may indicate either ignorance of authorship or indifference to it, or, alternatively, that the authorship might be known to the compiler, but that he or she did not bother to subscribe it to each poem.

ANSWER

As a legal document in a bill court (such as Chancery, Star Chamber, or the equity side of Exchequer), an answer is a written defence made by the defendant to the plaintiff's bill of complaint. It is the equivalent of the plea made orally by the defendant in a common-law court, which, however, might still be recorded in writing. In a bill court a written answer might also be made to interrogatories.

The sequence of any subsequent reponses and counter-responses by the two parties is replication (by the plaintiff), rejoinder (defendant), surrejoinder (plaintiff), rebuttal or rebutter (defendant), and surrebuttal or surrebutter (plaintiff). *See* INTERROGATORY, REJOINDER, and REPLICATION.

ANTHOLOGY

Deriving from the Greek *anthologia* ('a gathering of flowers') and *anthologiai* ('a collection of epigrams'), the term 'anthology' means a collection of different works, or extracts from works, by various authors, whether or not belonging to a particular literary genre or relating to a particular theme or subject. Anthologies, such as collections of epigrams and elegiac verse, date from classical times, although they are perhaps best known in printed versions, a well-known early modern English example being the so-called Tottel's Miscellany, *Songes and Sonettes* (1557). The anthology is perhaps distinguished from the miscellany (*compare* MISCELLANY), whether manuscript or printed, in that the former tends to have a more formal aspect, being a deliberately assembled collection, rather than a miscellaneous compilation which may have evolved somewhat randomly over a period, although this distinction is easily blurred.

ANTICIPATION

See SCRIBAL ERRORS.

ANTIPHONAL

The type of manuscript known since medieval times as an 'antiphonal', or 'antiphoner', or sometimes later as an 'antiphonary', is a liturgical volume containing antiphons, which are the responses sung by multiple voices or by choirs during a Catholic church service. Thus an antiphonal contains the music for the sung portions of the Divine Office (daily devotions at the fixed, or canonical, hours), being a collection of verses, stanzas, or sentences with musical settings, focused originally (in the fifth century) and still particularly (since the Council of Trent) on the recitation of psalms, as well as on the reading of lessons from Scripture. Such manuscript volumes can be very large in format, so that they might be readily used by the choir, or very grand and elaborate in design, possibly as a formal record of the sung responses. Often in heavy bindings and written on vellum throughout, antiphonals may well contain large rubricated lettering, coloured decorations, and historiated initials depicting saints or other religious subjects. Such features have led to many volumes being dismembered so that the decorative parts can be mounted separately or hung on walls.

ANTIQUARY

An antiquary—a figure caricatured by John Earle in the 1620s as a wrinkled old man who 'loves all things . . . the better for being mouldie and wormeaten'—is a collector of ancient relics and antiquities, or a scholar or researcher in such matters. Antiquaries—such as William Camden, Sir Robert Cotton, Sir William Dugdale, William Lambarde, John Aubrey, Sir John Dodderidge, Sir Henry Spelman, and many others—are among the most prominent collectors of old manuscripts in the early modern period. Some of their collections are among the most important of the period to survive, and indeed it is partly due to their enthusiasm and acquisitiveness that so many manuscripts do survive. In this respect, an especially important figure is John Leland (1506–1552), King's Antiquary to Henry VIII, who in 1533 was commissioned to make an examination of ancient writings in ecclesiastical and academic establishments throughout England. His great survey failed to prevent the dispersal and loss of vast numbers of medieval manuscripts during the havoc caused by the dissolution of the monasteries, but it helped to save some for the King's Library, it left historically important accounts of now lost manuscripts, and it established a precedent for the researches and collections of subsequent antiquaries. Although the original Society of Antiquaries founded in 1572 was banned by

James I in 1604 because of its supposed dangerous probing into the foundations of government and social institutions, it was revived in 1717 and still flourishes at Burlington House, London. A number of notable antiquaries, some of whom became Heralds or Kings of Arms, were associated with the College of Arms.

APOCALYPSE

See ESCHATOLOGY.

APOGRAPH

Derived from the Greek *apographon* ('copy'), the term 'apograph' denotes an exact transcript of an original manuscript. The earliest recorded use of the term (which is now virtually obsolete) is in Philemon Holland's published translation of Pliny's *Historie of the World* in 1601.

APPARATUS

In editing, 'apparatus' is a collective term, sometimes rendered in Latin as the *apparatus criticus*, for editors' textual notes, explanatory introductions, commentary, lists of variant readings, glossary, appendices, and other aids to the study of a text, provided in scholarly editions of literary works, or of historical texts or documents.

ARCHETYPE

Derived from the Greek *archē* ('first', 'original') and *typos* ('form'), the term 'archetype' is used in textual criticism to mean the original or prototype text from which all other copies in a given chain of transmission ultimately descend or are derived. If the archetypal text no longer survives, but is postulated hypothetically in a stemma (*see* STEMMA), it is usually represented by an italic capital such as *X*.

ARCHIVE

Archives, in the plural, are historical records and documents and, for the most part, are preserved as such in record offices, administered by archivists. An archive, in the singular, may be a quantity of papers, including muniments, associated with a particular family, institution, guild, company, or even individual, and it may survive in any one of a large number of county or city record offices, lawyers' offices, banks, commercial premises, or private houses and estates. An archive may be distinguished from a collection of documents in that the latter may be a select group of materials consciously compiled, and perhaps deliberately brought together from disparate sources, by one or more collectors, possibly even at a particular time for a particular project. By contrast, an archive is an organic entity that has usually evolved over a long period of time by natural accumulation and accretion, and is kept as a record or for reference purposes: for instance, a large family or estate archive, where documents have routinely been preserved perhaps over generations, usually in the same location, and which may also include papers of other families that were incorporated as a matter of course when they came to own the estate or married into the original family.

The term 'archive' also suggests a large quantity of documents. Many estate archives, for instance, occupy hundreds of boxes in record offices, while the records of law courts or government departments in the National Archives at Kew fill miles of shelving. However, the precise point at which a quantity of papers changes from being a collection of someone's papers to an archive is difficult to determine. It is not unusual to see in sale catalogues a relatively small group of papers of a writer, politician, or other notable figure described as an 'archive' whereas the more modest term 'collection', however the papers were preserved or brought together, might seem more appropriate. On the other hand, although the completeness or integrity of any important archive is highly prized, it may still appropriately be described as an 'archive' even if it has seriously suffered the ravages of time, provided it is all that now survives and is not just the residue of a recent dispersal (otherwise it would only be part of an archive).

By a metamorphoric extension of the term, large accumulations of other materials besides documents can today be called 'archives': e.g. a film or sound archive.

ARGUMENT

See PLOT.

ARMORIAL

An armorial, or armory, is a heraldic book, usually manuscript, containing coats of arms of particular families, or of series of families (such as the English nobility), or of individuals, which are usually arranged in sequence according to rank, from dukes to barons. They may also contain arms of institutions, such as colleges or City livery companies. The coats of arms are either emblazoned in their proper colours or else drawn in trick, sometimes with the arms drawn in hand-stamped shields. *See* Illus. 5, 7, and 18.

ARMS

See COAT OF ARMS.

ILLUS. 7 *A page in a heraldic illuminated genealogy and armorial of the Dudley family, presented to Robert, Earl of Leicester, by Robert Cooke, Chester Herald, in 1564. It is written on vellum in a professional secretary hand, the borders embellished with foliate decoration and coats of arms emblazoned in their proper colours.*

ARTICLES

Articles are clauses of a document, usually of a legal nature, setting out provisions, and the term is sometimes used to signify the document itself: e.g. articles of apprenticeship, of clerkship, or of partnership.

The term 'article', often abbreviated to 'art.', is also used in some institutions as an alternative to 'number' ('No.') to designate an item in a manuscript collection (e.g. Lansdowne MS 106, art. 55, in the British Library).

ARTICLES OF AGREEMENT

A legal document may be referred to as the 'articles of agreement' when it embodies a series of clauses, constituting the provisions of an agreement between two or more parties for a transaction or financial arrangement.

The articles may be signed and witnessed by the parties concerned, but more usually they are drawn up for purposes of negotiation as a prelude to the final agreed version, which takes the form of a contract. *See* Illus. 8.

ASCENDER

In palaeography, as also in typography, an ascender is the upward stroke or loop above the base line in letters such as *b, d, f, h, k,* and *l. Compare* DESCENDER.

ASCRIPTION

An ascription is an attribution of authorship as written in a manuscript. A manuscript text bearing such an attribution is said to be ascribed to the person whose name appears.

ASPECT

In palaeography, the term 'aspect' denotes the general appearance of a handwriting or script and its salient tendencies, such as its predominant uprightness or slope, its angularity or roundness, the tightness or spaciousness of the lettering, etc.

ASSIGNMENT

As a legal document, an assignment effects or authorizes the transference from one person or party to another of a right, interest (such as a leasehold or mortgage), or title to property.

ASSIZES

'Assizes', or 'courts of assize', are terms derived from Old French meaning 'sittings', or 'sitting', and denote a type of law court held in various towns in England and, from the time of Henry VIII onwards, also in Wales, on a visiting basis. By the late thirteenth century, they had largely replaced the earlier eyre courts (their name derived from the Latin *iter,* 'journey'). Though performing different functions, the eyre courts had been similarly peripatetic courts, convened by itinerant royal justices, but had become unpopular, not least because of the justices' remoteness from local affairs, their often heavy-handed and irregular procedures, and the lengthy delays involved in this system (the county visits customarily occurred only once every seven years). By contrast, assizes were held by commissioners appointed as judges of assize, who visited twice a year the main towns of four circuits (later extended to seven), two judges in each. Empowered to administer civil and criminal justice as representatives of the Crown, they had greater authority than local Justices of the Peace and could administer severe penalties. Courts of assize, which were not abolished until 1971, generated extensive records, many of which, dating from 1198 to 1971, are preserved in the National Archives at Kew (JUST and ASSI series).

ASSOCIATE

Among other meanings of the term, an associate is an officer of the higher courts of common law in England, whose duties include superintending the entering of causes, receiving and entering verdicts, and keeping, or supervising the keeping of, all records relevant to these proceedings. An associate was originally a clerk who worked with judges in a commission or official inquiry.

ASSOCIATION OATH ROLLS

The Association Oath Rolls are the official records of those who took the Oath of Loyalty to the Crown. This oath, erstwhile taken voluntarily, came to be compulsorily administered in May 1696. This was following the death of Queen Mary on 28 December 1694, the subsequent revival of Jacobite plots against William III, and the passing of the Act of Association: 'for the better Security of His Majesties Royal Person and Government'. The oath had to be taken by all holders of military and civil offices under the Crown, including members of parliament, the clergy, City guilds and livery companies, and local gentry. All men and some women householders were encouraged to subscribe if they wished, and in some places the names of defaulters were recorded as well. The records for England and Wales, arranged largely by county and diocese, are enrolled on some 474 rolls and books, of parchment and paper, now in the National Archives at Kew (C 213, C 214, C 220/9/7, KB 24/1, KB 24/2). Oaths were also taken in Ireland (for which no rolls survive), Scotland (for which only a few rolls survive in national and local archives), and elsewhere in the colonies, notably the British plantations in Virginia, New York, Barbados, Bermuda, and the Leeward Islands, as well as by British merchants in the Netherlands and other European countries (also recorded in the National Archives rolls). *See also* OATH ROLLS.

ASTERISK

The asterisk (*) is a familiar typographical feature used to refer to footnotes and the like; the word derives from the Greek *asteriskos* meaning 'little star'. In addition, it was used since medieval times to mark omissions in a text, and it sometimes occurs in marginalia by early modern readers to distinguish lines or passages of note, rather like a manicule or pointing hand. The asterisk was also frequently drawn as a small cross with a dot in each angle (✗).

ASTROLOGICAL MANUSCRIPT

An astrological manuscript is one dealing with the occult science, or pseudo-science, of astrology: that is to say, fortune telling, the divination of the future from the disposition of the stars and heavenly bodies, or from birth dates, with reference to the zodiac. The subject originally arose in ancient times as an application of astronomical observations to mundane affairs, and it incorporates the calculation and prediction of natural phenomena, tides, eclipses, meteors, etc., as well as certain measurements of time.

From the Middle Ages onwards, astrological manuscripts could take the form of learned treatises, bound compendia of discourses, notebooks, and other forms of writing. Some of them were illuminated, and they generally include calculations, tables, charts, diagrams, signs of the zodiac, and other symbolic figures, as well as horoscopes. *See* Illus. 34.

ASTRONOMICAL MANUSCRIPT

Until the end of the seventeenth century, astronomy, the study of the stars and heavenly bodies, and astrology, the pseudo-science of predicting the future from the disposition of such bodies, were virtually indistinguishable. From medieval times onwards, astronomical manuscripts, whether formal treatises or informal notebooks, were likely to incorporate astrological materials and interpretations as well. With the development of the telescope and other instruments, and the publication in 1543 of Nicolaus Copernicus's theory of the solar system, placing the sun rather than the earth at the centre, the two fields only gradually became distinct. The New Astronomy, leading in England to the creation of the Royal Observatory in 1675 and the work of Isaac Newton, John Flamsteed, Edmund Halley, and others, would stress the fundamental importance of observation with specialized mathematical instruments, rather than earlier forms of computation and interpretation. This is reflected in important manuscript writings—for instance, those of Jeremiah Horrocks, recording in 1639 for the first time an accurate prediction and sight of the transit of Venus. *See* Illus. 9.

ATLAS

The term 'atlas' is derived from the figure in Greek mythology, Atlas, brother of Prometheus and son of the Titan Iapetus and Clymene (or Asia), who was always represented as bearing the terrestrial globe or the heavens on his shoulders. The term was apparently first adopted to denote a large book of maps by the Flemish cartographer Gerard Mercator for his printed *Atlas sive cosmographicae meditationes de fabrica mundi et fabricati figura* (Duisburg, 1585). Collections of maps and portolans bound together

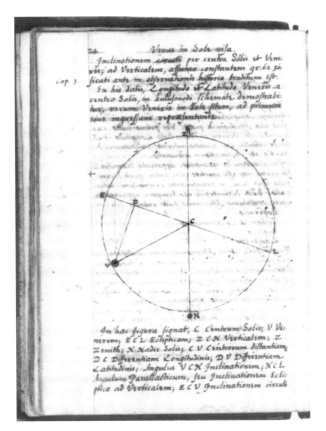

ILLUS. 9 *A page in an autograph astronomical manuscript by Jeremiah Horrocks, written in Latin in a predominantly italic hand and with a diagram, being his treatise* Venus in sole visa, *1639.*

date, however, from much earlier times, well before the invention of printing. The earliest printed atlas in all but name was Abraham Ortelius's *Theatrum orbis terrarum* (Antwerp, 1570). The figure of Atlas holding a globe appeared on the title-page of Antonio Lafreri's *Geographia, tavole moderne di geografia* published in Rome also in 1570, a feature which, whether on title-pages, frontispieces, covers, or elsewhere, subsequently became standard in printed atlases. The term 'atlas' was later adopted for other kinds of large books, usually double-folio size, containing plates, but only by reason of the similarity of size.

ATTESTATION

Attestation is the practice whereby deeds or other legal instruments are signed by the relevant parties in the presence of witnesses, who then themselves sign the document as evidence of its execution and authenticity. An attestation clause is the clause or clauses written at the end, or on the verso, of the document stating that the persons signing it were indeed witnesses to the signing by the parties concerned. *See* Illus. 93.

ATTESTED COPY

An attested copy of a document is a transcript that is formally subscribed and signed by a notary or other person, testifying that it is a true, authentic, and accurate copy (*vera copia*) of the original. Thus it might safely be used as valid evidence in the absence of the original itself. Besides having legal uses, various documents among state papers (such as transcripts of outgoing official letters) are docketed as being 'true copies'.

ATTORNEY

In England, an attorney, or attorney-at-law, is a type of lawyer that flourished from early medieval times, becoming after the mid-fifteenth century primarily based in the Inns of Chancery. Attorneys were officers of court, appointed to act for, and represent, parties in litigation. In lawsuits, they were appointed by warrant, which had to be enrolled in the official plea rolls. As their profession developed in the seventeenth century, they performed many of the standard tasks of solicitors, including framing clients' pleadings, instructing counsel, and conveying property. By the eighteenth century, many attorneys had three common-law practising certificates (for the King's Bench, Common Pleas, and Exchequer) and were also admitted as solicitors in Chancery: thus they could effectively perform all functions. The two professions of attorney and solicitor technically merged in 1875 when the old courts were abolished and the present Supreme Court of Judicature was established, whose officers are only solicitors. In the USA, however, attorneys have traditionally performed the functions not only of solicitors, but also of barristers, who can represent clients as advocates speaking on their behalf in court. *See also* POWER OF ATTORNEY and *compare* BARRISTER and SOLICITOR.

ATTRIBUTION

An attribution occurs when a text has authorship assigned to it, whether correctly or otherwise, and whether or not the alleged author's name actually appears in the text. Thus a work may be said to be attributed to a particular author as a matter of traditional or general belief, or because of claims made by certain people in earlier times, or because of arguments for authorship made by modern scholars. As such, an attribution may be distinguished from an ascription, in which the name is actually written in the manuscript text.

AUTHOR

An author is the person who creates, invents, or originates a text, as opposed to someone who only copies or transmits it. A literary work may have multiple authorship if two or more collaborators originally produced it (as, for instance, is the case with some Elizabethan and Jacobean plays).

Authorship as a concept has become a subject of some controversy among modern literary theorists, notably through influential writings published in 1968–9 by the French thinkers Roland Barthes (1915–1980) and Michel Foucault (1926–1984), and to some extent also through the philosophy of 'deconstruction' propounded by Jacques Derrida (1930–2004). It is argued that authorship is a problematic concept not only because of the occasional uncertainty as to who wrote what, but also because of the uses and appropriation of alleged authorship at different times; because of the possible contribution made to the text, in the transmission process, by other agents (copyists, compositors, actors, editors, etc.); and, above all, because the meaning of a work is quite independent of what the author may have intended. In the most extreme postulated scenario, this thinking leads to the so-called 'death of the author' and the contention that the meaning of a work is actually created by the reader. The case for 'the resurrection of the author' is argued by those who, granted the complicating factors of transmission and the instability of language, still recognize the author as the primary creator without whom the work and any meaning it may have would not exist.

AUTOGRAPH

Properly used as an adjective, the term 'autograph' means written by the person who composed or created the text embodied in the manuscript or document in question, as opposed to a copyist transcribing someone else's work. Thus, an autograph manuscript is one written in the author's own hand, not by a copyist. An autograph letter signed is a letter written and signed by the letter-writer himself or herself, rather than being in the hand of a secretary or amanuensis.

The term 'autograph' is also often used, somewhat imprecisely, as a noun: either as a substitute for 'holograph' (a text written entirely in the hand of its author) or, in popular usage, as a substitute for 'signature'. The latter usage is exemplified by the hobby of autograph collecting or autograph hunting, where the term may imply signatures that are collectable because they are by famous or distinguished people: hence the film director Billy Wilder's remark, 'One day you are a signature, next day you're an autograph.' On the other hand, the bogus term 'autographed', meaning 'signed', should be avoided. For various examples of autograph or partly autograph documents, *see* Illus. 1, 9, 21, 23, 24, 35, 43, 44, 49, 54, 64, 77, 80, 86, 89, and 90.

AUTOGRAPH ALBUM

'Autograph album' is a common modern term denoting any kind of album used for, or intended to be used for, collecting personal signatures and inscriptions. They tend to be commercially produced stationery products designed for that purpose. Depending on the taste of the collector and circumstances of compilation, the contributors might be family members, friends and colleagues, or, alternatively, famous people (writers, politicians, show-business personalities, film-stars, musicians, sportsmen, etc.). Contributors might inscribe the blank album leaves directly for the collector; alternatively signatures and inscriptions might be written on separate pieces of paper (including letters, cards, signed menus, programmes, and photographs) and pasted into the album afterwards. Although the origin of such albums lies in the *libri amicorum* of the sixteenth century (*see* LIBER AMICORUM), the great vogue for autograph albums developed in the nineteenth century and in great measure persisted in the twentieth century. The use of the word 'autograph' as a synonym for 'signature' has popular currency in this context, although the term has a technically more correct application.

B

A badge is a device, emblem, or distinctive piece of insignia that denotes a person's office, his or her membership of a society, regiment, or other body, or else allegiance to a particular individual, house, or family. Originally heraldic devices primarily to identify a particular knight and secondly to distinguish his followers, badges are granted by the College of Arms to individuals and corporations by patent. They are often represented in heraldic manuscripts, although they form no part of an achievement, but are traditionally worn on clothing. Like coats of arms, badges are occasionally found represented in books and manuscripts to denote particular ownership of the volumes.

Baga de Secretis

The *Baga de Secretis* (Latin for 'bag of secrets') is a series of records in the National Archives at Kew relating most notably to trials for high treason, sedition, and other offences of particular concern to the state. They belong to the King's Bench, but also include important proceedings before the Lord High Steward. They date from the reign of Edward IV (although lacking some of the early bags or *bagae*) to that of George III: from 1477 to 1813. Once literally preserved in canvas bags or pouches, they were evidently segregated from other state papers because of their political importance and sensitivity. This was sufficient for them, for many years, to be preserved in a closet under three keys, kept respectively by the Lord Chief Justice, the Attorney-General and the Master of the Crown Office or Coroner. Nevertheless, many relatively insignificant writs and court records were also transferred to the *Baga*, or, alternatively, important documents failed to be transferred there, simply as a matter of practical convenience.

These records, as well as those original bags that survive after being repaired in 1934, are now mounted in a series of ninety-one bundles and files (series KB 8). Generally containing formal records in Latin of the proceedings, including the indictments, they relate to some of the most famous trials in British history, including those of Sir Thomas More in 1534–5 (KB 8/7), Anne Boleyn in 1536 (KB 8/8, KB 8/9), Thomas, Duke of Norfolk, in 1572 (KB 8/42), Anthony Babington in 1586 (KB 8/48), Sir Walter Ralegh in 1603 (KB 8/58), Guy Fawkes in 1605 (KB 8/59), the murderers of Sir Thomas Overbury in 1615 (KB 8/62), the regicides in 1661–2 (KB 8/64), and the leaders of the Jacobite rebellions of 1715 and 1745 (KB 8/70 and KB 8/69).

BALLOON LETTER

A balloon letter is a letter, usually stamped *par ballon monté*, sent out by balloon from the besieged city of Paris during the Franco-Prussian War. During the siege, which lasted from 19 September 1870 to 28 January 1871, the French postal service planned a fleet of sixty-five balloons, carrying out of Paris altogether twenty-nine passengers, as well as a number of pigeons to bring messages back, and nearly eleven tons of mail. Examples of these letters are prized today by postal collectors, their value depending on the distance they eventually travelled after being unloaded from the balloons away from Paris. Many reached England, but a few rare items, now worth tens of thousands of pounds each to postal collectors, reached as far as Japan.

BALLPOINT PEN

The ballpoint, or ball-point, pen as known today was first patented in 1938 and developed in the 1940s by a Hungarian refugee to Argentina, László Bíró, who formed a manufacturing company with his brother. Their type of pen (often called a 'biro') was based on the principle of a small tungsten carbide or steel ball-bearing revolving in the mouth of the barrel of a pen fed with ink by gravity or capillary action. Prototypes of this pen were developed experimentally, but less successfully, in the late nineteenth century.

BANDEROLE

A banderole is a ribbon-like scroll bearing an inscription or a device, usually seen as a representation in heraldic, medieval, and early modern manuscripts and art. *See* Illus. 18, 30, and 65, and *compare* PHYLACTERY.

BARGAIN AND SALE

A bargain and sale is an agreement between two or more parties for a sale of property. Hence it is any kind of document recording the terms of that sale, authorizing it, or bearing witness to its completion or enactment. Laws governing bargains and sales, particularly respecting how the use or benefit of land might be converted to possession, were enshrined in the Statute of Uses in 1535 and, with respect to freehold property, in the Statute of Enrolments of 1536. The latter determined that in order to free a freehold, bargains and sales should be executed by deed and made public by being enrolled in one of the King's courts of record. *See also* LEASE AND RELEASE.

BARRISTER

Since the fifteenth century, a barrister in England is a lawyer who has been called to the bar of the Inns of Court: i.e. has a degree in law conferred by one of the Inns of Court. Since the sixteenth century, this was a prerequisite for practice at the bar of the central courts, although, from at least Tudor times to the mid-seventeenth century, regulations forbade barristers practising in these courts until they had several years of legal experience acting as solicitors. Once called, they could specialize in advocacy and represent clients as their legal counsel in the superior courts, speaking on their behalf. Although in the seventeenth century barristers were supposed to take instructions from clients in person, they have since traditionally been barred from performing the functions of solicitors, but may receive instructions and advice from solicitors, who are generally responsible for preparing their briefs.

Since the end of the sixteenth century, on the recommendation of the Lord Chancellor, highly qualified and experienced barristers have been honoured with the title of Queen's Counsel (QC) or King's Counsel (KC), the earliest person so honoured being Sir Francis Bacon in 1597. Those awarded this honour are traditionally said to 'take the silk'. Rolls of Queen's Counsel in England and Wales, Scotland (since 1898), and Northern Ireland (since 1921) are preserved among the Public Records. *See also* SERJEANT-AT-LAW and *compare* ATTORNEY and SOLICITOR.

BEAD-ROLL

A bead-roll, or bede-roll, is a list or catalogue of persons for whose souls prayers are to be said in the Catholic Church. From early medieval times, it could be particularly a parchment roll on which prayers and commemorative verses were inscribed to honour a deceased abbot, the roll being carried from one monastery to the next for each to make additions. Sixteenth-century examples might also contain drawings depicting the deceased's abbey and his life and death.

BEATUS

See PSALTER.

BIBLIOGRAPHY

Deriving from the Greek *biblios* ('book') and *graphē* ('writing'), the term 'bibliography' denotes the branch of learning devoted to the historical study of books, both printed and manuscript, as physical objects or artefacts. Descriptive bibliography involves detailed scrutiny, collation, analysis, and description of the form and structure of books; of paper, ink, script, or type; of binding; and of other components, as well as of material evidence of provenance (readers' annotations, inscriptions, bookplates, shelf-marks, etc.).

What is sometimes called 'analytical bibliography' involves much of the same evidence, but it is analysed in order to make deductions concerning printing-house practices and to identify compositorial characteristics. Certain of these aspects, throwing light on the way the text was transmitted or presented in the book, may then be relevant to textual criticism. *See* TEXTUAL CRITICISM.

Enumerative bibliography is the listing of books or printed articles on a particular subject or that have some formal relationship, such as books relating to a particular author, language, or historical period, or else a list of sources used for, or cited in, a particular book.

BIFOLIATE

See BIFOLIUM.

BIFOLIUM

Although the term 'bifolium' (plural: bifolia) is sometimes thought to apply specifically to folio-size leaves, a bifolium is a pair of conjugate leaves (i.e. four pages), of paper or vellum, of any size. A sheet of paper or vellum so folded can be called 'bifoliate'.

BILL

Etymologically linked to the old French words *bille*, *billet*, and also *libelle*, as well as to the Latin *bulla*, the term 'bill' is used at different times over the centuries to denote various kinds of document, including, in its most general use, any kind of written statement, letter, list, memorandum, or formal proposal, especially one containing some kind of seal. The term is perhaps most commonly used to denote a document in which is set out the details of a debt, charge, or obligation to pay money (*see* Illus. 10). In a legal context, a bill is commonly a petition or complaint.

Some particular types of bill are:

Bill of complaint: a formal, written petition or declaration to a monarch, lord chancellor, or other civil, legal or ecclesiastical authority—most commonly to a bill court (such as Chancery, Star Chamber, or the equity side of Exchequer)—in which a person (the plaintiff) makes a complaint against someone (the defendant) for an alleged wrong or injury and requests justice or redress, thereby initiating a lawsuit. It is the equivalent of the count or declaration made orally in a common-law court, which, however, still had to be recorded in writing. *See also* ANSWER.

Bill of exchange: a type of financial document used to facilitate commercial transactions, originally an exchange of currency for overseas transactions, before bank cheques became the standard form of making payments. It consisted of a written and signed order or request made by one person (the drawer) to another (the drawee) for a payment to be made to a third person (the payee) on demand or at a specified time. Such payment would obviously involve some standing arrangement, such as money held by the drawee on behalf of the drawer. If the payee endorsed the bill in favour of a fourth person, the latter became the endorsee and the original payee the endorser.

Bill of lading: a type of document of title, constituting a formal and detailed receipt given to a person consigning goods for transport on a merchant ship by the master of the vessel, the term 'lading' meaning the 'loading of a ship with freight or cargo'. He thereby acknowledged their receipt and accepted responsibility for their safe delivery to a consignee. It would usually be drawn up in three copies: one for the consignor, one sent to the consignee, and one kept by the master of the ship. The document would constitute legal proof of the consignor's ownership of the goods and might be used as security for any money advanced, as well as for redress if the goods were not properly delivered to the consignee.

Bill of sale: a written document testifying to the sale of goods or property by one person to another and to the transference of title to that property. When the transaction involves the borrowing of money, the document constitutes legally binding security for the sum borrowed and authorizes the lender or creditor to seize the property concerned in the event of non-payment by the debtor.

BILLA EXPENSARUM

Billa expensarum (the Latin means 'schedules of expenses') were drawn up at the conclusion of a law case to itemize the legal costs of the successful party when the costs were awarded against their adversary. Surviving examples (at the University of Cambridge, for instance) date back to the sixteenth century and up to 1681.

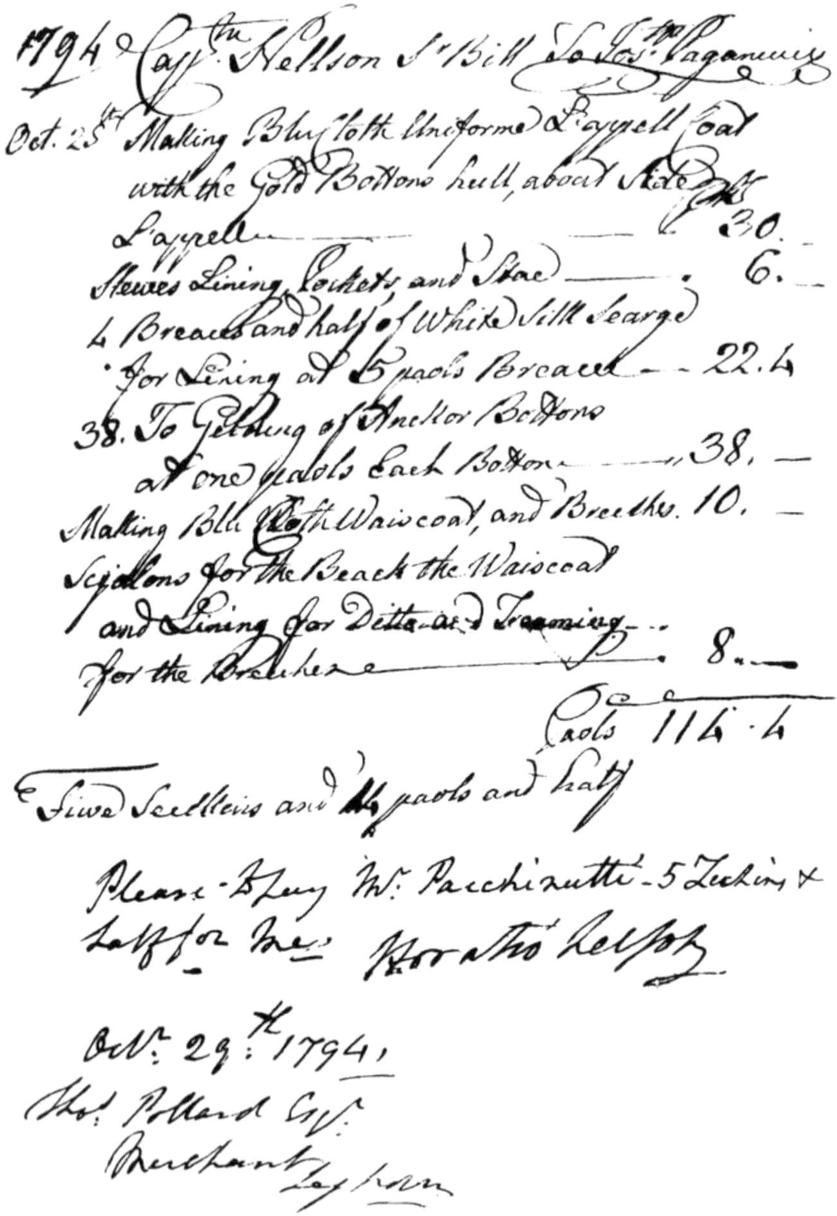

1794 Capt. Hellson's Bill To Jos. Paganini

Oct. 25 Making Blue Cloth Uniform & Lappell Coat
with the Gold Bottons full, about Side
Lappell — 30. —
Sleeves Lining, Pockets, and Stae — 6. —
4 Breacts and half of White Silk Searge
for Lining at 5 paols Breace — 22.4
38. To Gilding of Anchor Bottons
at one paols Each Botton — 38. —
Making Blue Cloth Waiscoat, and Breethes. 10. —
Scjallons for the Beach the Waiscoat
and Lining for Ditta as Trimming
for the Breethes — 8. —

Paols 114. 4

Five Scelleus and paols and half

Please to pay Mr. Pacchinutti — 5 Zechins &
half for me   Horatio Nelson

Oct. 29th 1794,
Th. Pollard Esqr.
Merchant Leghorn

ILLUS. 10 *A bill submitted by the Italian tailor Jos. Paganini to Captain Horatio (later Lord) Nelson for making a formal naval uniform. It is subscribed and signed in Nelson's own hand (his right hand) asking Thomas Pollard at Leghorn to settle the bill for him, 29 October 1794.*

See COURTS OF LAW.

BINDERS' WASTE

Binders' waste is the paper or parchment leaves or fragments traditionally used by binders, from medieval times onwards, as filling to pad or reinforce the binding of a book inside the spine and covers, or on or beneath the paste-down, or else to line the endpapers. Some bindings bestowed upon medieval and early modern manuscript volumes may themselves constitute binders' waste in so far as they are vellum or paper leaves taken from earlier documents considered redundant and recycled to save expense. Such material may, on occasions, throw light on the dating or early history of the manuscript with which it is bound: for instance, the fragments of an indulgence printed by Caxton in 1489 in the Winchester manuscript of Malory's *Morte d'Arthur* (British Library, Add. MS 59678), or a letter of 1440 bound in the dictated manuscript autobiography of Margery Kempe (British Library, Add. MS 61823). With the dissolution of the monasteries, the dispersal of monastic libraries, and the prohibition in 1550 of 'all books . . . heretofore used for service of the Church', the old medieval manuscript service books provided a particularly rich supply of material for such use.

Whether blank, printed, or manuscript, binders' waste has accordingly been the source of many interesting discoveries. Quantities of leaves from early manuscript bibles and other religious, classical, and secular works have been found in the bindings of books in libraries and by private collectors and booksellers, often when the books were rebound. Other items found include proof-sheets, among them whole uncut formes, of early editions of Elizabethan and Jacobean plays and of other works, as well as examples of early printed and manuscript music. Notable discoveries made in recent years include an early to mid-seventh-century bifolium from a *Historia ecclesiastica* by Eusebius Pamphili, one of the oldest surviving examples of Anglo-Saxon manuscripts; a manuscript fragment of an unknown Elizabethan play, with a tavern scene similar to one in Shakespeare's *Henry IV, Part I* (*see* Illus. 11); and two documents relating to transactions in 1610 involving the *Mayflower*, the ship that carried the Pilgrim Fathers to America in 1620. It is likely that more such discoveries will be made as old books wear and are disbound or repaired.

BINDING

The binding of books and manuscripts is a major feature of the object as a physical artefact, subject to an almost infinite variety of styles and materials determined by function, cost, and differing aesthetic taste, among other factors. Binding is consequently a bibliographical subject in its own right.

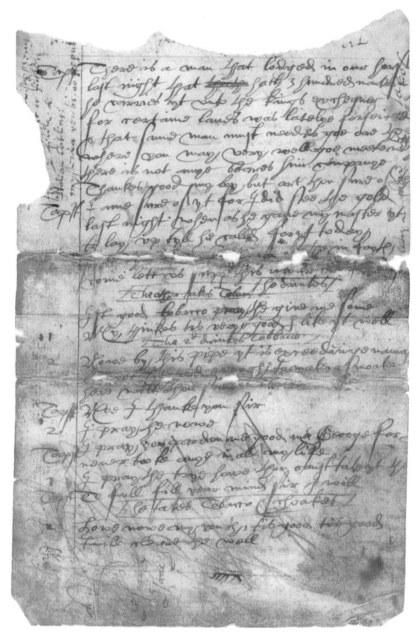

ILLUS. 11 *One page of a piece of binder's waste used in the contemporary Oxford binding of a copy of C. Gessner's edition of Homer's* Odyssea *published in Geneva in 1586. The manuscript, written in secretary script, is a two-page quarto fragment of the text of a late Elizabethan or early Jacobean play and contains altogether fifty-seven lines of blank verse dialogue for an inn scene somewhat similar to Shakespeare's* Henry IV, Part I, *(II, i).*

With respect to manuscripts, the binding can, on occasions, be a very important feature of the original production—if, for instance, it is a constituent of
an elaborately prepared volume made for presentation to a monarch or
high-ranking official. When the binding is original (in so far as this can be
determined), even with more modest items, such as a commonplace book, it
may help to define the character of the manuscript and its original owner, how
it was regarded, and the purpose it served—perhaps, for instance, a relatively
cheap wrapper for a casual notebook for daily use as opposed to a fine, sturdy,
or expensive one for a library manuscript that was seriously compiled and
expected to last. However, the majority of early modern manuscript volumes
that survive are likely to be in bindings supplied by subsequent owners,
reflecting their individual tastes or circumstances, or else, often combined
with other texts, in standard library bindings that bear little or no relation to
the character of the particular manuscript.

The range of materials used by binders over the centuries is wide, but
those most commonly encountered with manuscripts include vellum (or
limp vellum if it is not covering boards), calf, sheep, morocco (an expensive
leather from goatskin), pigskin, marbled boards, and, in more modern
times, the cheaper tree-calf, roan, buckram, and cloth. In an exceptional
case, even rat skin could be used (*see* PRISONER OF WAR MAGAZINES),
while, yet more extraordinary, a number of extant library books were bound
in the eighteenth or nineteenth centuries, if not earlier, in human skin. Each
normal type of leather is subject to a variety of forms and treatments: thus
morocco can be hard-grained, pebble-grained, diced, niger, etc.; calf may be
reversed (if the soft inner suede-like side is exposed), mottled, sprinkled,
and so on. A satchel or wallet binding, in whatever material, is one in which
the back cover is extended to enclose the fore-edge and fasten into a slot or
metal clasp in the front cover.

As for the tooling and decoration that might be bestowed upon the binding
by craftsmen (some of them known by name, highly valued for their skill and
artistry, whose work is collected in its own right), the range of features and
styles themselves give rise to a whole vocabulary. Commonly applied terms
found in descriptions of bindings include blind-stamped, cartouche, dentelle,
doublure (a leather paste-down), embossed, fillets (lines or parallel lines), gilt,
inlaid, lacquered, panel, raised bands (horizontal ridges on the spine for
sewing bands), semé (with small sprinkled ornaments), and sombre (black),
among many others. More expensive or elaborate binding materials might
include linen fabric heavily embroidered in gold and silver threads (such as
devotional manuscripts prepared for her family by Elizabeth I in her youth);
or velvet (such as the weighty manuscript discourses Lord Henry Howard

presented to Queen Elizabeth and other eminent persons); or tortoiseshell; or even jewelled bindings (like various books presented to Queen Elizabeth as New Year's gifts). The term often applied to the most expensive, elaborate, and luxurious bindings, exhibiting exemplary displays of craftsmanship, is 'sumptuous'.

Books may also be described as half-bound (half-morocco, half-calf, etc.) when only the spine and outer corners of the covers are bound with the specified leather or material. Less common, quarter-bound is when only the spine is so bound.

BIRO

See BALLPOINT PEN.

BIS

The word *bis* (the Latin for 'twice') is commonly used in pagination or foliation to indicate either that two pages or leaves have been mistakenly given the same number or else, alternatively, that one has been overlooked in the numbering sequence. Thus, for instance, 'fol. *2 bis*' means that the sequence of foliation for four leaves that should properly run from 1 to 4 runs here either 1, 2, 2, 3, the second '2' now being called '2 *bis*'; or, alternatively, 1, 2, [unnumbered], 3, the unnumbered leaf now being assigned the number '2 *bis*'.

BISHOP MARK

A Bishop mark is the earliest type of hand-stamped dated postal mark struck on letters. Named after Henry Bishop, the first Postmaster General after the Restoration, it was introduced in 1661. The mark comprised a small circle incorporating the month and day on which the letter was posted in London or received there. This type of postal mark, varying in size and colouring of ink, lasted for well over 100 years, being used in London until 1787, in Dublin until 1795, and in Edinburgh until 1806. Versions were also used in various towns in America, Canada, and India.

BISHOP'S TRANSCRIPT

A bishop's transcript is a copy, usually in the hand of a parish clerk, of one year's entries in a parish register that the vicar or other incumbent was obliged to send each year, usually at Easter, to his bishop (or, in some areas, archdeacon). This was a custom in some dioceses since the beginning of the reign of Elizabeth I, but was made general after an archiepiscopal order issued in 1597. Bishops' transcripts, now preserved chiefly in county record offices, are useful historical sources which supplement the information found in parish registers, or serve as partial substitutes for registers no longer extant. They may bear the signatures not only of local churchwardens, but also of notable clerics: for instance, the poets Robert Herrick, as vicar of Dean Prior, Devon, and Thomas Traherne, as rector of Credenhill, Herefordshire.

BITING

In palaeography, the term 'biting' is applied to occasions when two adjacent letters (such as *bo* or *po*), formed of contrary curved strokes, merge or overlap one another.

BLACK BOOK OF THE TOWER

See PARLIAMENT ROLLS.

BLACK-EDGED PAPER

See MOURNING STATIONERY.

BLANK

As an adjective, 'blank' means 'left white', 'not written or printed upon'. As a noun, a 'blank' is a leaf of paper left white, not written or printed upon. The term is also used to denote an empty space left in a written or printed document, or else a document, such as a blank charter, written with vacant spaces left for the person to whom it is given to fill in as seems fit. Commonly blank leaves in both printed books and manuscripts occur in the preliminaries, at the end, or as dividers between different sections of the text, in addition to the endpapers supplied by the binder. Leaves or pages are still technically described as blank if they bear no text integral to the book's original production or use, but only minor subsequent additions, such as page or folio numbers or very brief inscriptions, signatures, or scribbling.

BLAZON

In heraldry, a blazon is a shield, coat of arms, or banner bearing arms, or else a description in the proper terminology of armorial bearings drawn up in accordance with the formal rules of heraldry as instituted by the College of Arms. To 'blazon' (as distinct from 'emblazon') is to describe arms or other heraldic devices in accordance with these rules.

BLIND

The terms 'blind' and 'blind-stamped' are used in connection with book-binding to describe any non-gilt ornamentation or lettering that is stamped, blocked, or tooled so that only an indented impression is left in the binding.

A type of bibulous unsized paper used to absorb superfluous ink on freshly written documents, blotting paper has been in use since at least the fifteenth century. It was an alternative to early methods of absorbing ink such as sand or pounce shaken from pounce pots, which gradually became obsolete. Blotting paper, of various colours and sometimes bearing printed pictorial images or advertisements, was being developed and manufactured on a large scale by the mid-nineteenth century.

The term 'boards' is commonly used to denote the stiff card or panels at the front and back (but not the spine) of a hard-bound book, including their covering, although, technically, boards are the base for these sides and exclude the covering material. They may, however, be characterized by the covering: e.g. marbled boards. Since the early sixteenth century, boards have tended to be pasteboard, or, from the late seventeenth century, rope-fibre millboard, or, from the eighteenth century, strawboard. Before then, in medieval manuscript volumes, wood was generally used. The covering material has varied from types of leather and vellum to cloth, fabric, and paper. *See* BINDING.

In palaeography, as well as in typography, the body of a letter such as *b* or *p* is that part of the letter resting on the base line exclusive of the ascender or descender.

A bond, or bond and obligation, is a formal legal document or deed acknowledging an indebtedness by one person to another and also acknowledging a payment to be made as a penalty for default. The bond proper is the obligation, recording the penalty for default. Since at least the fourteenth century, the document also contains, usually written (or in more recent times printed) beneath the obligation and sometimes on the dorse, the condition setting out what the bonded person has agreed to commit himself to. This condition annuls the bond when performed. Except for a brief period in the 1650s, the obligation was traditionally drawn up in Latin, in a standard formula beginning *Noverint universi per presentes* (generally rendered in legal documents in

English as 'Be it known to all men by these presents'), and the condition was in English. From 1733 onwards, bonds were written entirely in English.

The various species of bond, entailing authorizations or legally binding engagements, include bonds to perform covenants, which often accompany leases; bonds to appear in court; the bail bond (surety for the release of a ship, a prisoner, or some other commodity pending judicial judgment); and the mariners' bond (a certificate given to a Justice of the Peace for the transportation of felons overseas).

BOOK

Apparently deriving from forms of the Germanic *bok*, originally meaning 'beech' (the wood of that tree traditionally providing the tablets on which runes were carved), the word 'book' is today most commonly understood to be a bound printed volume. Although a bound manuscript volume can technically be described as a codex, the term 'book' is applicable to it as well, as indeed it was before the invention of printing. Certain divisions of literary texts (in the Bible or in Virgil's *Aeneid*, for instance) denote units that might (though not necessarily) once have been separate and independent, or which are now conceived as metaphorically so, originally because a book often represented the contents of a single papyrus scroll.

The term 'book' has, however, been applied historically to almost any kind of written document, both bound and otherwise. If a common feature may be detected it is not anything to do with its physical form, but rather a sense of authority that the record in question has: i.e. that it is the main or official source of reference or finality. Thus, for example, a commercial company's books are the definitive, neatly drawn up accounts of its financial transactions, which may be open to inspection. The book in the Elizabethan and Jacobean theatre was the full and final text of the play provided usually by its author(s) and used as the exemplar for all subsequent copies of actors' parts and during rehearsals and performances by the theatre's manager and stage prompter. A book in the parlance of government officials, at least in Elizabethan times, was the document relating to a particular matter (the warrant, commission, instructions, or whatever) formally drawn up or engrossed for the attention of a lord chancellor or other eminent official, or else prepared for the monarch's seal of approval. The book in a related legal and administrative context was the engrossed charter, grant, letters patent, or other formal instrument embodying the final text and arrangements authorized (as opposed to preliminary drafts of it). The book in gambling parlance also means a bookmaker's register or record of the bets on a given race, match, or other contest or prediction; hence it can symbolize those bets, so that the book might, for instance, be bought by another party who will thereby take responsibility for paying out or reaping the benefits of the bets depending on the result.

No doubt many other uses of the term 'book' can be found, including the naming of particular classes of records kept by departments of state or local government; branches of the military; or professional organizations such as livery companies (e.g. freedom books recording the names of apprentices admitted to the freedom of the company).

BOOK-HOLDER

See BOOK-KEEPING and PROMPTER.

BOOK-KEEPING

In an administrative or business context, book-keeping is the practice or process of keeping accounts, which in general are neatly entered in commercial or company books as formal or official records of financial transactions, payments, and receipts. A book-keeper is the person responsible for keeping such accounts.

BOOK-LABEL

A book-label is a small label attached to a printed or manuscript book, usually on the paste-down inside the cover or on one of the front endpapers, to identify ownership of the volume. Normally oblong in shape (though roundels, ovals, and other shapes are known), a book-label is generally no more than an inch or two in width. It is a smaller label than a bookplate and usually contains little more than the owner's name. What may be the earliest known printed book-label in England is a small typeset black-letter one, reading 'John Bickner owneth this Booke', probably produced by the John Bickner who flourished at Oxford in 1554–61. This is on a copy of Erasmus's *Institutio principis Christiani* (Basle, 1518), now privately owned in Japan. Book-labels in subsequent periods have also tended to be printed, while other details of the owner's library, such as shelf-marks or press-marks, are relegated to inscriptions.

BOOKLET

A modern term, the diminutive form of 'book', 'booklet' simply means a 'small book', generally a thin pamphlet, which is sewn, stapled, or glued. As applied to manuscripts, it may mean a thin unit or sheaf comprising not much more than one or two gatherings. The term is also sometimes used by medievalists to denote a single gathering or quire.

Bookmarks, or bookmarkers, are items loosely inserted into a book to mark a particular place for reference or for easy return and continued reading. As a bibliographical tool, they are of considerable antiquity, their use dating back at least to the twelfth century. Extant examples include strips of parchment, some of them coloured, leather thongs, strips of paper, and linen or silk ribbons, sometimes attached to the spine or headband and hanging down in any chosen opening. Examples of medieval bookmarks exist that are somewhat more elaborate and serve in effect as column markers. They comprise a revolving parchment disc bearing numbers indicating columns, which may be turned to indicate the one selected, attached to a small strip of parchment capable of being moved up and down a cord suspended from the headband to signal the required line of text. By contrast, modern bookmarks may be strips of leather, silk, plastic, card, or other material, plain or elaborate, manufactured and printed as decorative items, as advertisements, as souvenirs of places, exhibitions, or celebrations, or as sources of other information.

In principle, any suitably sized object whatsoever may be used as a bookmark. As early as the fourteenth century a bishop (Richard de Bury, 1287–1345) could deplore the use of straws as bookmarks, since they were apt to decay. Books bequeathed by the jurist John Selden (1584–1654) to the Bodleian Library, Oxford, were found to contain dozens of pairs of spectacles that he had used as bookmarks. In a poster displayed in more recent years by the British Library, examples of objects found in books and used as markers included a rasher of bacon and a jam sandwich.

BOOK OF CONCORDATUMS

A concordatum (the Latin *concordatum* means 'something agreed') was an order by the Privy Council regarding money set aside for particular matters relating to state affairs outside normal routine business. Hence a book of concordatums is an official register recording extraordinary disbursements. Books of this kind are found among the State Papers relating to Ireland in the National Archives at Kew (in the SP 63 series). Both they and the practice of special payments they record seem to have flourished particularly with respect to Irish affairs in the reign of Elizabeth I, although the term 'concordatum' in connection with special funding was used at least until the mid-nineteenth century. Equivalent books recording extraordinary state expenses exist under different names on the continent, including, for instance, registers in the Venetian archives recording secret payments for assassinations ordered by the State Council in the 1620s and 1630s.

The term 'book of entries' can be applied to various types of registers, ledgers, and memorandum books that record on a regular or day-to-day basis official business or proceedings of some kind. Examples are those relating to certain merchant companies, the control of imports and exports at specific ports, naval prizes, and taxation on births, marriages, and burials.

A book of entries in a legal context is specifically a collection of pleadings (or 'counts', as they were called, from the French word for 'story', rendered in Latin as *narrationes*), in law-French and Latin. These were copied principally from the records of the Common Bench or Common Pleas, as also to a lesser extent of the King's Bench, formally entered in the official plea rolls. Such collections of precedents were probably produced for the guidance of court officers, attorneys, and special pleaders. Books of entries flourished in manuscript form from the early fifteenth century. One was first printed, by Richard Pynson in London, as *Intrationum excellentissimus liber*, in 1510. They continued to be produced, in one form or another, until about 1700, petering out in the eighteenth century. The manuscript volumes, which involved much labour to produce, were evidently much valued by early owners and a considerable number were bequeathed in wills. A book of entries is to be distinguished from a book of forms and precedents. *Compare* BOOK OF FORMS AND PRECEDENTS.

'The Book of Entries' in a government context specifically denotes the Registers of the Privy Council (National Archives, Kew, PC 2). *See* PRIVY COUNCIL.

BOOK OF FORMS AND PRECEDENTS

A book of forms and precedents, whether manuscript or printed, is a legal formulary. Since the early thirteenth century such compilations, which often preserve legal texts found in no other source, have been made to serve as models of form and wording for the practical use and guidance of lawyers, law students, and other practitioners. Over the years, the size of the volumes produced increased considerably, especially as they came to incorporate additional notes and rules. The result was that books of forms and precedents were the commonest species of medieval English legal manuscripts after statute books. Their usefulness was such that the practice of compiling one's own manuscript formulary continued well after the advent of print, and they were the subject of occasional bequests even as late as the seventeenth century.

There are two principal types of formulary. The earlier one recorded examples of Latin writs as embodied in official Chancery rolls or in Year Books. A fifteenth-century collection of such writs was eventually printed in 1531 (*see* REGISTRUM BREVIUM). A second type of collection contained examples of deeds, bonds, bills, and other legal instruments for conveyancing, as well as wills and other settlements, in Latin and English. Such collections evidently appealed not only to law students and law clerks, but also to practitioners on the fringes of the legal profession, such as scriveners. Their utility was amply extolled in the printed versions that subsequently appeared, such as Thomas Phayer's *A Newe Boke of Presidentes in Maner of a Register* (1543), or publications such as *The Compleat Clark, and Scriveners Guide* (1655) and *The Perfect Conveyancer* (1655). *Compare* BOOK OF ENTRIES.

From medieval times until the seventeenth century, the word 'precedent' itself denoted enrolled legal precedents, generally meaning examples from the official plea rolls, but since the late seventeenth century has meant reported judicial decisions.

A precedent (as used in Shakespeare, for instance) might also mean the original document from which a copy is made.

BOOK OF HOURS

Horæ (Latin for 'hours'), more commonly known as 'books of hours', or sometimes 'primers' (Latin: *primaria*), are a type of devotional volume in Roman Catholic use. Although they were based on texts that were in ecclesiastical use by the tenth century and in popular use by the late twelfth century, and originally formed parts of psalters, *horæ* flourished in manuscript form especially from the fourteenth to sixteenth centuries. They incorporate a shorter version of the devotions performed at the eight canonical hours (Matins and Lauds, Prime, Terce, Sext, None, Vespers, and Compline), specifically the Little Office of the Blessed Virgin (the Hours of the Blessed Virgin or *Horæ Beatæ Mariæ Virginis*). *Horæ* are attractively produced prayer books, which could also include a calendar, almanac, hymns, psalms, and meditations. While the main texts would be in Latin, some of these supplementary devotions, from the late fourteenth century onwards, were occasionally in English. Books of hours were produced in vast numbers by commercial workshops for a popular market among the laity throughout Europe, most especially in France and Flanders (many of which came to England). Usually relatively small and portable in size—for the most part not much more than about 6¾ × 4¾ inches (17 × 12 cm), although exceptional examples are larger—books of hours are almost always well bound, decorated, and illuminated; are frequently written on vellum throughout; and are often embellished with full-page miniatures portraying the Virgin, or depicting other biblical scenes or saints. Some examples, usually of a grand or elaborate character, also include portraits of the patron by or for whom they were commissioned.

Like breviaries and missals, books of hours are often distinguished by the particular diocese whose forms and precepts they follow. Thus, a manuscript characterized as 'use of Sarum' is one basically conforming to the Roman rite as used in Salisbury Cathedral from about the twelfth century onwards. Other major cathedrals and geographical locations by which the use of liturgies incorporated in *horæ* were commonly distinguished include York, Rome, Paris, Rouen, Amiens, Rheims, Liège, Bourges, Besançon, and Utrecht, as well as those service books characterized by religious orders, such as Ambrosian, Carthusian, or Bridgettine.

Chiefly because of their visual appeal, as well as their relatively modest commercial value (although exceptionally fine examples can sell for huge sums of money), these volumes remain one of the most popular and most widely collected genres of late medieval manuscripts.

Books of hours were also produced by early printers. The printed versions were as popular as the manuscript volumes, with well over 530 different European editions of *horæ* published before 1500 (the majority French, a few English). These editions were copied from manuscript exemplars (though French versions sometimes introduced printers' innovations); were of similar pocket-book size; were generally illustrated with woodcut miniatures, which were coloured or illuminated by hand; and were often also decorated or rubricated by hand, the exempla of any particular edition usually bearing decorations in different styles by different hands. Both manuscript and printed books of hours had ceased being produced by the end of the sixteenth century.

BOOKPLATE

A bookplate, or book-plate, is a label attached to a printed or manuscript book, usually on the paste-down inside the cover or on one of the front endpapers, to identify ownership of the volume. Like a book-label, it is generally printed, but will tend to be of larger format, ranging from 2 or 3 inches in height to the size of a whole page. Bookplates are generally of rectangular shape, although variations are known, and contain not only the names of the owner, or of his or her family, but also a graphic design. This will often incorporate a personal or family coat of arms, crest, or motto, sometimes even a depiction of the owner's estate, and maybe emblems of his principal interests or profession, as well as perhaps an *ex libris* heading. The plate may also contain manuscript additions, such as a signature or shelf-mark. Bookplates, often with woodcuts, which are sometimes hand-coloured, are known to date from as early as the mid to late fifteenth century (in Germany); early bookplate designers include Albrecht Dürer, Lucas Cranach the Elder, and Hans Holbein. They seem to have become popular in England from about the mid to late seventeenth century onwards.

BOOKWORM

Besides its literal meaning (*see* WORMHOLE), the term 'bookworm' may also colloquially be applied to a habitual, avid, or voracious reader of books.

BORDER

See MARGIN.

BOSS

A boss is a prominent, raised stud or ornament, usually of metal, on the wooden or leather binding of a manuscript or early printed volume. An occasional feature, which helps to strengthen and protect the volume, bosses are most commonly found on fifteenth-century bindings, but occasionally elsewhere. They can often be taken as an indication that the book was either kept shelved horizontally or, like certain university proctors' books, designed to be carried in public. In the latter case, bosses will have had short chains attached to them at the centre-top of the front and rear boards (a feature that can mistakenly be interpreted as evidence that they were part of a chained library).

BOWL

See LOBE.

BREVE

Breve (plural: *brevia*) is the Latin form of the word 'brief' (*see* BRIEF). A breve is also a diacritical mark that, placed over a vowel, indicates that it is a short vowel (e.g. ă) as opposed to a long vowel signified by the use of a macron (e.g. ā, where the vowel is pronounced 'ah').

BREVIARY

A breviary (Latin: *breviarium*, originally meaning 'summary' or 'abridgement') is a liturgical book, either manuscript or printed, containing texts for the celebration of the Divine Office of the Catholic Church for each day of the calendar. It includes Latin prayers, psalms, hymns, collects, lessons, and readings from the Scriptures or from lives of saints. The term is related to the Latin *brevis* ('short') because the breviary is in some sense an abbreviated amalgamation in single portable form of several types of liturgical book, serving from the eleventh century onwards as a useful service book for clerics who were obliged to recite all the appropriate offices for each day. Varying in text and form over the years according to geographical location and religious order (*see* BOOK OF HOURS), breviaries as manuscript volumes are sometimes highly decorated, with historiated initials, and, in elaborate examples, with illuminated miniatures.

BREVIATE

A breviate is a brief statement, summary, or abridgement, usually of an official nature, such as a breviate of parliamentary papers. The term 'breviate' was also once used as an alternative to 'brief', both in the sense of a short letter or note and also in the legal sense of a lawyer's brief.

BREVIGRAPH

'Brevigraph' is a term sometimes used to denote a type of abbreviation in which two or more letters are represented by a single symbol: for instance, the elongated ℮ to represent *es*, or the various types of *p* with curls or cross-strokes on the descender to represent *par*, *per*, *pre*, *prae*, or *pro*.

BRIEF

In the most common use of the term today, a brief is a short summary, especially a summary of the facts of a case prepared by lawyers for the instruction of legal counsel for their appearance in court and which might include other papers relevant to the case. This practice has flourished despite the advice of a chief justice in 1640 recommending new serjeants (a superior order of barristers) not to rely on briefs prepared by solicitors, but to draw up their own.

In the Middle Ages, the term 'brief' (a French word), or its Latin form *breve* (plural: *brevia*), could also mean any kind of written note, letter, or dispatch, but came to mean more specifically a letter of authority issued by a royal, government, legal, or ecclesiastical official ordering people to do things. A Church Brief, or King's Brief, was a mandate addressed to each parish incumbent and churchwardens and read out from the pulpit, authorizing a collection in churches throughout England for a particular charity or deserving cause, the brief being returned to the relevant authorities, together with the funds collected at the church door, with an endorsement specifying the sum raised.

A papal brief, or *breve*, was a letter sent by the Roman Curia to some individual or religious community, generally concerning matters of ecclesiastical discipline. Usually a somewhat less formal or widely significant pronouncement than a bull, the document would be written on vellum by a clerk of the Papal Chancery, subscribed by the Pope's Secretary of Briefs, dated, and (at least from about 1265 onwards) sealed with an impression in red wax of the Pope's signet ring, the seal of the fisherman. By the sixteenth century, such *brevia* would commonly be issued in printed broadsheet form.

BRITISH LIBRARY

Among the many important libraries in the English-speaking world, the British Library must stand pre-eminent as the largest and most significant, containing as it does upwards of 150 million books, manuscripts, maps, drawings, musical scores, and other artefacts. Originally part of the British Museum, which was founded in 1753, the 'foundation collections' include the books and manuscripts of the politician Sir Robert Cotton (1571–1631), which, among the huge number of significant state papers and historical documents he owned, include the Lindisfarne Gospels and *Beowulf*; of the physician Sir Hans Sloane (1660–1753); and of the politician Sir Robert Harley (1661–1724) and his son Edward (1689–1741), which, among much else, includes *The Booke of Sir Thomas Moore* containing three pages very probably in the hand of Shakespeare. Among the many other important collections of manuscripts subsequently acquired are the Royal Manuscripts, comprising collections of British monarchs since Edward IV, presented in 1757 by George II; the King's Manuscripts, the library of George III, presented in 1823 by George IV; the Lansdowne Manuscripts, collected by William Petty (1737–1805), first Marquess of Lansdowne, including many state papers of William Cecil (1520–1598), Lord Burghley, purchased in 1807; the Burney Manuscripts, of the schoolmaster Charles Burney (1757–1817), purchased in 1818; the Arundel Manuscripts, of the art collector Thomas Howard (1585–1646), fourteenth Earl of Arundel, purchased from the Royal Society in 1831; and the Stowe Manuscripts, of Richard Temple-Nugent-Brydges-Chandos-Grenville (1776–1839), first Duke of Buckingham and Chandos, purchased from Bertram Ashburnham (1840–1913), fifth Earl of Ashburnham, in 1883.

All these, and other collections, have been catalogued in some detail over the years, including the series of Egerton Manuscripts, extended from the original collection bequeathed by Francis Henry Egerton (1756–1829), eighth Earl of Bridgewater (up to 3,882 by the year 2000), and the Add-itional Manuscripts (currently extending to well over 81,500 manuscripts), as well as the separate series of Additional Charters and Rolls (currently approaching 80,000). However, while some (such as the Royal Manuscripts) have been catalogued exceptionally well, the antiquated cataloguing of some of the most important—including the Cotton and Harley collections, last catalogued in 1802 and 1808–12 respectively—remains less than adequate for modern scholarly use, and well below the cataloguing standard of the more recent Additional Manuscripts. It is hoped that the process, begun in recent years, of entering these catalogues online will continue and that the older catalogues will soon be updated accordingly.

The British Library was established as a separate body, distinct from the British Museum, in 1973, and it moved from Bloomsbury to its present new premises at St Pancras in 1997. Although its still limited storage facilities continue to necessitate the housing of many books and some more recently acquired manuscript collections (such as certain booksellers' archives) in a number of off-site locations (in Yorkshire and elsewhere), the great majority of manuscripts are still preserved and accessible at St Pancras.

BULL

A bull, or *bulla* (the Latin originally denoting a circular or global object), was in early times any seal attached to an official document. From the sixth century onwards, although bulls were also used by Byzantine emperors, the term became more specifically applied to the leaden seal of authentication attached to an edict by the Pope issued by the Papal Chancery. Later, from the thirteenth century onwards, it denoted the papal document itself. Invariably written in Latin, and originally dealing with a variety of administrative matters, bulls became more generally, by the fifteenth century, formal and solemn edicts on serious doctrinal or ecclesiastical matters of wider significance, as opposed to briefs, or *brevia*, which generally dealt with local matters and bore a different, wax seal.

Although early papal bulls were written on papyrus (the earliest recorded extant examples are a fragment of one by Pope Adrian I, of 22 January 788, now in the Bibliothèque Nationale, Paris, and one by Pope Paschal I, of 11 July 819, in the archives of Ravenna), bulls and the official copies of them came to be commonly engrossed on vellum, the formulaic wording generally beginning with the name of the Pope, followed by *Episcopus servus servorum Dei ad perpetuam rei memoriam* and then by the text, ending with the date. By at least as early as the twelfth century, bulls would be signed not only by cardinals and other officials, but also by the Pope himself, whose signature would appear at the foot of the document beside an impression of a *rota*, or wheel of concentric circles, within which was written his motto. Later bulls were generally signed by functionaries of the Papal Chancery. Engrossed official copies were issued to the archbishops or other leading ecclesiastical authorities throughout the Catholic world, while the signed originals were retained in Rome.

The circular leaden seal that was attached to each would, by about the thirteenth century, bear on one side the images of Saint Peter and Saint Paul and on the other the name of the reigning pope and, in later years, his date of accession. This seal would be attached by a silken cord for a Bull of Grace—i.e. one conferring rights, benefices, etc. in favourable response to petitions—or by a hempen cord for a Bull of Justice—i.e. one (liable to be folded and sealed so that it could be opened only by cutting the cord or parchment) conveying administrative orders, or appointing judges in ecclesiastical cases that had been referred to the Curia. In rare cases, for exceptionally important bulls, the seal might be not of lead but (adopting a practice also used by Byzantine emperors) of gold.

The most famous and perhaps most consequential papal bulls relating to England are that by which Leo X bestowed on Henry VIII the title *Fidei Defensor* ('Defender of the Faith') on 11 October 1521; the bull of excommunication issued against Henry VIII by Clement VII on 11 July 1533, following the king's divorce and remarriage; and the bull of excommunication that Pius V issued against Elizabeth I on 27 April 1570, because of her 'heresies' and 'monstrous' crimes against the Church, which released her Catholic subjects from any oath of fealty and obedience to her.

BULLARY

A bullary (Latin: *bullarium*) is a volume or collection of transcripts of papal bulls, including those that appeared in print from the late sixteenth century onwards.

BUREAU

A bureau (the word is French) is a type of furniture used for writing. It usually incorporates a writing surface, generally a hinged flap which pulls down flat, over sets of drawers, with pigeon-holes and inner compartments for storing papers, and also sometimes kneeholes underneath to accommodate seated writers more comfortably. Various prototypes of the bureau were developed in France and Italy in the sixteenth century, but its main development dates from the late seventeenth century. The bureau was subject to numerous refinements over the years, including elaborately veneered parquetry and other decorative features, and even smaller portable versions were manufactured. In its various forms, this type of furniture was also widely known in England as a 'secretaire', 'escritoire', 'scriptor', 'scrutoire', and 'secretary'.

Since the eighteenth century the word 'bureau' has also been applied to an office, usually one dealing with public business, most especially a branch or department of government administration (such as the US Federal Bureau of Investigation).

BURSE

The term 'burse' (etymologically related to, and sometimes synonymous with, the word 'purse', meaning a bag or pouch to hold money) has more than one application. The Burse in London, for instance, is the Royal Exchange built in 1566 by Sir Thomas Gresham, and Britain's Burse was the New Exchange built on the Strand in 1609 by Robert Cecil, Earl of Salisbury. The term is also related to 'bursar', meaning a treasurer, one in charge of finances, especially in a college.

In addition, 'burse' is the term used for the square-shaped case or bag that has customarily been used to hold the matrix of the Great Seal in the custody of the Lord Chancellor or Lord Keeper. Originally made of white linen or leather, since the time of Henry VIII the burse has been elaborately embroidered with regal arms and emblems worked in gold or silver thread, with sequins and other decorative needlework, on a velvet and silk ground. A rare surviving Elizabethan example, once owned by Lord Keeper Thomas Egerton, later Lord Chancellor, is in the British Museum. Since at least the seventeenth century, the burse has also traditionally been kept hung on a rigid frame about 16 inches (40 cm) wide.

C

CABINET

Since at least the sixteenth century, the type of usually expensive furniture known as a cabinet, comprising a form of upright chest with drawers, shelves, compartments, and perhaps doors with locks, has been associated with the storage of personal letters and other documents, as well as assorted curiosities and such valuable items as jewellery—to be kept private and confidential apart from being displayed to select guests. Because of its connotation of both value and exclusiveness—reflected also in the modern use of the term denoting the most confidential government council—the word 'cabinet' often appears in the titles of seventeenth-century books supposedly revealing sensational political information, secret documents, or otherwise risqué texts ('The Cabinet of the Parliament', 'The Cabinet of the Jesuits' secrets opened', 'The cabinet of Venus unlocked, and her secrets laid open', etc.).

CADEL

A cadel is a decorative flourish on certain lettering in medieval or later manuscripts, characterized by the extension and elaboration of the penstrokes on letters, usually at the beginning of particular lines. The more convoluted examples include features such as human heads or other figures and designs.

CALAMUS

A *calamus* (a Latin word) was a type of sharpened, split reed pen used for writing in ink on papyrus or parchment in ancient times. *See* its use in CURRENTE CALAMO.

CALENDAR

A calendar is some kind of tabular booklet or chart showing the days and months in a year or, alternatively, a section tabulating such information within a book. Most familiar today as commercially printed products, calendars may be designed to stand up on a desk where, perhaps, each day occupies a leaf that may be readily detached after expiry. Alternatively, and more commonly, they are colourful items that may be pinned up on a wall. Such calendars may also be used as a type of diary or journal, when the spaces allowed for each day are inscribed with entries recording appointments to be kept or events that have occurred. US submariners, for instance, often used their pin-up calendars for this purpose in the Second World War, when the page for each month was liable to have the central illustration of an attractive girl surrounded by manuscript entries recording their vessel's battle successes, etc. (Examples of these are preserved in the Bowfin Museum at Pearl Harbor, Hawaii.)

Earlier manuscript types of calendar date from the medieval period onwards. They usually identify local saints' days and church festivals (features that help scholars to determine their provenance). Some of them are illuminated, and some incorporated in books of hours and other devotional books. *See also* DATES.

In other contexts, a calendar may also be any kind of list or register, but most specifically a catalogue of documents, generally arranged chronologically with short summaries of them. Well-known examples are the printed Calendars of State Papers, Patent Rolls and Charter Rolls of the Public Record Office (now National Archives, Kew). Most county and civic record offices have typescript or computer print-out calendars (of varying quality) of their archival collections.

'Calendar' is also a term applied to a list of prisoners brought to trial at a criminal court.

CALF

See BINDING.

CALL BOOK

See VISITATION.

CALLIGRAPHY

Deriving from the Greek *kallos* ('beauty') and *graphē* ('writing'), the term 'calligraphy' means the art of beautiful penmanship, and a calligraphic manuscript is one characterized by fine writing, design, or ornamentation, executed with skill and elegance. Calligraphic script differs from mere neat handwriting in the extent to which its principal object is its physical or visual appearance, in the degree to which it is consciously prepared, and in the extent to which it draws attention to itself as an attractive and aesthetic piece of artistry in its own right, as a material artefact worthy of display, whatever its text. Notable calligraphers flourished in both the medieval and early modern periods, continuing well after the invention of printing. Some of them, from the late sixteenth century onwards, were writing masters who produced books of specimen writings as models or wrote treatises on the subject.

An example of a highly gifted calligrapher is Esther Inglis (1571–1624), of Edinburgh, whose many manuscript copies of largely devotional texts could each exhibit a variety of styles of script, up to more than forty in a single manuscript, including imitations of typefaces. Some were written in minute lettering on leaves scarcely more than 4 × 6 cm in size (*see* Illus. 12); yet others contained a self-portrait, elaborate decoration, and dedicatory verses. For further examples of calligraphic writing, *see* Illus. 21, 35, 54, and 95.

The art of calligraphy in England, as well as of letter and type design, has had something of a renaissance in modern times, partly due to the huge influence of Edward Johnston (1872–1944), whose almost equally influential pupils included William Graily Hewitt (1864–1952), Eric Gill (1882–1940), and Irene Wellington (1904–1984). A notable Modern Calligraphic Collection is at the National Art Museum at the Victoria and Albert Museum, London.

CALL NUMBER

The call number in a library is the registered code or official numbering used to identify the particular book or manuscript, which must be cited by a reader when submitting an order to see it. The call number may be synonymous with its press-mark or shelf-mark, which identifies the book's actual location, but it is often instead simply a number assigned in a catalogue within an accumulated series (such as 'Additional MS 25247') regardless of shelf location. *Compare* PRESS-MARK and SHELF-MARK.

CANCEL

The word 'cancel' derives from the Latin *cancellus* or *cancelli* denoting a lattice or cross-bars. To cancel written text is to cross out or delete it, most commonly by drawing lines through or across it, whether or not as a series of *X*s (*see* Illus. 58 and 73).

A cancel may also be text that is physically substituted for previous text. Thus verbal changes that are written or printed on small slips of paper pasted over text in a manuscript or printed book may be called 'cancels'. Alternatively, especially in printed books, a cancel (or *cancellans* in its Latin form) may be a leaf or series of leaves that are bound- or tipped-in to replace original leaves that, for some reason, have been removed (perhaps because badly printed or because of subsequent revision or censorship). The original

ILLUS. 12 *An example of the calligraphy of Esther Inglis, showing an opening in a tiny 32mo book (each page c.1½ × 2½ inches or 4 × 6.2 cm, and with ruled margins) containing her copy of the* Quatrains du Sieur de Pybrac. *The book is written in a minute hand in a variety of different scripts, some imitating typefaces, for presentation as a New Year's gift to Henri, Vicomte de Rohan, 31 December 1600. The page on the left, at the end of her dedicatory epistle, bears her flourished signature in its French form.*

leaf or sheet replaced (not to be confused with the cancel) is called a 'cancelland' (or *cancellandum*, meaning 'to be cancelled').

In philately, a postage stamp is cancelled—usually with a hand-stamped or mechanically applied cancellation—when it has some kind of marking or design or perforation imposed upon it so that it cannot be used again.

CANCELLAND

See CANCEL.

CANCELLARESCA

See CHANCERY HAND.

CAPITAL

Deriving from the lettering that sometimes appears at the head, or *capitellum*, of Roman columns, the term 'capital', or 'capital letter', means a large letter (an upper-case one in typography). It is the same as a majuscule, as opposed to a minuscule. *Compare* MINUSCULE.

CAPTION

Deriving from the Latin *captionem* ('taking' or 'capture'), the term 'caption' denotes the text forming a heading, subscription, or label to describe something graphic on a page, such as a drawing or features of a map (*see* Illus. 30 and 35). Such features might then be described as 'captioned'.

In older legal use, caption meant a judicial arrest or seizure. Alternatively, it was that part of a legal instrument such as a commission or indictment, the wording of which begins *Inquisitio capta coram . . .* ('An inquiry held in the presence of . . .'), stating the authority by which it was executed. *See also* LETTERS OF CAPTION.

CARBON COPY

A carbon copy, or carbon-copy, is the under-copy of a typescript, as opposed to the top copy, when a text is typed in duplicate. Whereas the lettering on the top copy is produced on the typewriter by the keys striking the inked ribbon directly on to the sheet, the under-copy bears the same impressions via the use of carbon paper interlaid between the two sheets (and a second under-copy would be produced if a further layer of carbon paper and under-sheet were used). The lettering on a carbon copy, usually in blue or black ink, is generally a little less distinct and clear-cut than that on the top copy, and may also show marks or smudging because of rubbing of the carbon paper against the under-sheet(s) (*see* Illus. 13).

There is also a modern type of stationery for writing and recording purposes comprising a bound account book or letterbook in which blank pages alternate with sheets of carbon paper, each top page being perforated at the inner edge for easy removal after being written on while each underlying page retains the text by virtue of the intervening carbon paper.

The invention of carbon, or carbonated, paper (sometimes also called 'sponge paper'), which was originally paper soaked in printer's ink and dried, dates back at least to 1806 when Ralph Wedgwood obtained a patent for its use in what he called his 'Stylographic Writer', a kind of writing board with metal wires invented primarily to help blind people to write. The use of such paper allowed duplicates to be made without further use of ink. Indeed, an early example of a hand-written document produced as a carbon copy is a letter sent to Wedgwood himself by the poet P. B. Shelley in February 1811 (now in the Bodleian Library, Oxford). Comparable methods, for a similar purpose, were independently devised at about the same time by Pelegrino Turri in Italy. Other types of carbon paper, including the familiar one-sided paper to reduce smudging, were then commercially developed in America and elsewhere.

CARET

Originally a Latin word meaning 'it needs', the term 'caret' denotes the symbol ^ used by scribes since at least the thirteenth century to mark the place in a

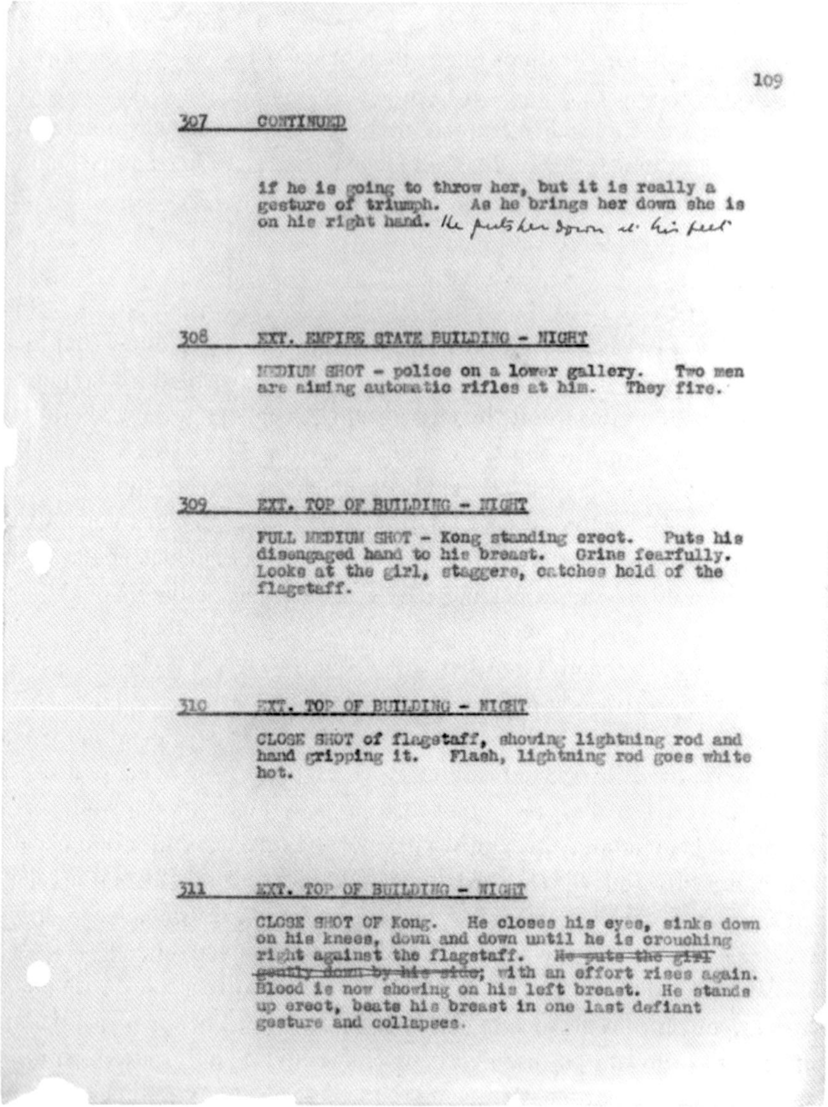

307   CONTINUED

if he is going to throw her, but it is really a
gesture of triumph.   As he brings her down she is
on his right hand. *He puts her down at his feet*

308   EXT. EMPIRE STATE BUILDING - NIGHT

MEDIUM SHOT - police on a lower gallery.   Two men
are aiming automatic rifles at him.   They fire.

309   EXT. TOP OF BUILDING - NIGHT

FULL MEDIUM SHOT - Kong standing erect.   Puts his
disengaged hand to his breast.   Grins fearfully.
Looks at the girl, staggers, catches hold of the
flagstaff.

310   EXT. TOP OF BUILDING - NIGHT

CLOSE SHOT of flagstaff, showing lightning rod and
hand gripping it.   Flash, lightning rod goes white
hot.

311   EXT. TOP OF BUILDING - NIGHT

CLOSE SHOT OF Kong.   He closes his eyes, sinks down
on his knees, down and down until he is crouching
right against the flagstaff.   ~~He puts the girl~~
~~gently down by his side~~; with an effort rises again.
Blood is now showing on his left breast.   He stands
up erect, beats his breast in one last defiant
gesture and collapses.

ILLUS. 13 *A page of the carbon-copy typescript of Edgar Wallace's original film-script of* King Kong, *bearing two autograph revisions (one an insertion, the other a deletion), January 1932. This is the copy retained by Wallace after the top copy had been submitted to the RKO studio in Hollywood a month before his death.*

line of text where something was to be inserted. The new text would usually be written supralineally above the caret or else in the margin (*see* Illus. 8). A version of this symbol is still used by printers in proof correcting.

CARTA EXECUTORIA DE HIDALGUÍA

See GENEALOGY.

CARTE-DE-VISITE

A carte-de-visite, or visiting card, is a small card on which are printed the name and often other relevant details of a particular person, who will usually possess multiple examples of the card for occasional distribution. Such cards serve purposes relating both to social etiquette and to practical business, being a ready means of establishing a person's credentials and status in society and making possible further communication between him or her and the recipient of the card. Cartes-de-visite date from at least as early as the sixteenth century, when their use by German students is recorded, and their use by Englishmen dates from at least *c*.1605 when Sir Charles Cornwallis, Ambassador to Spain, had one printed.

The fashion for them flourished especially from the eighteenth century onwards, when stationers produced vast quantities of custom-made cards, in various types of font, for the socially established or aspiring professional classes, who, as visitors to grand or respectable houses, might be expected to place their cards on a silver tray at the entrance hall to be conveyed by a servant to the host or hostess for scrutiny before they were admitted. By the mid-nineteenth century, the card also tended to correspond to the standard size for photographic portraits (in the region of 4 × 2 inches, 100 × 55 mm) and were likewise often collected for mounting in albums. It was fashionable for the card to be minimalist, containing only the name of its owner (the more important, the less need to proclaim), although it became increasingly practical for it to contain additional information, such as his or her status or position, address, and so on. Some cartes-de-visite, with perhaps printed borders, were left deliberately blank so that the owner could inscribe his or her name by hand, and it was in any case common for printed cards to be personalized by their owners' inserting hand-written messages to particular recipients. Some of the inscriptions used might take the form of standard shorthand messages, such as 'ppc' (meaning *pour prendre congé*); the card would be left on the tray when the person was leaving town and had no time to say 'goodbye'.

The term 'carte-de-visite' may perhaps also be extended to other types of small presentation cards that do not relate specifically to visits, but which are

ILLUS. 14 *A partly printed card, c.2½ × 3¾ inches (6.5 × 9.5 cm), with engraved vignette and manuscript insertions, serving as a kind of carte-de-visite for Omai, the Polynesian who enjoyed a successful year's stay among London high society in 1775–6.*

of similar size and serve the purposes of these cards in other respects, such as formally answering enquiries. Cards for these, as for many other contingencies, were produced by stationers, with printed lettering and with spaces left for particular details to be entered by hand. One, for instance, used by Omai, the Polynesian brought by Captain Cook to England in 1775–6, was printed with an engraved vignette and borders and with standard lettering leaving spaces for manuscript insertions: thus (the manuscript insertions here rendered in italic) 'M'. Omai presents *his* Compliments to M'. *Way* and Returns *him* many thanks for the Favor of *his* obliging Enquiry's'. *See* Illus. 14.

CARTOGRAPHY

Cartography is the study of maps and their history. The term is also applied to the practice of drawing maps and charts. A cartographer is a chart- or map-maker. The early modern period produced a number of innovative cartographers, the most important being Gerard Mercator (1512–1594), who developed his own revolutionary projection method for representing the earth's sphere on a flat surface and whom his distinguished colleague Abraham Ortelius (1527–1598) called 'the Ptolemy of our age'. Mercator's own collection of fifty maps of Europe bound together as an atlas, with his autograph annotations, including his wall-map of the British Isles (1564) and two manuscript maps in his own hand, is preserved in the British Library (Maps C.29.c.13). *See also* MAP and PORTOLAN.

CARTOUCHE

A cartouche is a decorative ornament in the form of a representation of a scroll, tablet, shield, or other enclosed figure, sometimes bearing an inscription. Cartouches are found commonly on maps (*see* Illus. 48), occasional letters patent, heraldic documents, and on book or manuscript bindings. In Egyptian hieroglyphics, cartouches surrounded the names of royal personages.

CARTULARY

A cartulary, or chartulary, is a manuscript book or formal register in which are copied *in extenso* the texts of charters, deeds, and other records relating to the foundation, land, property, privileges, and legal rights of a particular abbey, monastery, college, or manorial estate. Some (especially later ones) also contain drawings of seals or other features of the original documents copied, and even maps of the land described. Chiefly produced from about the twelfth century onwards, more modern examples including those commissioned by particular landed families, cartularies are of various sizes, but from the fourteenth century onwards have tended to be large folio or large quarto coucher-sized volumes, more often than not written on vellum throughout, and sturdily bound in parchment or leather. Drawn up as a detailed and permanent account of a particular owner's or community's rights and possessions, and incorporating the full historical evidences for them, such registers clearly served a practical function in their time, and they often remain a source of considerable value to local historians.

A particularly notable example in the early modern period is provided by the 'Great Books' of Lady Anne Clifford (1590–1676), who spent thirty-eight years of her life establishing her rights of inheritance to family estates in Yorkshire and Westmorland. She commissioned a set of three large and illustrated cartularies, or 'Books of Record', to be drawn up, each measuring over 18 × 15 inches (46.5 × 38 cm), with between *c.*200 and 460 pages in each, containing transcripts of relevant historical accounts, genealogies, and family and land documents, including drawings of their seals, from medieval times onwards. This voluminous series was produced in triplicate by various scribes, with her own autograph additions and annotations, all three sets of which are now in the Cumbria Record Office, Kendal. *See* Illus. 30.

CASE PAPERS

'Case papers' is a generic term denoting all the documents that relate to a particular lawsuit, including bills of complaint, depositions, interrogatories, answers, replications, briefs, and summaries, prepared by or for legal counsel.

In commercial book-keeping and accountancy, a cash-book is a book in which is kept a usually continuous, daily record of money paid and received.

CASTING-OFF MARKS

Casting-off marks are characteristics of printer's copy and were written usually in the margin of the manuscript, typescript, or printed text (if an earlier edition was being used as copy) from which the printer's type was to be set. Usually comprising slashes, sometimes parallel slashes (//), or else a step-like figure (⌐) or a wavy line transected in the middle by a Z (~ ~ ~ ~ ~ ~ ~ Z ~ ~ ~ ~ ~ ~), these marks indicated page breaks, where each new printed page should (or did) end, after the printer or typesetter had estimated the page area to be covered taking into account the given type size. The copy—generally known as 'cast-off copy'—might also be numbered to show the pages it would occupy within the printed forme. This kind of preparation facilitated printing by multiple compositors working simultaneously on a single text. *See* PRINTER'S COPY.

CATALOGUING AND DESCRIBING OF MANUSCRIPTS

There are various schools of thought on the proper ways of describing or cataloguing manuscripts of different kinds and different periods. Nevertheless, a full and detailed description of a manuscript, whether a literary work or a legal, scientific, or other miscellaneous document, is likely to include, where applicable, particulars of features such as the following:

title of work(s) (with first line if a poem, or incipit if a medieval text or a song);

genre (e.g. poem, sermon, tract) or type of document (e.g. indenture, letters patent, manorial roll);

contents (a full or selective list of the individual items in a composite volume, or of the multiple texts contained in a verse miscellany, etc.);

authorship of the text(s) (identified, attributed, or ascribed);

material (paper, parchment, etc.);

watermark(s) (in paper);

identity of handwriting (autograph if by the author; identity of the scribe if known, recognizable, or mentioned in a colophon; whether in a professional or non-professional hand, etc.);

script(s) employed (e.g. secretary, italic, court hand);

special or characteristic features of the handwriting (e.g. cursive, sloped or upright, peculiar letter-forms);

leaf size or format (e.g. folio, quarto, duodecimo; or specifying horizontal and vertical measurements in inches and millimetres);

foliation or pagination (how originally and/or presently numbered);

total number of leaves, pages, or membranes;

layout (e.g. written in double columns, rubricated, with ruled margins);

decoration, illustration, or illumination (e.g. geometrical diagrams, historiated borders, arms emblazoned in their proper colours);

collation (a book's structure in terms of quires, inserted leaves, cancels, etc.);

binding (e.g. contemporary limp vellum, late seventeenth-century red morocco gilt, eighteenth-century mottled calf);

evidence of provenance (e.g. coats of arms or devices stamped on the binding, bookplates, inscriptions, early shelf-marks, scribbling);

any other features of interest (e.g. elaborate title-page, lacunae in text, annotations, side-notes, glosses, index);

condition (e.g. complete, imperfect, damp-stained, wormholed, gnawed by rodents);

present location and press-mark (e.g. Bodleian Library, MS Don. b. 8; British Library, Cotton MS Cleopatra A. IV).

CATCHWORD

Catchwords have been used in manuscripts since early medieval times and were later adopted as useful devices also by printers, English printed books commonly bearing them from about 1500 to 1800. A catchword is a word that generally appears isolated at the bottom right-hand corner of a page as an aid to continuity, since it anticipates the first word that appears on the next page. In medieval codices, a catchword was introduced at the end of each quire (overlapping with the earlier system of numbering quires or lettering them *A, B, C,* etc.) to indicate the opening of the next quire. Later scribes and printers could use them in similar fashion to facilitate the sequential arrangement of leaves and ensure that the sheets of the book were gathered and bound in the correct order by the binder.

CENSORS' MARKS

Censors' marks, or marks of censorship, meaning inscriptions or markings made on letters by official or self-appointed censors, date from the eighteenth century, when Jacobites in the 1745 rebellion endorsed letters they detained as 'Open'd by Rebells'. A more formal mode of censorship was applied to letters by servicemen in subsequent wartime, generally by local superior officers, who read the letters and obliterated compromising text by heavy inking, after which the envelopes were hand-stamped as having been officially censored. Such procedures were implemented from at least the Boer War (1899–1902) to the Second World War (1939–45).

Censors' marks, of one kind or other, would also be imposed by their captors on mail sent by prisoners of war from Napoleonic times onwards. *See* PRISONER OF WAR MAIL.

CENSUS

A 'census', the term derived from the Latin, is an official enumeration of the population of a given country or area, in which details of individuals, their occupation, and their property might also be gathered for possible taxation purposes; hence it is also the register setting out the results of this exercise. Although types of population registration (for baptisms, marriages, and burials according to parish or diocese) were known since 1538, the first census as such in Britain (covering England, Wales, the Isle of Man, and the Channel Islands) was undertaken in 1801. A census has generally ensued thereafter every ten years, the first truly modern one, giving details of individuals rather than just statistics, being undertaken in 1841. The process involved a series of Census Returns made by each registration district, comprising lined printed forms, with headings and columns, filled in by clerks with the relevant details. These were submitted (until 1970) to the General Register Office, which was established in 1836 under the direction of a Registrar General. The returns were then sorted out and copied by clerks into books of similar forms which would comprise the General Register. These census records, which are preserved in the National Archives at Kew (and those from 1841 to 1901 are available online), are the single most important source for genealogists, at least relating to the past two centuries. Because a census is closed to the public for 100 years, however (even under the Freedom of Information Act, 2000), they have some years to wait before they have full access to most of the twentieth-century ones.

CERTIFICATE

A certificate is a document—whether written, printed, or a combination of both—in which something is formally certified or attested as being true: for example, the certification of someone's credentials or authority, of a degree or award made to him or her, of his or her naturalization (rights to the civic privileges of an adopted country), of his discharge (as a record of a seaman's

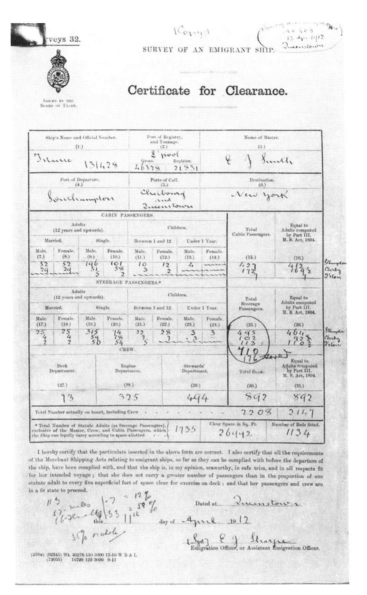

ILLUS. 15 *An official Board of Trade copy of the Certificate of Clearance of the* Titanic, *certifying that the ship was 'seaworthy, in safe trim, and in all respects fit for her intended voyage', a partly printed form with manuscript insertions, including details of passengers and crew, totalling 2,208. This is the copy, issued from Queenstown on 13 April 1912, used, and annotated in pencil, by W. D. Harbinson, advocate for the third-class passengers at the subsequent official inquiry into the sinking.*

service on board ship), of his or her membership of a particular society, or of other important facts for which a testamentary document is deemed to provide useful material evidence. Certificates are usually signed by someone who has appropriate authority to verify the stated facts. *See* Illus. 15.

CERTIORARI

See WRIT OF CERTIORARI.

CHAIN-LINES

Chain-lines, or chain lines, are the prominent, wide-spaced, parallel lines in laid paper, used in both manuscripts and printed books, left by the wire mesh across the bottom of the mould or tray in which the paper was made. They are to be distinguished from the lighter, close-set lines running perpendicular to them called 'wire-lines'. The chain-lines are visible when the paper is held up to the light. The original tray had the wires responsible for chain-lines running across its width; thus a full sheet of paper, held up lengthways to the light, will show chain-lines running horizontally. When folded in half to form a bifolium, each folio leaf will have the chain-lines running vertically; when folded again, each quarto leaf will have the chain-lines running horizontally; folded again to octavo size, they will run vertically, and so on. Chain-lines do not appear in wove paper, unless through some modern mechanical imitation process. *Compare* WIRE-LINES.

CHANCERY

The Chancery (Latin: *cancellaria*) at Westminster is, along with the Exchequer, one of the two most important departments of government involved in the preparation and preservation of public records, including writs, charters, and letters patent. From medieval times it was the office of the Chancellor, at that time effectively the principal secretary of state appointed by the sovereign. Because the Chancellor, who had custody of the Great Seal of England, had power to dispense royal justice by overseeing writs that instigated legal actions in other courts, as well as his arbitrating on procedural matters, his jurisdiction developed what is known as the 'common-law' or 'Latin side' of the Chancery (all records being kept in Latin). From about the mid-fourteenth century, however, a distinct Court of Chancery developed as what is called the 'English side' of Chancery, where bills and pleadings were written in the vernacular, and this came to deal with matters of equity outside the common law.

The Chancery was always noted, among other things, for the large staff of clerks it employed, headed by twelve so-called Masters in Chancery, and for the immense amount of documentation it generated every year. The Chancery papers were originally kept in the Tower of London, and much later in the Public Record Office. The many thousands of Chancery documents now in the National Archives at Kew (C series) date from *c*.1085 to the present day, while those for the Court of Chancery date up to its abolition in 1875. The majority of the texts are entered by clerks on rolls each of which comprises membranes of parchment sewn together head to foot in a continuous scroll, 'Chancery-style', as opposed to head to head, 'Exchequer-style'.

The Vatican also has a chancery, the Papal or Apostolic Chancery, responsible for its official documentation.

CHANCERY HAND

Chancery hand, or *littera cancellaresca*, is the type of cursive or documentary script originally used by the Apostolic Chancery in the Vatican for papal documents. Derived from Gothic *bastarda* script, it spread rapidly across Europe in the late medieval and early modern period and was also adopted for a style of typeface used by early sixteenth-century Italian printers.

In England, by the sixteenth century, a distinctly English type of Chancery hand was the stylized set hand used by Chancery clerks for the engrossing of letters patent and enrolments. Although, like court hand, it was abolished by Parliament in 1650, restored after 1660, and abolished again in 1733, a degenerate and somewhat disconcerting form of this elaborate and antiquated script continued to be used in legal and government circles, notably for the enrolment of Acts of Parliament. It was finally abolished by Parliament in 1836, but examples of the hand can still be found even up to the twentieth century.

CHANCERY ROLLS

See CHANCERY.

CHAPTER BOOK

See CONCLUSION BOOK.

CHARGE

In heraldry, a charge is any figure, emblem, device, or bearing whatsoever on an armorial shield or coat of arms. The commonest charges are beasts or creatures of some kind, such as lions or stags.

CHART

A chart is a type of map, either manuscript or printed, drawn up largely in outline, for geographical or navigational purposes or else in order to delineate a route or a plan of military dispositions or the like. A maritime navigational chart, or sea chart, would usually show far less detail than a full-scale map, giving only the coastlines and key ports relating to a particular voyage.

In a more general sense, a chart can be any sheet of information, either verbal or diagrammatic, drawn up in tabular form. The astrologer and mathematician John Dee (1527–1608), for instance, drew up in 1570 a large chart of five sheets pasted together with a series of captions bracketed or connected by vertical lines in columns representing his synopsis of the state of England ('To make this Kingdome florishing, Triumphant, famous, and Blessed'). This manuscript is now in the British Library (Cotton Charter XIII, No. 39).

The term 'chart' is also occasionally used in the early modern period as a shortened form of 'charter'.

CHARTER

A charter, in the most general sense, is an authorized document granting land, rights, privileges, or honours to a person, family, or other corporate body. Most specifically, charters are grants made by the Crown, drawn up in Chancery as a type of letters patent under the Great Seal. Charters differ from normal Royal Letters Patent by virtue of their elaborate address to the leaders of society and because they are always executed in the presence of witnesses, long lists of whose names sometimes appear. Since medieval times charters would most commonly apply to institutions, such as religious orders, abbeys, monasteries, boroughs, towns, guilds, universities, and other corporations, sometimes formally recognizing or establishing their foundation and setting out details of their property and of the special powers, privileges, benefits, liberties, and immunities received by them. Charters considered particularly important (such as borough charters, which might be sometimes hung up on display) could be very elaborate, written on large membranes of vellum with perhaps an initial letter portrait of the monarch and borders heavily decorated in colour.

What is distinguished in legal terminology as an 'original charter' is that first issued and making the original grant. A 'charter by progress' is one renewing the original grant in favour of an heir or successor to the original subject, and a 'confirmation charter' is one confirming the continued validity and authority of the original charter. Until the eighteenth century charters were largely drawn up in Latin and written on parchment. Copies were enrolled as a public record.

Charters might also serve to enshrine certain other solemn acts by the Crown or state. Charters of Liberties, for instance—of which the most famous example is the Magna Carta ('Great Charter'), reluctantly granted by King John to the barons at Runnymede on 12 June 1215—are royal charters made in the twelfth and thirteenth centuries whereby English monarchs were persuaded to establish or define their subjects' rights and obligations under feudal law. The term 'charter' is also used for certain types of formal declaration, treaty, or international agreement: e.g. the 1945 Charter of the United Nations.

CHARTERPARTY

The term 'charterparty' was formerly used to denote an indenture that was written out in duplicate on a single membrane of parchment and then cut in two in a wavy or jagged line to produce an indenture and its counterpart that would fit each other exactly and prove their authenticity if the two were reunited. From the early modern period onwards, the term has more frequently been applied to a type of commercial charter drawn up between merchants and shipowners relating to the hire of a ship and safe delivery of a cargo.

CHARTER ROLLS

The Charter Rolls in the National Archives at Kew (C 53) are enrolled copies of royal charters from 1199 onwards made and preserved as an official public record. They were copied by Chancery scribes on large membranes of vellum sewn head to tail to form a series of continuous rolls and were usually arranged by regnal year (1 Henry III, 2 Henry III, etc.).

CHARTULARY

See CARTULARY.

CHECK

'Check' is the American spelling for 'cheque'. The word is also used in the USA to denote a bill, setting out what someone owes, usually for food consumed in a restaurant.

CHEMISE

The term 'chemise' derives from, or relates to, the French word for 'shirt', and denotes a protective slip-on cover for a book or manuscript, generally kept as a loose, fitted, enclosing wrapper, although in medieval times it might be secured to the wooden boards of a book with bosses. From about the twelfth century onwards, such covers could be made of fabric, linen, velvet, silk, sheepskin, chevrotain (a type of deerskin), or other leathers and textiles. They might vary in style from basic functional wrappers to expensive display items, luxuriously embellished. The chemise was the precursor of the modern dust-jacket, but still survives in the form of soft silk or acrylic fitted folders which some collectors have made to protect particular books or manuscript materials, including their fore-edges. They usually serve to cushion the item before its placement in a fitted box or slip case.

CHEQUE

A cheque, or check (as the word is spelt in North America), is a written and signed order, or bill of exchange, whether on a printed form or otherwise, authorizing a bank to make a payment on the writer's account (*see* Illus. 16). The earliest known at present dates from 22 April 1659, instructing 'M^r: Mauris [John Morris] & m^r [Robert] Clayton' to 'pay this bearer Tenn Pounds forY^{rs}: Nic[hola]s Vanacker'. In the early eighteenth century, as a precursor to its modern use, the term was used to denote any financial bill, note, or draft that had a counterfoil.

CHIROGRAPH

Deriving from the Greek *cheir* ('hand') and *graphē* ('writing'), the term 'chirograph' denotes a document, especially a deed or indenture on parchment, on which the text is written twice, head to head, the word *CHIRO-GRAPHUM* (or sometimes other capital letters of the alphabet) being commonly written between the two parts of the membrane. It would then

ILLUS. 16 *A cheque issued by Messrs Coutts & Co., partly printed with manuscript insertions, here made (in the sum of £150 payable to the solicitor Frederic Ouvry) in the hand of Charles Dickens. It was signed by him probably on 8 June 1870 but post-dated, the date (the 'Tenth') for which it is made out being the day after his death, for which reason the cheque was never presented and cashed.*

be cut in two, in a wavy or zigzag line through that word, so that each party would have a copy (which might itself be called a chirograph) that could be matched up to the other, if need be, to prove its authenticity. Commonly, however, the deed would be prepared in triplicate on a T-shaped membrane of parchment and divided accordingly, the bottom portion being known as the 'foot of the fine', which was filed with the King's court as a public record. *See also* COUNTERPART, FINE, and INDENTURE.

CHRYSOGRAPHY

'Chrysography' (Greek: *chrysographē*) is the technical term for writing in gold, a feature of certain elaborate or important manuscripts from the early Christian era onwards.

CHURCHWARDENS' ACCOUNTS

Since possibly as early as the twelfth century, churchwardens (or 'reeves', as they were also called in medieval times) have been traditionally the principal lay officers of a parish, their prime duties being the collecting of church rents and representing the lay congregation in its dealings with the clergy. Each parish normally had, and still has, two churchwardens, although there might be as many as six for especially busy parishes. Churchwardens' accounts, usually set out systematically in formal account books, are the official records of their financial dealings, detailing both their income and money-raising activities and also expenditure on church fittings, services, etc. Dating from as early as the fourteenth century onwards, such records are the oldest parish accounts to survive, as well as being among the most numerous. Preserved for the most part in local record offices, they are a major source of information about local church affairs. *See also* VESTRY DOCUMENTS.

CIPHER

A cipher, or cypher as the word is sometimes spelt, is a form or system of writing in code, by the use or substitution of alphabetical characters, numbers, or other symbols or signals, to disguise the meaning of the script to everyone except those who are entrusted with the key to it. A cipher list is a list of the letters or symbols used in a particular system and of the letters they represent, by means of which the writing may be deciphered and understood (*see* Illus. 17). A cipher book may contain a series of such lists, when various different systems are employed: e.g. for diplomatic, spying, or secret-service activities.

The use of codes and ciphers for secret communications dates back to ancient times, but was developed particularly in Italy in the thirteenth century. The earliest known treatise on the analysis and breaking of codes, by Sicco Simonetta, dates from 1474. Numerous systems developed throughout Europe, including various methods of letter substitution and the use of grilles that could be laid over pages of writing to highlight particular words that, in their proper sequence, would form the intended secret message. Besides their use for private letters and dispatches—including confidential communications by Henry VIII, Mary, Queen of Scots (who used over 100 different ciphers), Elizabeth I, James I, and their ministers—ciphers were also employed from the late seventeenth century onwards to protect rights in connection with mathematical discoveries and inventions. These might be written up in cipher and deposited for safety with a learned society (such as the Royal Society) while the discovery was developed. If it were ever challenged, the inventor would be able to establish his priority by publicly deciphering the relevant documents held on deposit. *Compare* ENCODED MESSAGE.

CIRCA

The Latin term *circa*, usually abbreviated to *c.*, is still widely employed in descriptions of manuscripts, as well as in other matters of dating, to mean 'about' or 'approximately'. Thus 'circa 1558' or 'c.1558' means 'approximately 1558'. How approximate *circa* is depends upon the authority venturing to supply the date or the context in which it is cited.

ILLUS. 17 *One of the many Royalist manuscript ciphers captured by the Parliamentarians from Charles I's Secretary of State, Lord Digby, at the Battle of Sherburn on 15 October 1645. This one is headed 'Sʳ Th: Roe The Alphabet implies the lettrs signified'.*

See VISITATION.

CLAIMANT

See PLAINTIFF.

CLASP

Clasps are fastenings, usually made of metal, sometimes with connecting strips of leather, fitted at the fore-edge of the bindings of many manuscript volumes from the medieval period onwards, as well as of many early printed books. They served to keep the volume closed, to reduce strain on both boards and joints, to help prevent warping of the boards or cockling if covered in vellum, and to keep dust and dirt out of the book. Clasps usually take the form of two interlocking parts, one on each cover. One of them would be hinged to reach across the depth of the volume to snap into place on a catch-plate on the opposite side (which in England, as opposed to most of the continent, tended to be on the lower board) or else to snap on to a projecting pin on that side. At first they were a combination of metal fittings with leather straps, but entirely metal clasps subsequently came to predominate. In expensively produced books and codices, from about the late fourteenth to the early seventeenth century, the clasps might be made of brass or silver, elaborately chased or engraved.

CLERK

Etymologically linked to the word 'cleric' in the ecclesiastical sense, the term 'clerk' in medieval times denoted someone who had clerical status: one who, though possibly of lowly station or even married, was literate, could write and perform secretarial, notarial, or accountancy work, and was in some sense a scholar. Hence developed the more modern concept of a clerk as someone in secular life able to perform a variety of functions involving writing.

They might include such functionaries as parish clerks, responsible for keeping registers of baptisms, marriages, and deaths; legal officers, such as a Clerk of the Peace, the principal director of court proceedings in quarter sessions who kept county records; or government and parliamentary officials, such as a Clerk of the Signet, a Clerk of the Rolls, a Clerk of the Privy Council, a Clerk of the Council in Ordinary, who summons meetings of the Privy Council, or a Clerk of the House, who advises the Speaker in the House of Commons, or a Clerk of the Parliaments, who directs procedures in the House of Lords. Other clerks include recorders or keepers of accounts in other civic, administrative, legal, ecclesiastical, or commercial offices, and numerous employees who handle routine office transactions, correspondence, copying and accounting tasks in various other businesses, corporations and institutions.

Despite their occasional rise to superior status, clerks, particularly lawyers' clerks, were, like scriveners, a common subject of satire in the early modern period, generally mocked for their lowliness, ignorance, sharp practice, and venality.

CLERK OF COURSE

See CURSITORS

Close Rolls

The Close Rolls in the National Archives at Kew (C 54 and C 55 series) are principally the official enrolment of letters close. They constitute official copies by Chancery scribes of private letters and writs issued by the Crown, chiefly giving orders or instructions to specified individuals, from 1204 to *c.*1542. They also came increasingly to include documentation relating to a variety of other official and miscellaneous business, including private deeds and conveyances, and these extend up to 1903. The rolls take the form of a long series of membranes of parchment stitched head to foot, Chancery-style, and rolled up, each year of a monarch's reign being represented by one or more rolls.

CLOTH

See BINDING.

CLUBBED

In palaeography, particular letters or features are described as 'clubbed' when, for instance, the stem terminates in a heavily inked inverted triangle, or else the loops on ascenders or descenders are filled in, for decorative effect.

COAT OF ARMS

A coat of arms is the distinctive heraldic bearings of a gentleman or nobleman incorporated in a shield or escutcheon, and forms the central component of an achievement (*see* ACHIEVEMENT). Such bearings are depicted, either drawn in trick or emblazoned in their proper colours, in armorials and in other heraldic and genealogical manuscripts. *See* Illus. 5, 7, 18, 30, 48, and 76.

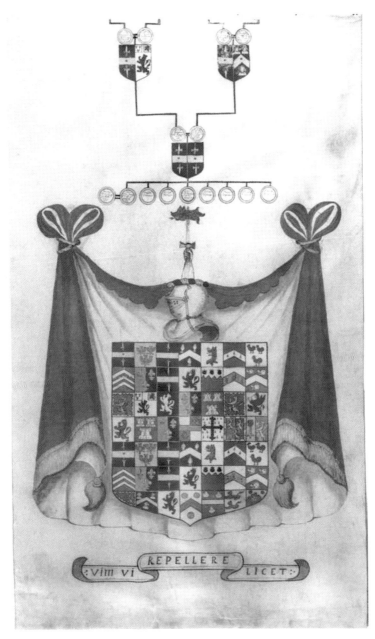

ILLUS. 18 *A coat of arms emblazoned in its proper colours, with crest and mantling, the motto in a banderole* Vim vi repellere licet *('To repel force with force is permissible'). This forms one of 117 such arms on a seventeenth-century Welsh genealogy or pedigree of the Gwynne family, on a vellum roll nearly 13 feet (c.4 metres) long.*

COCKET

Since the thirteenth century, a cocket was a type of seal applied to permits of various kinds, most especially one used by the King's Custom House. Until at least the seventeenth century, the term could also signify a document sealed by Officers of the Custom House and delivered to merchants as a certificate confirming that their merchandise had been duly entered and the appropriate duty paid.

COCKLING

Cockling is a condition afflicting paper or, more frequently, parchment or vellum documents when they warp and become wrinkled, puckered, or wavy, so that they will not lie flat and even. This usually results from poor storage or changes in temperature or humidity over a period, causing shrinkage and instability in the material.

CODE

See CIPHER and ENCODED MESSAGE.

CODEX

Deriving from the Latin *caudex* ('tree bark') and most commonly applied to ancient and medieval written books, whether on papyrus, vellum, or paper, the term 'codex' (plural: codices) denotes a manuscript volume, comprising quires sewn together at the fold and usually also bound, in contrast to the tablet or scroll of earlier usage. The earliest codex forms were probably wax-covered or ivory tablets hinged together like the leaves of a book.

Although any subsequent manuscript book is technically a codex, the word is most frequently found today in connection with especially import-ant, named examples—such as certain early scriptural texts (e.g. the Greek fourth-century Codex Sinaiticus, which is now divided between St Cathe-rine's Monastery in Egypt, where it was discovered in 1859, the British Library, and libraries in St Petersburg and Leipzig, or the similar Codex Vaticanus in the Vatican Library) or various medieval collections of legal texts. The term is also applied, somewhat selectively, to certain fifteenth- and sixteenth-century continental manuscript books or booklets of distinc-tion—such as the Codex Leicester of Leonardo da Vinci (named after its purchaser in 1717, Thomas Coke, later first Earl of Leicester of the fifth creation, and now owned by Bill Gates) or the various pictorial codices relating to Mesoamerican civilizations (the Codex Mendoza, Codex Borgia, etc.). With very few exceptions (such as the Lindisfarne Gospels, which are occasionally cited as the Codex Lindisfarnensis), the term 'Codex' is not commonly applied to any 'named' manuscripts produced in Britain.

CODICIL

Deriving from the Latin *codicillus* ('a short writing'), the term 'codicil' means an addition to a will, made to record alterations in the original. This may be written because the person concerned has changed his or her mind, or wishes to add supplementary provisions as an afterthought or owing to changed circumstances. If brief, a codicil may be subscribed to the original will. Alternatively, many wills have more than one codicil, in which case the codicils will tend to be written on separate sheets or membranes and attached to the original by cords or by other means. Such additions are legally construed as integral parts of the will.

CODICOLOGY

A term of modern coinage, 'codicology' denotes the study of manuscript books, or codices, in all aspects, including their physical structure, texts, script, binding, decoration, and other features of their production. Codicology is therefore the manuscript counterpart to bibliography, the study of printed books, but, like palaeography, it does not embrace the study of manuscripts in general, a subject that lacks any single-word term of classification.

COLLATION

In the field of textual criticism and editing, when there are two or more extant texts of a particular work or document, whether manuscript or printed, to collate them is to make a detailed comparison and to record systematically the differences between them. The prime focus will usually be on the verbal (substantive) differences, but a thorough collation will also pay attention to incidentals such as punctuation and spelling, as well as details of layout and format of the different texts. The collation of variants will be the detailed list, or parallel lists, resulting from this comparison.

In the field of bibliography, to collate a manuscript or printed book is to determine its current or earlier physical structures: specifically, its format and the arrangement of its leaves and quires, including its signatures, the number and sequence of the quires, and units (such as sheets, partial sheets, bifolia, and single leaves) within or supplementary to the quires. This kind of technical collation is often presented as a formula. Thus, for example, the formula a^4 b^2 $c–d^8$ $e–h^{10}$ $i–k^{12}$ would mean that the volume comprised eighty-six leaves, gathered as one quire of four leaves, one bifolium, two quires of eight leaves each, four quires of ten leaves each, and two quires of twelve leaves each (i–k representing two quires, since the letter *j*, as well as *u* and *w*, are not traditionally used in bibliographical collation because those letters were not in the Latin alphabet). There are many complicating factors, especially in printed books (such as mis-signed leaves, paste-downs, pre-liminaries, inserted leaves, excised blanks, cancels, etc.), which may render such collation formulae considerably more complex and elaborate than this example. Different editors also have differing views on how such formulae should be presented, although the commonly accepted authority on such matters (at least for printed books) is Fredson Bowers.

Bibliographical investigation of printed books may also usefully involve comparison of two or more exempla of a book to check that all the pages that should be there in the edition are present and in the order intended by the publisher. The resulting collation will be a record of the differences, which may be faults or deficiencies, if the exempla do not correspond exactly. When booksellers use the terms 'collate' and 'collation' it is usually in this sense of checking the book's condition and completeness: i.e. whether it is 'perfect'.

COLLECTANEA

The Latin term *collectanea* is sometimes encountered as a rather formal version of the word 'collections', occasionally applied to someone's miscel-laneous collections, writings, or gleanings in manuscript form.

COLLECTOR

In a bibliographical context, a collector is one who is devoted to acquiring or assembling a collection of books or manuscripts, generally as artefacts in their finished form, as opposed to a writer, compiler, or anyone else who has anything to do with their original production. There have been many col-lectors, from ancient times onwards, some rich, some relatively poor, who have appreciated and helped to preserve important books and manuscripts, and many libraries, or collections within libraries, are named after them.

COLLEGE OF ARMS

See HERALDIC MANUSCRIPTS.

COLOPHON

Deriving from a Greek word meaning the 'summit' or 'finishing touch', or possibly from a town of that name (because the Colophonians were warriors who could tip the scale in favour of one side and finish the battle), the term 'colophon' denotes a kind of tail-piece sometimes added to manuscript books, from the ninth century onwards, or in later times to printed books, supplying details about the production of the book. These might include information such as the title of the work, names of author, scribe, person who commissioned it, or printer, and place and date of production, as well as sometimes threats, or anathemata, against unauthorized copyists, and even personal comments by the scribe himself. It thus gives the kind of information that, from the early sixteenth century onwards, became usually (though not always) incorporated in a title-page. The wording was sometimes embodied in, or accompanied by, an emblematic or pictorial device or flourish. *See also* EXPLICIT and SCRIBE.

COMMISSION

A commission is any kind of document or warrant issued by an authority embodying an order, charge, or instruction, or else it is one vesting authority in someone to perform a particular role, function, or service—usually judicial, civic, ecclesiastical, or diplomatic. One of the most commonly encountered types of commission is that signifying the rank to which an army or naval officer has been appointed.

COMMISSION OF ARRAY

A commission of array is a formal instruction emanating directly or indirectly from the Crown (except in the Interregnum, when Parliament implemented the Militia Ordinance of 1641) for the raising of a force of militia by local officers or gentry. The term is also applied to the body of men so charged. *See also* MUSTER ROLLS.

COMMITMENT

'Commitment' is a term sometimes used for a warrant that sends someone to prison. The committal proceedings in a magistrates' court are those to decide if a case should go to trial.

COMMON PAPER OF THE SCRIVENERS' COMPANY

'Common Paper' is the term used by the Scriveners' Company of London to denote the book or register in which, since the late fourteenth century, the Company recorded particulars of early ordinances (since 1357) leading to its foundation (1373), with the texts of subsequent related charters, ordinances, oaths, and memoranda. It also records the names of apprentices and others admitted to the craft of Writers of the Court Letter since 1392, together with, in many cases, their individual notarial signs or marks, entered either by the members themselves or as copies. Members with entries include John Milton, father of the poet, on 27 February 1599/1600 and 4 April 1615. The Common Paper as it now survives is a sturdy volume of 296 pages, measuring 15 ½ × 11 ½ inches (39.5 × 29.5 cm), bound in leather with a strap and buckle, and is on deposit in the Guildhall Library (MS 5370). It goes up only to 1628. The original continuation is now lost, but a 41-leaf folio copy made between 1664 and *c.*1680 of various entries, related letters, reports, and lists of apprentices, from 1615 to 1678, is preserved in the Bodleian Library, Oxford (MS Rawlinson D 51; a photostat copy is in the Guildhall Library, MS 8721A). This is supplemented by a 32-leaf folio copy, made between *c.*1636 and 1640, of petitions and ordinances relating to the Company in 1616–35, now in the British Library (Harley MS 2295). The full text of the Common Paper, including the continuation to 1678, was edited, with illustrated examples, by Frances W. Steer in 1968, and it is extensively illustrated in Illustrations I–XXI of Hilary Jenkinson's *The Later Court Hands in England* (1927).

COMMONPLACE BOOK

A commonplace book in its original form is a manuscript book in which quotations or passages from reading matter, precepts, proverbs and aphorisms, useful rhetorical figures or exemplary phrasing, words and ideas, or other notes and memoranda are entered for ready reference under general subject headings, these headings often having been systematically written in advance of the main entries. The practice of keeping such volumes dates back to antiquity, when, for instance, Aristotle's educational methodology included attention to *topoi*, meaning topics or subjects (the singular form is *topos*), which could in turn be subdivided into other categories. Cicero later enjoined legal advocates to collect *loci communes*, literally 'common places', meaning information or materials relating to general topics and principles that could usefully be applied to particular cases as they occurred. In medieval times and especially in the sixteenth century, students and scholars were encouraged to keep such compilations as aides-memoire and as a mode of storing information, and organizing it methodically, for ready retrieval and effective use in their studies.

Although many compilers sought to find quotations etc. illustrating universal truths or general observations, different types of commonplace books developed according to specific categories—thus there are legal, theological, philosophical, medical, literary, historical, and even artistic commonplace books, as well as others that tend to concentrate on particular disciplines. Different methods or systems of organizing, classifying, and indexing materials (alphabetically or otherwise) developed similarly, as well as a variety of physical forms, ranging from small portable notebooks to huge leather-bound folio volumes kept in studies.

Popular anthologies of quotations known as *florilegia* (meaning 'gather-ings of flowers') appeared from medieval times onwards and flourished in the early modern era of printing, when they could be used as ready source material for commonplace books or alternatively save readers the trouble of compiling their own commonplace books altogether. Besides such publica-tions as John Foxe's *Locorum communium*, a series of blank leaves with systematically ordered theological headings first published at Basle in 1557, stationers were also kept busy supplying blank paper books for common-place-book use. Other types of commonplace books printed in various sizes with introductions, tables for indexes, and blank pages with ruled margins— especially those extolling the compilation 'method' advocated in the late seventeenth century by the philosopher John Locke—flourished from the early eighteenth century until well into the nineteenth.

Although the principles of compiling commonplace books systematically under pre-arranged headings were steadily advocated by certain scholars and publishers throughout this period, their use by compilers was often far from consistent or systematic in practice. This development (towards freedom or indiscipline, depending on one's perspective) perhaps also coincided with a reaction against rigid scholastic methods by the early seventeenth century— Bacon, for instance, rejected the practice of filling 'the Index with many idle Heads' for their own sake. Thus, even in the early modern period, the term 'commonplace book' could be very loosely applied to notebooks, miscel-lanies, and other types of manuscript compilation in general, whether their contents were formally arranged under headings or not. It is in this sense, as a jumble of snippets of information in no particular order, that the term has come to be used metaphorically as a literary genre. Various examples of disorganized memoirs, random observations, or miscellaneous anthologies have been published under titles incorporating the words 'Commonplace Book'. *Compare* ANTHOLOGY, *FLORILEGIUM*, and MISCELLANY.

COMMON RECOVERY

In a legal context, a recovery is a judgment to recover property. From the fifteenth century onwards, a common recovery was specifically a type of conveyance of property involving a complicated and fictitious legal proced-ure designed to clear away problems of entailment. It took the form of a collusive action whereby someone sued the tenant on the land for having no title to it. The tenant would then introduce another party (the vouchee), who had supposedly given him warranty of the title, but who would fail to appear in court to prove it, whereupon a judgment barring all contingent remainders and heirs would be given in favour of the recoverer, who might

83

then be free to convey the land back to the tenant or else other land of equal value. The case was entered on the court rolls and a copy, or exemplification, of the entry, in the form of a royal writ, was given to the recoverer. These cases were heard in several courts, including manorial courts, but principally in the Court of Common Pleas, whose recovery rolls, from 1583 to 1838, are preserved in the National Archives at Kew (CP 43). This convoluted legal procedure was technically abolished in 1834.

COMMUNITY

See TEXTUAL COMMUNITY.

COMPANY OF SCRIVENERS

See SCRIVENERS' COMPANY.

COMPASS CHART

See PORTOLAN.

COMPASS-ROSE

In cartography, a compass-rose is the pointed star at the centre of a depicted compass dial that is a common feature of medieval and early modern maps and portolans (*see* Illus. 48 and 63). Derived from the ancient Greek concept of the eight named winds in the Tower of Winds at Athens, early prototypes of compass-roses, generally known as 'wind-roses', featured eight points, the north in the form of a spearhead. By the thirteenth century, they were divided into thirty-two points, all projecting or radiating rhumb-lines, although the number of points represented in any given example might still vary between eight, sixteen (the sixteen-pointed version sometimes cited as a half compass-rose), and thirty-two. By at least the sixteenth century, they could be represented in elaborate form, with their concentric circles and stars in multiple colours and patterns, even on occasions in gold leaf. Also, the north point would generally be in the form of a (sometimes enlarged, extended, and decorated) fleur-de-lis. Probably because of this feature, as a corruption of 'fleurs-de-lis', mariners sometimes referred to compass-cards (compass discs with magnetic needles) and compass- or wind-roses as 'flys' or 'flyes'.

COMPENDIUM

A compendium is an abridgement, abstract, epitome, precis, or summary of a larger written work, which conveys its substance and essence in a smaller or more compact form. The term appears to date from the sixteenth century.

COMPILATION

A compilation is usually a miscellaneous collection of texts from different sources, and generally by different writers, set out in a single manuscript or printed book. The compiler may or may not be himself or herself the scribe in whose hand the texts are entered, but is the person responsible for the overall gathering, selection, and possibly arrangement of those texts or textual extracts.

COMPLAINT

See BILL OF COMPLAINT.

COMPOSITE VOLUME

A composite volume of manuscript or printed materials, as distinct from a compilation or miscellany, is a volume made up of various physically and textually independent units bound together: e.g. a volume of separate paper or pamphlets. Such volumes are sometimes described as 'nonce' volumes. *See also* SAMMELBAND.

COMPOSITION PAPERS

Composition is the making of an agreement, contract, or settlement of some kind between two parties. The term has a specific application, however, in the context of the English Civil War and Commonwealth period, during which, in 1646, a parliamentary Committee for Compounding with Delinquents (i.e. Royalists) was set up. The defeated Royalists who wished to avoid prosecution or confiscation of all their property 'compounded' with the Committee to reach a compromise settlement, usually involving limited fines. The related documentation is sometimes classified as 'composition papers'.

COMPOTUS ROLLS

The term 'compotus rolls' is a generic one sometimes applied to the many hundreds of estate accounts relating to Crown lands prepared by royal officials that are not part of sheriffs' annual accounts and which are other-wise known as 'Ministers' and Receivers' Accounts'. Dating from the thir-teenth to the eighteenth century, and now in the National Archives at Kew (SC 6), many of them are records of royal escheators, the officials who ascertained the lands and rightful heirs of deceased tenants.

COMPUTUS TEXTS

Deriving from the Latin *computus* meaning 'calculation', the generic term 'computus texts' is sometimes used to classify a range of manuscript texts, from medieval times onwards, involving calculations of some kind, principally relating to time. Such texts include calendars, almanacs, and astronomical and alchemical works.

CONCLUSION BOOK

In university colleges, a conclusion book, sometimes also known as a 'chapter book', is one recording formal decisions of the Masters and Fellows.

CONCORD

Of Latin and French origin and meaning 'heart together' (i.e. 'of one heart' or 'of one mind'), the term 'concord'—usually in legal parlance the 'final concord' (Latin: *finalis concordia*)—is an agreement between two or more people, usually ending actual or fictitious litigation, set out as a type of conveyance. It was usually engrossed on parchment by the chirographer of the Common Pleas in triplicate in the form of a chirograph (*see* CHIROGRAPH and FINE). Such documents are among the commonest muniments of title.

The term 'concord' may also be applied to a peace treaty between contending parties or nations.

CONCORDANCE

The term 'concordance' may sometimes be used as an alternative to 'concord'. Alternatively, in more general modern use, concordances of particular authors (such as Shakespeare) are a type of printed compilation or index in which particular words are arranged alphabetically with citations showing lines or passages in which each word is used in the author's works.

Other types of concordance were those printed in the sixteenth and seventeenth centuries, and sometimes also known as 'harmonies', in which passages of the Bible or various Protestant dogmas or catechisms, perhaps set out in parallel columns, were compared or effectively collated. A singular example of a cottage industry in such things, produced basically for devotional purposes, is those produced by the religious community founded by Nicholas Ferrar (1592–1637) at Little Gidding in Cambridgeshire (a community celebrated in T. S. Eliot's poem on this subject in his *Four Quartets*, 1943). At their clumsiest, these concordances (as Ferrar himself called them) were each basically a kind of large folio scrapbook in which relevant passages cut from printed pages of the Bible were pasted together side by side, usually embellished with the application of religious engravings, and with some would-be calligraphic manuscript additions, such as title-pages, headings, and rubrics. They also progressed, however, into more sophisticated and elaborate compilations, worthy at their best of presentation to members of the Royal Family and other eminent dignitaries.

86

(One lent to Charles I was returned with his own marginal annotations; a more elaborate one, 'bound in crimson velvet and richly gilded', was subsequently given to him.) According to Ferrar, the art of binding was taught to the community by 'a Cambridge bookbinder's daughter' and the bindings of the concordances, which took various forms, seem to have been partly if not wholly produced by women in the community, including his niece Mary Collet. Some twelve or thirteen examples of these concordances are known to survive, four of them in the British Library (C.23.e.2–4 and Royal MS App. 65).

CONCORDAT

See TREATY.

CONCORDATUM

See BOOK OF CONCORDATUMS.

CONFIRMATION ROLLS

The Confirmation Rolls in the National Archives at Kew (C 56) are a series of enrolments made between 1483 and 1626 of confirmation charters whereby earlier grants, charters, letters patent, and other royal and private deeds were confirmed by fresh letters patent. The need for confirmation arose when an imperfection or deficit in title became apparent and an estate might therefore otherwise have become voidable (i.e. of no legal validity). Certain bodies and institutions (universities, for instance) also thought it wise to seek a charter of confirmation of their rights and privileges at the beginning of a new reign. The confirmation in each case generally took the form of an inspeximus (*see* INSPEXIMUS), reciting verbatim the text of the earlier charter or letters patent, the validity and authority of which was confirmed. Despite this official record, some of the earliest grants (to monasteries, etc.), predating the Norman Conquest of 1066, are suspected of being spurious. Some confirmations also appear in the Charter Rolls.

CONFLATION

In textual criticism, conflation occurs when two or more texts of a work, or parts of them, are merged together to form a new composite text. This happens when, for instance, scribes copy a text from more than one exemplar, or at least introduce into their copy variant readings from different exemplars, as opposed to restricting themselves to one exemplar and maintaining a single line of descent. For the equivalent of conflation in editing practice, *see* ECLECTIC.

CONJUGATE

In a bifolium, or sheet folded in two, one leaf is said to be conjugate, or conjunct, with the other. It matters in detailed collation of a book or codex to understand which leaf is conjugate with which in order to determine the structure and even completeness of the book. *Compare* DISJUNCT.

CONJUNCT

See CONJUGATE.

CONSERVATION

'Conservation' is the common term used by archivists, bibliographers, librarians, and museum curators for the proper preservation, for future generations, of artefacts, including books and manuscripts. It implies considerations of storage, temperature- and light-control, dehumidification, and other aspects of physical condition, involving, among other things, the use of acid-free, protective materials for wrappers or containers, as well as repairs, restoration, remounting, rebinding, washing, bleaching, and even sometimes freezing (to eliminate fungal mould or bacterial infection or to kill insects, bookworms, and their larvae). While, as in the case of archaeological or painting restoration procedures, some 'conservation' practices (especially nineteenth-century ones) have proved to be controversial, if not fairly disastrous, however well intentioned, it is to be hoped that the technology of archival conservation developed in the late twentieth century will prove to be of rather more enduring success.

CONSTAT

A constat (the Latin word meaning 'let it be established') is a certified or attested copy or exemplification of an official record, such as the enrolment of a letters patent under the Great Seal, made for legal purposes. Most especially, it is a certificate in which is duplicated the text of the official record concerning a particular matter and which is issued by the Clerk of the Pipe or Auditors of the Exchequer for use as evidence by someone who intends to plead in the Court of Exchequer for a discharge or acquittal.

CONTAMINATION

'Contamination', like the term 'corruption', has a pejorative connotation as used by editors. A text is said to be contaminated when it appears to be subject to a significant number of scribal errors, or has been sophisticated, or subject to alteration that editors might conclude to be non-authorial, unauthorized, or lacking legitimacy. The term may also be applied to textual traditions when, for instance, one independent line of descent becomes, in a particular copy, contaminated by the introduction of readings from another independent line of descent, as a result of which conflation a new, contaminated tradition is created by the texts that then descend from that copy. The textual history may, of course, become extremely complicated if an author effectively contaminates his own work by introducing into a fresh text readings from different copies or versions of his work, each of which had initiated its own textual tradition.

CONTEMPORANEOUS

See CONTEMPORARY.

CONTEMPORARY

In descriptions of manuscripts, 'contemporary' means dating from the same time or belonging to the same period. Thus a contemporary manuscript copy of an Elizabethan poem is a transcript written in the Elizabethan period itself (1558–1603), or at least very close to that period, rather than at a much later date, and a contemporary reader's annotations in a book printed in 1660 are annotations made by a reader round about that time and not many years afterwards. Since the term effectively derives its meaning from the context— so that, for instance, a current exhibition of contemporary calligraphy would show calligraphy produced at the present time—it is sometimes open to misunderstanding, since 'contemporary' may erroneously be construed as always meaning 'modern' or 'produced today'. This ambiguity may perhaps be avoided by applying instead the less common synonym 'contemporaneous', which does not have the connotation of modern. Neither term is precise, and a cataloguer or bookseller who is not quite sure how much later than the composition of its text a manuscript may have been written may hedge his or her bets by describing it as 'contemporary or near-contemporary'.

CONTENTS

See TABLE OF CONTENTS.

CONTRACT

A contract is a legally binding agreement between two or more parties, which usually involves financial arrangements, the transference of property, or other specified commitments and obligations similar to a covenant. It may or may not be embodied in a written document. In earlier times, the term 'contract' denoted more specifically a transaction involving the transference of property or a debt rather than a consensual agreement.

CONTRACTION

See ABBREVIATION.

CONTROLMENT ROLLS

'Controlment rolls' is a generic term applied to a class of records in the National Archives at Kew (KB 29) in which a succession of Clerks of the Crown, from 1329 to 1843, kept account of the progress of Crown cases in the King's Bench. Although the accounts were kept and arranged term by term, the rolls were made into bundles according to the regnal year. They contain details of the prosecution, court proceedings, and special writs involved. The rolls include other related memoranda rolls, although the Controlment Roll proper, which is sometimes also called the 'Roll of Entries', is that which contains minutes of the appearances and pleas in each term.

CONVENTION

See TREATY.

CONVEYANCE

A conveyance is a deed, or formal written document, whereby property, rights, or title are legally transferred from one party to another.

COPPERAS

Copperas (the term subject to variant spellings, including 'copprice') is an iron sulphate, which is one of the traditional main constituents of one of the two principal types of ink. Like gall, the term occasionally appears in seventeenth-century satires on clerks and scriveners in which the materials of their profession are elaborated and subjected to mockery: for instance, in Jeremiah Wells's *A London Scrivener*, where a scrivener's ink is described as '*Poyson* had it neither *Gall* nor *Copprice*'. *See* GALL.

COPY

In a manuscript context, a copy is generally taken to be a written document in which is transcribed the text of another document; hence a reproduction or duplicate of the text rather than the original. However, the term 'copy' could also be used more widely simply to signify the text of a work, usually with the connotation that it is the authentic or original text, if not the original document itself. This sense is implied when, for instance, Elizabethan lawyers or politicians wish to see 'the copy' of a text or document (meaning the exact text in, preferably, its original authentic form), and it persists also in the numerous sixteenth- and seventeenth-century works given titles beginning 'The copy of': for example, *The Copie of a Leter, Wryten by a Master of Arte of Cambrige* published in 1584, or scribally circulated texts such as *The Coppie of the Speeche Deliuered by S^r. Francis Bacon* and *The Coppye of a Letter Wrytten to the Lower Howse of Parliam^te '*. The term 'copy' persists to the present day as denoting the actual written or typed text submitted to a publisher or printer.

Besides its additional use as meaning a particular example (the copy or exemplum of a book), the word 'copy' may be distinguished from another earlier use of the term (in various spellings), from medieval times onwards, derived from the Latin *copia*, meaning 'copiousness', 'richness', or 'abundance': for instance, when Francis Bacon extolls the usefulness of a commonplace book as 'that which assureth copiè of invention'.

COPYIST

A copyist is a person who produces written copies or transcripts of texts or documents. A copyist is the same thing as a scribe, except that the person's role may be restricted to the mechanical task of transcribing alone, without performing other possible functions of a scribe, clerk, or secretary.

COPYRIGHT

Attempts to license and control printing and publication date back to the early sixteenth century. Copyright in the modern sense, however, did not come into force in England until the Statute of Anne was passed by Parliament in 1709, being 'An Act for the Encouragement of Learning, by Vesting the Copies of Printed Books in the Authors or Purchasers of such Copies, during the Times therein mentioned'. As the law evolved, copyright became the exclusive legal right for the author or creator of a work or for his or her immediate family or executors to publish that work. This right exists for a legally stipulated number of years regardless of the ownership of the manuscript of the work in question. Thus a letter written and sent by A to B is owned by B as a physical object, but the copyright in the text still resides with A. Similarly, B may acquire, and be in legal possession of, an unpublished manuscript by A, but the copyright still resides with A or his or her heirs or executors and cannot legally be published without their permission.

The actual length of time for which copyright exists after the death of the author is subject to the law, which varies from country to country and is also occasionally changed (resulting, for instance, in the reimposition of copyright by European Community legislation upon works that had temporarily come out of copyright in England under the previous fifty-year rule). Generally speaking, the publication of newly discovered manuscript texts by medieval and early modern writers will not be affected by hereditary copyright issues except that, in practice, use of the manuscript is effectively controlled by its current private or institutional owner.

The term 'copy-text' is used by modern editors to denote the particular text, whether printed or manuscript, adopted as the principal or base text for an edition or part of an edition. This will, in principle, be the text that the editor deems to be the one closest to the author's holograph (or to the author's supposed 'final intentions', in the event of more than one authorial version or edition of the work existing), or to the original version, before, in the course of transmission, the authorial text was contaminated by scribal corruption or emendation by others. In practice, with frequently edited texts, it may well be based only on that produced by the editor's predecessor. Variants in other manuscripts or editions might be collated, or even sometimes incorporated in the newly edited text, but the usual impetus for editors is to avoid producing eclectic texts (editions pieced together or conflated from two or more textual sources) and to adhere as far as possible to the one selected copy-text unless there are compelling reasons to do otherwise (such as identifying stop-press variants in different exempla of a printed edition or turning to another manuscript when the copy-text is clearly garbled or defective at some point).

The term has, however, been subject to varying and more specific uses and definitions since it was first adopted by R. B. McKerrow (1872–1940) to address problems in the editing of early printed texts. It was expounded in its most influential form by Sir Walter Greg (1875–1959). Greg's definition varied over the years, but in his classic essay 'The rationale of copy text' (1950) he defined 'copy-text' as specifically the printed edition of a work most likely to preserve the author's accidentals (i.e. incidentals: spelling, punctuation, capitalization, etc.), as opposed to the substantive or verbal components of the text, which might well be supplied from a later corrected or enlarged edition. Greg's theory has been adopted, with variations and refinements, by subsequent major bibliographers such as Fredson Bowers and G. Thomas Tanselle, although it has been rejected by others, who question whether any printed texts are very likely to retain authors' incidentals, since compositors will adjust spelling and punctuation at will to justify their lines. In the case of manuscripts, however, Greg was uncertain whether the same editorial theory—with its distinction between one authority for incidentals and another authority for substantives—was applicable. More recent editors have, in fact, tended to think that it is not. In the case of scribal manuscripts, it seems evident that incidentals usually reflect the habits of the scribes rather than those of the author; moreover, but for exceptional cases, a proliferation of manuscript copies and versions may especially complicate the process of deducing or reconstructing any author-ial original, or archetype, let alone authoritative incidentals. This therefore remains a contentious area, and scholarly debates about the nature and rationale of copy-text and the correct definition and application of the term are likely to continue.

What is, however, a common misuse of the term is calling a scribe's or compositor's exemplar his 'copy-text'.

CORDS

In a manuscript context, cords are the strings or laces by which certain kinds of pendent seals are attached to parchment documents. Such cords are usually made of white or coloured thread, cotton, silk, or other material, usually plaited, and sometimes wrapped in silver or gold thread, depending on the nature of the document. Especially grand or elaborate patents, such as patents of nobility, way well have plaited cords terminating in large gold thread tassels. *See* Illus. 84.

CORONER'S INQUEST

See INQUISITIO POST MORTEM and INQUISITION.

CORRECTION

A correction is a textual alteration made to rectify a mechanical error, such as an unintentionally omitted word or a misspelling, in the writing or copying of a document. The term implies that the alteration simply amends a mistake and entails no textual rethinking by the author or scribe, nor any substantive change, such as verbal deletion or rephrasing, made to the text as originally intended. *Compare* EMENDATION and REVISION.

CORRESPONDENCE

A correspondence is a series of letters that pass between two or more people writing to each other. It therefore represents both sides of a (usually prolonged) process of epistolary communication, not, as is sometimes mis-takenly thought, just a series of letters written by one person (which is only one side of the correspondence).

CORRIGENDA

See ERRATA.

CORRUPTION

A corrupt reading, or textual corruption, is a mistaken or inaccurate reading, the result of faulty copying or transmission—or at least what is deemed by a textual editor to be so. The terms 'corrupt' and 'corruption', as also 'contamination' (*see* CONTAMINATION), imply a pejorative or judgemental view of the reading in question, based on assumptions that may or may not be warranted. For this reason, these terms tend to be used less readily and more circumspectly by modern textual critics and editors than they used to be, especially when individual texts of a work are viewed as legitimate subjects of study in their own right. Even by traditional standards, however, what may seem to be corruptions may occasionally prove to be alternative readings, belonging to a different line of descent from an original, perhaps authorial, source, rather than subsequent copying errors or contamination. *See also* SCRIBAL ERRORS, SOPHISTICATED, and UNEDITING.

COTERIE

A coterie, in a literary context, is a social group, set, or circle of people, generally of a somewhat exclusive nature, joined by friendship, class, and common cultural, literary, political, or intellectual interests. Examples in the early modern period include the Great Tew circle, centred in the 1630s on the Oxfordshire manor of Lucius Cary, second Viscount Falkland, and including figures such as Thomas Hobbes, Edward Hyde (later Earl of Clarendon), William Chillingworth, George Morley, Gilbert Sheldon, John Earle, Edmund Waller, and Sydney Godolphin, as well as the so-called 'Society of Friends' centred in the 1650s and 1660s on the poet Katherine Philips ('the Matchless Orinda'). Various circles were also initially centred on such writers as Sir Philip Sidney (family and social networks who secured copies of his unpublished *Arcadia*) and John Wilmot, Earl of Rochester (in the purview of the court of Charles II after the Restoration). Other relatively limited or enclosed communities were in academic and ecclesiastical institutions, in the Inns of Court, and in provincial family circles. Most, if not originally all, of the literature produced within such coteries had restricted circulation in manuscript form, and was possibly valued to some extent for that very reason. *See also* TEXTUAL COMMUNITY.

COUCHER

Deriving from a French word meaning 'to lay down', the term 'coucher' denotes a large book, such as a cartulary, antiphonary, ledger, or register of some kind, that tends to be kept lying down on a flat or sloped desk, a table, or other surface, as opposed to standing upright on a shelf or being portable.

See BOOK OF ENTRIES.

COUNTERFOIL

A counterfoil today is generally that small appendage to a cheque that is retained as a record by the payer when the cheque itself is extracted for financial use. It is intended for the duplication of essential information in the main portion of the document (such as date, sum made payable, to whom it is paid, and the number of the cheque) and is usually marked off by machine-made indentation or perforation so that the cheque can easily be separated. Types of counterfoils were introduced by the early eighteenth century to prevent forgery or cheating. Other kinds of financial documents, such as bills, receipts, and tickets, for which retained evidence of the transaction was thought necessary, could similarly have counterfoils. The part of a wooden tally retained by the debtor, the counter-stock, might also be called a 'counterfoil'. *See* TALLY.

COUNTERMARK

In paper, a countermark is part of the watermark (*see* WATERMARK), being an extension or appendage to it, sometimes connected by lines, in the second half of the sheet opposite the main, patterned watermark. Often it embodies simply the papermaker's initials. Those in early French paper were also used to denote the quality of the paper, the different grades of fine, second, and ordinary paper being each distinguished by its own countermark.

COUNTERPART

The counterpart of a deed or indenture is its exact duplicate, the copy that is retained by one of the parties to the deed as a security. In earlier times, the text would be written out in duplicate, usually head to head, on a single membrane of parchment and then cut in two in a wavy or indented line to produce an indenture and its counterpart which would fit each other exactly if the two were reunited. This practice declined in the early modern period, although it is not unusual to encounter indentures of the seventeenth-century and later with the traditional scalloped edges. *See also* CHIRO-GRAPH, INDENTURE, and LEASE.

Also, in a bifolium, one conjugate leaf can be called the counterpart to the other.

COUNTERSIGN

When a signature is added to a document already signed by someone else, the document becomes countersigned, the purpose of countersigning being to confirm or reinforce its authenticity. Many legal documents are counter-signed, as are official and government warrants and commissions such as those signed by monarchs and then also by certain of their ministers, secretaries of state, Treasury officials, or private secretaries. Documents are generally described as countersigned even when they have actually been drawn up and signed by such officials before being presented to the monarch for his or her signature to be entered in the appropriate space.

COUNTER-STOCK

See TALLY.

COURSE OF THE SEALS

The course of the seals is the procedure leading to the attachment of the Great Seal to a royal document. The first step was the Sign Manual, the draft warrant actually signed by the monarch. This was usually taken to the Signet Office where a fresh document was drawn up and the Signet Seal attached. This would then go to the Privy Seal Office where yet another document was engrossed and the Privy Seal attached, usually (if there was one) by the Lord Privy Seal, otherwise by the Principal Secretary. This would serve as warrant for a final document, usually engrossed on parchment, for the Great Seal to be attached by or at the direction of the Lord Chancellor or (if there was no Chancellor) the Lord Keeper of the Great Seal. Although certain of these steps, particularly the Privy Seal, might occasionally be bypassed, the purpose of this elaborate bureaucratic procedure, which originated in 1444 and was re-established by statute in 1536, was to prevent fraud and error and allow opportunity for checking. It was also lucrative for the various officials involved, who each received a fee, and it kept numerous clerks employed.

COURT

See COURTS OF LAW.

COURT BARON

A feudal institution, a court baron was the principal type of manorial court that flourished especially in medieval and early modern times. It comprised an assembly of the freehold tenants of a manor under the presidency of the lord or his steward. It was convened periodically to deal with manorial administration and to settle land disputes and civil matters relating to the lord's or tenants' rights and duties within the manor, having jurisdiction in that regard. It is not unusual to find a single session defined as both a court baron and a court leet. Proceedings of such courts are recorded in court books or court rolls.

COURT BOOK

See COURT ROLL.

COURT CUSTOMARY

A court customary was the same thing as a court baron except that the steward of the manor presided as judge and the assembly was of copyholders: i.e. tenants who were not free but occupied land from the lord of the manor upon certain conditions. The court was convened for purposes of establishing copyhold tenure and transfers of tenure and for recording the particulars in manorial rolls. Copies of the relevant entries were usually given to the tenants as evidence of their holdings and its terms.

COURT HAND

'Court hand' is a generic term that has traditionally been applied (although no longer) to types of cursive and documentary script, including the cursive form of Anglicana, that developed in England from the thirteenth century onwards and were commonly used for official, business, or accounting purposes, especially by the legislative and administrative offices of government. The script was commonly employed, for instance, from the late fourteenth century by the guild of Writers of the Court Letter (*scriptores litterae curialis civilitatis Londoniensis*). It was thus distinct from the book hands or text hands (such as those known as 'Textura' and 'Gothic') traditionally used for engrossing manuscripts of a literary or liturgical nature by Writers of the Text Letter, although in practice it did evolve into a type of book hand itself (*Anglicana formata*).

Court hand, which by 1571 could be called somewhat misleadingly 'Bastard Secretary', came to be used especially by the four central law courts at Westminster, each of which adapted the script to their own particular set hand for their individual enrolments and record purposes. Its somewhat convoluted and antiquarian letter forms, not always easily comprehensible to common people by the mid-seventeenth century, led in part to the Commonwealth Act of Parliament, of 22 November 1650, whereby 'all Proceedings whatsoever in any Courts of Justice' were to be henceforth 'in the English Tongue onely, and not in Latin or French' and to be 'written in an ordinary, usual and legible Hand and Character, and not in any Hand commonly called *Court-hand*'. Following the Restoration, however, court hand was reintroduced and used as before until it was abolished, along with the use of Latin, in 1733.

COURT LEET

A feudal institution, a court leet was a type of manorial court held by right of franchise that flourished especially in medieval times, falling into decline from the sixteenth century onwards (although a few do still exist). It was a court of record held periodically, supposedly once or twice a year, in a hundred (a subdivision of a county), a lordship, or a manor, before the lord of the manor or his steward, and was attended by the residents of the district. It had jurisdiction to settle local civil affairs, elect various officials, and adjudicate over minor offences and nuisances. It is not unusual to find a single session defined as both a court leet and a court baron. Proceedings of such courts are recorded in court books or court rolls.

COURT OF RECORD

See COURTS OF LAW.

COURT ROLL

A court roll is a roll or book (the latter sometimes specifically distinguished as a 'court book') kept in connection with a manorial court: i.e. a court baron, court customary, or court leet. Written by the steward or his clerk, generally on parchment, and kept by the steward or the lord of the manor himself, an original court roll constitutes a record of the court's proceedings, usually respecting administrative rulings on rights, holdings, and rents, the roll itself serving as evidence of the holdings of copyholders (the lord's non-free tenants), to each of whom was usually given a copy of the relevant roll as his record of title (he might then be technically known as a 'tenant by copy of court roll'). Court rolls were always written in Latin until the Commonwealth period, when English was briefly introduced before Latin was reintroduced at the Restoration in 1660, Latin being finally abandoned in 1733. Court rolls, or copies of them kept by copyholders, from their proliferation in the thirteenth century until as late as 1925, are among the commonest kinds of manorial document to survive, large numbers being preserved in local record offices and estate muniments and archives (*see* Illus. 19). A substantial series, dating from *c.*1200 to 1900 and principally relating to manors belonging to the Crown, is in the National Archives at Kew (SC 2), as are a separate number relating to the Duchy of Lancaster and to the Principality of Wales.

COURTS OF LAW

Over the centuries, the principal or central law courts and ecclesiastical courts of the realm have been among the main sites for the production of records and documents. The four principal superior courts at Westminster

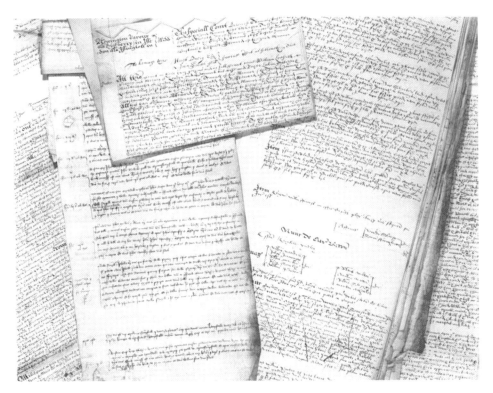

ILLUS. 19 *Selection of court rolls relating to Islington, in Latin and English, all on parchment (fifteenth- to seventeenth-century).*

Hall, London (i.e. King's Bench, Common Pleas, Exchequer, and Chancery), flourished from medieval times until they were abolished between 1875 and 1880 and their jurisdiction transferred to a single High Court following the Judicature Act of 1873. Those that are commonly called 'bill courts' had their business conducted almost entirely through manuscript submission rather than through litigants' personal appearance, although even then in some cases petitions might once have been made orally. Prerogative courts are those that were created under the royal prerogative, but which nevertheless were supposed to operate judicially. Most of the various courts' surviving records are housed in the National Archives at Kew.

They are, in alphabetical order:

Court of Chancery: from the fourteenth to nineteenth century the principal court of equity for cases largely outside the scope of the common law, although it also dealt with common-law cases with limited jurisdiction on its Latin side. The court is marked by the huge number of court officials it employed, and is that for which there is the greatest number of surviving records (C series: *see* CHANCERY).

Court of Common Pleas: a fixed and independent court from the thirteenth century onwards relating to common-law civil litigation between subjects in which the sovereign had no interest, although the sovereign could, and on occasions did, bring suits there (CP series). In medieval times it was the *curia domini regis de banco*, meaning 'the King's court of the Bench', usually called simply the Bench or Common Bench (not to be confused with the King's Bench).

Court of Exchequer: the oldest common-law court (on its 'plea side'), its name derived from the chequered cloth on the table originally used for calculating. It was the main court for collecting royal revenues and determining Treasury and taxation matters, but later dealt with general cases on its equity side (E series). It is to be distinguished from Courts of Exchequer Chamber which have been established at various times between 1357 and 1830 as courts to rectify on appeal errors made by other courts.

Court of the King's Bench: originally dealing with pleas of the Crown, later the highest court of common law in England and Wales dealing with both civil and criminal actions (KB series).

Among the other principal courts of the realm were:

Court of Admiralty: relating to maritime matters, including claims for prizes (HCA series).

Court of Arches: so-called because it sat in the church of St Mary-le-Bow in London which was built over arches; the ecclesiastical court of appeal for the province of Canterbury (its surviving records are now held chiefly at Lambeth Palace, a few in the British Library).

Court of High Commission: a prerogative court established in 1559 to enforce the Acts of Supremacy and Uniformity, and deal with related ecclesiastical matters, when the Crown assumed the position of supreme head of the Church. It was abolished in 1641 (among SP 16 and SP 46 series).

Court of Requests: a popular but minor prerogative court of equity in the sixteenth and early seventeenth centuries originally dealing with suits by poor men or by the King's servants. It was abolished in 1641 (REQ series).

Court of Star Chamber: a prerogative court named after a room with a star-spangled ceiling built in 1347 in the Palace of Westminster. It traditionally involved judicial sessions principally held by members of the King's Council and originally dealt with criminal offences of a public or extraordinary character or relating to the safety of the state. It was a bill court, and its business was conducted primarily through manuscript submission, but it could also summon litigants to appear in person. It came to deal with a wider range of matters outside the common law (which, however, it applied on its Latin side), often providing justice not available elsewhere. Its judgments were not subject to appeal, however, and it eventually became unpopular because of its alleged 'tyrannical' and politicized exercise of prerogative powers. It was abolished in 1641 (STAC series).

Court of Wards and Liveries: an unpopular court, which flourished from 1540 to 1646, whose main business was to deal with wardships and to assert certain feudal rights of the monarch relating to them (WARD series).

In addition to these, besides assizes and manorial courts, there were numerous provincial magistrates', municipal, commissary, diocesan, and consistory courts, as well as special courts that flourished in earlier centuries for only brief periods, such as the Court of Augmentations (1535–54) and Court of First Fruits (1540–54) relating to consequences of the Act of Supremacy and the dissolution of the monasteries. Yet further courts were held in Scotland, Ireland, and Wales, such as the Court of Session (the supreme civil court) and Court of Exchequer in Scotland.

Those courts, including the central high courts and some county and special courts, whose proceedings are enrolled as a permanent public record, are known as 'courts of record'.

COVENANT

A covenant, or deed of covenant, is a legal document formally embodying an agreement. From the time of Edward III in the fourteenth century, a writ of covenant (alleging breach of a covenant by one party to it) could not be enforced in the central courts without the evidence of a deed under seal. This gave rise to the modern meaning of 'covenant', which is a written agreement executed as a deed and witnessed. The term may also be applied to a particular undertaking contained or implied in the deed.

COVERS

The upper (front) and lower (rear) covers of a manuscript or printed book are the sides of the binding, as opposed to the spine at the back between them. *See* BINDING.

CRADLE

A cradle, a term generally associated with babies' cots, can also be a larger structure or frame designed to support something (such as a boat under repair). In the context of libraries and other institutions, cradles are types of support for books or codices, whether for the use of readers or for display or exhibition purposes. While varying in size and material (they can be made of wood, foam rubber, brass, or plexiglass), they are generally wedge- or V-shaped so that a book can be rested in the cradle with its boards opened at an angle, thereby reducing strain on the spine, rather than lying flat on the desk. A cradle is therefore to be distinguished from a rest or stand (such as a music stand) where the book stands or is opened up against a flat surface.

CRAYON

A French word used as early as the seventeenth century, the term 'crayon' generally means an implement used for drawing rather than writing, although it is often used for marking in copy-editing and the like. It comprises a kind of pencil or stick made of, or incorporating, chalk or some other coloured substance capable of leaving a thick mark on paper. By the nineteenth century, crayons incorporated a mixture of charcoal and oil, or other pigments of various colours, the oil component being subsequently replaced by wax.

CREST

In heraldry, a crest is a figure or device, one originally borne by a knight on his helmet, mounted above the helmet and shield in an achievement (*see* ACHIEVEMENT). The crest, often in the form of a lion or other striking figure, generally rests on a wreath or twisted silk base, coronet, or chapeau (*see* Illus. 18). Coats of arms are not always surmounted by crests, but in the late Elizabethan period many men already armigerous (bearing arms) had crests granted to them, and in due course new grants of arms would invariably include crests as well. The devices chosen for crests could sometimes reflect on aspects of the family name, perhaps even in a punning manner: e.g. the boar crest found stamped in gilt on books owned by Sir Francis Bacon.

In more general use, crests may also be custom-made devices used on personal articles to identify their ownership, including stationery with black or coloured crests imprinted or embossed in them.

CROSS-HATCHING

Cross-hatching, or what is sometimes called 'cross writing', is the form of writing and layout that results when a page is filled with normal horizontal writing and then turned sideways and filled or partly filled again with writing inscribed along the length of the page in a direction perpendicular to the previous writing. This practice, which often makes the congested page very difficult to read, flourished particularly in nineteenth-century letter-writing. Since the cost of postage depended on weight, it was thought practical, especially when the letter was being sent abroad, to cram as much writing as possible on to a single folded sheet of lightweight paper to minimize the postal charge. This practice may, however, be distinguished from the common instances when letters are written as usual and then turned sideways and continued in the margins. This would not constitute cross-hatching unless the main written text itself is intersected.

The term 'cross-hatching' is also encountered in descriptions of late medieval and early modern manuscripts, where it denotes a type of decoration involving crossed sets of parallel lines. In addition, but less commonly, the type of cancellation in which text is struck through with diagonal lines or multiple *X*s may sometimes be called 'cross-hatching'. *Compare* HATCHING.

CRUX

In the context of editing or textual criticism, whether relating to printed or manuscript materials, the term 'crux' (plural: cruces), derived from the Latin *crux interpretum* ('interpreter's cross'), means a reading in the text that is difficult to interpret or explain satisfactorily. It is some puzzling word or phrasing whose meaning is obscure, or which may result from the author's original having been misread, misunderstood, or simply altered in the process of recopying or transmission. Such readings may therefore be subject to differing theories and explanations by editors and scholars struggling to make sense of them. The most famous cruces occur in Shakespeare, such as the much disputed readings in *Hamlet* (I, ii, 129), 'O that this too too solid flesh would melt', where 'solid' in the First Folio text of 1623 reads in the first two Quartos of 1603 and 1604/5 'sallied' (i.e. 'sullied'); or in *Henry V* (II, iii, 16–17), the phrase 'a babbled of green fields', where 'babbled' ('babeld') is an eighteenth-century editorial emendation of the word 'Table' in the Folio text; or in *Othello* (V, ii, 356), where 'the base Indian' in the 1622 Quarto reads 'the base Iudean' in the Folio.

Many other works throw up such features, not least those found in multiple manuscript copies. In Sir Philip Sidney's well-circulated letter of advice to Queen Elizabeth on her proposed marriage with the Duc d'Anjou in 1579, for instance, a reading found at one point in the majority of manuscript texts—the word 'ivy' in the phrase 'ivy knots'—is rendered in various other manuscripts as 'slight', 'keye', 'high', 'eight', 'unkindly', 'indissoluble', 'Gordian', 'united', and 'oveon'.

CRYPTOGRAM, CRYPTOGRAPHY, CRYPTOLOGY

These terms derive from the Greek *kryptos* ('hidden'), *graphē* ('writing'), and *logos* ('word') respectively. 'Cryptography' denotes any mode or example of secret writing, such as in code or cipher, that is only intelligible to those possessing the key to it, or else the art of writing or solving such codes. A cryptogram is a piece of writing thus encoded. 'Cryptology' is a generic term meaning secret writing, communication, or language, or, more specifically, the study of it.

CURIA REGIS

See PRIVY COUNCIL.

CURRENTE CALAMO

A piece of script is described as being written *currente calamo* (the stress in the second word generally placed on the first syllable in pronunciation) when it was written rapidly (the Latin means 'with a running pen'), with words formed without lifting the pen. Such features usually characterize writing produced by an author in the throes of composition, with corrections or revisions made immediately rather than later (*see* Illus. 23 and 28). The sense of something produced speedily to grasp a fleeting moment of inspiration is conveyed in Arthur Hugh Clough's poem *Currente Calamo* (*c*.1861), beginning:

> Quick, painter, quick, the moment seize
> Amid the snowy Pyrenees;
> More evanescent than the snow
> The pictures come, are seen, and go:
> Quick, quick, *currente calamo*.

CURSITORS

From about the fourteenth century until 1835, when their function was taken over by the Petty Bag Office, Cursitors, or Clerks of Course, were Chancery clerks who wrote out writs *de cursu*: i.e. writs 'of common course', involving routine (rather than extraordinary) official business. Cursitors, who each dealt with a particular shire or shires, had to serve a seven-year apprenticeship to perfect their knowledge of precise Latin and the correct formulation of legal writs. A substantial number of records of the Cursitors from 1558 to 1888 are in the National Archives at Kew (principally in the C 207 and C 220 series). *Compare* EXIGENTERS, FILACERS, and PROTHONOTARY.

CURSIVE

Script is described as 'cursive' (the word is derived from the Latin *cursus*, a 'running') when it shows signs of having been written rapidly, with, for instance, the characters hurriedly formed, minimal separate strokes and pen-lifts, linked lettering, loops, and often a pronounced slope to the right. *See* Illus. 1, 28, and 53.

CUSTOS BREVIUM

See WRIT.

CUSTOS ROTULORUM

See ROTULUS.

CUT BOOK

In the context of printers since the nineteenth century, a cut book is one, usually very large, into which are pasted copies or drafts of art work (drawings, engravings, photographs, etc.) of or for books in production. They sometimes bear annotations indicating authors' suggestions for improvements.

CYCLOSTYLED

See FACSIMILE.

D

DAMP-STAINING

A fairly common feature of old documents, whether on parchment or paper, damp-staining, or water-staining, occurs when they have been exposed to humidity over a period, whether in a cold cellar, attic, outhouse, muniment room, or elsewhere. Damp-stained documents will tend to have patches of light brown discoloration, sometimes affecting the ink to produce a mauve or purple hue. This results primarily because damp provides good growing conditions for fungi, which produce matabolites stimulating reactions in the writing material. The documents worst affected by damp, especially those on paper, may partly have crumbled away or else matted to a wet, or subsequently dried, pulp so that the leaves cannot be opened without crumbling. *Compare* FOXING, OXIDATION, and STAINING.

DATES

Dates in old letters and documents take various forms, not always consistent with the modern calendar. There are also discrepancies between English and continental dating systems.

Throughout the Middle Ages and most of the early modern period, the standard calendar adopted in Europe was the Julian Calendar, based on that introduced by Julius Caesar in 45 BC. Because this was slightly out of synch with the solar year, every fourth year ('leap year') had 366 days instead of 365. As used in England, it also entailed different dates for the beginning of the year. New Year's Day originally fell on 25 December; then, from the fourteenth century onwards, on 25 March (Lady Day). All dates cited in accordance with the Julian Calendar came to be classified, or qualified, as 'Old Style' (often abbreviated to OS).

A new, Gregorian Calendar, was introduced by Pope Gregory XIII in 1582. With this calendar, among other differences, the New Year began on 1 January. Although England did not officially adopt the Gregorian Calendar until 1752, in practice the two calendars coexisted, the new being increasingly, if inconsistently, used in the British Isles from the end of the sixteenth century onwards. Dates cited in accordance with the Gregorian Calendar are New Style (or NS).

Since the two systems coexisted for so many years, however, with different dates for New Year's Day, the form of any date between 1 January and 24 March had, properly, to be cited as, for example, '10 January 1600/1' and '19 March 1600/1'. This means that the year in each of these dates was 1600 according to the Julian Calendar, but 1601 according to the Gregorian Calendar. From 25 March to 31 December, there was no confusion since only one calendar year applied whichever system was used. Confusion does, however, occur in the dating of letters and documents when the writer fails to indicate which calendar he is using: thus the date '19 March 1601', with no indication of whether this is OS or NS, might mean that the year is 1601 if the writer is conforming to the new calendar, but 1602 if he is abiding by the old calendar (since the year would not become 1602 until 25 March). This confusion is extremely common in the seventeenth century, especially since individual writers are not always themselves consistent in using one system or the other—for which reason, the year in old dates is sometimes cited by modern historians in inverted commas (e.g. 19 March '1601'). Some later English dating of documents is also complicated by the persistence of the Old Style among certain groups: for instance, Quakers, members of the Society of Friends, continued to date the calendar year from 25 March until well into the nineteenth century, so that, for example, their date '22/10/1825' would be, by the modern calendar, 22 January 1826 (the tenth Quaker month of the year running from 25 December to 24 January).

A further discrepancy introduced by the Gregorian Calendar in 1582 was its adjustment of earlier miscalculations of the solar year by having 4 October of that year jump to 15 October. This meant that there was, initially, a ten-day gap between English and most continental dating. Thus 1 January in England would be 11 January in Italy, France, or Germany. Diplomats and other writers sending letters internationally tended to be conscious of this distinction and therefore might cite the day in their date as, say, '1/11', meaning that it was the first of the month in England, but the eleventh on the continent. This discrepancy, which by then had increased even further, was removed in 1752, and the two calendars brought into alignment, when, to considerable public outcry (including 'give us back our eleven days' riots), eleven days were officially omitted from the English calendar and 2 September of that year was immediately followed by 14 September.

Among other types of dating found in old British documents, perhaps the most common, at least since the time of Richard I, is by regnal year. Most royal and official documents from medieval times onwards were dated according to the reign of the monarch computed by the date of his or her accession. Thus, for instance, '21 November 27 Elizabeth' and '21 July 27 Elizabeth' mean '21 November 1584' and '21 July 1585' respectively, the 27th year of the reign of Elizabeth (who came to the throne on 17 November 1558) running from 17 November 1584 to 16 November 1585. Two days in each reign usually (but not always) overlap: i.e. the two days when one sovereign died and another acceded to the throne. Thus, for instance, the last day of Elizabeth's reign (24 March 1603) was the day of James I's accession, and the date of James's death (27 March 1625) was the day of Charles I's accession.

Another frequently encountered dating system, from at least as early as the twelfth century up to 1830, is that applied to legal records and relating to law terms. These, named after traditional Church festivals, are the periods when the Common Bench and King's Bench at Westminster held court. The exact dates vary from year to year and in different reigns, but the terms are, namely: Michaelmas (ranging from 9 October to as late as 29 November), Hilary (23 or 24 January to 12 or 13 February), Easter (varying periods between 9 April and 17 June), and Trinity (varying between 28 May and 18 July).

When someone attempts to date a manuscript, or anything else for that matter, by referring to the earliest and latest dates that could apply to that particular item, the Latin terms *terminus a quo* ('boundary from which') and *terminus ad quem* ('boundary to which') may be used. Thus it might be said that the *terminus a quo* for an undated letter written by John Smith is 4 December 1844 and its *terminus ad quem* is 15 January 1846, because, perhaps, it is addressed from where he is known to have been living between those two dates.

Those who need to distinguish between dates in the past two millenia and those earlier have a choice between AD (*Anno Domini*, 'in the year of the Lord') and BC (before Christ) on the one hand, and CE (Christian, Common, or Current Era) and BCE (before the Christian, Common, or Current Era) on the other, the latter having been formulated in the late twentieth century by self-appointed arbiters of political correctness and having gained considerable currency among academics and non-Christian pressure groups, if not with the public at large.

The new dating introduced during the French Revolutionary period, with months renamed Vendémiaire, Brumaire, etc., and year I beginning (backdated to) 22 September 1792, lasted fourteen years before its abandonment. The dating in the Muslim world remains officially the Hijri calendar (its years cited in the West as 'AH' from the Latinate *Anno Hegirae*), 1 AH being calculated from the beginning of the first lunar month of the year of Muhammad's flight from Makkah to Madinah, corresponding to 16 July 622 AD. For its part, the Jewish dating system, its months determined by complicated astronomical calculations, is based on the numbering of years from the supposed creation of the world 5700-odd years ago (thus, for instance, AD 2007 corresponds to twelve months in the Hebrew years 5767 and 5768).

DATE-STAMPED

A letter is date-stamped when it bears a hand-stamped postal mark, as opposed to a hand-written annotation, containing a date, whether on an address leaf, address wrapper, or envelope. The practice of postal date-stamping dates from 1661. *See* BISHOP MARK.

DAVENPORT

A davenport is a type of writing table, comprising a set of relatively square-shaped drawers surmounted by a sloping surface for writing on. This type of furniture dates from the late eighteenth century.

DAY BOOKS

Day books are commercial registers or account books recording business on a strictly daily basis, including details of such things as sales or work done. When devoted primarily to financial matters, the contents of day books would usually be entered afterwards in summary form in more formal ledgers at weekly or monthly intervals. *See also* WASTE BOOK.

DEAD LETTER

'Dead letter' is a Post Office term, used since at least the late eighteenth century, for an item of mail that is undeliverable because the address is incorrect, or incomplete, or else because the addressee is deceased or no longer at the specified address and therefore untraceable. The Dead Letter Office is the Post Office department that deals with such items, which, if undeliverable and unclaimed after a certain period, are generally returned to their senders or else destroyed.

The most famous dead letter office is the fictional one depicted in Herman Melville's short story 'Bartleby the Scrivener' (1853). Among a number of other fictional works under the title *Dead Letters* is Maurice

Baring's *Dead Letters* (1910), with its amusing letters supposedly by or relating to famous figures of ancient and later history and literature, such as Helen of Troy, Cleopatra, King Arthur, King Lear's daughters, Hamlet, Lady Macbeth, and Sir Walter Ralegh.

DEATH WARRANT

See EXECUTION WARRANT.

DEBENTURE

Adapted from the Latin word *debentur* ('they are owing'), the term 'debenture' denotes a certificate of indebtedness. It is a formal or official document or voucher acknowledging and certifying that a sum of money is owed to someone for some reason (whether for goods, service, salary, etc.), the document serving as that person's authority for claiming payment. Different kinds of debenture were issued, from the late Middle Ages onwards, with different wording, application, and conditions, as well as rates of interest granted, depending on circumstances. They include those given by various government offices, such as by the Ordnance Office as payment for supplies, by the Customs House in relation to money returnable on the export of imported goods, and by Trade or Treasury commissioners with respect to loans made to the Government, as well as by naval and military bodies. When issued by private companies, they may be equivalent to share certificates.

DECKLE EDGES

When a leaf or sheet of paper has deckle edges, the edges are rough, uneven, and uncut. Such edges are usually a feature of hand-made laid paper, caused in the manufacturing process by seepage of surplus pulp underneath the deckle (the thin rectangular frame supposedly confining the pulp to the mould), the paper then being left untrimmed. Deckle-edged pages are sometimes reproduced by mechanical means in writing paper sold by stationers or, very occasionally, to cater to a certain book-collecting fashion, in relatively modern press books.

ILLUS. 20 *First page of the Declaration of Breda, granting 'a free & generall Pardon' to all former rebels apart from those 'excepted by Parliament', signed in the upper border by Charles II and with his papered 'Privy Signet' seal, 4/14 April 1660. It is neatly written in a professional scribal hand and is the official document sent by Charles to General Monck, forwarded to Edward Montagu, General of the Fleet, and read out to the Fleet by his Secretary Samuel Pepys.*

Charles R

Charles by the Grace of God King of England
Scotland, France and Ireland, Defender of the
Faith &c   To all Our loving Subjects of what degree
or quality soever, Greeting.   If the generall Distracti-
on and Confusion which is spread over the whole Kingdome, doth not awaken all men to a desire and longing that
those Wounds which haue so many yeares together been
kept bleeding may be bound up, all We can say will
be to noe purpose; However after this long silence
We haue thought it Our Duty to Declare how much
We desire to contribute thereunto, and that as We
can never giue over the hope in God time to obteyne
the possession of that Right, w:ch God and Nature
hath made Our Due; soe We doe make it Our dayly
suite to the Devine Providence, That he will in Com-
passion to Vs and Our Subjects, after so long misery
& sufferings, remitt and put Vs into a quiet & peace-
able possession of that Our Right with as little blood
and dammage to Our People, as is possible: Nor doe
We desire more to enjoy what is Ours, then that

DECLARATION

In a legal context, a declaration is the plaintiff's opening pleading in a personal action at common law. In a wider context, a declaration is a formal and public announcement or proclamation, whether made orally or in writing and embodied in a document. Numerous declarations have been made throughout history. The Declaration of Breda, for instance, restored Charles II to the throne, and in effect the British monarchy, in 1660 (*see* Illus. 20), and the Declaration of Rights in 1689, of which an emended parliamentary draft is preserved in the House of Lords Record Office (T/6), was the basis of the Bill of Rights of the same year, establishing freedom of speech, etc. Perhaps the most famous is the Declaration of Independence, drawn up chiefly by Thomas Jefferson and signed by the American Continental Congress on 4 July 1776, the principal signed copy of which is in the National Archives, Washington DC.

DECORATION

Scribal decoration of texts is common throughout the history of writing. At its simplest, it may comprise the calligraphic accentuation, extension, elaboration, flourishing, engrossing, or rubrication of certain letters for visual effect. More pronounced ornamentation, extending into the margin, might take the form of tendrils, tracery, strapwork, bezants (circular gold shields), or other patterns. Even more ambitious decoration, some in colour, some possibly by professional limners, might include such features as historiated initial letters and borders, with graphic depictions of scenes, coats of arms, flowers, foliage, animals, shells, heads, and other figures.

Manuscripts of all kinds may be so decorated for a variety of reasons, both aesthetic and practical. Decorations may be added or incorporated, for instance, for the casual amusement of particular scribes; for serious religious or political purposes (such as the great monastic manuscripts of the Scriptures or manuscripts prepared with special care for presentation to rulers or patrons); for diplomatic purposes (such as ornate letters sent to foreign potentates); or for purposes of social aggrandizement (such as heraldic grants of arms or Royal Letters Patent for particular noblemen bearing initial letter portraits of the monarch).

A decoration is generally distinguished from an illustration in so far as the latter is a self-contained depiction of a scene or figure of some kind within its own frame or border rather than an ornamental extension of, or addition to, some other feature. For examples of decorative features, *see* Illus. 7, 31, 37, 38, 40, 48, 63, 87, and 95.

A decretal, or decretal epistle, is a letter or document issued by the Pope or Roman Curia containing a papal decree or authoritative ruling on some point of doctrine, clerical discipline, or ecclesiastical law. In medieval times, decretals were often written in response to specific appeals and might have either local or general application. The term 'decretal' is also used to denote a manuscript collection of transcripts of such decrees, since they were taken to form part of canon law and were used or studied in universities or by ecclesiastical and civil authorities. The term 'Decretals' was also commonly applied to the particular collection of papal decrees issued in 1234 by Pope Gregory IX. Notable collections of decretals in general, many of them glossed, include examples concerning England. Some are even illuminated with depictions of scenes from saints' lives or other subjects which may or may not be relevant to the text. Fragments of decretals are among the commonest materials used as binders' waste, both before and after the Reformation, as printed editions came to supersede the manuscripts.

DEDICATION

Many manuscript literary works in the early modern period bear an author's dedication, or dedicatory epistle, among the preliminaries to the main text, as do many printed books. They will tend to be addressed to patrons or persons of influence whose support the author is soliciting, or else to family, friends, or other persons of note within the author's circle (*see* Illus. 12, 21, 54, and 78). The presence of a dedication does not necessarily signify that the particular manuscript is a presentation copy to that person unless there is additional evidence to that effect. The work itself may be dedicated to a particularly eminent person—such as the sovereign—while the particular manuscript is one of a number presented to other dignitaries as well—as is the case, for instance, with certain of the lengthy manuscript tracts produced by Lord Henry Howard in Queen Elizabeth's time.

Some prefatory epistles, which are effectively dedications, are also written in manuscripts by persons other than the author. Certain scribes dedicate hand-written presentation copies to particular recipients. For instance, Ralph Starkey (describing himself as 'a gleaner in other mens harvests of this kinde') dedicated his semi-calligraphic copy of a legal treatise by Arthur Agard to the Lord Chancellor Lord Ellesmere, and in 1624 Ralph Crane dedicated his copy of John Fletcher's play *Demetrius and Enanthe*, as 'a Matter Recreatiue', to Sir Kenelm Digby.

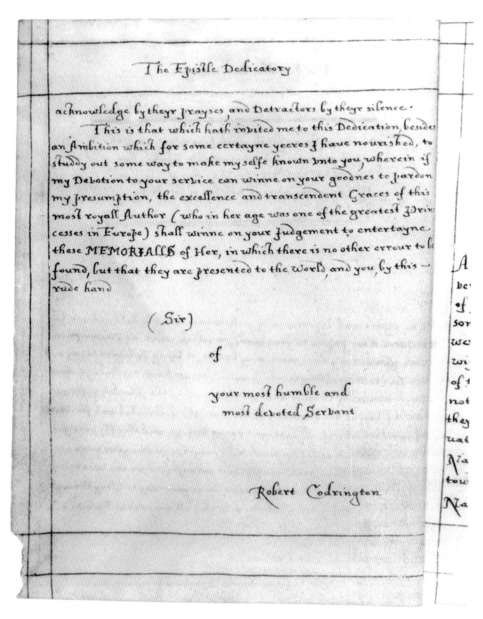

ILLUS. 21 *The last page of the autograph dedication to Sir Thomas Nott signed by Robert Codrington in an autograph manuscript of his translation of* The Memorialls of Queene Margaret *(Marguerite de Valois, first wife of Henri IV), c.1640. It is written by Codrington in virtually calligraphic, predominantly roman script, the letters largely separate, within ruled margins, and is possibly the manuscript presented to Nott.*

Although the term 'deed' is commonly, but inaccurately, used to denote any kind of land or estate document, a deed, since medieval times, is a legal instrument that is technically sealed and delivered as a deed, being then *factum*, something done, and not mere words in writing. There are two principal types of deed. One is an indenture, which is made by, and expresses the intentions of, two or more parties (the 'party of the first part', 'party of the second part', etc.). The other is a deed poll, which is by one party only. The latter was traditionally 'polled', meaning that the document was cut even, whereas an indenture was indented with zigzag, wavy, or scalloped edges (*see* INDENTURE).

Most frequently until modern times written on parchment, deeds embody various kinds of legal disposition, agreement, or arrangement concerning property, money, or related matters and obligations, including conveyances, leases, and other property transactions. Unless they are transcripts (or sometimes counterparts), deeds will not only be generally signed and sealed by the parties concerned, but often also countersigned (at the foot of the document or else endorsed on the verso) by witnesses to the arrangement. Various kinds of deed are known by the nature of the transaction: e.g. a deed of exchange, for a reciprocal conveyance of property by two parties, or a deed of partition, for an agreement to divide an estate. The texts of innumerable deeds are preserved in official enrolments. *See* ENROL.

DEED BOX

Boxes designed specifically to contain and preserve deeds are of considerable antiquity. They are especially associated with locations where large numbers of such documents were produced or accumulated over a period and needed to be stored as permanent records—such as civil, government, legal, and ecclesiastical repositories, as well as the muniment rooms of large private estates. Although, in different periods, such boxes might have been made of different materials, including wood and leather, the most common kind of deed box encountered, since at least the eighteenth century, is the black-japanned tinned-iron variety, the size varying from relatively shallow boxes some 30 inches (76.5 cm) long to huge trunk-size containers. When subject to dampness, they are not immune to rusting.

A smaller type of deed box, similarly of black-japanned tinned iron, was used by certain late nineteenth- and twentieth-century literary agents for storing the contracts and other papers relating to their authors. Each box bore the name in clear lettering of the author concerned.

DEED OF COVENANT
See COVENANT.

DEED POLL
See DEED.

DEFEASANCE
Deriving from the Old French meaning 'defeat' or 'undoing', the term 'defeasance' denotes a deed or legal instrument setting out a condition, the performance of which will render null and void some other deed. The term is also applied to the condition in a deed the performance of which will nullify that same deed.

DEFENDANT
In a lawsuit, the defendant is the person being sued by a plaintiff. In a Chancery suit, both parties might be obliged to provide written answers to questions or statements put to them, although in common law, until 1851, neither party could be asked questions.

DELETIONS
Deletions (the term derives from the Latin *deletio*, 'destruction') are a common feature of manuscripts, especially of working drafts written when the process of creative composition was still in progress and subject to the writer's second thoughts and revisions. Alternatively, text can be heavily deleted by subsequent readers by way of expurgating offensive matter. Text may be deleted—i.e. rejected, erased, or obliterated—in any number of ways, including rubbing out words or lettering by scraping the paper or parchment with a knife or abrasive implement, by covering over text with a block of heavy inking, with pasted-over slips of paper, or, in modern times, with liquid 'white-out'. The most frequent type of erasure, however, is made by leaving the rejected text legible on the page, but simply crossing it out or striking through it, whether with a horizontal line, or with large crosses, or with vertical, oblique, or wavy lines, through words, lines, or passages to indicate their elimination (or, in the case of certain accounts, that entries are cancelled because the relevant payments have been made or received). In certain cases, such as late sixteenth- and seventeenth-century playscripts submitted to the official censor, text may be marked for deletion, with minimal disfigurement, simply by a vertical line drawn down the margin.

There are other circumstances when deletions are less frequently employed in earlier periods than they would be today: for example, early modern writers or scribes sometimes record a revision or alternative reading by writing it directly over the wording they wish to see substituted, but without actually deleting the original reading. This practice, which can be a source of occasional confusion for subsequent copyists and editors, may result either from a writer's or scribe's reluctance to mar his copy aesthetically or because he consciously wants alternative readings to be preserved. For examples of deletion, *see* Illus. 8, 13, 23, and 28.

DEMANDANT

See PLAINTIFF.

DEPONENT

See DEPOSITION.

DEPOSITION

A deposition, made by a deponent, is a statement on oath in a court of law or a written statement to be used as testimony and evidence in court or in a lawsuit. From the fifteenth century onwards, depositions were generally made by witnesses in writing, or at least by appending their signature or mark to a scribal account of their replies, in answer to interrogatories.

DESCENDER

In palaeography, as also in typography, a descender is the downward stroke or loop below the base line in letters such as *g, j, p, q,* and *y. Compare* ASCENDER.

DESK

The type of furniture most commonly associated with writing, the desk has a history dating back to ancient times. Of the various forms that developed over the centuries, the common factor is that it is a table designed specifically for reading or writing purposes, whether in monasteries, schools, universities, libraries, offices, private studies, or other locations, where books and writing materials may be rested and used by the (generally) seated reader or writer, either on a sloped or flat working surface (*see* Illus. 79).

Desks of various shapes and sizes, some of them revolving or multi-sided to seat several writers at once, sometimes with built-in book rests, shelves, and other fittings, are featured frequently in medieval and later illustrations of scribes at work. From at least the early seventeenth century until Dickensian times, English scribes and clerks have been depicted or described as sitting on high stools at tall slanted desks (*see* Illus. 22). The importance of such furniture to the practical process of writing or copying by clerical and secular men and women, who might spend a major part of their lives in this

ILLUS. 22 *A scribe seated at his high, sloped desk and engaged with a client, the back of the desk with a frame to support his exemplar, as depicted on the engraved title-page of* The Compleat Clark, and Scriveners Guide *(1655).*

activity, is self-evident. It is also known that certain writers paid special attention to the design and function of their private desks. For instance, the philosopher John Locke (1632–1704) had a large, flat-topped desk fitted with a set of drawers to each side, built to his specifications, which enabled him to create his own filing system.

An alternative use of the term, which is occasionally found even as late as the nineteenth century, but which is now obsolete, is 'desk' meaning a shelf, case, or press on which books stand in a library.

DESPATCH
See DISPATCH.

DEVICE
See PLOT.

DIACRITIC
A diacritic is a sign or mark used to distinguish an alphabetical letter or character in terms of its sound value, notably (at least in non-English

words) with the use of accents (ç, é, è, etc.). In manuscripts, it is common to see early modern scribes either ignore such markings or else misapply them.

DIAERESIS

A diaeresis is a diacritical mark comprising two horizontal dots, akin to the German umlaut, placed over the second of two adjoining vowels to show that each must be pronounced separately rather than as a diphthong: e.g. in the proper noun Noël. Such marks are rarely picked up or reproduced by early modern English scribes.

DIAGRAM

A diagram, a common feature in certain kinds of manuscripts, is a drawing in which only the outline of the subject is given, or alternatively a general shape or symbolic representation of it: e.g. scientific, geometrical, or navigational figures in notebooks, exercise books, or treatises devoted to such subjects. *See* Illus. 9 and 34.

DIARY

Deriving from forms of the Latin words *dies* ('day') and *diaria* ('daily allowance'), the term 'diary' generally denotes a manuscript book in which the writer keeps, or sets out to keep, a daily record of events in his or her life. The entries may be made on a consistent day-to-day basis or else at irregular intervals, and they may be lengthy and detailed or only brief jottings. Alternatively, a diary is a book in which are recorded memoranda relating to forthcoming dates and appointments, such as a modern commercial desk diary. The practice of keeping diaries dates back in England at least to the sixteenth century, extant examples including that of the young Edward VI for 1549–52 (British Library, Cotton MS Nero C. X, art. 7). Early diaries chiefly began as blank 'paper books', entries in which could be arranged however the writer wished. By 1565 the prototypes of printed diaries appeared when, in printed almanacs, blank pages were left for the users' own entries against the calendar of each month. Thence developed in succeeding centuries the various types of diary published and retailed by stationers, setting out the forthcoming full year's dates, supplemented by other relevant details (holidays, saints' days, etc.), with a blank space or page left for each day for the user's own manuscript entries. Numerous diaries, some covering extensive periods, have been written since the seventeenth century, many of them by well-known figures, many others by otherwise obscure people, valued for the personal light they throw on contemporary life. The most famous remains the multi-volume diary kept in shorthand by Samuel Pepys from 1660 to 1669, preserved in the Pepys Library at Magdalene College, Cambridge, and not deciphered until 1825. *Compare* JOURNAL.

DICTATION

Dictation is the process by which someone reads out words orally so that someone else can write or copy them down. This might involve someone's reading out a pre-written text so that perhaps several scribes can copy it at the same time, or alternatively someone's giving utterance to originally conceived text so that it might be committed to writing by an amanuensis. Instances of the latter include the spiritual autobiography of the illiterate Margery Kempe, dictated to a priest of King's Lynn in 1436, and *Paradise Lost*, dictated by the blind John Milton to his daughters in the 1650s and 1660s. Besides countless office personnel, dictating letters to secretaries, some novelists have composed by dictation: e.g. Henry James, on occasions, and Agatha Christie, who in her later years composed into a dictating machine, which produced a cylindrical recording that could then be played and typed later by a secretary.

DIFFICILIOR LECTIO POTIOR

A Latin maxim meaning 'the more difficult reading is stronger' used by early editors of classical texts, *difficilior lectio potior* is one of the traditionally basic, most frequently cited principles of textual criticism. It means that if different manuscript (or printed) exempla of a text have different readings at a particular point, and one reading is more difficult to understand than the others, then that is most likely to be closest to the correct or original reading, given copyists' tendency to simplify rather than complicate the thought processes embodied in a text. The principle is hardly infallible, but, in the absence of any other satisfactory explanations for the variant readings, it remains a useful point of reference for editors when making judgements to establish viable texts. *Compare* UTRUM IN ALTERUM ABITURUM ERAT?

DIGEST

A digest is the same thing as an abridgement or abstract, namely a shortened or condensed version of a work or text, being a substitute that enables the original to be more easily 'digested', assimilated, or understood. It is upon this principle that the magazine *Reader's Digest* has flourished for so long.

In medieval times, digests could denote more specifically formal compilations of legal rules and statutes, generally based on, or copied from, those made by classical Roman jurists (in particular 'The Digest' produced by a team for the Emperor Justinian in AD 530). Medieval copies are sometimes illuminated and contain explanatory glosses.

DIGIT

See MANICULE.

DIGRAPH

A digraph is the symbol produced when two letters are written as one, such as *ae* as *æ* and *oe* as *œ*.

DIMISSORIALS

From medieval times onwards, dimissorials (from the Latin *litterae dimissoriae*), or letters dimissory, are a type of licence issued in the Catholic Church by the Pope, bishops, abbots, or other superiors of religious orders, formally allowing ordinations to take place. After the Reformation, in the Church of England, they generally involved the bishop of one diocese arranging for the bishop of another diocese to ordain a candidate for Holy Orders when it was not convenient or possible for the first bishop to do so.

DIPLOMA

Deriving from a Latin word meaning an official letter or document of recommendation, or one conferring some favour or privilege, the term 'diploma' most commonly denotes a type of certificate, signifying an award to a particular suitably qualified person, such as an honorary appointment, a university degree, a licence to practise in a particular field, or a medal of some kind for a military, sporting, academic, or other achievement. Almost invariably printed, usually with manuscript insertions, sometimes decorated, diplomas commonly take the form of single sheets or scolls, and, depending on their nature, tend to be signed by monarchs, presidents, university chancellors, or other distinguished officials representing the awarding body.

DIPLOMATIC

The term 'diplomatic' can have three different, if related, meanings in a manuscript context.

'Diplomatic', the term used in this sense from the seventeenth century onwards, is the science or study of documents and records, including their forms, language, script, and meaning. It involves knowledge of such matters as the established wording and procedures of particular kinds of document, the deciphering of writing, and document analysis and authentication.

A diplomatic transcription of a document is one that reproduces faithfully and accurately, or as closely as is possible, *verbatim et literatim*, the exact form of the original, such as the precise original spelling and punctuation, including abbreviations, deletions, and word changes.

Diplomatic may also relate to the art of diplomacy in the political sense: i.e. concerning the management of international relations and negotiations. Diplomatic records and papers of various kinds, including ambassadors' and envoys' own letterbooks (*see* Illus. 44), are documents of an official nature that bear witness to such activity. Typical examples are formal letters by sovereigns or heads of state appointing ambassadors, envoys, or consuls; giving them instructions on their mission or duties; introducing them to foreign courts or governments; sending greetings or compliments to foreign potentates; soliciting amity, commercial rights, or other favours or privileges; arranging passports; seeking redress for injustices suffered by their citizens on foreign soil; and proposing settlements and treaties, as well as much other business.

Although highly formal in content, diplomatic letters and other instruments signed by British monarchs and addressed to other European sovereigns, whether written on paper or vellum, tend to be fairly circumscribed and conventional in appearance. Those sent to and from the rulers of distant lands, however, can be extremely elaborate and even spectacular, both verbally and visually, somewhat in the manner of Royal Letters Patent, this being a way of impressing upon the recipient the high status and importance of the sender. Thus, for instance, a letter by James I to an oriental ruler, soliciting friendship, could be on vellum and not only written in calligraphic script, but also with borders elaborately decorated in colours, the first line ('James, by the Grace') engrossed in gold leaf, with the initial *J* additionally enlarged and decorated. One by James II to an Ottoman Grand Vizier, replacing an ambassador, could be even more ornate, with flourished and engrossed lettering in gold leaf and illuminated arms in the borders. These, to some extent, replicate the level of grandeur found in similar letters sent to English monarchs in the sixteenth and seventeenth centuries by Russian, Turkish, Indian, and Far Eastern potentates.

DISBOUND

'Disbound' means that the book or booklet, whether printed or manuscript, was once sewn and bound, but has now lost its binding. The term may be distinguished from 'unbound', which means that the book was never bound.

DISBURSEMENT BOOKS

Disbursement books, or disbursements books, are ledgers or account books recording payments made. Those relating to old institutions, such as universities and colleges, may have considerable historical interest. The various disbursement books of Christ Church, Oxford, for instance, record detailed payments made in the first half of the seventeenth century to many well-known literary figures of the period, who were then students or in some way associated with the college, and who signed the entries in person by way of officially acknowledging or authorizing receipt. These records, with the clusters of signatures on particular pages, bear vivid witness to an active contemporary academic and literary community, including such notables as Richard Corbett, Robert Burton, George Morley, William Strode, Brian Duppa, Jasper Mayne, William Cartwright, Barten Holyday, Thomas Goffe, Henry King, and, in 1660–1, Izaak Walton.

DISCHARGE

A discharge is a document, receipt, or legal instrument certifying the fulfilment or termination of an obligation or liability, usually because the relevant payment has been made to satisfy a debt.

DISINFECTED MAIL

Disinfected mail is letters sent from plague-infected countries which, in accordance with the Quarantine Act of 1710, had to be fumigated at quarantine stations before delivery in Britain. The letters were liable to be opened to expose them to air, or to be slit or cut to ventilate them, or to be dipped in vinegar (which generally left stains), or to be exposed to sulphurous fumes (leaving some stains), or else to be held over a brazier (which would leave scorch marks). Eighteenth- and nineteenth-century letters so treated in various maritime countries would often bear special postal marks signifying that they had been disinfected.

DISJUNCT

When a leaf originally forming half of a bifolium, or sheet folded in two, has been physically separated from its counterpart, it is said to be disjunct. *Compare* CONJUGATE.

DISPATCH

Deriving from the Portuguese and Spanish word *despacher* ('to hasten, speed, expedite or get rid of'), the term 'dispatch' (properly so spelt, although the spelling 'despatch' entered general currency in the mid-eighteenth century) denotes an official written message, communication, or report, generally relating to public affairs, sent off promptly or speedily, usually by means of a special messenger or courier. The term is generally employed in connection with political, diplomatic, military, or naval communications of that character. Examples of famous dispatches include the Waterloo Dispatch written by the Duke of Wellington immediately after the Battle of Waterloo on 18 June 1815, informing Lord Bathurst, Secretary of State for War, of the victory. The possibly tear-stained draft of this is in the British Library (Add. MS 69850) and the fair copy actually sent is in the National Archives at Kew (WO 1/205/2).

DISPATCH BOX

A dispatch box is a box designed for carrying confidential dispatches, usually of a formal or official nature, used for travelling or for delivery. The nineteenth- and twentieth-century examples most commonly encountered belonged to government ministers, politicians, or other public figures or men of business. They are generally made of wood covered in leather (normally morocco), black, dark brown, or red in colour, bearing the name of the owner and possibly the manufacturer in gilt lettering, the interior lined with marbled paper, velvet, or other material, with a brass or leather handle to the top and a brass plate to the front with lock and key for security purposes. They vary in size, but some characteristic examples measure as follows: David Lloyd George's, *c.*11½ × 5½ × 3¼ inches (29.25 × 14 × 8.25 cm); Isambard Kingdom Brunel's, *c.*15¾ × 11¾ × 5½ inches (40 × 30 × 14 cm); and Winston Churchill's, as Minister of Munitions, 1917–18, *c.*17¾ × 12 × 5¾ inches (45 × 30.5 × 14.5 cm).

DISPATCH SLITS

Dispatch slits are slits cut into a letter before sending to accommodate a ribbon or ribbons which would enclose or be tied around the letter and their knots sealed by wax. Such slits are generally a feature of early modern letters of a more formal nature, such as dispatches sent by monarchs or state officials (*see* Illus. 3). *Compare* FUMIGATION SLITS.

DISSEMINATION

Deriving from a form of the Latin *disseminare* ('to scatter seed'), the term 'dissemination' means, in connection with manuscripts, the distribution or circulation of copies of a particular work. *See also* TRANSMISSION.

DISTRIBUTION

See DISSEMINATION.

DISTRIBUTIVE COPYING

See PECIA SYSTEM.

DITTOGRAPHY

See SCRIBAL ERRORS.

DIURNAL

Deriving from the Latin *diurnum* ('something pertaining to the day'), the term 'diurnal' may denote the same thing as a diary or journal, although it is a term less frequently used. In medieval times, a diurnal was commonly a type of service book containing only the daytime offices (Lauds, Prime, Terce, Sext, None, and Vespers). The word 'diurnal' also became popular in the seventeenth century and was frequently incorporated in the titles of printed newsletters or political pamphlets giving news of current parliamentary or public events. *See* Illus. 6.

DIVIDER

A divider is a type of compasses, with a sharp point at both ends and sometimes shaped with handles like scissors, used by map-makers and possibly scribes for measuring or regulating spaces on their writing or drawing material. *See* Illus. 48 and 79.

DOCKET

The word 'docket', or in its older form 'docquet', has various applications in different contexts, including types of legal briefs, memoranda, and customs certificates. Most commonly, it denotes an annotation inscribed on a letter or other document briefly summarizing its contents or recording some information relating to it, such as the name of the writer, date of writing or receipt, or a reference for filing purposes. More formally, dockets might be made by secretaries, as Robert Beale wrote in 1592, 'on the backside of the le*tt*res' in order to 'abbreviate . . . the substantiall and most materiall pointes w*h*ich are to be propounded and answered' in case their superiors had not 'leisure' to read them in full themselves. A document may thus be docketed on its back or verso (the docketing thereby corresponding to an endorsement), at the head, at the foot, in a corner, or down the side, a matter sometimes determined by filing considerations. *See* Illus. 27 and 69.

At their most formal, in documents of state, dockets are abstracts or summaries of contents written on Kings' bills as part of the process of authorizing and preparing letters patent under the appropriate royal seal. These abstracts were copied for the record into a register or docket book. Docquet Books, so-called, in the National Archives at Kew exist, for instance, in connection with the Signet Office from 1584 to 1851 (SO 3) and Privy Seal Office from *c.*1327 to 1884 (PSO 5).

DOCKWRA MARK

The earliest type of hand-stamped postmark struck on letters and denoting prepayment for delivery, the Dockwra mark was named after William Dockwra, who, with Robert Murray and Dr Hugh Chamberlen, started a London local postal service, originally based in Lime Street, in May 1680. Although Murray soon developed a rival service of his own, letters associated with one or other of the companies, between December 1680 and September 1682, bore variant forms of a common hand-stamp always known as the 'Dockwra mark' or 'Dockwra stamp'. It takes the form of a triangle within a larger triangle whose corners are rounded, bearing the words 'PENNY / POST / PAID' and at the centre the letter 'L' (for Lime Street) or 'P' (for St Paul's). Following the suppression of these private postal services in November 1682, they were restarted by the Post Office using a similar type of stamp. Extant examples of letters bearing the original Dockwra stamps are preserved chiefly in institutional archives and collections; they are otherwise rare and are highly sought after by postal collectors, who may pay tens of thousands of pounds each for them.

DOCQUET

See DOCKET.

DOCUMENT

A document is any kind of material bearing text, whether it be paper or parchment, manuscript, typed, or printed. Indeed technically a document may be any physical artefact whatsoever bearing text and providing information about something, including coins, public monuments, and tombstones. The term used as a verb means to prove or give evidence in support of a case, statement, historical account, interpretation, or proposition.

DOCUMENT OF TITLE

A document of title is one that establishes evidence or proof of someone's ownership of commercial goods or that transfers rights of possession or responsibility for custody to someone else, such as, for instance, a bill of lading. *Compare* TITLE DEED.

DOG-EARED

'Dog-eared' is a distinctly unrespectable, but, in the absence of anything better, a nevertheless common and useful term applied to books that have had the corners of leaves turned down by readers. This practice has been an occasional feature of readership since at least the early modern period, and probably earlier, as a substitute for the use of bookmarks to signal pages of particular interest or to which the reader may wish to return. It is obviously frowned upon by librarians and most bibliophiles since it disfigures the book, weakens the corners of the leaves concerned, and is apt to lead to their breaking off altogether. Distinguished persons who were in the habit of 'dog-earing' their books include Sir Isaac Newton, a significant portion of whose library is now at Trinity College, Cambridge. Newton's method was to fold the leaf so that the corner pointed to the particular passage that had caught his interest.

DOODLE

A doodle is a piece of random or casual scribbling or drawing, a common feature of manuscripts, whether inscribed whimsically or absent-mindedly by their original writers or added by other owners or users at a later date. When doodles are inscribed on working manuscripts by creative minds such as Leonardo da Vinci, for instance, or Samuel Beckett, they may throw fascinating light on the writer's thought processes. *See also* PEN TRIAL.

DORSE

Deriving from the Latin word *dorsum* ('back'), the term 'dorse' denotes the same thing as 'verso', meaning the back or reverse side of a leaf of parchment or paper. It is more commonly applied, however, to single leaves or membranes of vellum and to rolls rather than to leaves in a bound book or codex. *Compare* ENDORSEMENT.

DOSSIER

Originally a French word and adopted into English in the nineteenth century (and still retaining its French pronunciation, *doss-i-ê*), the term 'dossier' means a bundle of papers. It is most commonly used to denote a file of documents appertaining to some particular person, case, or subject.

The judicial and administrative procedure adopted by the Indian Civil Service, whereby officials tended to deliberate on cases at hill stations by reviewing dossiers sent up from the plains, is sometimes known as the 'dossier system'.

DOUBLE ELEPHANT FOLIO

See FOLIO.

DOUBLE-FOLIO

See FOLIO.

DOUBLURE

See PASTE-DOWN.

DRAFT

A draft is a working manuscript or typescript, roughly written or produced, usually with deletions and revisions, during the actual composition of a work. The final draft is that reworked, refined, and completed by the author before any fair copying or printing takes place.

The term 'draft' is also used to denote certain documents that are specifically prepared as first or preliminary versions as a basis for discussion and subsequent amendment: e.g. draft Bills or Acts of Parliament, or draft deeds or other formal instruments from which fair copies, or officially engrossed versions, will subsequently be prepared for execution.

The term is often used more loosely and imprecisely as a general synonym for 'version'; however, a version may be a finished entity in itself (*see* VERSION) whereas a draft, even a final draft, embodies a composition still in a potential state of incompleteness. For examples of drafts, *see* Illus. 8, 23, 28, 44, 89, and 90, and, for a particular type of draft, *see* FOUL PAPERS.

In a financial context, a draft is a written order by one person to another for payment of money, as in a bank draft. Such drafts may include bills of exchange and cheques.

DRY POINT

Dry point, or hard point, is a mode of writing or drawing with the use of a stylus or other pointed metal, lead, or bone instrument, as opposed to a pencil or pen and ink, so that the writing surface is simply scored with blind impressions, furrows, or ridges. As a less conspicuous method of marking guidelines, dry point was commonly used by scribes for the ruling of manuscripts in the medieval and early modern periods. Dry point is usually distinguished from metal point in that the latter is more pronounced, a visible trace of brown, grey, or other tincture appearing on the surface depending on the type of metal used (lead, silver, copper, tin, etc.). Metal point was sometimes used in the Middle Ages for both ruling and annotating purposes,

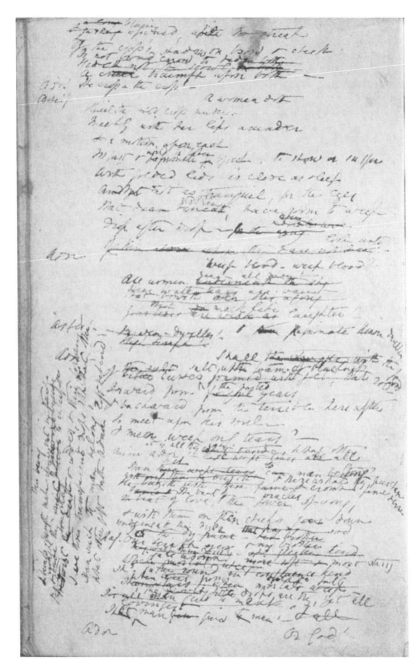

ILLUS. 23 *A page in an octavo autograph working notebook of Elizabeth Barrett (later Browning), containing her draft, with extensive* currento calamo *revisions and deletions, principally for* The Seraphim, and Other Poems *published in 1838.*

as well as drawing. Lead point in particular (also known as 'plummet') was widely used from the eleventh century onwards and served as a precursor of the pencil before the discovery of plumbago in the sixteenth century.

DUANAIRE

A *duanaire* (pronounced 'dóo-na-ra'), the term meaning literally 'poem-book', is a book of poetry in Irish Gaelic. It is a genre of manuscript devoted principally to bardic verse, most of it originally delivered orally, celebrating, for instance, the heroic deeds and fortunes of particular Irish chieftains or families, as well as verse on religious and other subjects. *Duanaireadha* (pronounced 'dóo-na-rāā') flourished from medieval times until the seventeenth century, when bardic culture largely withered under English domination. Such manuscript volumes, which may contain poems dating over a period of several centuries, are generally written by professional scribes, in an Irish majuscule or uncial script, with occasional light decoration or rubrication, on often primitive, rough-cut leaves of parchment. There is also evidence that some of these volumes had for their contemporary users a talismanic significance. The majority of surviving *duanaireadha* are preserved in the Royal Irish Academy and National Library of Ireland, in Dublin; some rare examples are found in libraries and private collections elsewhere.

Although there exist manuscript collections of poetry, bardic or otherwise, in Scotland and Wales, there would appear to be no generic term equivalent to *duanaire* in either Scottish Gaelic or Welsh.

DUCT

In palaeography, 'duct' or *ductus* (the Latin meaning 'leading' or 'conduct') are terms used to denote the distinctive features of the strokes in a particular hand. These include the way in which the letters are formed, the sequence of the strokes creating a letter (such as whether the bowl or the ascender is written first in a *d*), how the pen was cut and held, how much pressure was applied to it, how quickly or in what direction the hand moves, how carefully or carelessly the penmanship is executed, and any other characteristic or distinguishing aspects of the writing.

DUODECIMO

A Latin word meaning 'in twelfth' or 'for the twelfth time', the term 'duodecimo' (frequently rendered as 'twelvemo' and abbreviated to '12mo') denotes the size of a leaf of paper produced when a standard papermaker's sheet is folded twice across its length and three times across its width into twelve leaves (twenty-four pages), being a twelfth of the sheet. An alternative folding, which still produces twelve leaves (twenty-four pages), is when the sheet is folded once across its width and five times across its length to produce what is known as 'long twelves'. The size of a duodecimo leaf will vary according to the paper manufacturer and to trimming by the papermaker or binder, but the average size for the early modern period is from very approximately 5–5½ inches (12.5–14 cm) in length and 4 inches (10.25 cm) in width to approximately 6–6½ inches (15–16.5 cm) in length and 4½ inches or so (11.5 cm) in width for the 'long' format.

Because of the wires across the width of the papermaker's tray, duodecimo leaves will have the chain-lines running horizontally across the page for the normal 12mo and vertically down the page for the long 12mo. A printed or occasional manuscript volume made up of gatherings of such leaves (which will most commonly comprise gatherings sewn in twelves: i.e. six pairs of conjugate leaves per gathering, subject to occasional variation) is itself called a 'duodecimo' or 'twelvemo' as a means of distinguishing it by size and basic format.

There are alternative foldings of each sheet which produce smaller formats than duodecimo (notably 18mo and 24mo), but these seem to feature with manuscripts on only very rare occasions. For the more common different-sized leaves and volumes, *see* FOLIO, OCTAVO, QUARTO, and SEXTODECIMO.

DUPLICATE

In a manuscript context, a duplicate is the exact copy of a letter or other document. It might be made either as a standby substitute for the original (having, perhaps, equal legal authority) or for retention as a record. A duplicate letter or other document might also be sent independently, when or after the original was sent, in order to increase the chances that the message would get through if one or the other were actually delivered: e.g. official letters sent to English diplomats abroad in the early modern period, or by the Admiralty to naval commanders on various ships in foreign waters during the Napoleonic Wars.

DUST-JACKET

The dust-jacket is a well-known feature of modern printed books, dating back at least to the 1830s. On them are commonly displayed the name of the author, the title, an engaging, usually colourful design, and advertising blurb about the book or select reviewers' comments on it. As adjuncts to books, rather than integral parts of them (though some collectors and bibliographers would disagree), dust-jackets are often worn away or else discarded, especially in libraries, where they are usually removed as a matter of course. Some dust-jackets for certain books that are prized by collectors are therefore extremely rare, a fact occasionally resulting in extraordinary prices at auction. For instance, a first edition of Sir Arthur Conan Doyle's *The Hound of the Baskervilles* (1904), worth normally about £3,000–4,000, sold for over £80,000 in London in July 1998 because it was one of apparently only three surviving examples in the original dust-jacket.

Dust-jackets would be irrelevant to manuscripts except, perhaps, for occasions when they become 'doctored' by hand by certain users. A notable example is those embellished with humorous or indecent cut-outs pasted on by the dramatist Joe Orton and his partner Kenneth Halliwell in 1962. Since they happened to be on books belonging to Islington Library (where they still are, kept on exhibition in the Islington Local History Centre), the men were sentenced to six months' imprisonment for defacing public property. Other cases include examples of dust-jackets of later editions of James Bond novels by Ian Fleming to which inking has been applied to make them look like first-edition dust-jackets, thereby greatly increasing their commercial value when wrapped around first editions lacking their original dust-jackets.

DUST-STAINING

Manuscripts, both on paper and on parchment, are described as 'dust-stained' when they are heavily soiled, dirty, or blackened because of prolonged exposure to dust. This is a condition common to archives and muniments that have not been adequately preserved and protected from atmospheric pollution. The term implies a slightly harsher, darker, even more ingrained type of discoloration than is implied by the word 'soiled', which may betoken relatively superficial sullying.

DUST-WRAPPER

The term 'dust-wrapper' can be applied to any unattached sheet of paper of some kind that is loosely wrapped around a book or manuscript of any period for protective purposes.

E

ECLECTIC

An edition of a text is described as 'eclectic' when the editor combines readings from more than one exemplar, rather than adhering to a single copy-text and recording separately in a commentary or appendix the variants in other texts. Often this is inevitable when existing texts are in some way defective or when no one text has overriding authority. Editors will defend ecleticism if there is good reason to believe that the original text was 'maimed, and deformed' (to quote the editors of the First Folio of Shakespeare) or interfered with in a manner inconsistent with the author's intentions, such as when censorship was imposed (the deposition scene in Shakespeare's *Richard II*, for instance, appears only in later editions, having been obviously censored in the early Quartos). Critics of the practice argue, for their part, that an eclectic text is an artificial editorial confection, which bring into existence a text that had never previously existed and is in no sense authorized.

EDIT

To edit a work is to prepare it for publication, whether for a general or a scholarly readership, by establishing an accurate or acceptable text of the work from surviving witnesses (whether printed or manuscript), with such introductions, notes, and commentary as may help readers to understand or appreciate it. In scholarly editions, the notes and commentaries are likely to include attention to such features as the nature and provenance of the available textual witnesses, a collation of these texts, and explanatory comments elucidating the meaning of words, passages, or references in the text. The person with overall responsibility for such an enterprise is the editor, or the general editor of a series, although detailed checking of the text(s) established may also be undertaken by one or more copy editors. The principles involved in editing, in such matters as choice of copy-text, whether parallel texts should be printed where multiple texts of a work exist, whether the text should be transcribed diplomatically or in modern-ized spelling, the nature of the textual apparatus, whether comprehensive or selective, how much collation of variant texts should be included, and other related matters, are among the most controversial subjects in modern textual criticism. An explicit statement as to the editorial policy and procedure adopted is de rigueur for a truly scholarly edition.

EDITORIAL INTERVENTION

Editorial intervention (or, in more pejorative parlance, interference) is the process by which an editor alters or emends a text for a published edition. This step is likely to be taken when there are different readings in different texts of the work or when a reading in the text does not make sense and looks as if it may be the result of corruption. The editor may intervene and emend if he or she feels it necessary to decide which of various options is likely to be the most accurate or original reading, or if it seems imperative to clarify phrasing that seems garbled, or if the editor's brief is to present a single, even eclectic text of the work based on all the textual witnesses regardless of the differences they embody. Such procedures, involving value-judgements, will depend upon factors including the publisher; the general editorial policy of the edition or series to which it belongs; the editor's personal sense of mission to present as uncluttered and readable a text as possible; and the intended use and reader-ship of the edition, such as whether it is for a general or a scholarly readership, or for particular educational age groups, or subject to other special interests.

Even the tiniest alteration by an editor, made perhaps unconsciously, may constitute intervention. For instance, in Shakespeare's Sonnet 129, line 11, 'A bliss in proof, and proud, a very woe', the word 'proud', which appears in the 1609 edition, is ambiguous, meaning either 'proud' in our sense or else 'prov'd' (i.e. 'proved') if the printer's *u* represents *v*, as is common. Thus if the spelling of the text is modernized, the editor is obliged to 'disambiguate' the word, choosing one reading or the other. Similarly, there is a slight but telling shift of emphasis in the opening line of John Dryden's great verse satire *Absolom and Achitophel* (1681) when the original 'In pious times, e'r Priest-craft did begin' is modernized by an editor to 'In pious times, ere priestcraft did begin', for the latter's bland 'priestcraft' (as opposed to 'Priest-craft') tends to gloss over the author's subtle hint at the craftiness of priests.

Like all editorial procedures, editorial intervention and emendation is consequently the subject of debate and controversy among textual critics. For the school of thought that opposes all forms of editorial intervention, however well intentioned, *see* UNEDITING.

ELEPHANT FOLIO

See FOLIO.

ELLIPSIS

See SCRIBAL ERRORS.

EMBELLISHMENT

Embellishment is the process or result of the attempt to beautify a manuscript text with decoration, ornaments, or other graphic features, including colouring. It is an aesthetic phenomenon most readily associated with various kinds of medieval manuscripts, many of which are embellished to a famously spectacular degree. Early modern manuscripts, however, particularly when prepared for presentation to royal, noble, or distinguished patrons, can also sometimes bear illustrations, coats of arms, calligraphic and other decorative features that constitute embellishment.

EMBLAZON

'Emblazon' (as distinct from 'blazon') is a heraldic term meaning to represent, portray, or display conspicuously and colourfully, which is applied to such things as coats of arms. The term 'emblazoned in their proper colours' denotes coats of arms painted in a heraldic manuscript with accurate or appropriate colouring. Emblazonry is the display in manuscripts of bright, gorgeous, or colourful pictorial representations, generally of a heraldic nature. For examples, *see* Illus. 7, 18, 30, and 31. *Compare* BLAZON.

EMBLEM

An emblem is a picture of some kind intended to have symbolic significance, representing an allegory, moral, token of status, or other coded message, including sometimes a particular person, family, or even nation. Emblems, sometimes accompanied by mottos, occur commonly in heraldry (coats of arms, *imprese*, etc.); in letters patent (Tudor roses or the like in decorated borders); in poems (where the lines are set out in a particular shape that visually represents the subject of the poem: e.g. George Herbert's 'The Altar'); and in paintings, textiles, jewellery, and many other material artefacts. *See* Illus. 35, 40, 65, and 76.

Emblem books, comprising series of symbolic pictures, with mottos and verses explaining their meaning, are usually printed books and date from the early sixteenth century (notably Andrea Alciato's *Emblematum liber*, 1531), the earliest English emblem book being Geffrey Whitney's *A Choice of Emblemes and other Devises* (1586). Manuscript emblem books are occasionally found, however. One was produced, for instance, by Thomas Palmer in 1598, originally intended as a gift for Lord Burghley, and it is bound with another produced by the poet William Browne of Tavistock, now in the Bodleian Library (MS Ashmole 767). Yet another, an illustrated translation of James I's *Basilicon doron*, one of several produced by Henry Peacham, was presented to Prince Henry in 1610 and is now in the British Library (Royal MS 12 A. LXVI).

EMBOSSED

The adjective 'embossed' is applied to paper that is stamped in blind with lettering, ornaments, monograms, arms, or other personal emblems, which stand out from the paper in relief. Embossing is a form of lettering and decoration generally associated with modern customized stationery, but was also commonly used from at least the late seventeenth century onwards on certain kinds of financial and official documents (for instance, to indicate stamp duty on legal instruments, certificates, etc.), as well as later on postal stationery and postage stamps. The first philatelic use of an embossing process occurred in New South Wales in 1838 and it extended to Britain in 1841.

EMBROIDERED

See BINDING.

EMENDATION

Deriving from the Latin *emendare* ('to remove faults'), the term 'emendation' denotes a deliberate textual alteration or interpolation made by someone other than the author of the work in order, in principle, to rectify, amend, or improve its text. Thus it is a function of an editor, or of a scribe or copyist effectively performing a role analogous to that of an editor, rather than the original writer or author. Editorial emendation may comprise the correcting of obvious scribal or compositorial errors. It may also involve dealing with more substantive errors based in some measure on conjecture, as well as on deduction from palaeographical, compositorial, or other evidence. This is when the surviving text of the work is physically defective or else words or phrases in the copy-text do not make sense and something appears to have gone awry in the process of transmission. *Compare* CORRECTION and REVISION.

ENCHIRIDION

An enchiridion (plural: enchiridia; the Greek term means literally 'a little thing in the hand' and is also applied to a dagger) is a manual or handbook. From ancient times the term was applied to brief religious or philosophical treatises or epitomes intended to be used as handy guides or references—for instance, the *Enchiridion* of Epictetus (written AD *c*.135), or the *Enchiridion* of St Augustine (written after AD *c*.420), which were copied and circulated widely in medieval manuscripts throughout Europe, as were various other enchiridia on grammar, metrical verse, medicine, and other subjects. However, the term was applied most commonly to any kind of brief devotional handbook. With the coming of printing, many enchiridia were published on religious and other subjects, celebrated and influential examples including Martin Luther's *Enchiridion der Kleine Cathechismus* (Wittenberg, 1529). Enchiridia might also include collections of proverbs and the like, such as John Leycester's *Enchiridion . . . or a Manuall of the Choysest Adagies* (1623) extrapolated from the Adagies of Erasmus.

ENCODED MESSAGE

An encoded message is one written wholly or partly in cipher or else incorporating signals recognizable only to the recipient. Such encoding might be a means of keeping the communication private, confidential, or secret, or else of conveying special dimensions of meaning in otherwise straightforward messages. For example, in a letter by the Earl of Leicester to Queen Elizabeth from Tilbury in July 1588 at the time of the Spanish Armada, he writes the word 'most' as 'mõõst' and signs himself as her 'most obedient õõ R. Leycester'. The superscript swung dashes or tildes here represent eyebrows and constitute an 'in-reference' to the Queen's nickname for Leicester as her 'Eyes', thereby reinforcing his message that he is ever watchful for her safety.

ENCYCLICAL

A word originally meaning 'circular letters' (Latin: *litteræ encyclicæ*) and applied in the early Church to generally circulated letters written by archbishops, bishops, or the Pope, 'encyclical' is a term that was adopted about 1740 for a type of papal letter, then issued in printed form, for distribution throughout the Catholic Church, concerning particular issues of great general importance relating to doctrine, morals, or discipline. In effect, encyclicals performed the same function as papal bulls except that the latter might also deal with limited or specific ecclesiastical matters, not necessarily affecting the Church at large. Normally addressed to the archbishops, bishops, patriarchs, and primates of the Church, and usually in Latin, each encyclical takes its title from the first words of the official text.

ENDNOTE

See FOOTNOTE.

ENDORSEMENT

An endorsement is an inscription, annotation, or docketing written on the back (or dorse) of a letter, deed, or other document (*see* Illus. 3). Documents are generally endorsed to indicate the nature of their contents or to record other relevant information—which in the case of some indentures may amount to entirely fresh transfers of title to property. In more modern times 'endorse' is a term applied to the inscribing of a cheque or other financial document to make it payable to another person. In general use, to endorse is also to back, in the sense of to confirm, sanction, or support: e.g. someone's candidacy at an election.

ENDPAPERS

Endpapers, or end-papers, are the pairs of conjugate leaves usually added by binders at the front and back of a bound printed or manuscript volume, partly to help reinforce the joints, the two sets being properly called the front (or upper) and rear (or lower) endpapers. The outer leaf of each bifolium is usually pasted to the inside of the cover and is called the paste-down; the inner leaf is called the front or rear free endpaper. The free endpapers, especially the front one, are also popularly called flyleaves. These leaves are to be distinguished from preliminary blanks, which are integral to the main paper stock of the book and not supplied by the binder. Endpapers are usually blank, except for owners' subsequent inscriptions or additions, but from the mid-seventeenth century onwards some leather-bound volumes were given marbled endpapers (*see* LINERS). From the nineteenth century onwards, printed books have been frequently subject to a variety of patterned, decorated, or pictorial endpapers (as the present volume has).

ENGROSS

When a text is engrossed (meaning literally 'enlarged') it is written or copied out by a scribe as a legal or official document in the proper recognized form and script. An engrossed document is thus prepared as the authoritative or (usually) final copy, as opposed to a draft version or some other copy. A particular script, or wording or lettering within a document, is described as engrossed when the text in question is distinguished or highlighted by being written in a larger, bolder, or more ornate style: e.g. the engrossed lettering usually found in the first line of a Royal Letters Patent. For examples of engrossing, *see* Illus. 8, 36, 40, 45, 65, 87, and 95.

See SEAL.

ENROL

To enrol, enroll or inroll, is to enter or copy the text of a document as an official record. The term derives from the fact that such records, in medieval times, took the form of parchment rolls. The enrolment of deeds became more widespread as a result of the Statute of Enrolments in 1536, which determined that bargains and sales should be executed by deeds enrolled as public records in courts of record. Many series of enrolments of deeds, as well as of a multitude of other public records, are preserved in the National Archives at Kew. Many others, registered with the local Clerk of the Peace, are found in city and county record offices.

ENTRIES

See BOOK OF ENTRIES.

ENVELOPE

The envelope, as commonly used today, as a commercially produced piece of stationery, is a sheet of paper folded and gummed to serve as a separate cover enclosing a letter. Envelopes, generally of small size, were introduced in the early eighteenth century. Before then, letters were simply folded and sealed with the address written on the outer leaf (*see* LETTER) or else folded and sealed within a separate addressed wrapper. The use of envelopes only prevailed gradually, especially since it added to the weight and therefore to the cost of postage. Until the Uniform Penny Postage of 1840 standardized the basic postal charge, many letters continued to be sent with the address written simply on the exposed panel of the last folded leaf.

Variant forms include envelopes illustrated by the senders by hand with pen and ink or watercolour drawings, with a space left for the address, and sent through the post (*see* Illus. 24). The fashion for these, among both juvenile and older letter-writers, prevailed particularly in the nineteenth century.

EPHEMERA

Deriving from the Greek *ephēmeros* ('subject to what the day may bring' or 'lasting only a day'), the generic term 'ephemera' denotes artefacts, especially printed or manuscript ones, that have only a brief or short-lived usefulness before they are discarded, as opposed to more ambitious literary or other productions that may be expected to have a long-lasting if not permanent interest. Ephemera include items such as notes, postcards, telegrams, trade cards, greetings cards,

ILLUS. 24 *Autograph envelope addressed and illustrated by the 18-year-old Edward, Prince of Wales (later Edward VII), to his sister Princess Helena, embellished with his watercolour drawing of a girl riding a dragon, its looped tail wrapped around the address below, which is initialled 'AE' (for Albert Edward). The envelope bears a Penny Black postage stamp and hand-struck date-stamps, 27 November 1859.*

bills, receipts, tickets, theatre programmes, advertising posters, and a host of other articles of generally limited and transitory interest. Often ostensibly trivial, ephemera are, however, valued by many people as curiosities and as items that have historical and educational significance as witnessing to the tastes, habits, preoccupations, etc. of particular people and societies at particular times. There are several Ephemera Societies that exist to promote the preservation and study of such things, catering to a substantial body of collectors.

EPHEMERIS
Derived from the Greek *ephēmeros* ('subject to what the day may bring' or 'lasting only a day'), the now obsolete term 'ephemeris' (plural: ephemerides) denotes a calendar, diary, or almanac, especially one setting out the predicted daily positions of heavenly bodies in a particular period.

EPISTLE
Derived from the Latin *epistola*, the term 'epistle' tends to be applied to particular letters of a formal, public, or literary nature. Hence the word 'epistles' (or its Latin form *epistolae*) commonly denotes a literary genre rather than actual written letters, the physical artefacts themselves.

EPITOME

An epitome (the Greek word means a 'cutting short') is an abridgement, precis, summary, or condensed version of a work or text in which the original text is reduced in size to the bare essentials or substance.

ERRATA

Errata (Latin for 'errors') or *corrigenda* ('corrections') are generally a feature of printed books, when misprints or other mistakes discovered after the book has been proof-read and printed are recorded and corrected in a separate list. It is usually printed on an otherwise blank space in the preliminaries or else on a separate sheet or slip of paper tipped into the volume. *Errata* of sorts are also, however, occasionally found in manuscripts when the scribe, having copied a text, records separately (in a margin, border, or on some other page) the mistakes found afterwards. These may, perhaps, give instructions to readers as to how the text should be read: when, for instance, stanzas of a poem have been copied in the wrong order or some text has been entered on the wrong page. *See also* SCRIBAL ERRORS.

ESCHATOLOGY

Deriving from the Greek *eskatos* ('last'), the term 'eschatology' denotes the study of the theological doctrine of the 'Last Things': i.e. of the end of the world and the Last Judgement, as embodied in the Book of Revelation, the last book of the New Testament. This book, the revelation of St John the Divine, is narrated in dramatic and vividly symbolic terms. The destruction, for instance, is unleashed when the seventh seal is broken on a scroll held by God, releasing seven angels whose trumpets signal the partial burning of the earth, the turning of the sea into blood, and the summoning of locusts, an army of horsemen, and other plagues to afflict mankind.

Not surprisingly, the subject has inspired many artistic representations, the study of which also comes within the purview of eschatology. Of these the best known in manuscript form remain those volumes known as 'apocalypses' (the Greek *apokalypsis* meaning 'revelation'). Because of the religious fears, calamities, and preoccupations current in medieval Europe, apocalypses were among the most popular and most frequently produced types of manuscript of the period, in England particularly in the second half of the thirteenth century. Generally written in Latin or Anglo-Norman, they not only incorporated commentaries, but were also invariably illustrated or illuminated, often elaborately so, with lurid depictions of dragons, beasts, flames, and other images of the universal holocaust. Apocalypses were also occasionally produced by early printers, the earliest versions, some hand-coloured, appearing in the Netherlands and Germany in the 1460s.

ESCRITOIRE

See BUREAU.

ESCROW

A term sharing the same etymological derivation as the word 'scroll', an escrow is a document intended to become a deed, and sealed as a deed, but embodying inchoate (i.e. incomplete) obligations between two or more parties and which is given to another party. The latter is under obligation to deliver the document to one of the parties only when a specified condition is fulfilled – such as when a payment is made or when someone dies. In that case, having been executed conditionally as a deed, the document has the power and legal validity of a deed.

ESCUTCHEON

In heraldry, an escutcheon is a shield bearing a coat of arms.

ESSOIN ROLLS

In legal parlance, an essoin (the word derived from the Medieval Latin *essonium*) was an excuse (such as sickness or absence overseas) for non-attendance in court (including manorial courts) given by or on behalf of someone summoned to appear. From at least the late twelfth century until the end of the eighteenth century, official court records of these excuses were kept and enrolled on essoin rolls. Notable series relating to the Court of Common Pleas and its precursors are in the National Archives at Kew (CP 21 and KB 26 series).

ESTABLISHMENT BOOK

'Establishment book' is a term applied to a formal register or account book listing in detail, with their respective fees and order of precedence, the principal offices of the realm, both civil and military, maintained at the expense of the sovereign or state. These will include officers of the Admiralty, of fortified towns, fortresses (such as the Tower of London), royal palaces, forests, and Duchies of Cornwall and Lancaster. They may well also include Royal Household accounts (*see* ROYAL HOUSEHOLD ACCOUNTS and Illus. 25). Such books are usually folio-size, formally drawn up in ruled columns, with particulars entered in neat, even stylish, secretary script by official scribes, and bound in vellum.

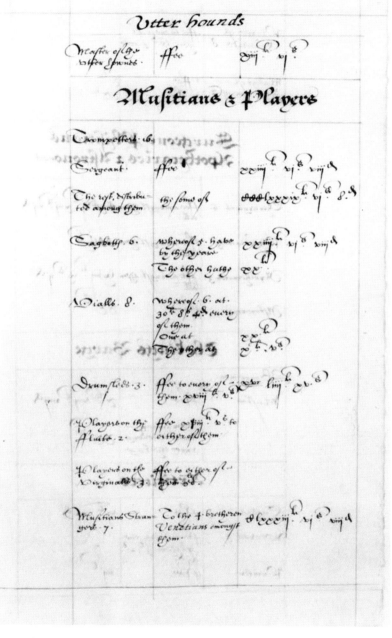

ILLUS. 25 *A page in an Elizabethan establishment book incorporating Royal Household accounts. The folio page, ruled in tabular form, is written in the secretary hand of an official scribe and records expenses principally for 'Musitians & Players'. It lists their various employments (sixteen 'Trompotters', six 'Sagbottes', etc.), explanatory comments on their rates of pay, etc., and the sums paid to them. (Thus xxiiij^{li}. vj^s. viij^d. = 24 pounds 6 shillings and 8 pence; ccclxxxix^{li}. vj^s. 8^d. = 389 pounds 6 shillings and 8 pence.)*

Among the most copious extant archives in Britain are estate records: i.e. account books, ledgers, deeds, surveys, rentals, vouchers and receipts, maps, plans, and other documents relating to landowners' estates, many of them dating from early feudal times onwards. Substantial quantities of such records are still retained by great houses, including those of well-known noble families; many others are preserved in county or other local record offices. With the extensive and specific information they can provide about land, tillage, wages, buildings, ownership, and local communities, including particulars of tenants and retainers, and descriptions and contemporary valuations of property, these records are a prime source of research for local historians.

ESTREAT

Deriving from the Latin *extracta* ('extract'), the term 'estreat' denotes a copy of, or copied extract from, a court record, usually one specifying or listing fines or amercements to be levied and collected by a bailiff or sheriff on behalf of the Crown or Exchequer. Estreats relating to courts leet or courts baron are generally written on both sides of long narrow scrolls.

EVIDENCES

Evidences are legal records or documents that prove someone's title to rights or property. General recognition of the importance of such materials in establishing or confirming ownership is the reason why so many deeds and instruments of property transaction have been so widely and so extensively preserved. An exemplary lesson in their significance is provided by the case of James Wood, Laird of Bonnington, who was executed by James VI of Scotland in 1601 for stealing his father's 'evidents [i.e. evidences] of lands'.

EXCHEQUER

The Exchequer in England, along with the Chancery, is one of the two most important departments of government involved in the preparation and preservation of public records. The Exchequer is the Treasury where

ILLUS. 26 *An Exchequer warrant authorizing a payment by Sir William Herrick, one of the four Tellers of the Exchequer, to Sir Lewis Stucley for sequestering Sir Walter Ralegh's ship the* Destiny *at Plymouth on his return from his disastrous expedition to Guiana. It is drawn up in formal fashion in the secretary hand of an Exchequer clerk, signed by Sir Fulke Greville and Sir Julius Caesar, and was issued on 29 December 1618, two months after Ralegh's execution. The sum to be paid is £566 8s. 3d., here rendered as* $v^{li}lxvj^{li}$ *[= 5 × 100 + 66]* $viij^{s}$ iij^{d}.

Sr Lewes Sturley Knight
for moneys disbursed for
and conterninge Sr Walter
Raliegh Knight deceased

Order is taken this 4th day the 14th of December 1618 by
vertue of his Mate leters of Privie Seale dated the 20th
of the same That wheras Sr Lewis Sturley Knight
Lutenante of the Countie of Devon by his Mats
comandnt Castle arestd being by letters out of
Devonshire by reson of Sr Walter Raleigh Knight
lately returned, and did thereto make stay of the shi
called the Destiny within the harborow of Plymouth
uppon the returne of the said Raleigh from his late
voyadge from Guiana In the performance of w
service the said Sturley disbursed sondry somes of
money, as well to pay Marrinors of the said ship uppon
their discharge & other occations of that shi, as also
for other charges of the said Raleigh, at Plymouth
& in his Countie letter, and for his own attendance
& ... untill the 20th of this present December amounting
in all to nyne hundred thertene ... pownds ...
as he hath made appere unto his Mats relates by the
said Sturley hath obtained ... w ... raised by the
sale of a quantitie of Tobacco ... taken aboard
the said ship as also ... for further ...
beste of ... empty caske and other provisions
belonging to the ship by him likewise ... at Ply
mouth, to the w ... , due to him the some of five
hundred thertene ... pownds ... his Mats
is graciously pleased shll be paid unto him
These are therfore to require you of his Mats
Treasurer as ... in ... charge to deliver and
pay to the said Sr Lewis Sturley the said some
of five hundred thertene ... pownds out of the
same to be taken ... of ... iijli ... ... by him
... and ... his said accompt ... or other
charge to be ... by you his ... ...
or of ... the some or any ... a parcell
therof. And this together with his or his
Assignes Acquittance shalbe your discharge herein

Arth Ingrum
Jul Cesar

Sr William Herrick I pray pay this order

Accordatm viij December 1618

18

state finances and accounts were managed and where Crown revenues were received or monies dispensed for public services. Like the Chancery, the Exchequer also developed its own law court, dealing from the thirteenth century with Crown revenues, auditing and debt-collecting (the Exchequer of Receipt side) and with suits of debtors and accountants (the Exchequer of Pleas side). It acquired general common-law jurisdiction in the seventeenth century, while a distinct equity side of the Exchequer had developed in the sixteenth century. The vast number of Exchequer documents in the National Archives at Kew (E series) date from 1086 (the Domesday Book: E 31) to 1880, although many warrants and other documents issued by the Exchequer are now widely dispersed (*see* Illus. 26). The huge number of large Exchequer rolls from 1279 onwards contain entries made by official clerks on both sides of membranes of parchment sewn together head to head, 'Exchequer-style', as opposed to head to foot in one continuous scroll, 'Chancery-style'.

EXECUTION WARRANT

An execution warrant is an official warrant or commission ordering or authorizing the death by execution of an offender. Since at least early medieval times, those found guilty of criminal offences were subject to judicial execution by authority of the sovereign or his or her judicial deputies. While sentence of death for a range of routine local offences, including theft and poaching, as well as murder, was perhaps rarely referred to the monarch in person, at least by the early modern period those cases of public interest involving treason or serious crimes against the state, or by nobles or prominent public figures, were certainly a matter for the sovereign's ultimate judgement and determination, especially if he or she received petitions for mercy.

The execution warrant would initially be drawn up by officials or secretaries for the sovereign's sign manual under the Privy or Signet Seal; then the text would be engrossed on parchment under the Great Seal by the Lord Chancellor or Lord Keeper for the actual enactment of the execution. The text in these cases usually conformed to a traditional formula, including a brief recital of the arraignment and conviction of the guilty party, with reference to the lawful authority of the peers who passed judgment, and then a declaration of the sentence itself, which might be expounded in gruesome detail if it were hanging, drawing, and quartering (to 'give example of terror dread and fear' to others), followed, if the traitor was of noble rank, by the mitigation of the sentence to beheading alone, the text possibly also including set phrases justifying the execution ('for the safety of the realm', etc.). Famous examples of such execution warrants that are preserved in some form include those for Mary, Queen of Scots, in 1587 (known from contemporary transcripts), for the Earl of Essex in 1601 (the warrant signed by Queen Elizabeth is now on deposit in the British Library, Loan MS 34), and for Charles I in 1649 (the warrant signed by Oliver Cromwell and the fifty-eight other parliamentary regicides is now in the House of Lords Record Office).

Executions in general were commonly authorized by courts alone, and by George III's time the monarch was involved only when recommendations for mercy were received (a number of death sentences being commuted, for instance, to transportation to Australia). The execution warrant was drawn up by the clerk of the court, usually signed by the judge, and issued to the relevant sheriff or keeper of the prison in which the offender was an inmate. In Britain, executions mostly took place in public until 1868, thereafter only within prison walls, until the death penalty was finally abolished in 1969 (the last actual execution occurring in 1964).

EXEMPLAR

An exemplar is the particular manuscript of a text used by a scribe for making a copy or transcript (*see* Illus. 22). In medieval times, an exemplar was the official copy of a scholastic text produced by a stationer under the authority and control of a university. The term should not be confused with 'copy-text'.

EXEMPLIFICATION

An exemplification is an official attested copy or transcript of a deed, record, or enrolment of some kind and bears the seal of a court, a public official, or, in the case of certain state documents such as Acts of Parliament, the Great Seal. Such exemplifications generally served as written evidence of title. What is in effect an exemplification may sometimes be incorporated in another document, such as an inspeximus (*see* Illus. 40). The commonest type found in muniments is the exemplification of a common recovery under the seal of the Common Bench or Court of Common Pleas (often mistaken for the Great Seal since it was of the same size). *See* RECOVERY.

EXEMPLUM

The term 'exemplum' (the Latin word means 'example') is occasionally used by bibliographers to denote a particular example of a book, thereby avoiding the term 'copy' in a context where 'copy' might mean 'transcript'. However, the term 'copy' remains that most commonly applied to particular examples of a book. Elsewhere, the term 'exemplum' can denote a story illustrating some particular matter.

EXERCISE BOOK

An exercise book is a book or booklet of blank pages, often ruled or lined, designed usually for school or other academic use to accommodate written exercises, sums, diagrams, graphs, compositions, translations, etc. Many family archives, chiefly from the eighteenth century onwards, include such items, preserved perhaps partly for nostalgic reasons, partly because of the amount of work that went into them and the information they might contain.

EXHIBITA

In lawsuits, *exhibita* (the Latin term meaning 'things exhibited') are the original documents or copies of documents produced in court. They might include documents such as depositions, bonds, deeds, or other covenants relating to the case, as well as bills of expenses.

EXIGENTERS

Exigenters were clerks of the Common Pleas who wrote and enrolled writs of exigent concerning defendants who were summoned to appear in court upon pain of outlawry. *Compare* CURSITORS, FILACERS, and PROTHO-NOTARY.

EX LIBRIS INSCRIPTION

The phrase *ex libris* (the Latin means 'out of the books') was often printed on bookplates before the name of the owner or library and is now often used to mean the bookplate itself. In medieval times, books in monastic libraries were often so inscribed on an endpaper or on the first page of the text. *Ex libris* inscriptions also occur on preliminary blanks or title-pages in various printed or manuscript books owned by private collectors in the early modern period. The presence of such a feature is obviously valuable evidence of provenance.

EXPLICIT

Deriving from the Latin *explicitus est* ('it is unrolled', as originally applied to scrolls), the term 'explicit' usually means the same thing as a colophon: namely, an announcement or explanation made by a scribe at the conclusion of a specific text or textual unit, in forms such as 'Here endeth …', in which is sometimes cited the name of the author or scribe (*see* COLOPHON). As adopted in early printed books, the explicit or colophon might also include the place and date of publication and name of printer. Alternatively, cataloguers of medieval manuscripts tend to apply the term 'explicit' (as opposed to 'incipit') to the last few words of the main text itself, before any colophon. *Compare* INCIPIT.

EXPUNGE

To expunge is to erase or wipe out, something so obliterated being an expunction. In a manuscript context, particularly in medieval times, expunge may mean marking letters or words with dots underneath to indicate that they are to be regarded as eliminated.

EYESKIP

See SCRIBAL ERRORS.

EYRE

See ASSIZES.

F

FACSIMILE

Deriving from the Latin *fac simile* ('make similar'), the term 'facsimile' means an exact copy, representation, or reproduction of a piece of writing or printing, imitating in every detail the original physical artefact. The facsimile may be produced by hand, as a manuscript imitation (for instance, when missing pages in early books have been supplied by hand-written copies closely simulating the printed characters), but is usually produced by engraving, or by lithographic, photographic, or other printing processes. Some particularly well-known and widely distributed printed examples are so convincingly executed that they are very frequently taken to be original manuscripts. Such facsimiles include: that for Lord Byron's letter of 27 April 1819 to the publisher Galignani disclaiming authorship of a play called *The Vampire*, a fine engraving of which was first published in Galignani's Paris edition of Byron's *Works* in 1826; Queen Victoria's 1887 and 1897 Golden and Diamond Jubilee letters to the people of England; George V's welcoming letter to homecoming servicemen in 1918; 'thank you' letters by Winston Churchill, particularly from when he was Prime Minister in 1940–5 onwards, sent out to individual well-wishers by his secretaries; the frequently reproduced American Declaration of Independence of 4 July 1776; and the poster declaring Irish independence in the abortive Easter Rising of 1916. A vividly produced publication in 1936, *Some Stirring Relics of English History*, which is also sometimes mistaken for originals, contains detachable reproductions, complete with fraying and staining (though on rather stiff paper), of famous autograph letters or signed statements written by Lady Jane Grey, Sir Philip Sidney, Guy Fawkes, Oliver Cromwell, Charles I, the first Duke of Marlborough, Lord Nelson, the first Duke of Wellington, and Napoleon.

Printed facsimiles are not a purely modern phenomenon, however. Earlier examples include a petition to Parliament by the London Carpenters printed in 1593 in a perfectly formed secretary script (known as '*civilité* type'). Another is the letter that James I sent out in great numbers to various counties to request loans, which was engraved to look like a professional scribal hand with spaces left so that particular details (name of collector, date, county, sum requested) could be filled in by hand. Stamped royal signatures, used since at least the sixteenth century, may also be regarded as facsimiles of a kind. *See* Illus. 81.

Since the early modern period, various mechanical processes have been invented for producing facsimiles of manuscripts, and in later times typescripts, in multiple copies for distribution or publication. These have included the use of polygraphs (devices for moving another pen parallel to that held by the writer, such as one used by Thomas Jefferson); diagraphs (for making larger-sized copies of maps or drawings); carbonated paper; stencils; and letter- and roller-press copying machines, such as the model patented by James Watt in 1780, all precursors of modern photostat machines and electronic photocopiers, besides the various methods used in printing. The names given to the types of facsimile they produce generally derive from their trade names: hence duplicated reproductions described as 'cyclostyled', 'roneoed', 'mimeographed', 'xeroxed', and so on.

There is also a type of publication that may be called 'quasi-facsimile', in that, using recognized conventions, a text is printed to reproduce in some measure the form of the original—such as certain scholarly editions with 'type transcripts' of manuscript texts, or formal bibliographies that incorporate type representations of features such as a book's title-page.

FAIR COPY

A fair copy, as opposed to a working draft or foul papers, is a neat, or at least legible, copy or transcript of any kind of text, made by its author or by a scribe as an acceptable version of it, deemed fit to be read by others. In some modern discussions of Elizabethan and Jacobean dramatic documents, where the use of this term is especially debated, it is often assumed that 'fair copy' implies the complete text of a play, or what the dramatist Robert Daborne, writing in 1613 to the impresario Philip Henslowe, called a 'finished and perfected' playscript. It seems clear, however, that the term 'fair copy' might also be applied to only part of a play, consisting perhaps of a few legible 'sheets . . . fayr written', in Daborne's words, representing perhaps the play as composed, and in that sense 'completed', so far, although not yet in its finished or 'complete' state. A manuscript may also be fair copy even if it bears corrections, revisions, or deletions, so long as it is evidently designed to be a reasonably clear and legible transcript for use by others. *Compare* FOUL PAPERS.

FALSE START

A false start by a writer or scribe occurs when an opening to a text has been abandoned: i.e. the writer or scribe has had second thoughts about it, or has recognized mistakes in it, or has perhaps realized that it is a text already copied elsewhere, or some other consideration has occurred to him. A false start, which may be a matter of a few words, is most commonly deleted in the manuscript and the text begun afresh. Occasionally what was probably a false start is left suspended and unmarked on a page otherwise left blank.

FAMILY TREE

See GENEALOGY.

FASTENER

A modern fastener is a small metal clip with bifurcated tails used to hold sheets of paper together when inserted through a spindle hole and the tails opened out to hold the paper fast.

FEATHERING

'Feathering' is a term used to denote a type of decoration in medieval and later manuscripts in which particular letters are formed with fine wispy trailers and pen strokes or else elaborated in the border with elongated stems fringed with curled barbs, features also characteristic of spraywork (*see* SPRAYWORK). One particular anonymous professional scribe who flourished in London from the 1620s to 1640 and whose script is characterized by such light, fine-nibbed ornamentation has been dubbed 'the Feathery Scribe' and appears under that designation in the *Oxford Dictionary of National Biography*.

FEES BOOK

See VISITATION.

FIAT

A fiat (Latin for 'let it be done') is an official warrant or authorization, by a public authority such as a judge, attorney-general, or university vice-chancellor, allowing something to be done.

FIBRE-TIP PEN

The fibre-tip pen is a twentieth-century invention, although its principle of storing ink in a brush-like absorbent material is based to some extent on the reed pen of ancient times.

FIELD

In heraldry, the field is the background of a coat of arms.

FILACERS

From medieval times until their abolition in 1837, filacers, or filazers, were among the clerks of the King's Bench and Common Pleas who wrote out and enrolled judicial writs, generally of a routine nature. Their name derives from the Latin *filum* ('thread'), because of the way they kept the original writs on file as their warrants. *Compare* CURSITORS, EXIGENTERS, and PROTHONOTARY.

FILE

Deriving from the Latin *filum* ('thread'), the word 'file' in the sixteenth and seventeenth centuries and probably earlier meant a series of papers strung together on a string, wire, or twisted leather cord terminating in a metal point (many documents still filed on their original cords are preserved, for instance, in Cambridge University Archives). Alternatively, the term denoted the string itself that kept the papers in order. This system of filing papers is seen in many contemporary paintings, especially Dutch and Flemish examples, depicting lawyers, scholars, clerks, or merchants sitting in rooms or offices where sheaves of documents are strung together and hanging on the wall. Other filing systems so depicted include bundles of folded documents stacked on shelves, in pouches hanging from pegs, or else folded over or behind straps or belts against the wall (*see* FRONTISPIECE and Illus. 79). Yet another system involved the use of mounted spikes or sharp points on which letters and papers might be kept together, perhaps on a desk. The presence of a hole in a document, even when later preserved in some other form (such as in a guard-book), is evidence of its earlier filing on a string or a spike.

The term 'on file', denoting the accumulation and keeping of certain information as a permanent, or at least continuous, record for reference, presumably derives from some such practice whereby certain documents were retained and distinguished from those rendered obsolete, which were removed elsewhere or discarded. Since then the term 'file' has come to mean a relatively small collection of papers, especially one arranged more or less systematically on a particular subject. Modern files tend to be groups of documents within a folder or hanging-file kept in a filing cabinet. The terms 'file', as also 'folder', are used in this sense metaphorically in modern computer terminology.

In addition, the term 'file' could formerly be used to denote a list or catalogue of documents.

FILLER

In manuscripts, from early medieval times onwards, a filler, or line-filler, was some kind of decorative device or flourish used by a scribe to fill up a blank space left at the end of a line (usually of prose). Various decorative or foliate patterns occur over the years, including small drawings of figures. What would seem to be the most common type used by professional scribes by the seventeenth century is a sequence of swung dashes (~ ~ ~) or else wavy lines transected by pairs of parallel oblique strokes (~# ~ ~# ~ ~# ~). Such features could be satirized as means by which (according to an anonymous writer in 1615) a 'Clarke of a swooping Dash', like the 'large taile' of a 'Flanders horse', spread the words and extended the length of a document to increase his fee.

FILOFAX®

Filofax®, a word derived from the term 'file of facts', is the commercial brand name for a type of personal organizer, in the form of leaves within a ring binder, launched by Norman & Hill Ltd in London in 1921 (the brand name itself was registered in 1930). It, and other brands, were based on a system originally designed by the American engineer J. C. Parker in 1910 and used by the military in the First World War. Its purpose was to combine in a single portable and flexible volume a series of loose leaves on which could be entered all the personal useful information someone might want to keep to hand for ready reference, including a diary for recording appointments, addresses, telephone numbers, and so on. Filofaxes vary in size and quality, from relatively inexpensive little pocket books to luxurious, leather-bound, large desk versions. Their usefulness, and the extent to which people could become dependent on them to organize their lives, are evident from the newspaper advertisements that appeared when people were frantically seeking to recover their lost Filofaxes® and offering rewards for their return. Filofaxes® perhaps reached the height of their popularity in the late 1970s and 1980s just before their functions were largely usurped by the rapid development and huge popularity of personal computers, especially the portable laptop, notebook, or BlackBerry® versions.

FINAL CONCORD

See CONCORD and FINE.

FINE

Derived from the Latin *finis* ('end'), the term 'fine', commonly used to mean a charge or penalty entailing a payment, also denotes a type of freehold land conveyance that, for technical reasons, takes the form of a written agreement or final concord (*finalis concordia*) between a seller and buyer resulting from a legal action, this action being (at least since 1300) largely fictitious. The agreement, with reference to the relevant writ, licence, and payment made to the Crown, was normally written out three times on a single, usually T-shaped membrane of parchment, or chirograph, two copies head-to-head at the top and one written at the bottom, each of which was then cut out in a wavy or zigzag line. The bottom copy, with a full narration of the proceedings, was known as 'the foot of the fine', and it is this that was filed with the King's court to be kept as a public record of the conveyance and as a safeguard against subsequent fraud or false claims. Many 'feet of fines' from 1182 to 1833, the majority up to 1733 written in Latin, are in the National Archives at Kew (CP 25/1–2).

FINE ROLLS

'Fine rolls' is a generic term applied to a range of several hundred rolls and records in the National Archives at Kew (C60 series), largely covering the period 1199–1641, detailing payments made to the Crown for a variety of services. These included the Chancery's issuing of writs, charters, grants, pardons, licences, franchises, and other tokens of royal favour, as well as warrants of appointment, which constituted a major source of Crown revenue.

FINGERPRINT

Fingerprints and thumbprints are the marks or stains left on paper, or on any other surface, when handled, by the ridges on the skin at the tips of the fingers and thumb respectively. As any aficionado of police investigation fiction or films knows, the pattern of ridges is unique to each individual. Because of this—ever since Scotland Yard secured its first conviction on purely fingerprint evidence in 1902 and adopted the Galton-Henry system in 1907—fingerprints are capable of being classified and used as a forensic means of identification.

This is pertinent to manuscripts in so far as it has sometimes been wondered whether any of the great writers or historical figures have left any traces of their fingerprints on their papers, thereby providing evidence by which other documents or books handled by those persons could be identified. The possibility of such intriguing investigation proves, however, to be restricted by factors such as the limited durability of the oils in the skin, of which most fingerprints are comprised, as well as the staining consequences of such forensic methods as the application of ninhydrin. The chances of normal fingerprints surviving are likely to be measured in years, by two or three decades at the very most, rather than in generations or centuries. A more enduring base is ink, if the writer happened to leave his or her fingerprint in an ink smudge on the page. A likely instance of this is found on folio 65 in a manuscript of verse written *c.*1700 by the poet and novelist Jane Barker, now in Magdalen College, Oxford (MS 343). Such examples are, however, rare.

FINIS

The word *finis* (the Latin term means 'finish' or 'end') is occasionally subscribed by scribes in centred position at the end of a text in order formally to signify its conclusion and sometimes also to distinguish and separate it from an ensuing text. *See* Illus. 91.

FIST

See MANICULE.

FLORIATION

Floriation refers to aspects of a manuscript book, in the medieval period and later, that are decorated with ornaments in the shape of small flowers, stems, leaves, and tendrils. Features most likely to be subject to floriation include initial letters and borders.

FLORILEGIUM

Since medieval times, a *florilegium* (plural: *florilegia*; the Latin word means 'gathering of flowers') is a compilation of miscellaneous texts, or extracts from texts, in the nature of an anthology or commonplace book, although not necessarily arranged systematically under subject headings. Sometimes quite encyclopaedic in scope, *florilegia* provided a source of material for quarrying by preachers, clerics, students, and other people. *Florilegia* in various languages, some of considerable size, were also popular early modern printed books. *Compare* COMMONPLACE BOOK.

FLORUIT

Floruit (usually abbreviated to *fl.*; the Latin word means 'he [or she] flourished') is commonly applied to dates given to a particular person in, for example, biographical dictionaries. Thus if a citation reads 'Thomas Tomkis (*fl.*1597–1615)' it means that the dates of Tomkis's birth and death are currently unknown, but that there is evidence (probably from dated documentary sources) that he was alive and active at least between 1597 and 1615.

A flourish is an ornament or embellishment. Flourished writing is character-ized by the scribe's elongation, elaboration, or exaggeration of some letter forms or diacritic marks for stylistic effect, or else by added or accentuated pen-strokes, such as a spiral swirl or other decoration at the beginning or end of a text or as a line-filler (*see* Illus. 12, 69, 78, and 95). Royal signatures, most notably that of Elizabeth I, may also be heavily flourished (*see* Illus. 41 and 82).

FLY

See COMPASS-ROSE.

FLYLEAF

A relatively modern term, 'flyleaf', or 'fly-leaf', most commonly denotes a blank leaf at the beginning of a printed or manuscript book, before any title-page, or else at the end of the book. When (as is normal) it is supplied by the binder rather than being part of the main paper stock of the book, the leaf corresponds to what is more generally described in bibliographical descriptions as an endpaper. *See* ENDPAPERS.

FOB SEAL

A fob seal is a small, usually hand-held, seal matrix with a metal mount designed for suspension. The term derives from its subsequent connection with the fob watch in the Regency period (1810–20) when, for the most part, it too was worn suspended at the front of the waistcoat as an article of adornment. Fob seals in all but name developed in the eighteenth century, the earliest usually mounted on a ring and hanging from a chain. They were variously made of carnelian or other semi-precious coloured stones, and silver, gold, copper, brass, steel, or other metal. They would generally be engraved with the owner's crest or monogram, sometimes with a portrait or other device, and be used to impress the chosen device into hot wax to seal personal letters or documents.

FOLIO

Derived from the Latin *folium* ('leaf'), the word 'folio' has different appli-cations in bibliography. One is that it is synonymous with a leaf of paper or vellum, whatever its size or format, comprising both recto and verso sides: i.e. two pages. Foliation is thus the numbering of the manuscript according to its leaves (generally cited as 'fol. 1', 'fols 1–2', etc., or alternatively 'f. 1', 'ff. 1–2', etc., or, if rectos and versos are specified, 'fol. 1r', 'fol.1r–v', 'fol. 2r', 'fols 2r–3v,' etc.). Foliation is thus distinct from pagination (where 'fol. 1r–v' would be represented as 'pp. 1–2', 'fol. 2r–v' as 'pp. 3–4', and so on). Examples of early modern scribal manuscripts can be found, however, where foliation and pagination are not consistently segregated, but get confused, a page being numbered as if a folio and vice versa, or where a manuscript is partly paginated, partly foliated.

In other contexts, a folio is a leaf of paper (i.e. two pages) in which, if it is laid paper, the chain-lines run vertically down the page. Unless cut as a separate leaf, this will usually be one half of a sheet folded in two (a bifolium). The size of the sheet before folding will correspond to the size of the paper maker's mould or tray, in which the wires forming the chain-lines run across the tray's width, less trimming of the edges by the paper-maker or binder. Depending on the manufacturer, the trimmed sheet-size for laid paper can vary from as little as c.15 × 11½ inches (39 × 30 cm) to as much as c.35 × 23 inches (90 × 60 cm). The average size of a folio leaf found in English manuscripts of the early modern period, whether in separate bifolia for letters or sewn in gatherings for books, is very approximately 12 × 8 inches (31.5 × 21 cm).

A printed or manuscript volume made up of gatherings of these folded sheets is itself called a 'folio' as a means of distinguishing it by size and basic format: for example, the First Folio of Shakespeare's works (1623), the Second Folio (1632), and so on. For other-sized leaves and volumes, result-ing from further folding of each sheet, *see* DUODECIMO, OCTAVO, QUARTO, and SEXTODECIMO. These various sizes and formats often corresponded to particular types of book, as is indicated by Lord Chester-field's comment in the eighteenth century: 'I converse with grave folios in the morning, while my head is clearest and my attention strongest; I take up less severe quartos after dinner; and at night I chuse the mixed company and amusing chit-chat of octavos and duodecimos.'

The term 'double-folio' is also used to denote a large sheet, being the equivalent of a broadsheet or of what a large bifolium would be if it were not folded in the middle. It normally measures in the region of 26 × 17 inches (66.5 × 43 cm). The term can hence be applied to large books of this size such as atlases.

A further term used by some bibliographers and booksellers is 'elephant folio', which has been coined not only as an alternative to 'double-folio', but to denote even larger books, which are two or more times the size of standard folio volumes, and even the term 'double elephant folio' can occasionally be found applied to volumes of exceptionally large size. An example of the latter is the first edition of J. J. Audubon's celebrated *The*

Birds of America (1827–38), each of the four hand-coloured volumes of which measures approximately 39 × 27 inches (*c*.99 × 68.5 cm).

FONDS

The French word *fonds* ('collection' or 'archive') has been adopted by archivists to denote a discrete collection of papers created or assembled by a particular person or organization.

FOOLSCAP

Foolscap is a long sheet of paper characterized by a watermark in the shape of a fool's or jester's cap, with its triangular points and bells. The paper varies in size, but, from the fourteenth century onwards, a foolscap sheet was likely to measure approximately 16–18 inches (41–46 cm) in length by 12–13½ inches (30.5–34.5 cm) in width. The term was subsequently applied to the long folio size of paper traditionally associated with that watermark (whether a watermark was actually present or not) e.g. Oxford pads and long typing paper.

FOOTNOTE

Since the early modern period, the footnote, commenting on, or citing references to support, an argument or allusion made in a discourse, is a common feature of printed books, especially scholarly works. Footnotes are technically explanatory notes and references keyed to particular points in the text and set out at the foot of each page. Those relegated to the end of each chapter or to the end of a book are more correctly called 'endnotes'. Since they effectively came to supersede the glosses, sidenotes, etc. found in earlier manuscript treatises, footnotes generally play little part in manuscripts except for the typescripts of modern scholars. Although an essential feature of responsible discursive literature, which aims to signal where the evidence for its assertions is to be found, there seem to be plenty of general readers who wish that what has sometimes been called 'the tyranny of footnotes in contemporary publishing' was just as scarce as in manuscripts.

FOOT OF THE FINE

See FINE.

FORE-EDGE LETTERING

Although in modern times we normally expect books to be stored on shelves with their spines outwards, suitably lettered with author/title of the book, it was common practice, from medieval times to at least the seventeenth century, to have books shelved with their spines to the wall and their fore-edges outwards. The fore-edges would commonly be lettered in ink by hand (it being easier to letter fore-edges in this way than spines). Owners would add lettering or marking in accordance with their own categorization or practical concerns, whether according to author, title, location, or other private library system (using individual letters of the alphabet or asterisks, for instance). Such volumes, both manuscript and printed, are seen on shelves in depictions of scribes and writers from medieval times onwards (e.g. in seventeenth-century editions of Bacon's *Advancement of Learning*).

FORE-EDGE PAINTING

Some medieval manuscript volumes and a number of books, usually printed, from the early modern period onwards have figures, scenes, or designs painted on their fore-edge (the front or outer edge of the book opposite to the spine), usually in colours. They might be made by early owners of the books or, more commonly perhaps, by professional limners on a commercial basis. Although in many cases the edges of the pages have to be slightly splayed or retracted for the painting to become visible, in other cases the painting would be visible in a library if the books were kept on a shelf with the fore-edge, rather than the spine, turned outwards. This fashion may itself be a development of the common early practice of inscribing the fore-edges of books in ink with lettering for identification purposes and keeping them on shelves with this lettering exposed for ready recognition. Fore-edge painting, especially in the seventeenth and eighteenth centuries, could at times be extremely ambitious and elaborate, comprising not only intricate foliate or scrollwork designs, but also depictions of biblical or other figures, scenes, landscapes, and the like, usually relevant to the subject of the book itself. Books with contemporary embellishment of this kind are prized by collectors and can fetch high prices at auction. This fact has also prompted instances of forgery, when old books have had fore-edge paintings applied to them in the present day to increase their sale value.

FORGERY

In a manuscript context, a forgery is usually understood to be a false or inauthentic document fabricated with the deliberate intention of deceiving people into thinking it is genuine. Forgery is, indeed, endemic to the nature of documents, which are inherently unstable as embodiments of authority, given the relatively limited nature of the materials and of the skills needed to counterfeit them, as well as the personal inducements for such a practice.

Forgery is consequently a phenomenon of great antiquity. The foundation charters of many medieval monasteries, for instance, were forgeries, not necessarily because the rights they embodied were spurious, but simply because in each case the original had disappeared and it was felt proper to manufacture a replacement charter to fill the void and confirm the accepted tradition of foundation. Similarly, chronicles, maps, genealogies, and other accounts of the period could include features that might be seen as purely fictitious, but which embodied contemporary conceptions of how something was or should have been, at least in spirit. Thus, the writer of an early fifteenth-century history of the University of Cambridge did not hesitate to support his case for the university's traditional independence from ecclesiastical control by introducing a few fabricated documents, such as an alleged charter to the University granted in 531 by the legendary King Arthur. Cambridge University Archives also retains bulls, evidently forged for the same reason, supposedly by Pope Honorarius I in 624/5 and by Sergius I in 689, both genuinely confirmed by Martin V (r. 1417–31) and by Eugenius IV (1433). Oxford has similar examples.

Such cases inevitably complicate any categorization of what a forgery is, since the term covers practices ranging from the criminally fraudulent at one extreme to what was, in effect, socially acceptable at the other, depending on their intention and context. It would not, for instance, be appropriate to describe an official document signed and sealed by subordinates on behalf of an issuing authority as a forgery simply because the signature is not the original as it seems, when the document successfully performs its intended official function. Neither would an apparently hand-written thank-you letter by Winston Churchill be accounted a forgery because it is not, as the recipient may have believed, an original, but rather a printed facsimile sent out by a secretary as an assuring response to someone's letter expressing good will. Such examples do involve elements of intentional deception, but are also, in a sense, authorized.

On the other hand, certain types of deliberately fraudulent documents prove to be a social menace. These include such things as false title deeds, establishing non-existent ownership rights to property; authorization warrants with a fabricated text spuriously validated by a genuine seal transferred from another document; or false writs summoning unsuspecting victims to appear before, say, the Privy Council and charging them fees for delivery. It was partly to counteract the increasing forgery of legal documents, and to establish controls over the processes of authentication, that the profession of scriveners developed in the Middle Ages. The seriousness of the problem was also reflected in the penalties meted out to offenders. In the fourteenth century, a forger might receive a fine, imprisonment and/or have to stand in the pillory for two hours with the forged document around his neck. In subsequent years up to the seventeenth century, the penalties for forging became harsher, for offenders on the pillory could have their ears cut off and nostrils slit and seared with red-hot irons. More consequential or repeated offences could incur a death sentence.

Criminal forgery—of cheques, financial documents, etc., motivated by avarice—has persisted in most societies. Some major forgeries, with huge consequences for the lives of those concerned, have been politically motivated. These include the journalist Richard Pigott's forgeries of letters by the Irish patriot Charles Parnell in 1887 purporting to show Parnell's approval of recent republican murders (Pigott shot himself when he was exposed, had fled to Spain, and police came to arrest him); certain of those used in the case begun in France in 1894 against Alfred Dreyfus supposedly establishing that he was passing French military intelligence to the Germans (for which Dreyfus spent five years in the penal colony on Devil's Island); and the Zinoviev letter, which supposedly linked British socialists with an Anglo-Soviet Communist conspiracy and which brought down the first Labour government in the 1924 general election. More recent forgeries include the 'Hitler Diaries', sixty manuscript volumes supposedly written by Adolf Hitler, but actually forged by Konrad Kujau, the 'discovery' of which, as well as its supposed authentication by 'experts' and then rapid exposure, created a press sensation in 1983, and the numerous forgeries made by the American dealer Mark Hofmann, in Utah, including the so-called 'Salamander Letter', intended to discredit the Mormon Church (which bought it through an intermediary). Hofmann's over-extended financial dealings and the suspicions he raised in associates led to his murdering two people with pipe bombs in 1985.

Not least interesting, if only because of their sometimes complex motivation, are the great literary forgeries. These include the manuscript poems by the supposed fifteenth-century poet Thomas Rowley 'discovered' in Bristol in the 1760s by the young Thomas Chatterton (who committed suicide before his eighteenth birthday in 1770); the cache of documents supposedly by Shakespeare 'discovered' by William Henry Ireland (1777–1835) in the 1790s (see Illus. 27); and the various Shakespeare and Elizabethan 'discoveries' by John Payne Collier (1789–1883), who also made pseudo-Elizabethan manuscript insertions in some genuine documents (such as in the Henslowe-Alleyn Papers at Dulwich College and in the Ellesmere Papers now in the Huntington Library, California).

For sheer audacity and industry, however, it would be difficult to surpass the work of the French legal clerk Vrain-Denis Lucas who, in the 1850s and 1860s, produced over 27,000 letters by many of the most famous figures in

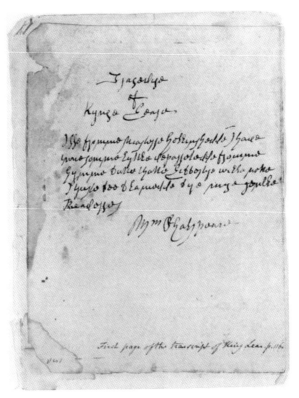

ILLUS. 27 *A forgery by William Henry Ireland, in pseudo-Elizabethan script, supposedly an autograph introduction to the 'Tragedye of Kinge Leare' signed by William Shakespeare, docketed in another hand at the foot, c.1790s–1800s.*

history, including Alexander the Great, Cleopatra, Caligula, Mary Magdalene, Pontius Pilate, Judas Iscariot, the prophet Muhammad, Petrarch, Machiavelli, Galileo, Bacon, Hobbes, and Newton. These managed for some years to dupe gullible members of the Académie des Sciences in Paris, even though all were written in French and on near-modern paper.

FORMULARY

See BOOK OF FORMS AND PRECEDENTS.

FOUL PAPERS

The term 'foul paper', or 'foul papers', and even 'foule sheet', used by Elizabethan and Jacobean dramatists, scribes, other theatrical personnel, and censors, evidently denotes a piece of writing characterized by deletions, blots, corrections, and revisions. Hence it is a writer's rough draft, untidily

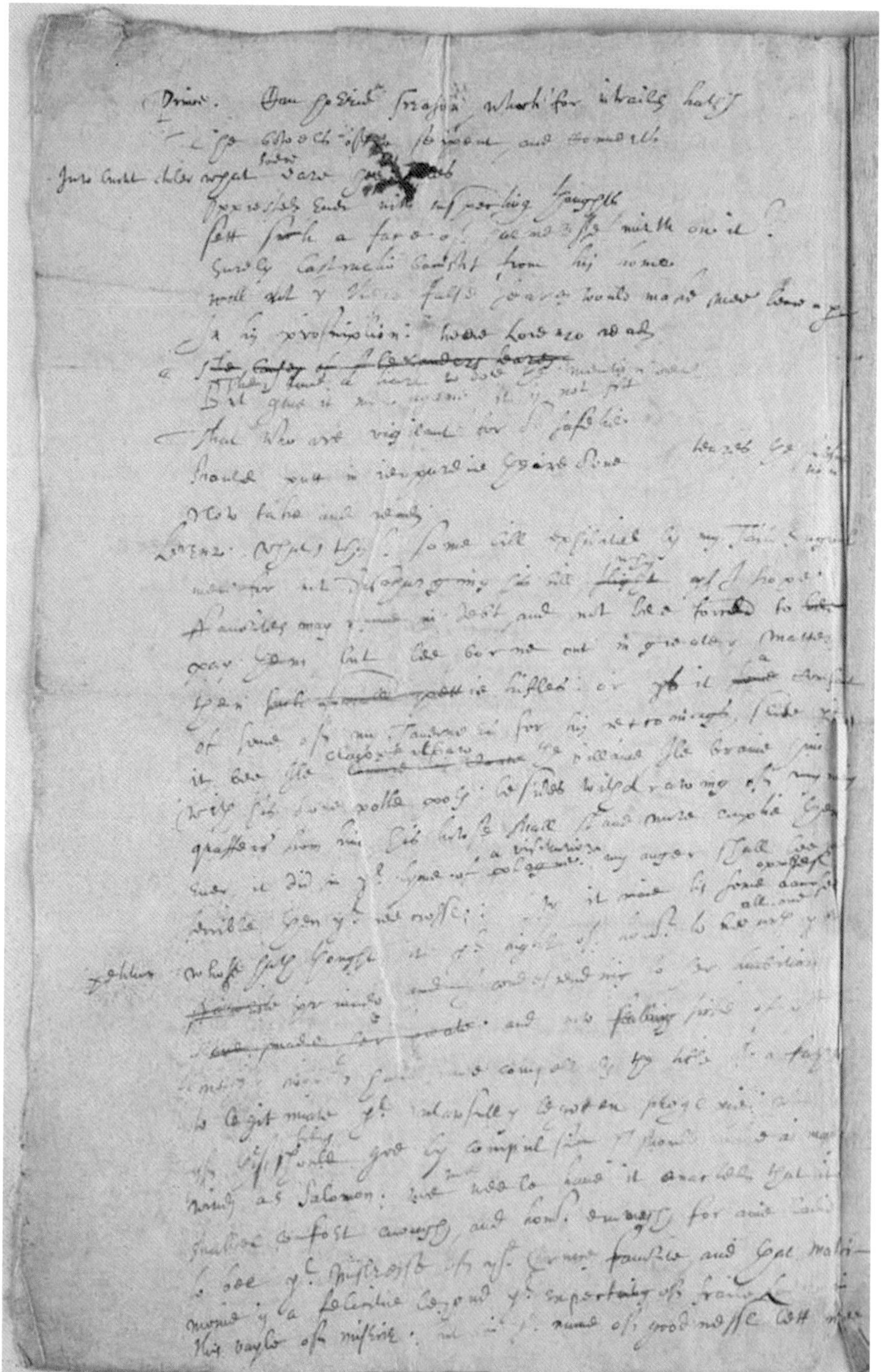

written, as opposed to fair copy. Foul papers thus show the writer in the throes of composition, as opposed to a transcript made of a text, or part of a text, whose composition is essentially complete. As an author's own working papers, foul papers would probably not have been primarily intended for others' eyes: hence the need for a fair copy to be made, either by himself or by a scribe, for anyone else to read the text properly. A manuscript might, alternatively, be something of a hybrid in that what started as foul paper was touched up, or only partly recopied, so that it could serve as a fair copy: e.g. Thomas Heywood's *The Escapes of Jupiter*, *Sir Thomas More* by Anthony Munday, Heywood, and others, and Philip Massinger's *Believe as You List*. Surviving examples of manuscripts that are basically foul papers include Heywood's *The Captives*, Walter Mountfort's *The Launching of the Mary* (a manuscript that the theatrical censor complained about because it was not fair copied) and the anonymous fragment of a tragedy about Alessandro de' Medici discovered in 1985 among the archives of the Marquess of Lothian and conjecturally attributed at that time to John Webster: see Illus. 28. (All these manuscripts are now in the British Library.)

The bookkeeper and scribe Edward Knight who wrote *c*.1625 a fair copy of the Beaumont and Fletcher play *Bonduca* (now British Library, Add. MS 36758) said that he was obliged to summarize one scene because it was 'wanting' in his exemplar, which was 'the fowle papers of the Authors wch were found' in place of the lost 'booke' from which the play was 'first Acted'. It has been conjectured that some of Shakespeare's plays, such as the second Quarto of *Romeo and Juliet* (1599) and the first Quarto of *King Lear* (1608), were printed from his foul papers in view of the unresolved errors, repetitions, and contradictions they contain, flaws that might have been ironed out when fair copies were made.

John Dryden could still refer to a 'foul draught' as late as 1690, as did Anthony Wood a year later. Otherwise, outside the theatrical sphere, writers seem to have used terms other than 'foul papers' to denote their drafts. The poet and polemicist George Wither, for instance, speaks in 1631 of his 'blurred papers' before they were 'made legible to others'. *See also* FAIR COPY.

ILLUS. 28 *A page of the foul papers of a Jacobean tragedy about Alessandro de' Medici, Duke of Florence, murdered in 1537 by his kinsman Lorenzo de' Medici. It is a working draft in the cursive secretary hand of its unidentified author, with* currente calamo *revisions and deletions. The page is part of a single bifolium (four-page) fragment used later in the 1630s as wrapping paper. The fragment was discovered in 1985 among family archives of Sir John Coke (1563–1644) at Melbourne Hall, Derbyshire. The otherwise unknown play influenced c.1631 James Shirley's tragedy* The Traitor.

FOUNTAIN PEN

A fountain pen is a type of steel-tipped reservoir pen equipped to carry ink, thereby avoiding the necessity of constantly dipping the nib into an inkwell. Prototypes of portable metal pens with their own supply of ink date back as early as the tenth century (fourteenth-century Italian ones, for instance, incorporated ink-soaked felt), and they were certainly in use in England by the seventeenth century. Various developments aimed at improving the retention and flow of ink in the eighteenth and early nineteenth centuries led to the first self-filling fountain pen patented in 1832 by John Jacob Parker. This type of pen did not really reach a mass market, however, until the invention and commercial exploitation by Lewis Edson Waterman in 1884 of his 'Ideal' pen, the first really modern, reliable, leakproof, and popular fountain pen.

FOXING

'Foxing' is a relatively modern term, generally used by booksellers. A book, or pages in a book or manuscript, are described as foxed when they are spotted or stained a brownish colour, the discolouration caused by fungal and biological activity in the paper.

FRAGMENT

A fragment is a portion of a text, the remainder of which is lost (such as some ancient texts that survive only because passages were cited by later writers); or else a work that was never finished, but survives only in an incomplete state; or, alternatively, a portion of a manuscript that has otherwise physically decayed or become detached. Common examples of what are in effect fragments are signatures ('autographs') and miniatures or other pictorial features that have been deliberately excised from manuscripts for separate preservation, framing, exhibition, or mounting in albums.

FRANKING

Franking was a process whereby a letter was signed on the outer address leaf or envelope by a Member of Parliament so that it could be sent without postal charge. It was a privilege claimed by MPs following the Restoration in 1660, and it persisted until its abolition in 1840 following the introduction of the Uniform Penny Postage. The regulations for franking, specifying what additional information the MP had to write on the letter, where and when it had to be posted, how many letters he could send or receive free of charge each day, and whether he could sign on behalf of others, varied over the years, and the privilege was also extended to the Clerks of the Post Office.

In the early nineteenth century, as part of the cult of 'autograph' collecting, it became a popular practice to acquire examples of letters franked by all current MPs in order to get as complete a set of their signatures as possible. Each signed address panel would generally be cut out by the collector and mounted in an album to form a collection of what were then known as 'free fronts'.

FREE FRONT

A free front is an address panel, or the addressed front of an envelope, that has been signed, or franked, by a Member of Parliament for free postage.

FREE HAND

'Free hand' is a term used to denote the rapidly cursive, irregular, and relatively undisciplined script, or style of writing, that was in general use in England from the twelfth to sixteenth centuries, as opposed to the more rigidly formal, regular, and uniform set hand that was generally prescribed in each of the courts and government departments. *Compare* SET HAND.

FREEMASONRY

See MASONIC DOCUMENTS.

FUGITIVE

'Fugitive' is an adjective sometimes applied to literary or archival texts that are, or have been, scattered about or subject to random or uncontrolled distribution, as opposed to texts kept under control or consistently gathered together. What were referred to as 'fugitive' verses in the seventeenth century, for instance, might be poems that were distributed in separate manuscript copies or which were widely copied by others. Alternatively, they might appear in printed miscellanies or other publications beyond the authors' control. At least one author in this period, Katherine Philips ('Orinda'), bitterly regretted letting 'those fugitive Papers' escape her hands when copies of her poems were printed in 1664 without her authorization. The term 'fugitive pieces' could still be used, somewhat in self-deprecation, by writers in the eighteenth and nineteenth centuries when assembling volumes from texts scattered in obscure publications or not thought worthy of inclusion in earlier volumes.

FUMIGATION SLITS

In the eighteenth and nineteenth centuries, fumigation slits were slits made by postal officials in letters delivered from plague-infected countries so that they could be fumigated, or otherwise disinfected, as a protection against carrying diseases such as typhoid. The quarantine process would generally leave traces of browning in the paper. Such slits may thus be distinguished from dispatch slits. *See* DISINFECTED MAIL and *compare* DISPATCH SLITS.

G

GALL

Gall is one of the principal traditional constituents of ink, derived from oak-galls, which are excrescences produced on oak trees by the action of insects. Like copperas, the term occasionally appears in seventeenth-century satires on clerks and scriveners as one of the materials of their profession. Gall is also subject to puns because of its other meaning of bile secreted from the liver, and hence bitterness. Thus, in *Twelfth Night* (III, ii, 52), Sir Toby Belch gives instructions for writing a challenge by saying 'Let there be gall enough in thy ink', and in *Cymbeline* (I, i, 101), Posthumus tells the Queen 'I'll drink the words you send / Though ink be made of gall'. *See* COPPERAS.

GALLEY PROOF

See PROOF.

GALLIMAUFRY

The term 'gallimaufry', which in the sixteenth century was a dish comprising a hodge-podge of miscellaneous scraps of food, generally denotes a heterogeneous, random, unsystematic collection of material of any kind, lacking any common or unifying character or theme. The term is sometimes encountered in booksellers' and auction catalogues applied to miscellaneous, unorganized collections of albums, letters, and other documents.

GALLOWS LETTER

What is commonly known as a 'gallows letter' is an official letter or dispatch, generally of a type occasionally issued by the Elizabethan Privy Council, in which an extreme degree of urgency of delivery is signified, usually by the exposed address panel bearing a rough sketch or sketches of a gallows, sometimes bearing a hanging body. These sketches would be accompanied

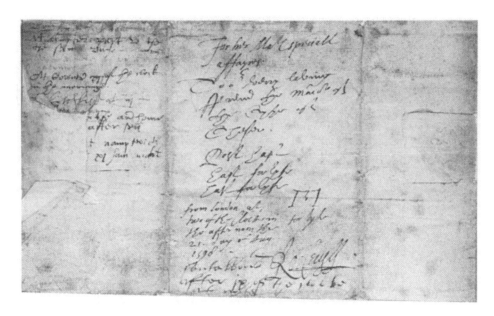

ILLUS. 29 *The address leaf of an Elizabethan gallows letter, sent by the Privy Council as a matter of utmost urgency conveying a packet of letters to Chester for sending to the Council in Ireland, 21 August 1598. The address panel bears the postal instructions 'For her Mats [Majesty's] speciall / affayres / To o' very loving / ffrend the Maior of / the Cytye of / Chester. / Post hast / hast for lyfe / hast for lyfe', with a gallows mark subscribed 'for lyfe', signed by Robert Cecil. Ten endorsements (three affected by the seal tear) were made by postmasters at various points along the route from London, via Towcester, Coventry, and Lichfield, to Chester, where it arrived at 6 a.m. three days later.*

by such repeated written directions as 'haste haste', 'post haste', 'haste for life', 'for life haste', with other indications of the importance of the letter and the official authority for it, such as 'For Her Majesty's special affairs'. Such letters could be literally a matter of life or death when they were reprieves for prisoners condemned to be executed—such as one sent by the Council on 27 June 1600 to reprieve Alexander Newbury, due to be executed at Maidstone Gaol for murder—and at least one example is recorded of a letter that arrived too late to save a man because it was mistakenly delivered to another town of the same name. The markings and directions might also emphasize to the postal agents the urgency of the communication in relation to state business: e.g. one sent by Sir Robert Cecil on 21 August 1598 to the Council in Ireland following news of the disastrous defeat of the English army at the Blackwater River (*see* Illus. 29). To have any validity, these letters had to be signed on the address leaf by an official of sufficient authority, such as a Privy Councillor or Master of the Posts, and they would also bear a series of endorsements recording the towns and times of arrival every time the courier stopped. Extant examples of such letters are rare and are highly prized by postal collectors. There are also modern forgeries of such letters, sometimes when counterfeit gallows marks have been added to genuine original letters. Their non-authenticity is usually recognizable when they fail to include convincing docketing recording the courier's itinerary.

GATHERING

A gathering, or quire, in a manuscript or printed book is a discrete group of leaves, a series of which units sewn together makes up the volume. A gathering results from the folding of a sheet or sheets so that they 'nest' inside one another (as opposed to being arranged adjacently as a series of separate bifolia). They are then sewn at one side through the principal fold, and the folds at the top, bottom, or fore-edge are cut (usually after sewing) to produce the separate leaves of the book. Since at least as early as the thirteenth century, the gatherings in a book were lettered or numbered, largely to ensure that they were bound in the correct sequence. These markings, which involved sometimes different systems of letters and numbers, are known as 'signatures'. This practice persisted in early modern printing. *See also* QUIRE.

GENEALOGIST

A genealogist is a person who makes a study of genealogies or family pedigrees. Genealogists include certain heralds in the College of Arms, as well as assorted persons who are engaged, whether in an amateur or professional capacity, in tracing people's forebears or ancestors. Genealogists of one kind or another constitute perhaps the single largest group of people who use local record offices.

GENEALOGY

Genealogy is the study of family pedigrees. A genealogy is also a particular pedigree or family tree, tracing someone's descent from his or her ancestors or else the descent of various people from a common ancestor. Genealogies usually take the form of a summary on a diagrammatic chart. Sometimes they are not much more than a simple list, but commonly they take a more elaborate form, being often in the shape of a tree, either upright or inverted, in which the earliest ancestor is represented at the root or trunk and his descendants, named in captions often in roundels, in the various branches and twigs. Connections by marriage are indicated by an equal (=) sign. A vertical line from the names of each married couple descends to their issue, which if multiple is then linked together by a horizontal line, with eldest to the left, youngest to the right, their issue set out after further drop lines, and so on. Illegitimate issue is usually denoted by a wavy drop-line and unconfirmed issue by a broken line. Other details may be incorporated, such as dates of birth, marriage, and death of the person named, if known.

Genealogies can be very picturesque and colourful documents, especially if they relate to very distinguished, wealthy, or noble families, when they may well contain figures, portraits, depictions of seals, and emblazoned coats of arms, as well as other insignia, decorations, and embellishments. They are sometimes of immense size, whether on rolls of parchment or linen-backed paper. Alternatively, very grand pedigrees can on occasions take the form of illuminated and decorated manuscript volumes, set out as a series of names listed in more or less chronological order with appropriate commentary or else incorporated in a cartulary (such as the 'Great Books' of Lady Anne Clifford: *see* Illus. 30). If drawn up by the College of Arms, a genealogy may well contain the signatures of the Kings of Arms responsible for it, usually subscribed at the end.

Many late medieval and early modern genealogies are also of great interest in the degree of inaccuracy or sheer fiction of the information they contain. A number of pedigrees, for instance, purport to represent a family line descending from Adam and Eve, other biblical or mythical figures, or from ancient or legendary kings. Certain heralds in Elizabethan times are notorious for their tendency to invent lines of descent from such figures to humour eminent patrons, especially aristocratic newcomers or parvenus, for whom proof of noble lineage, perhaps to disguise actual humble origins, was a serious social and political consideration. An example is that drawn up by the Chester Herald Robert Cooke in 1564 for Robert Dudley, Earl of Leicester, tracing his descent from various ancient English, Welsh, and Scottish rulers and peers, including monarchs and princes from whom Queen Elizabeth was also supposedly descended. *See* Illus. 7.

Among the most elaborately illuminated and ostentatiously grandiose examples of European genealogies, which also serve as patents of nobility, are those produced in Spain from the late fifteenth to eighteenth century, known as *cartas executorias* (or *ejecutorias*) *de hidalguía*. Drawn up by professional notaries, they usually comprise a series of folio leaves of vellum in the form of a gilt leather- or velvet-bound booklet, with silk cords or ties. Besides heavily decorated calligraphic text, they normally contain lavish coloured depictions of a nobleman's or gentleman's portrait, arms, and family tree, with related miniatures (landscapes, etc.). Such patents, which were signed at the end by civic or ecclesiastical authorities testifying to the accuracy of the pedigree, were granted, upon petition, to a rising class of country squires who

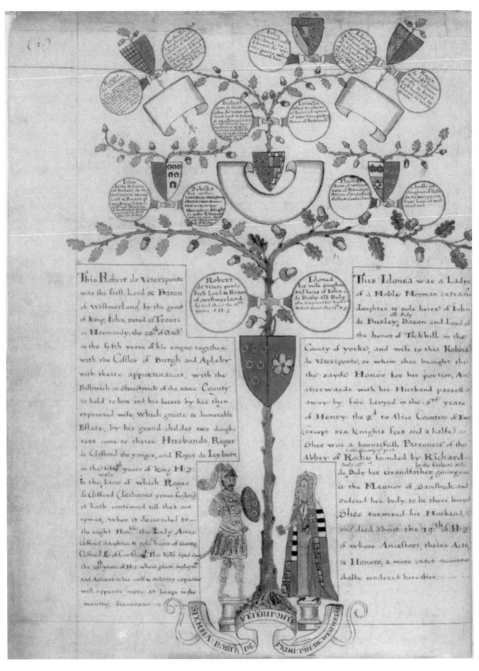

ILLUS. 30 *Part of a genealogy of the Veteripont family of Westmorland, in the form of a tree, including painted figures, the family motto in a banderole, coats of arms emblazoned in their proper colours, and captions within roundels, the margins and boxing-off of the text ruled in red. This appears in one of the 'Great Books', or cartularies, of Lady Anne Clifford, the large folio page measuring c.18 ¼ × 15 inches (46.5 × 38 cm), c.1649.*

were of ostensibly 'pure' blood and of old Christian stock. They were allegedly 'untainted' by Moors, Franks, or Jews, but were not necessarily of ancient noble lineage. The benefits of having such a *carta* would include exemption from taxation in return for military service, which might itself be commuted.

GENERAL REGISTER OFFICE

See CENSUS.

GENERAL REGISTER OF SASINES

See SASINE.

GILT

An object is described as 'gilt' when it is gilded, or covered with a thin layer of gold or gold colouring. Many expensive manuscripts, from medieval times onwards, are embellished in gilt. Select lettering in the text and details in illuminations are gilded by means of specially prepared ink containing powdered gold or by the application of gold leaf. Bindings may also have decoration or lettering tooled in gilt. A volume is described as 'gilt-edged' when the outer edges of the leaves, usually on all three sides, have been cut smooth and gilded by a binder.

GIRDLE BOOK

A girdle book is a small portable book, usually manuscript, designed or bound for attachment, generally by a chain, to a girdle or belt. Such books date from late medieval monastic times, when breviaries and other devotional books were endowed with bag-like leather protective covers extended so that they could be so attached and hung from the waist to allow ready use at any time for private reading and meditation. The most common types of manuscript produced or used as girdle books are books of hours and prayer books, which seem to have been particularly popular in the fifteenth and sixteenth centuries, especially with wealthy women. Such books—for instance, a prayer book in Berkeley Castle apparently given by Queen Elizabeth to her kinsman Lord Hunsdon—could be richly decorated, with fine-quality precious metal- and enamel-work, sometimes even with jewelled bindings. Other types of book might occasionally be worn on the belt, such as notebooks and small wax tablets. They can usually be identified as girdle books when the binding has a metal ring at the top for suspension purposes.

A glebe is all the land and buildings that form part of an ecclesiastical benefice: i.e. the landed property that a beneficed clergyman may cultivate and, subject to certain conditions, lease, mortgage, exchange, or even sell. A glebe terrier is a document that describes such land, specifying its acreage, boundaries, and the holders of adjacent lands.

GLOSS

A gloss is a word, or words, inserted—usually in the margin, sometimes between lines, and in more modern printed editions generally as a footnote or in an appendix—to clarify or explain the meaning of a difficult or obscure word in the adjacent or relevant text, by citing a more familiar or more easily understood equivalent term. The relevant word in the text is therefore said to be glossed as (such and such). Glosses may be added by the original writer or else by a subsequent reader or editor. A glossary is a collection of glosses, being usually an alphabetical list of difficult or abstruse words and their explanations, incorporated as a reading aid in some part of a book or manuscript, or else constituting a separate work in itself (*see* Illus. 54).

Glosses may be found in any kind of printed or manuscript text, but are especially common in medieval theological and legal texts, where they can sometimes take the form of extended exegesis, interpretation, and commentary wrapped around the text and filling the margins and lower border on each page. A glossator was a medieval legal scholar who specialized in producing elaborate glosses and glossaries. From about the fourth century onwards, a glossarium was a kind of dictionary or lexicon of the most difficult words in a language. The various cognates of 'gloss' have their origin in Greek words, *glossa* meaning 'tongue' and *glossēma* the 'explanation of a strange word'.

GLYPH

See PICTOGRAPH.

GRACE BOOKS

Grace Books (Latin: *libri gratiarum*), as they are known at the University of Cambridge, or Registers of Convocation and Congregation, as they are known at the University of Oxford, are official registers of the degrees conferred by the university, as well as records of other financial and administrative matters, elections to office, and changes to statutes. Those at Cambridge, numbering thirty-three volumes in Latin and English, date from 1454 to 1943; those at Oxford date from 1535. For lists of degrees, the names on each page, or for each date, are supposedly arranged 'in order of seniority' (*ordo senioritatis*). The right of the Vice-Chancellor, proctors, and Senior Regent to insert names of 'honorary optimes' into the *ordo* was stopped in 1827, although it seems not to have been exercised after 1797. Otherwise, the list is one in order of merit up to the point where men are listed in college groups, which is a sign that order by merit has been abandoned.

From 1748 to 1894, lists of successful honours examination candidates were printed as 'tripos lists': i.e. on the back of the traditional satirical tripos verses in Greek or Latin that a senior Bachelor of Arts would deliver at commencement of a term on a three-legged (tripod) stool. Some tripos verses also survive in manuscripts.

GRAFFITI

The term 'graffiti' (the Italian word means 'scratches') was adopted apparently in the eighteenth-century, and denotes the crude inscriptions drawn, scratched, painted or sprayed on walls and buildings so familiar in urban life today. Such features date back to ancient times and many, such as those on certain Roman ruins and catacombs, are still preserved, as well as examples such as crosses carved in castle walls by medieval crusaders. As mementos of particular people or communities, graffiti scratched or carved on walls, windows, or other surfaces range from those by prisoners in fortresses or dungeons to those by students over fireplaces in university colleges. Workmen might also leave their names, marks, or doodles, as well as sometimes more advanced designs, on parts of buildings, including cathedrals, near the roof where they would generally never be seen by anyone except subsequent workmen: e.g. those carved and painted on the oak beams and plaster in the roof of the late fifteenth-century Duke Humfrey's Library in the Bodleian Library, Oxford. The term is thus especially applicable to inscriptions on walls and buildings, as opposed to the kinds of casual scribbling by readers that may deface books and manuscripts.

GRANT OF ARMS

A grant of arms is a formal document issued by the College of Arms granting a coat of arms to a particular person or corporation or else confirming or augmenting an earlier grant of arms. Usually set out on a single, sometimes large, sheet of vellum or paper, the grant, neatly written by a scribe according to a set formula, will tend to incorporate a design of the arms in question, emblazoned in their proper colours, as well as the seal(s) and signature(s) of the King(s) of Arms issuing the grant. Some more

ILLUS. 31 *Part of an illuminated grant of arms by Robert Cooke and William Flower,*
Kings of Arms, to John Harington, 12 February 1568/9. It is written and limned on
vellum (c.11 × 22 inches, 28 × 56 cm, in full), the arms emblazoned in their proper
colours, partly in gilt, the borders decorated, and with a coloured initial letter portrait of
the principal herald in his tabard.

elaborate examples are decorated with coloured or gilt initial letters and borders, possibly even with a portrait of the reigning monarch, and there are even grants of arms bearing an illuminated portrait of the issuing King of Arms himself in his official tabard (*see* Illus. 31). Grants of arms could at one time be issued by a single King of Arms, but were later each issued by two or, for large corporations (such as livery companies), three Kings of Arms.

GRAPH

Deriving from the Greek *graphē* ('writing'), the term 'graph' means a drawn diagram symbolically representing something. It may, for instance, be types of diagram used in science and mathematics, or else the curved, saw-toothed, or step-wise path that joins up dots on a chart and traces the rise and fall of a company's profits in the commercial world.

The term is also sometimes used in palaeography to denote a particular alphabetical letter or character as written in a manuscript. If two letters are written as one, such as *æ* or *œ*, they are digraphs. As an adjective, 'graphic' generally means drawn or painted, or else relating to drawing, painting, or diagrams, but may also sometimes refer to writing, which has itself some-times been described as a 'graphic art'.

GRAPHIOLOGY

'Graphiology' is a term apparently coined in the mid-nineteenth century, though now obsolete, to denote the art of writing in general.

GRAPHITE

See PENCIL and PLUMBAGO.

GRAPHOLOGY

'Graphology' is a relatively modern term sometimes used to denote the study of handwriting, but more specifically to denote the supposed art or science of studying handwriting in order to infer the individual writer's character, personality, or disposition. Thus, a tendency in writing to exag-gerate the size of initial letters might be seen as a sign of egotism; wide spacing between lines a sign of an orderly, reasonable person; upright characters a sign of strong self-control; fluctuating slants a sign of instabil-ity; an accentuated right slope a sign of an active, but impatient and potentially irresponsible person; certain disjointed lettering as a tendency to indecision or prevarication, and so on. Other features of handwriting are variously interpreted as indicating intelligence, creativity, or initiative, or, on the other hand, a disposition towards aggression, alcoholism, suicide, or psychopathic behaviour, as well as differing sexual tendencies.

Although it is generally accepted that handwriting, like any other personal characteristic or pattern of behaviour, may reflect aspects of the individual's personality, the fairly rigid systems of interpretation or decoding invented or adopted by graphologists, practitioners in this field, are open to debate, in much the same way as psychoanalysts' interpretations of dreams. Graphology has, however, had considerable influence, and graphologists have often been employed by large business corporations, particularly in the USA, and even by police forces.

GREAT SEAL

Since the eleventh century, the Great Seal of England (later the Great Seal of Great Britain) was the most important royal seal whereby a monarch could formally authorize a document as being an expression or his or her will. Following authorization by a royal warrant under the monarch's sign manual or Signet or Privy Seal (*see* COURSE OF THE SEAL), an impression of the Great Seal was affixed by the Lord Chancellor, or else by the Lord Keeper of the Seal when there was no Chancellor (or else by temporary commissioners or custodians on certain occasions), to important types of public document. They included proclamations, letters patent, charters, and grants conferring titles and dignities or appointing diplomatic envoys and ambassadors, as well as certain kinds of writs and warrants, such as authorizations for ministers to sign treaties and to enforce execution warrants. Each English monarch had his or her own Great Seal. Since a statute passed in 1351 until, technically, the nineteenth century, the counterfeiting of the Great Seal, and also of the Privy Seal, was regarded as a form of high treason, subject to extreme penalties. From 1540, so was any misuse of it by Chancery officials.

The matrix (the seal proper) is made of heavy cast bronze or, more commonly (and nowadays), of silver, and actually comprises two interlocking matrices, one for each side. Always in the custody of the Chancellor or Lord Keeper, the matrix is traditionally kept in a square-shaped case or bag, known as 'the burse' (*see* BURSE). The seal matrix is redesigned and replaced not only for each new reign, but also when there is a change in the royal arms or when the matrix gets worn out through constant use.

The impression of the seal (commonly, if sometimes confusingly, referred to as the seal itself) is in wax. This was originally beeswax mixed with resin; in more modern times, it is cellulose acetate plastic. An impression of the whole seal, which is always circular in shape and, depending on the reign, may range in diameter from less than 3 inches (*c.*7.5 cm) to 6 inches (*c*.15.5 cm), is attached to the foot of the parchment document usually by pendent cords, thongs, or laces. Routine writs may, however, have only a partial impression (being *sub pede sigilli*, 'under the foot of the seal') when the edge of the matrix has been merely tipped on a blob of wax on the document itself. This practice may account for why documents are traditionally described as being 'under the Great Seal', even though it is much more common for the seal to hang physically under the document. The colour of the wax used (whether green, brown, yellow, black, or red) may vary from one reign to another and be determined by the type of document to which it is affixed. The cords may also vary in material according to the nature or importance of the document: thus an elaborately decorated patent of nobility, for example, is likely to have the Great Seal attached by laces incorporating intertwined gold and silver thread and possibly even terminating in tassels. Since wax is brittle and easily fragmented, pendent seals are commonly kept in special tight-fitting bags or skippets for protection. *See* SKIPPET and Illus. 84.

The sovereign is traditionally depicted on one side of the seal as crowned and enthroned in state and on the other side, since at least the time of King John, as mounted on horseback (seals with such depictions are called 'equestrian

ILLUS. 32 *The Great Seal of Henry VIII, this impression in white wax originally attached to Royal Letters Patent dated 3 June 1522.*

ILLUS. 33 *The second Great Seal of Elizabeth I (both sides), this impression in white wax with brown patina attached to Royal Letters Patent dated 15 March 1593/4.*

seals': *see*, for example, Illus. 32). In the Commonwealth period, this tradition was briefly interrupted when the Great Seal of 1649 represented an assembled Parliament. Although the most commonly encountered Great Seal is the large impression in red wax of Queen Victoria (who reigned from 1837 to 1901), perhaps the best-known example remains the second Great Seal of Elizabeth I designed in 1584–6 by the celebrated miniaturist Nicholas Hilliard. Elizabeth is depicted seated on a throne and holding the traditional symbols of royal power, the orb and sceptre. The reverse side shows her on horseback, but not in military armour, riding peacefully across a field of flowering plants and flanked by such symbols as the Tudor rose of England, the harp of Ireland, and the fleur-de-lis of France (*see* Illus. 33). The Latin legend around the edge reads *Elizabetha dei gracia Anglie Francie et Hibernie Regina Fidei Defensor* ('Elizabeth by the grace of God Queen of England, France and Ireland, Defender of the Faith'). *See also* SEAL.

GREEK

Outside Greece, Greek was much less known in Europe in medieval times than was Latin, and was largely limited to scholarly circles interested in classical texts, theology, philosophy, and science. Knowledge of Greek expanded from the mid-fifteenth century onwards with the development of the Humanist movement and the fall of the Byzantine Empire. Church reformers too wished to read the New Testament in its original language, finding that it differed in important respects from the Latin translation, the Vulgate, authorized and propagated by the Roman Catholic Church.

British manuscripts written in Greek are relatively uncommon, but Greek sometimes appears in early modern manuscript discourses in the form of titles or quotations, and Queen Elizabeth wrote at least one prayer in the language.

GRISAILLE

See ILLUMINATION.

GUARD

Guards in printed books are single leaves that are pasted into the volume on stubs and therefore not part of a quire or gathering. In a manuscript context, it is the stubs themselves that tend to be called guards. Thus leaves are said to be 'mounted on guards' when they are attached to stubs within an album or other volume especially prepared for conservation purposes (as opposed, for instance, to their being left loose in folders or laid-down). A volume in which documents are mounted on stubs may itself be called a 'guard book'. In medieval times, what could be called 'guards' were parchment strips that reinforced or were folded around the sewing edge of a manuscript bifolium or quire for protective purposes.

GUEST BOOK

See VISITORS' BOOK.

GUTTER

The gutter in a printed or manuscript book is the channel running down the middle of the book, against the spine where the folds of all the quires meet, when opened at any point.

HABEAS CORPUS

See WRIT OF HABEAS CORPUS AD SUBJICIENDUM.

HALF-CALF, ETC.

When the binding of a book is described as 'half-calf', or 'half-morocco', or 'half-' any other leather, it means that only the spine and the corners of both covers are bound in that material, the rest of the covers usually exposing paper- or cloth-covered boards.

HAND-STAMPED

'Hand-stamped', or simply 'stamped', means that the mark, device, or text in question has been applied to the document not by writing, but by means of a stamp: i.e. by a hand-held instrument, most commonly of wood or rubber, designed to leave an impression of the mark, device, or text usually after exposure to ink. The most commonly encountered hand-stamped documents are letters or envelopes bearing stamped postal marks (*see* Illus. 24). If they bear dates, they can also be called 'date-stamped'. From late medieval times onwards, however, various kinds of official documents could also be stamped. They include royal warrants, when clerks were sometimes allowed to use a stamp of the monarch's signature to save him or her the trouble of signing routine warrants in person (*see* Illus. 81). Modern documents commonly stamped include passports and telegrams (*see* Illus. 59 and 88).

HANDWRITING

Handwriting, or 'hand' for short, is any kind of writing on a document entered or inscribed by hand, as opposed to stamped or printed text. Although the term 'hand' is often used as a synonym of 'script', it usually has the connotation of a particular person's handwriting. Thus the handwriting on a document may conform to a certain script—its style, forms, and general characteristics belonging to a historical period or recognized generic type of writing (court, secretary, italic, etc.)—but it is the hand that has peculiar distinguishing features and personal idiosyncrasies reflecting the character or identity of the writer as an individual. To quote the palaeographer M. B. Parkes's definition, 'A *script* is the model which the scribe has in his mind's eye when he writes, whereas a *hand* is what he actually puts down on the page.'

The nature of a person's handwriting has traditionally been deemed of some importance, for a variety of practical, social, and even psychological reasons. While the privileged rank of aristocratic men and women might occasionally give them licence to write in haste letters scarcely legible, the importance of clarity and legibility of handwriting both of gentlemen (if not ladies) and of secretaries, or of others engaged in professional writing tasks was always acknowledged, and the virtues of a 'fair', 'gallant' or 'gentleman-like' hand were commonly cited as recommendations for those seeking such employment.

At least in the early modern period, if not earlier, it was also considered polite for personal letters between friends or persons of equal rank—whether of a particularly confidential nature or otherwise—to be written in the correspondent's own hand, rather than in that of an amanuensis. Hence, despite the increasing use of secretaries for even personal correspondence, there are numerous occasions when writers felt bound to apologise when the text of a letter was written by a secretary instead of the signer. Excuses were elaborated, such as the lameness of the signer's hand, the excessive current pressure of business, or the poor quality of his or her handwriting, for which a secretary's more legible hand was a substitute of greater convenience to the recipient. Some recipients would certainly have agreed with the last sentiment: for instance, Lord Burghley, who complained in 1587 of the 'paines' he was put to to read Robert Sidney's 'ciphres', and who desired Sidney to 'wryte a better hand' or else 'to let some other wryte them' for him. As for the psychological aspects of handwriting, *see* GRAPHOLOGY.

HARD POINT

See DRY POINT.

HARMONY

See CONCORDANCE.

HATCHING

Hatching, or hatchwork, is a form of ornamentation involving a series of parallel lines to produce the effect of shading. It is used sometimes in heraldry, variant modes denoting different colours in a coat of arms, for instance, and also, often in colour, in decorated manuscripts from the fifteenth century onwards. Hatching in texts may also be a form of cancellation. *Compare* CROSS-HATCHING and STRAPWORK.

HEADING

A heading is a title or inscription at the top of a page or above a particular text such as a poem, chapter, or division in a manuscript or book. The text in question may then be said to be headed (such-and-such). *Compare* TITLE-PAGE.

HEADLINE

See RUNNING HEAD.

HERALD

See HERALDIC MANUSCRIPTS.

HERALDIC MANUSCRIPTS

Heraldic manuscripts of various kinds, including armorials (*see* Illus. 7), genealogies (*see* Illus. 30), grants of arms (*see* Illus. 31), and visitations, as well as tracts and treatises on heraldic subjects, constitute a major class of historical documents encountered in local record offices, state libraries, and private archives. As the science of describing armorial bearings, heraldry was developed in the twelfth century, with official senior heralds known as Kings of Arms appointed as early as the reign of Edward I. This was in the context of feudalism, jousting tournaments, royal ceremony, and pageantry, as well as in the evolution of concepts of knighthood and chivalry. Kings of Arms, who are always depicted in their official role wearing elaborate, usually sleeveless coats emblazoned with the royal arms known as 'tabards' (*see* Illus. 31), were commonly entrusted with the delivery of important royal letters and challenges to foreign rulers—during the Hundred Years War, for instance—and played a role in regulating warfare, such as summonsing towns to surrender, arranging ransoms, and liaising with enemy heralds to keep mutual account of the noblemen killed during a battle—as they did at Agincourt in 1415.

Probably most extant British heraldic documents, however, have their origin in the College of Arms, which was founded in England in 1484 and incorporated by royal charter under Mary I in 1556. Under the Earl Marshall, the principal officers of the College are the Kings of Arms (Garter, Clarenceux, and later Norroy and Ulster), Heralds (Windsor, Chester, Lancaster, Somerset, York, and Richmond), and Pursuivants (Rouge

Croix, Rouge Dragon, Bluemantle, and Portcullis). The Ireland King of Arms since 1382 was replaced in 1553 by the Ulster King of Arms. In Scotland, the Lord Lyon King of Arms was supported by three Heralds (Albany, Marchmont, and Rothesay) and four Pursuivants (Carrick, Kintyre, Unicorn, and Ormond). Duties of the Kings of Arms and their deputies included administering strict regulations over the use of armorial bearings, preparing and issuing grants of arms, producing genealogies, and making occasional county visitations to record the arms and pedigrees of all those who could establish a right to the title of esquire or gentleman. The documents they produced, especially their descriptions of arms, are invariably couched in a specialized vocabulary adapted from Old French: thus 'argent' means 'silver', 'estoile' 'star', 'or' 'gold', 'sinister' 'left' (i.e. left from the viewpoint of the bearer of the shield, hence on the right to a viewer), and so on.

HERBAL

A herbal is a book, often elaborately illustrated, containing names and descriptions of herbs and plants and of their medicinal properties and virtues. Numerous herbals were produced as manuscripts, with botanical paintings, in the medieval and early modern periods, many of them copies or translations of ancient classical texts.

HERMETIC MANUSCRIPTS

Hermetic manuscripts are those incorporating or relating to the philosophy of Hermeticism. This cult philosophy presupposes the existence of the mythical figure of Hermes Trismegistus, identified with the ancient Egyptian god of wisdom and magic, Thoth, to whom various writings on the occult arts and sciences were attributed. Generally known collectively as the *Corpus Hermeticum* or *Hermetica*, these writings were collected in medieval manuscripts and then widely printed in the early modern period. Although they were supposedly written before the time of Moses, the scholar Isaac Casaubon famously demonstrated in 1614 that their language could date no earlier than the Christian era. Not surprisingly, as a cosmological philosophy, Hermeticism had an uneasy coexistence with Christianity. The Hermetically-influenced unorthodox views of the philosopher Giordano Bruno, for instance, led to his being burned at the stake for heresy by the Papal Inquisition in 1600.

Nevertheless, Hermetic teachings had considerable influence on European thought over the centuries, particularly in the Renaissance period through translations by Marsilio Ficino. The body of extant writings that can in some measure be classified as Hermetic, including many incorporating alchemical, Rosicrucian, and other esoteric teachings, is therefore large. A major collection of them, both in manuscript and printed form, made by J. R. Ritman is preserved in the Bibliotheca Philosophica Hermetica in Amsterdam.

HIEROGLYPHICS
See PICTOGRAPH.

HINGES
See JOINTS.

HISTORIATED
The term 'historiated' derives from the French *histoires* (meaning 'stories'). Features of a manuscript such as its upper border or certain initials or capital letters can be properly described as 'historiated' when they are decorated with images of living creatures, whether men or beasts, that in some sense tell a story or relate to a narrative scene, as opposed to their being embellished with purely floral, geometrical, or other abstract designs. Many medieval decorated manuscripts, from the eighth century onwards, are decorated with such figures and scenes. If the figures represented are for decoration and do not tell or relate to a story, then the borders or letters concerned are more properly described as 'inhabited'. Nevertheless, manuscripts in the early modern period and later, such as Royal Letters Patent, that have borders embellished with emblems including beasts that have heraldic significance are commonly, if not with strict accuracy, described as 'historiated'.

HISTORICAL MANUSCRIPTS COMMISSION
The Royal Commission on Historical Manuscripts, usually cited as the Historical Manuscripts Commission (often abbreviated to HMC), was founded by Royal Warrant in 1869 for the registering of privately owned archives. Since 1870, it has published approximately 250 volumes of reports on manuscript collections in Britain, including those of the majority of great family houses and estates. In 1945, as information about manuscript sources increased beyond what could feasibly be published, the Commission set up the National Register of Archives (NRA), with a National Register of Archives also established for Scotland (with records kept simultaneously in London and Edinburgh) in 1946. The NRA remains the largest registry of manuscript collections in Britain, with its unpublished lists and catalogues

of private muniments, as well as of holdings in local record offices, university libraries, companies, and other institutions, running to a total of well over 40,000. Since 1959, the NRA has also had custody of the Manorial Documents Register. Before 2004, the NRA was based in Quality Court, off Chancery Lane, London WC2. After then it came under the auspices of the National Archives and moved to Kew.

HOLOGRAPH

Derived from the Greek *holos* ('whole') and *graphos* ('written'), the term 'holograph', used as an adjective, means the same thing as 'autograph': i.e. written entirely in the hand of the author (as opposed to being written in any part by a secretary or copyist). The term is more commonly found used as a noun, however, to denote a literary manuscript in the author's own hand. Other kinds of documents may be described as 'holographs' in an archival or legal context, such as a conveyance or a will written at least principally in the hand of the granter or testator in whose name it appears or who has signed it.

HOLSTER BOOK

A term of modern coinage, a 'holster book' means a portable notebook or memorandum book characterized by its long, narrow format (somewhere in the region of 10¼ × 5½ inches or 26 × 14 cm), resulting from its sheets being folded by bisecting the shorter side, and by its generally overlapping leather or vellum wallet binding or leather carrying-case somewhat like the holster of a pistol. From late medieval times onwards, holster books were often used for accounts, but might also be used as miscellanies or even commonplace books.

HOMOIOARCHON

See SCRIBAL ERRORS.

HOMOIOTELEUTON

See SCRIBAL ERRORS.

HORÆ

See BOOK OF HOURS.

HORN BOOK

A horn book is a reading implement used in England from the fifteenth to the eighteenth century for the elementary instruction of children. It usually embodied the alphabet, some basic spelling, numerals, and the Lord's Prayer. The earliest examples were written by hand; virtually all later examples were in printed form. The text, usually on a label, was pasted on a wooden panel with a handle and the surface covered with a thin transparent veneer of cattle horn, whence derived the term 'horn book'. In its physical format, a horn book bears some resemblance to a tablet.

HORNING

See LETTERS OF HORNING.

HOROSCOPE

Deriving from the Greek *hora* ('hour') and *skopos* ('watching'), the term 'horoscope' denotes a diagram, chart, or zodiac, complete with astrological symbols and calculations, showing the disposition or configuration of the heavenly bodies at the time of someone's birth, from which are extrapolated astrological predictions about him or her (*see* Illus. 34). The casting of horoscopes by astrologers was common in the early modern period, as indeed it was since ancient times. Notable examples include surviving manuscript horoscopes for Sir Philip Sidney (Bodleian Library, MS Ashmole 356, item 5), for Robert Devereux, second Earl of Essex (British Library, Sloane MS 1697, fol. 57v), and for various prominent people who were clients of Simon Forman, Elias Ashmole, and other seventeenth-century astrologers. They are occasionally useful to historians in providing biographical information, notably when particular people were born.

HOURS

See BOOK OF HOURS.

HOUSEHOLD ACCOUNTS

Household accounts are written financial documents detailing expenses, or other monetary transactions, including sometimes receipts, incurred by a private household. Household account books are manuscript books or ledgers, drawn up in a generally standard manner, in which such accounts are entered. They may include details relating to a whole family estate, overlapping with purely estate records, concerning land, farming, tenants, and the like, but are more usually concerned with the running of a particular house. A typical early modern example is likely to relate to a family of the gentry class or nobility. It will most probably be drawn up systematically, on a daily, weekly, or other temporal basis, in a series of columns: one, perhaps, with a note of date and place; another with a series of brief explanations of

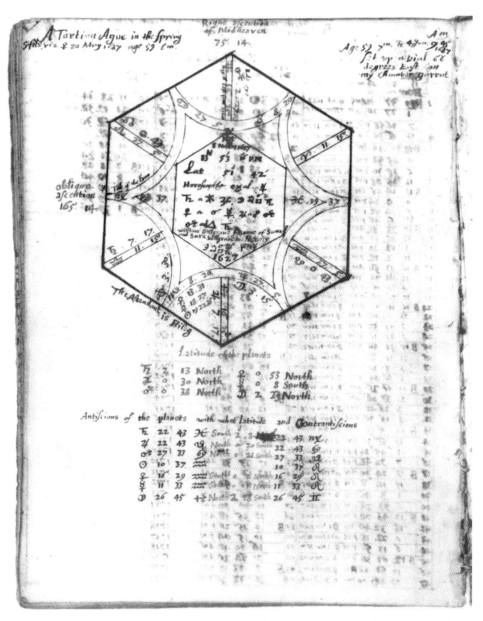

ILLUS. 34 *The horoscope of William Bellgrave (born 1 November 1627), shopkeeper of Chesham, Buckinghamshire, cast by himself, including a diagram and symbols, in his autograph astrological notebook, late seventeenth-century.*

what the expenses are for and to whom paid; others for figures denoting pounds (£), shillings (*s.*), and pence (*d.*), usually with a total at the bottom of each page; and sometimes subscribed with a signature by the master or mistress of the household, or their steward, by way of auditing, to record that the expenses and figures have been checked and approved as accurate.

Common disbursements would be for food and for wages of servants and employees (such as maids and cooks, butler, gardener, coachman, footmen, grooms, and other attendants and workmen), with occasional expenditure for such things as building works, repairs, clothing, household articles, books, or gambling debts. Such accounts were obviously made so that the household concerned could keep control over its finances and level of spending.

They can throw much light on the social history of the period, as well as on the individuals concerned and how they managed their households. They can also occasionally serve as prototype visitors' books in recording the names of guests for meals on particular dates. For a particular class of household accounts, *see* ROYAL HOUSEHOLD ACCOUNTS.

HUMANISTIC SCRIPT

The type of clear, elegant writing known at least since the nineteenth century as humanistic script, and linked to the development of italic, originated in Italy in the early to mid-fifteenth century as a consciously aesthetic reformation of writing style in reaction to medieval scripts such as Gothic. It was, to some extent, a revival of ninth-century Carolingian script (rechristened *littera antiqua*), which, it was mistakenly believed, was the script that early classical texts had been written in. It was thus symptomatic of the huge cultural movement commonly known as the Renaissance, marked, among other things, by the rediscovery of classical civilization in general, which spread from the late fourteenth century onwards from Florence, through Italy and then throughout Europe.

Humanistic script developed in variant ways over the years: for instance, from the disciplined, rounded, separately spaced lettering of *littera antiqua formata* to the more cursive *littera antiqua corsiva*, which entailed joined-up lettering. It was also related to innovations in book design. Humanistic script was in use in England, at least in the universities, by the mid-fifteenth century. *See also* ITALIC SCRIPT.

I

IGNOTO

See ANONYMOUS.

ILLUMINATION

Deriving from the Latin *illuminare* ('to light up'), the term 'illumination' means the decoration of manuscripts with gold or silver and with other bright, luminous colours (as opposed to monochrome black ink, or shades of grey known as 'grisaille'), the manuscript thus embellished being described as illuminated. Illumination can take the form of richly coloured and decorated lettering, elaborate tracery in the text, margins, or borders, and other ornamental or pictorial features, or else, most especially, miniatures (*see* MINIATURE). As a widespread phenomenon, illumination is most associated with medieval manuscripts, including the great monastic bibles and religious works, although illuminated manuscripts of various kinds, such as brightly coloured genealogies and chronicles, heightened with gold or silver, can still be found in the sixteenth and even seventeenth centuries.

An illuminator, or limner, is an artist who produces illumination. It may be a monk or other cleric, or else a lay craftsman, male or female, engaged in such work on a commercial basis. As works of art in their own right, illuminated manuscripts remain the most studied genre of manuscript, and every aspect of their style, production, physical components, etc. has long been subject to intensive scholarly scrutiny, analysis, and definition.

ILLUSTRATED ENVELOPE

See ENVELOPE.

ILLUSTRATION

Although any text bearing drawings or designs of any kind may generally be described as illustrated, an illustrated manuscript is properly one that is

Though pinching, WANT were not soe Ill a Thing,
Deiectednesse, and Scorne did Itt not bring.

DICKE.

IACKE! nay preethee come away!
This is noe time for sadnesse;
PAN's cheife Feast is kept to day,
Each Shepeard shewes his gladnesse:
W'are to meete All on the Greene,
To dance, and sport together;
O what Brau'ry will bee seene!
I hope t'will proue fayre Weather!

2. Looke! I'ue gott a new

ILLUS. 35 *A page of the autograph manuscript of 'Ballades dedicated to The Lady Victoria Uvedale by their Authour John Patricke Cary ... Writt All by the Authour's owne hand, An° (1653)', a calligraphic presentation manuscript designed for the author's sister, elaborately illustrated with captioned emblems. The text is written in a predominantly italic script, in imitation of a typeface, by Cary, who was brother of Lucius, second Viscount Falkland, of Great Tew. This page bears a pen-and-ink emblem in the form of a rural scene and an initial letter embellished with decorative foliation.*

embellished with pictures or illustrations, whether pencil, pen and ink or coloured, that are contained within frames or borders (*see* Illus. 24 and 35). An illustration may thus be distinguished from a vignette. Since an illustration is a self-contained depiction of a scene, figures, etc., rather than an abstract design or accretion on some other feature, it is also to be distinguished from decoration. If it is heightened with luminous gold or silver colouring, it can be described as illuminated.

IMPALED

In heraldry, arms are said to be impaled when a shield or banner bears two coats of arms side by side.

IMPERFECT

The adjective 'imperfect' applied to a manuscript text denotes one that is defective: that may have been complete originally but is now physically damaged, lacking leaves, portions of leaves, or even whole gatherings. A printed book may similarly be described as imperfect if it lacks any pages (including blanks) or perhaps even if it is bound partly out of order. *Compare* INCOMPLETE and UNFINISHED.

IMPOSITION BOOK

In an Oxford or Cambridge college, an imposition book was one that recorded students' delinquencies and the resulting 'impositions' or punishments. More often than not, the latter involved having to make a public Latin declamation in the college hall.

IMPRESA

An Italian word, occasionally Anglicized in the sixteenth and seventeenth centuries as 'impress' or 'impressa', the term *impresa* (plural: *imprese*) means an emblem, device, or badge, usually with a motto in Latin, found painted on shields in tournaments, as well as embodied sometimes in standards, helmets, and brooches, or embroidered on clothes or on horses' caparisons, and their use spread to portraits, tapestries, wall and ceiling paintings, jewellery, and other artistic productions. The emblem, an elitist symbol appropriate to the nobility, and sometimes also to scholars and divines, expressed a person's character, aspirations, or achievements, usually military or amorous, and was chosen specifically for each individual tournament or festive event. Subjects chosen for representation could include almost anything, including lions, unicorns, birds, mountains, castles, fire, trees, moon, stars, compasses, and many other devices with symbolic significance.

The motto, complementing the emblem, would usually express chivalrous sentiments, but could also be quite personal. One used on one occasion by Robert Devereux, Earl of Essex, read *Et tamen vincor* ('And nevertheless I am subdued'), accompanying the emblem of a pen and a cannon in a pair of scales, the pen weighing heavier. Another by the Queen's champion, Henry Lee, read *Premium patientia pena* ('My reward is patience and pain'). A particularly famous one was adopted by Philip Sidney at a tournament in late 1578 or early 1579, when his shield simply bore one deleted word painted on it, ~~SPERAVI~~ ('I hoped'). The meaning was that Sidney's hopes of being heir to his uncle Robert Dudley, Earl of Leicester, had been dashed by the birth of a son to Leicester's new wife, Lettice Knollys.

Although some *imprese*, such as Sidney's, were devised by the knight himself, it is clear that others were devised on the knight's behalf, which also indicates the importance attached to this practice and the care taken to select just the right symbolic emblem and motto for the occasion. A notable example of this is the documentary evidence that William Shakespeare was paid 44 shillings (£2 4s.) in gold in 1613 for composing an *impresa* for the Earl of Rutland. Inigo Jones was also employed to paint an *impresa* in 1610.

By the Elizabethan period, it was customary at tournaments to have *imprese* painted on cardboard shields which were presented by each knight's page to the Queen as part of the opening ceremony accompanying his entry into the tiltyard. By the 1580s, a collection of such shields was mounted on the walls of one of the galleries in Whitehall Palace, although none of these survives today.

Many *imprese* do, however, survive in representations in heraldic manuscripts, in the College of Arms and elsewhere. They also survive figuratively in early modern literature, such as Sidney's *Arcadia*, where their application to particular characters in the context of the story can be very sophisticated.

IMPRIMATUR

See LICENCE TO PRINT.

INCIDENTALS

Incidentals (or 'accidentals', though the former term is now more generally preferred) are what editors judge to be the subsidiary, non-essential, or less crucial elements of a written or printed text, such as punctuation, spelling, and capitalization, as opposed to the substantive, verbal elements. Editors have been traditionally keen to distinguish between the two, generally when in pursuit of authorial intention, taking the view that the incidentals are the least likely features of a text to be transmitted by agents, such as scribes or compositors, exactly as the author wrote them. In early modern scribal manuscripts, the punctuation, capitalization, spelling, etc. generally reflect the habits of the scribes, whatever their exemplars. Moreover, it is just as likely that compositors will have set up their type for printed editions according to practical criteria such as the type available, the page layout, and the need to justify their lines, rather than rigorously reproducing every tiny detail of their exemplars. Incidentals in certain circumstances, affecting the meaning, may, however, be termed 'semi-substantive' (*see* SUBSTANTIVE). Certain incidentals, such as curious spellings of proper names, may also be evidence of the textual descent of particular manuscripts. *See also* COPY-TEXT.

<h2 style="text-align:center">INCIPIT</h2>

The Latin word *incipit* ('it begins') was frequently used by medieval authors, the word sometimes highlighted in manuscripts by rubrication or majuscules, before or instead of a title, to denote the beginning of a new work or text. In modern scholarship, an incipit (as opposed to an explicit) is the initial or opening few words of a text that may serve to identify that text. This may include the first few words of poems and songs, if not the full first lines as they are listed in various published first-line indexes. For similar identification purposes, cataloguers of medieval manuscripts (though not necessarily cataloguers of incunabula) specifically apply the term to the first few words of the text proper, rather than to any introductory rubric (such as 'Incipit...'). *Compare* EXPLICIT.

<h2 style="text-align:center">INCOMPLETE</h2>

The adjective 'incomplete' applied to a particular text, manuscript or printed, denotes the lack of passages or sections that would be there if the text had been copied or printed in full. This means that the text in question is not necessarily defective or damaged, but that the scribe, editor, or printer did not in this instance choose to copy or print the work in its entirety. The term is sometimes used, less accurately, to denote a manuscript that is imperfect because damaged or one that is not complete because the work itself is unfinished. *Compare* IMPERFECT and UNFINISHED.

<h2 style="text-align:center">INDEMNITY CERTIFICATE OF SETTLEMENT</h2>

See SETTLEMENT CERTIFICATE.

<h2 style="text-align:center">INDENTURE</h2>

An indenture is technically a deed made by, and expressing the intentions of, two or more parties, as opposed to a deed poll, which is by one party only. Whereas the latter was traditionally polled, meaning that the document was cut even, an indenture was indented with zigzag, wavy, or scalloped edges (*see* Illus. 36). Such indentation resulted, at least in earlier times, from the practice of writing out the text in duplicate, head to head, on a single sheet of parchment, which was then cut in two in a wavy or jagged line to produce an indenture and its counterpart that would fit each other exactly and prove their authenticity if the two were reunited. Such an indenture was also formerly known as a 'charterparty'. From about the sixteenth century onwards, the practice of indenting became increasingly obsolete, although the term 'indenture' was still applied ('This indenture ... witnesseth ...') so long as more than one party was involved. An indenture involving an agreement between three parties is known as an indenture tripartite; one between four parties as an indenture quadripartite. *See also* CHIROGRAPH.

INDENTURE OF APPRENTICESHIP

An indenture of apprenticeship is an indenture, generally on parchment, whereby a person, usually a young man, binds himself to serve as apprentice to a merchant or craftsman for a specified number of years in order to learn his craft or business. It usually entails the apprentice's agreeing faithfully to serve and obey his master and to behave himself well during that period. One signed on 25 September 1607 by the sixteen-year-old future poet Robert Herrick, for instance, bound him to his uncle, the King's Jeweller Sir William Herrick, and entailed standard undertakings not to 'committ fornicacion nor contract matrimonye', 'playe at the cardes, dice, tables, or any other vnlawfull games', or to 'haunt Tavernes', among other stipulations. Apprentice binding books, listing the names of apprentices and their masters, are a common and informative feature of livery company archives.

INDEX

An index (the Latin meaning 'forefinger') is an alphabetical list of names, places, or other subjects treated in a book, with page or folio references, usually situated at the end of the book. It may be distinguished from a table of contents, which lists constituent parts of the book in the proper sequential order, not alphabetically. Indexes, or indices, were commonly provided in substantial manuscript treatises and other works long before the era of printed books, and numerous early modern volumes of manuscript tracts and account books have indexes written in by contemporary or subsequent owners. Many such indexes may, however, be semi-alphabetical, the words arranged according to first letter only.

An index can also be a substantial volume in its own right, as a type of catalogue. One particular example is sufficiently well-known to be sometimes cited as simply 'the Index': i.e. the *Index librorum prohibitorum*, the

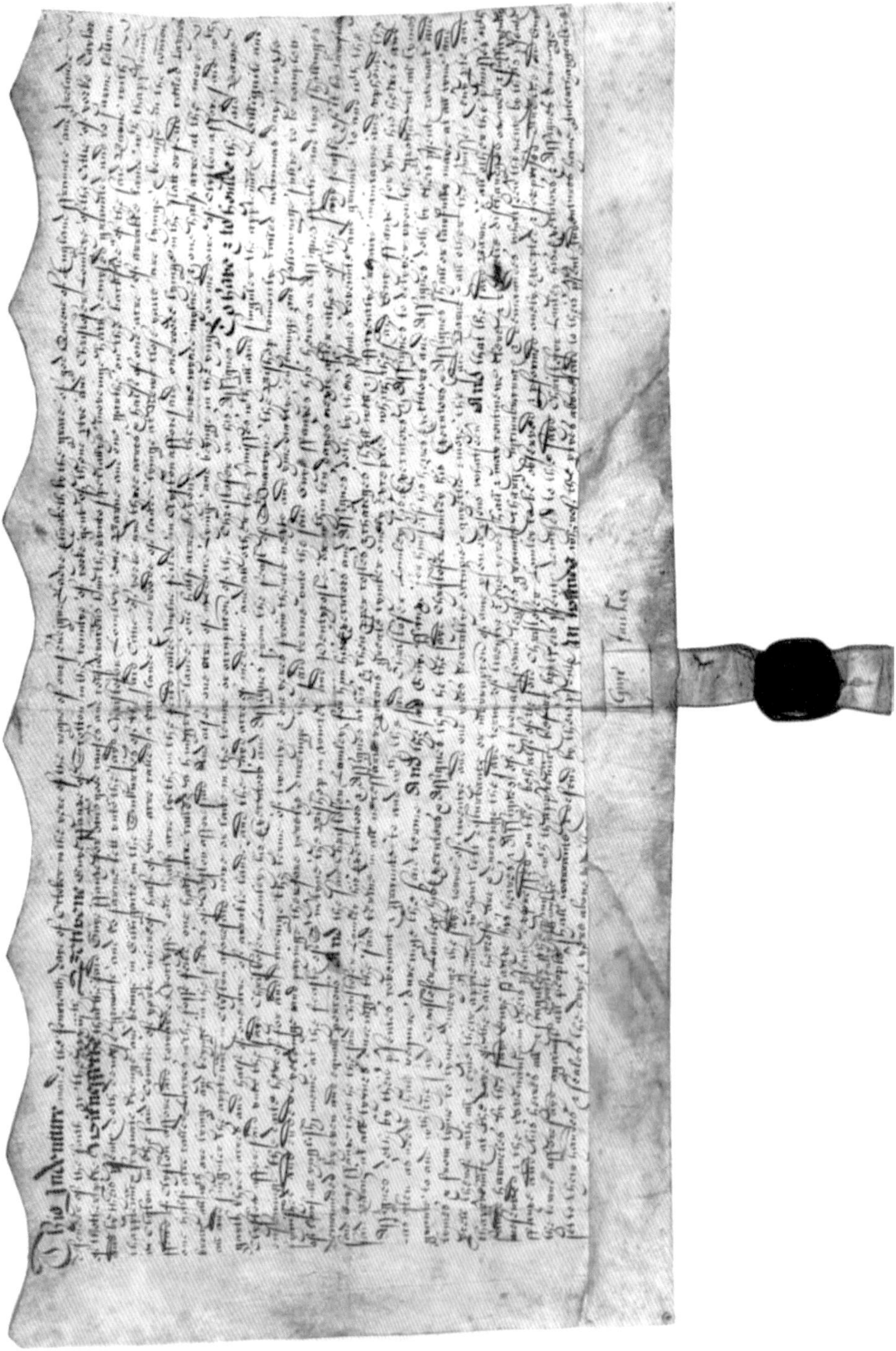

extensive and constantly expanding list of books (including some of the most famous ever written) forbidden to members of the Roman Catholic Church or that might be read only in approved expurgated versions. Established by the Vatican under Pope Paul IV and first published in 1557, this *Index* (which ran to forty-two published versions, containing eventually some 4,000 titles) was finally abrogated by Pope Paul VI in 1966, as was also the *Index expurgatorius*, the Vatican's list of passages in books that must be deleted before the books could be read by the faithful.

See also MANICULE and *compare* TABLE OF CONTENTS.

INDICTMENT

In earlier times, from at least the mid-fourteenth century, an indictment was an accusation by a grand jury (at assizes or quarter sessions), or by a coroner's jury, with regard to an alleged felony. A bill of indictment, with related evidence, was presented by the prosecutor to the jury. If they thought there was a case to answer, the bill was endorsed *billa vera* ('a true bill') and a trial ensued. If they did not think so, it was endorsed *ignoramus* ('we do not know') and there was no trial. In certain cases, indictments could be reviewed by the King's Bench to determine that their wording was technically in order. A large number of records of indictments in the various counties from 1675 to 1926 are preserved among the records of the King's Bench in the National Archives at Kew (KB 10, KB 11, and KB 12 series).

INDULGENCES

Indulgences (Latin: *indulgentiae*)—also technically called 'letters of indulgence'—are licences issued or sold by the Roman Catholic Church granting to penitent sinners the remission, either whole or partial, of temporal punishment still due for sins after sacramental absolution. Dating back at least to the eleventh century, indulgences were largely mass-produced in manuscript form in the medieval period, with formulaic text leaving spaces for relevant names to be entered, and written chiefly on parchment, with papal seals. Indulgences were also produced on paper in considerable numbers by early printers (including William Caxton), similarly with blanks left for particulars

ILLUS. 36 *An indenture signed by Guy Fawkes, being the lease of his property near York to Christopher Lomleye, tailor, 14 October 1591. The text is formally written in secretary script by a legal clerk, on a membrane of vellum, with occasional words engrossed and a pendent seal bearing on the tag or label an impression in wax of Fawkes's personal seal. The indenture is cut at the top with a scalloped edge (the semi-circles here being concave; those on the counterpart given to Lomleye would therefore have been convex).*

to be added by hand. Many indulgences were issued to raise money for particular causes, such as the rebuilding of St Peter's in Rome.

By the fourteenth century, there was a flourishing and unrestricted sale of indulgences by pardoners (the most famous fictional one being the narrator of the 'Pardoner's Tale' in Chaucer's *Canterbury Tales*). Abuses in the commercial exploitation of indulgences were, however, condemned in church councils as early as 1215 and most notably, as 'pious frauds', by Martin Luther in 1517. The Church's right to grant indulgences was, nevertheless, reaffirmed by the Council of Trent in 1563, although in 1567 Pius V prohibited the granting of indulgences for commercial profit.

Many original manuscript indulgences can be found in British local record offices dating as late as 1526. The texts of many others are found in copies in bishops' registers and other ecclesiastical records. Most original indulgences were probably destroyed in the Reformation or else after the death of the beneficiaries themselves. It is even possible that, after death, some people had their indulgences buried with them. According to the copyist in a seventeenth-century miscellany now in the British Library (Add. MS 28640, fol. 91v), one dated 1381 was found in a coffin in St Paul's, London, in 1608 when the ground was broken for the burial of the lawyer Sir Richard Swale. *Compare* LETTERS OF CONFRATERNITY.

INHABITED

See HISTORIATED.

INITIAL

Deriving from the Latin *initium* ('beginning'), the term 'initial' means the very first letter in the first word. This letter is that most likely to be engrossed or decorated in certain kinds of legal and official documents, such as indentures and letters patent, as well as in other types of formal or calligraphic writing (*see* Illus. 87 and 95), including medieval illuminated manuscripts. Other types of document are 'initialled' when they are signed by someone using only the first letters of his or her name: for instance, 'G.B.S.' for 'George Bernard Shaw'. *See* Illus. 8, 24, 59, and 86.

INITIAL LETTER PORTRAIT

From medieval times onwards, an initial letter portrait is a feature most commonly found in particularly elaborate Royal Letters Patent (*see* Illus. 37, 38, 40, and 76) and occasionally in other documents, such as grants of arms (*see* Illus. 31). The initial word of such patents, which are invariably on membranes of parchment, is always the name of the sovereign, or sovereigns in the case of

ILLUS. 37 *The initial letter portrait on Royal Letters Patent of Philip and Mary, issued on 2 July 1554, twenty-three days before they were married and their reign technically began. The portrait, measuring c.4 ½ × 3 ½ inches (11.5 × 9 cm), is executed in pen and ink within the initial M, with strapwork and foliate decoration.*

Mary and Philip, the first letter of which is engrossed and expanded to frame the top left-hand corner of the patent, leaving a space within which is drawn a portrait of the monarch(s). They are usually represented as seated in state and bearing the regal orb and sceptre, as well as generally the crown. The framing initial letter is usually decorated with heavily inked strapwork or other ornaments, the royal figures being drawn for the most part in pen and ink, with generally simple or crude representation of their features. In exceptional cases, much more elaborate portraits are limned in colours, which can occasionally reach very high artistic standards: for instance, a portrait of Henry VIII by the King's Limner Lucas Hornebolte, within a decorated capital *H* on a patent of 28 April 1524 (now in the Victoria and Albert Museum).

Since Royal Letters Patent were paid for by the person receiving the benefit of the patent, the quality of the portrait, if one were commissioned, as of any

ILLUS. 38 *The initial letter portrait on Royal Letters Patent of Charles I, issued on 19 April 1642. The portrait, measuring* c.6 × 5 ½ *inches (15.2 × 14 cm), is executed in pen and ink with plumbago shading within the initial C, with scrollwork and strapwork decoration.*

other emblems and decorations included, would depend on the importance of the patent and the size of the grantee's purse. Not surprisingly, patents bearing such portraits are quite well prized, even though most limners would never have set eyes on the monarchs themselves. However, by the time of Charles I, a cheaper, more mechanical form of Royal Letters Patent had come into use, whereby the decorated upper and side borders, including a portrait, could be produced by an engraved plate, the portrait itself being sometimes inked over or coloured by the scribe to give a false impression of originality. This type of patent became particularly common in the eighteenth century.

INK

The use of ink for writing dates back to ancient times. Its traditional ingredients, though subject to different recipes, include a type based on oak-galls (*see* GALL) and iron sulphate (*see* COPPERAS), a by-product of which is sulphuric acid, with gum arabic used as a binding agent. An alternative type was based on carbon, using lampblack or soot. The standard mixture was significantly varied in the nineteenth century with the reduction of the acidic constituents in order to eliminate rusting of the recently introduced steel-tipped pens. Even so, chemical changes in ink over the centuries have produced various effects and reactions in different qualities of paper and parchment. They range from fading (black turning to light brown, for instance, through the decay of vegetable matter) and discolouration (such as oxidation) to seepage into, and outright corrosion of, the writing surface when the acid content of the ink remained excessive.

INKHORN

An inkhorn, or ink-horn, is a small portable container for holding and carrying ink. Dating back to ancient Egypt, and certainly used by the Romans and throughout the medieval period, inkhorns were commonly made from the end of the horn of a cow, tapered to be held in the hand or else to be set into a hole in the scribe's desk. Other types of portable inkwells, serving the same function as inkhorns, might be small, lined pots, or leather or metal holders, sometimes decorated with stamped figures or ornaments, attached by drawstrings to a penner (*see* PENNER). The arms of the Worshipful Company of Scriveners, confirmed in 1634, but probably dating from medieval times, are, appropriately enough, an eagle holding in his mouth a penner and inkhorn.

These features were also seen as symbolic of the professional clerk, such as the one whom Jack Cade wishes to execute in *Henry VI, Part 2* (IV, ii, 108–9) simply because he can write ('Away with him, I say, hang him with his pen and inkhorn about his neck'). In similar vein, and generally in a satirical context, the word 'inkhorn' could also sometimes be used as an adjective to denote something bookish or pedantic. The use of inkhorns by itinerant scribes seems to have declined after the sixteenth century and they were finally rendered obsolete by the nineteenth-century development of the fountain pen.

INKPOT

An inkpot is simply a small pot for holding writing-ink. Types of inkpot date from at least medieval times and probably much earlier.

INKSTAND

An inkstand, or 'standish' as it was commonly called in earlier times, is a stand or tray for holding inkpots, bottles, glasses, a pounce pot, pens, or other writing materials, and is generally designed to rest on a desk. From at least the fifteenth century onwards, inkstands could take various forms and be distinguished by varying degrees of elaboration, ranging from plain tin, wooden, pewter, or brass models to luxurious porcelain, crystal, silver, or gold inkstands, some even with jewelled fittings. Some types could accommodate features such as a wafer box or drawer, a small candlestick for melting wax for seals, or even a small hand-bell to summon a servant to collect written letters.

INKWELL

Since at least the fifteenth century, inkwells were ink containers, originally made of lead or bronze. From the late seventeenth century onwards, an inkwell, as distinct from an inkpot, was generally made of glass with a hinged or screw-top metal lid. Subsequent types might also be made of stone, porcelain, or earthenware. The inkwell could either be fixed, as a fitting to a desk, or separate and portable.

INNS OF CHANCERY

The Inns of Chancery in London may be distinguished from the Inns of Court, to which they became subsidiary. Since medieval times they were primarily legal institutions serving as preparatory schools for students who would train to be called to the Bar at the Inns of Court, with which individual Inns of Chancery had particular affiliations. By 1600 there were eight flourishing Inns of Chancery: Barnard's Inn, Clement's Inn, Clifford's Inn, Furnival's Inn, Lyon's Inn, New Inn, Staple Inn, and Thavies Inn (one other, Strand Inn, having been demolished in 1549). In the seventeenth century, students came increasingly to enrol directly in the Inns of Court, and the Inns of Chancery became extinct by the nineteenth century. Unlike the Inns of Court, the Inns of Chancery have left no notable literary legacy.

INNS OF COURT

The Inns of Court in London, which still flourish, comprise the Honourable Societies of the Inner Temple, the Middle Temple, Lincoln's Inn, and Gray's Inn. To these four may be added the King's Inn, which was established by Henry VIII in Dublin and remains the Inn of Court of the Republic of Ireland. Since at least the fourteenth century (fifteenth for Lincoln's Inn), the Inns of Court in London—which once took their place among as many as twenty inns for apprentice lawyers—have been societies that served as major law schools for select students training to be called to the Bar. They conferred degrees and produced over the years an extensive legal literature.

Sometimes called the Third University (after Oxford and Cambridge), the Inns of Court could also sometimes be regarded by contemporary commentators as a kind of finishing school or fashionable venue for young gentlemen after leaving university (though many did not attend university), some if not many of whom were as much interested in the lively social life there as in the law. The result by the late sixteenth and early seventeenth centuries was that, besides turning out well-trained lawyers, some of them eminent future judges, legal writers, and legislators, versed in the arts of pleading and disputation, the Inns of Court became a significant cultural community and were, among other things, a notable centre of manuscript circulation. Many writings, largely unpublished in their own time, can be connected with members of the Inns of Court, including Francis Bacon, Francis Beaumont, Sir John Davies, and John Hoskyns, as well as writers who had their lodgings there or other associations, such as John Donne and James Shirley. A considerable number of surviving manuscript notebooks, commonplace books, and verse miscellanies, as well as political tracts, also show connections with the Inns of Court and suggest communal transcription and circulation, as well as some original literary production.

The Inns of Court were also responsible for putting on masques and other dramatic entertainments, the texts of which, when preserved, are often in manuscript form, or are known about through the surviving records of the Inns themselves. Examples of the entertainments put on by the Inner Temple include William Browne's *Ulysses and Circe* (13 January 1614/15) and Thomas Middleton's *Mask of Heroes* (6 January—2 February 1618/19); by the Middle Temple, a masque for the Duke of Buckingham (17 January 1616/17) and one before Ambassadors of the Netherlands (13 February 1620/1); and by Gray's Inn, *Gesta Grayorum* by Francis Davison, Francis Bacon, and others (20 December 1594 and later), a *Mask of Flowers* (6 January 1613/14), and an *Anti-Mask of Mountebanks* (2 and 19 February 1617/18). For some grand occasions the Inns combined forces: thus for the marriage of Princess Elizabeth (James I's daughter) and Frederick, Elector Palatine, one celebratory entertainment was put on by the Middle Temple and Lincoln's Inn (15 February 1612/13) and another by the Inner Temple and Gray's Inn (20 February 1612/13). The most spectacular and most expensive masque of all, mounted by all the Inns of Court in an attempt to regain the favour of Charles I, was James Shirley's *The Triumph of Peace* (staged by Inigo Jones on 3 and 13 February 1633/4), for which a huge number of records exist.

INQUEST

See INQUISITION.

INQUISITION

The term 'inquisition' is sometimes applied to the document recording the result of a formal inquiry or investigation. It may, for instance, be the certificate recording the conclusion or verdict of a public inquest conducted by a coroner into how a deceased person met his or her death.

In the context of the Roman Catholic Church, the Inquisition was the special tribunal established by Pope Gregory IX in 1231 to suppress heresy. This reached its most extreme development in the form of the Spanish Inquisition, responsible for many thousands of executions, usually by burning at the stake, from the late fifteenth century onwards. It was finally abolished in 1834. Because of this history, the term 'inquisition' today has a pejorative connotation, denoting a particularly harsh, aggressive, unrelenting inquiry.

INQUISITIO POST MORTEM

An inquisitio post mortem (Latin for 'inquiry after death'), sometimes called an 'inquisition post mortem' or simply an 'inquisition', is an official document recording the result of an inquiry following the death of a Crown tenant-in-chief. Such documents and records date from the early thirteenth century, when regional officials called 'escheators' were appointed to investigate and evaluate the lands and rights of any deceased tenant, and to ascertain any entitlements of the Crown. The latter might include the sovereign's right to assume wardship if the heir were a minor, aged less than twenty-one, and to extract appropriate revenues (such as profits for a year and a day). The escheators would send their report to the Court of Chancery, with a copy to the Court of Exchequer and, after 1540, also to the Court of Wards. Large numbers of these records, from *c.*1216 to the mid-seventeenth century, are preserved in the National Archives at Kew (C 132–142, E 149–150, WARD 7).

An inquisitio post mortem differs from a modern post-mortem or coroner's inquest in that it is not concerned with the cause of death.

INROLL

See ENROL.

INROLMENT OF ACTS OF PARLIAMENT

See PARLIAMENT ROLLS.

INSCRIPTION

Derived from the Latin *inscribere* ('to write in or upon'), the term 'to inscribe' means to write in or on something: for example, to write some words in a book, album, visitors' book, or greetings card. An inscription is the text or message itself: e.g. a presentation inscription written by an author or other person giving a book to someone as a gift (*see* Illus. 64) or an ownership inscription recording who owns it. From the sixteenth century onwards, one of the commonest types of inscription is found in bibles, where a series of entries record births, and sometimes also marriages and deaths, in the family owning

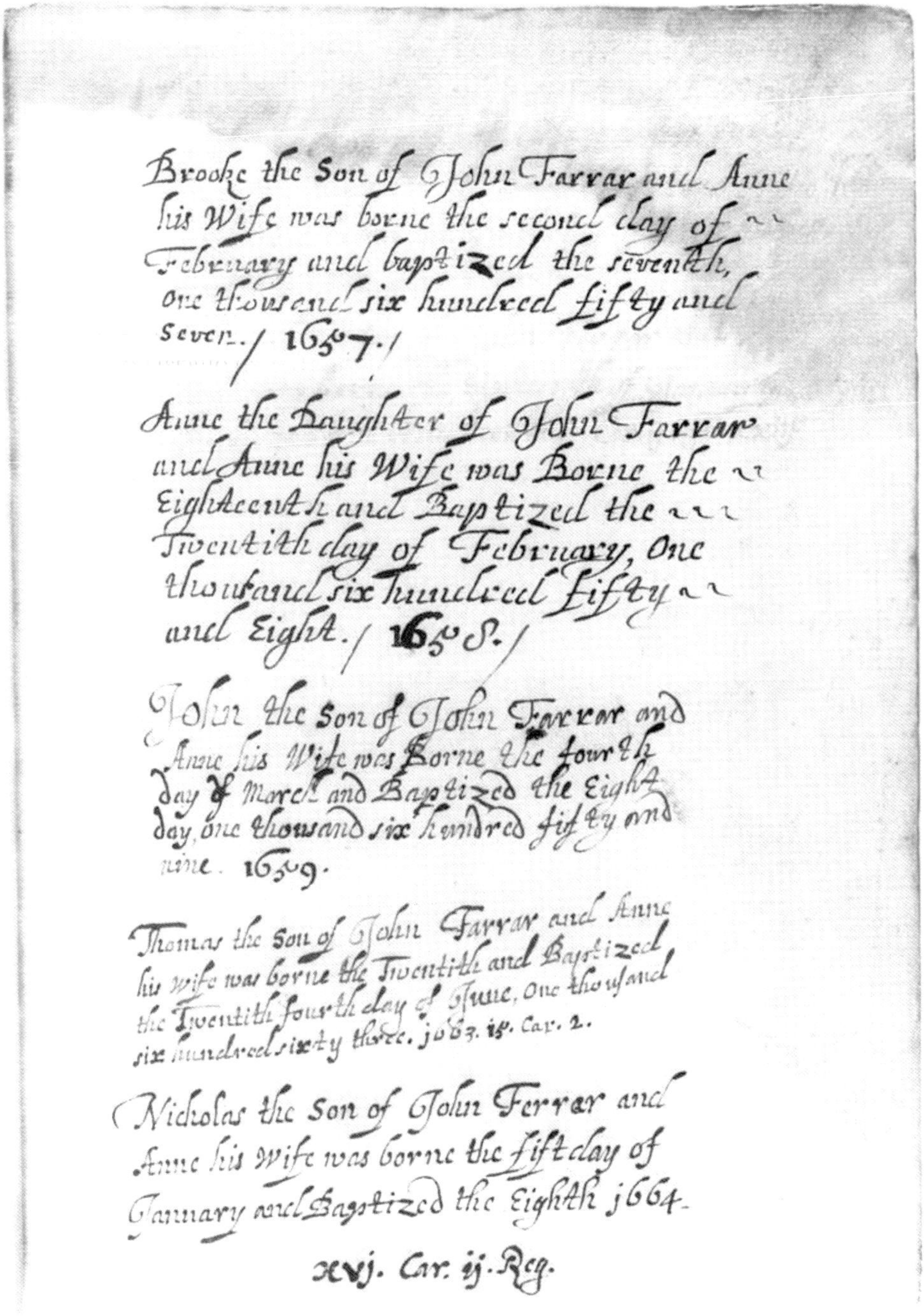

Brooke the Son of John Farrar and Anne his Wife was borne the second day of February and baptized the seventh, one thousand six hundred fifty and seven. / 1657. /

Anne the Daughter of John Farrar and Anne his Wife was Borne the Eighteenth and Baptized the Twentith day of February, One thousand six hundred fifty and Eight. / 1658. /

John the Son of John Farrar and Anne his Wife was Borne the fourth day of March and Baptized the Eight day, one thousand six hundred fifty and nine. 1659.

Thomas the Son of John Farrar and Anne his wife was borne the Twentith and Baptized the Twentith fourth day of June, One thousand six hundred sixty three. 1663. 15. Car. 2.

Nicholas the Son of John Ferrar and Anne his Wife was borne the fift day of January and Baptized the Eighth 1664.

xvj. Car. ij. Reg.

ILLUS. 39 *Entries recording births and baptisms between 1657 and 1664 in the Ferrar family of Little Gidding, Cambridgeshire, inscribed on the front free endpaper of a bible printed in Cambridge in 1637.*

the bible, often over several generations (*see* Illus. 39). The term 'inscription' usually implies that several words are written rather than just a name or signature. In a specialized sense, the term may also denote that part of a charter bearing the name of the person responsible for granting it.

INSPEXIMUS

An inspeximus is a charter beginning with the Latin word *Inspeximus* ('We have inspected'). It is declared in the charter that an earlier charter or letters patent, here quoted or summarized, has been examined and its validity confirmed. *See* Illus. 40.

INSTRUCTIONS

As a document, instructions commonly take the form of an official letter or warrant giving formal orders or directions for what the recipient is required to do: for instance, instructing an ambassador, diplomatic envoy, or legal counsel on his or her aims, duties, and responsibilities or on the particular mission, case, or matter in hand (*see* Illus. 41). Instructions may otherwise be directions on any practical matter, such as those given to a printer on how a writer wants his text set out, or those explaining how to play a game or to assemble a piece of equipment.

INSTRUMENT

In a manuscript context, an instrument is a formal legal writing or document, such as a deed or charter, that constitutes the means whereby a transaction, such as a transfer of property, is legally accomplished and of which it is evidence.

INSTRUMENT OF SASINE

See SASINE.

INSTRUMENT OF SURRENDER

See SURRENDER.

INTEGRAL

A term referring to what pertains to, or is part of, or intrinsic to, a whole entity, 'integral' is a useful word in describing certain kinds of manuscript: for instance, an integral address leaf is an address leaf that is attached to a letter and an essential component of it, not detached or just an appendage.

ILLUS. 40 *An inspeximus and exemplification of the various royal grants of Halesowen from King John to Edward I, on Royal Letters Patent of James I. It is written by a Chancery scribe on a membrane of vellum c.24 × 31 inches (61 × 78.7 cm), with an initial letter portrait of the King, the first line in engrossed decorated majuscules, the upper border adorned with heraldic beasts and royal emblems, the margins with floral decorations. It is signed at the foot by two clerks and bears a pendent impression in wax of the Great Seal, 31 May 1609.*

INTEGRITY

'Integrity' is a word sometimes used in connection with archives, the integrity of an archive being a desirable feature of it, when the archive has been kept more or less intact rather than split up or in any way dispersed.

Instructions gyven by her Matie
to Charles Lord Howard Lord
Admirall of England, beinge appoynted
to go to the Seas to rextaine his matie
[...] the twentith of Decembr
1587 in the [...] [...] his mate
[...]

Elizabeth R

Being sundry wayes most credibly given to understand of the great and
extraordinary preparations made by Sea, aswell in Spayn by the kyng [...]
as in the Low Countryes by the Duke of Parma, and that it is also ment
that the said forces shall be ymployed in som enterprise to be attempted eyther
in [...] domminions of England & Ireland or in the Realm of Scotland tending
principally to the disquietinge of o' estate, we have thought it very convenient
to provide all suche good meanes as God hath given us, to putt o' selves in
order of defence for the better withstanding of the said attempte.

And therefore fyndyng that the withstanding of the said intended attempte may in
no sorte be so well performed as by meeting by Sea, we have thought it
therefore most necessary to have in readines o' owne Shipps and certayn Shipps
apparteyning [...] o' subiectts, sett forthe to serve us, under yo' conduction, in
respecte of the place you holde, and the zeale and suffiency you have to
serve us [...].

Now forasmuch as it is to be doubted that the forces prepared aswell in Spayn as
in the Low Countryes may be ymployed in sundry attempts, som in Ireland or
Scotland, som against this Realm, we have therefore thought good that o' servant
S' Francis Drake with som of o' owne shipps, such as yo' shall thinke meete & others
apparteyning to o' subiectts could be ordered as well by instruction from yo' self

[...]

210

INTELLIGENCER

An intelligencer, at least from the sixteenth century onwards, was a species of spy or informer who gathered intelligence or information of some kind and was expected to send confidential reports to his paymaster. He might also be a writer of newsletters.

INTERLACING

See STRAPWORK.

INTERLEAF

Partly derived from the Latin *inter*, meaning 'between' or 'among', the term 'interleaf' means an additional leaf inserted between two other leaves in a book or manuscript. A volume is said to be interleaved when it contains a series of such extra leaves, which have been introduced and bound into the original. Interleaves are usually blanks for notes, comments, or additional text to be entered by hand by the reader or user.

INTERLINEAL

Words, such as corrections, revisions, or even glosses, inserted between lines of writing in a document, or else inscribed between lines in a printed text, may be described as interlineal, interlined, or interlinear. Interlineation is the act or process of such insertion or else the inserted text itself.

INTERROGATORY

As legal documents in bill courts (such as Chancery or the equity side of Exchequer), interrogatories are questions set out in writing and put by the plaintiff or defendant (or their counsel) to each other in a civil lawsuit, or else, more usually, put to witnesses or deponents who might throw light on the matter. They are questions that the court might require the relevant party to answer on oath. *See also* ANSWER.

INVENTORY

An inventory is a detailed list of items, usually of articles in a person's possession, such as household goods and chattels, and also of particulars

ILLUS. 41 *The first page of the formal instructions issued by Elizabeth I to Charles, Lord Howard of Effingham, Lord Admiral of England, to patrol the North Sea while Sir Francis Drake patrols the Irish Sea, in preparation for the anticipated invasion by the Spanish Armada. It is written in the secretary hand of an official scribe, with the Queen's flourished signature, or sign manual, near the top, 20 December 1587.*

of lands or properties owned. Inventories, especially in the sixteenth and seventeenth centuries, were most commonly drawn up after a person's death for probate purposes, and incorporated an itemized and attested appraisal of the goods and properties in question. Indeed, the submission of such a document to an ecclesiastical probate court by executors or administrators of any deceased person's estate worth more than £5 was obligatory under an Act of 1521 (framed primarily to enable a legatee to decline a *damnosa hereditas*, a 'cursed inheritance' that comprised more debts than assets). This remained so until 1782, being thereafter optional.

Inventories, which survive in considerable numbers written both on parchment and paper, can be interesting and informative historical documents, throwing light on individuals' occupations, circumstances, styles of life, social status, education, and other features. The inventory for a goldsmith, for instance, may include a detailed list of his jewels; one for a lawyer, cleric, or country gentleman a list of his books; one for a craftsman a list of his tools, and so on (*see* Illus. 42).

A number of inventories from the early thirteenth to late seventeenth century are preserved among Chancery and Exchequer papers in the National Archives at Kew. Many of them relate to persons attainted (such as the conspirators of 1586, Anthony Babington and Chidiock Tichborne: E 154/3/41).

INVISIBLE INK

In the history of secret written communication, so-called 'invisible ink' is one of the methods used as an alternative to encoded messages or cipher. If a letter or message was written in lemon juice, preferably overlaid with an innocuous text written in normal ink to avert suspicion, it would be invisible to the naked eye until placed over a flame, when the secret lettering would become apparent. There are examples of such messages, notably by royalists in clandestine communications at the time of the French Revolution. Intimate letters of other kinds might also be written in this form: for instance, love letters sent by the political writer Alexis de Tocqueville (1805–1859). Such letters are rare, however, probably because in practice the juice left only a faint, barely legible trace and the method proved less than satisfactory.

ILLUS. 42 *A page of the inventory compiled by the Commonwealth Committee of Trustees for the Sale of the Late King's Goods, showing a listing (items 340–352) of some of Charles I's paintings and embroidered portraits, with their estimated values. It is written by a clerk in a mixed hand and subscribed with the papered personal seals and signatures of four Commissioners including the poet George Wither, 1649.*

340 Lewis Games in Little enterd at o 01:00
341 Queen Elizabeth at — 00:02:50:
342: A Child on a blew wood at — 00:01:00
343. Lott done in Silke at — 00:03:00:
344 A Little dog. at — 00 01:00.
345 A greene Bullfinch. at — 00 02 00
346. A Little dog — 00 01 00
347: Christ on y Crosse at — 00 10 00
348 Christs Assention at — 00 01 00:
349 Christs Assention in Gild at — 03 00 00:
350 Mary y Child and some Angells at 50 00 00
By Cavalier Ballions at — 3
351 Mary Magdalen by Scipio Gaetano — 25 00:00:
352 Duroya a roytis after Tytsyan at 08 00 00:
8 picture frames gilt at — 09 00 00:

_____

The totall of this — 96 02 00
By estimate is — 1555 17 06

Geo: Wither

Jo: v: Belcamp

Monfrein

A Mildmay

INVOICE

Since at least the sixteenth century, an invoice (the word related to the French *envoyer*, 'to send') is a type of bill listing goods or other services provided, with their prices or charges. It is submitted by a supplier to the customer receiving them.

IOU

An IOU (meaning 'I owe you') is a document, usually written and signed, whereby a person acknowledges a debt and promises to pay someone a specified sum of money. Such documents are of a casual, fiduciary nature and are not negotiable, neither do they have the legal status of a promissory note.

ITALIC SCRIPT

A term deriving from the name of Italy (*Italia* in Latin and Italian), 'italic' (or 'Italic') denotes a style of script, and a type of printing font, originally associated with Italy and with Humanism (*see* Illus. 1, 9, and 54). Versions of it, with somewhat square-shaped lettering, are technically referred to (by the writing masters, for instance) as 'Roman' script (*see* Illus. 2, 21, 35, and 54 for examples that might be so categorized), although, in practice, this term could also be used loosely as synonymous with 'italic'. A style of sloped lettering still used today in printing (*this is italic*) and which approximates to basic modern character forms, italic, which developed in Italy in the early- to mid-fifteenth century, and which soon even gained some currency among scholars in England, had a major influence on the development of English script in the sixteenth and seventeenth centuries. It led to the development of a mixed or rounded hand by the mid-seventeenth century and then to the virtual extinction of secretary script by the 1700s (*see* SECRETARY SCRIPT).

In the sixteenth and early seventeenth centuries, many if not most literate Englishmen were able to write both secretary and italic, italic being a script favoured sometimes to the exclusion of secretary by a number of noblemen—as exemplified by the cursive italic used by Sir Philip Sidney or what was called the 'rugged Romane hand' of Robert Devereux, second Earl of Essex. With rare exceptions, italic was also the only script generally taught to women. Italic was commonly employed by scribes not only for various Latin texts, but also for some types of formal or semi-calligraphic writings in English. These include such texts as the preliminaries to manuscript tracts written for presentation. Italic might also be used to distinguish important or select words in a piece of otherwise secretary writing, such as headings, proper names, or foreign words, as an alternative to engrossing or underlining. *See also* HUMANISTIC SCRIPT.

Deriving from the Latin *itinerarium*, the term 'itinerary' means a record of a route or journey by land or by sea. It might be an account of a particular journey undertaken at a particular time, or else a description of a route written as a guide for future travellers, or alternatively the plan for an intended journey. An itinerary may, accordingly, be as extensive as, say, *The Itinerary of John Leland* written in the 1540s, the eight-volume autograph manuscript of which is in the Bodleian Library (MSS Top. gen. e. 8–15), or as brief as a small list of places to be passed through on a short excursion. An itinerary may also be a reconstruction by, say, a modern historian, setting out, in a list or chart, from available evidence, a particular journey or series of relocations undertaken by someone years ago.

.

J

JOINTS

The joints of a book are the hinges at the two edges of the spine allowing the covers to be opened. In strict bibliographical usage, the joints are the outside junctions of the spine and covers and the hinges the inside. The joints or hinges of a printed or manuscript volume are among its most vulnerable features, most likely to become cracked or broken over the years through wear.

JOTTING

Deriving from the Greek and Latin word *iota* (for the letter *i*, the smallest in the alphabet), the term 'jotting' means a brief, hastily written, scribbled note or inscription. Since they were produced for largely ephemeral purposes, jottings made in the early modern period are more likely to survive if they happen to be in substantial notebooks or commonplace books rather than on separate leaves, let alone on wax tables. Another rich site for jottings is books, in many of which the blank pages, spaces, or margins were used by early owners or their families, often juveniles, for random scribbling and pen-trials.

JOURNAL

A journal is substantially the same thing as a diary: i.e. a daily record of occurrences (*see* DIARY). While the terms are technically interchangeable, the word 'journal' has tended to be reserved for more formal types of diary involving more extended description or narrative (*see* Illus. 43). Journals may have a wider or professional application beyond the purely personal and, moreover, are not generally confined to the format of the printed stationery diary. Characteristic types of manuscript journal would include travel journals (detailing daily events and personal observations and impressions on an excursion or overseas tour), parliamentary journals (recording daily proceedings in the House of Commons or House of Lords), maritime journals (giving perhaps fuller or less formulaic accounts of daily events on

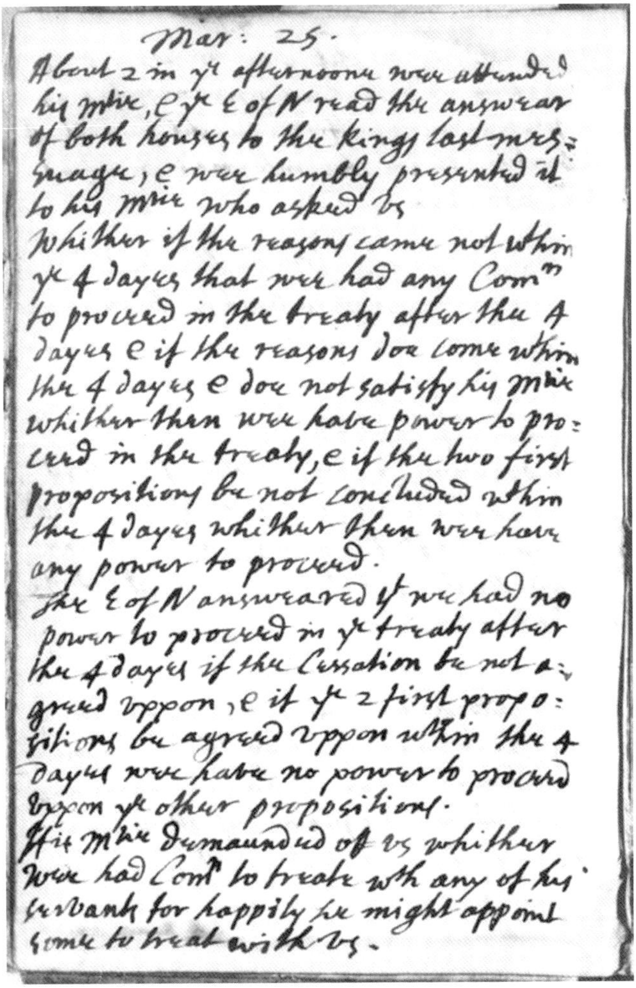
Mar: 25.
About 2 in ye afternoone wee attended
his mtie, & ye E of N read the answear
of both houses to the Kings last mes:
sage, & wee humbly presented it
to his mtie who asked vs
whither if the reasons came not wthin
ye 4 dayes that wee had any Comn
to proceed in the treaty after the 4
dayes & if the reasons doe come wthin
the 4 dayes & doe not satisfy his mtie
whither then wee have power to pro:
ceed in the treaty, & if the two first
propositions be not concluded wthin
the 4 dayes whither then wee have
any power to proceed.
The E of N answeared yt wee had no
power to proceed in ye treaty after
the 4 dayes if the Cessation be not a:
greed vppon, & if ye 2 first propo:
sitions be agreed vppon wthin the 4
dayes wee have no power to proceed
vppon ye other propositions.
His Mtie demaunded of vs whither
wee had Comn to treate wth any of his
servants for happily he might appoint
some to treat with vs.

ILLUS. 43 *A page of the autograph journal of Bulstrode Whitelocke, recording the Parliamentary Commissioners' negotiations with Charles I at Oxford on 25 March 1643 during the English Civil War.*

voyages than logs), and gardening journals, as well as certain business journals that record commercial transactions.

JOUSTING CHEQUE

From at least the thirteenth to the early seventeenth century, chivalric tournaments flourished, in which noblemen on horseback competed in lance and sword combats before large, often royal, audiences. Especially popular from the early fifteenth century was tilting, a form of jousting that involved mounted knights fighting each other with lances across a barrier (the tilt); without a tilt it was known as 'running at large'. When the contestants were separated by the tilt, which was generally made of wood, they rode against each other left arm to left arm, each lance angled across the barrier being more likely to snap on contact than to penetrate the oncoming knight.

A jousting cheque, sometimes known as a 'score cheque', was a document on which heralds noted the scores achieved by the knights. None is known to survive, however, before one for Prince Arthur's marriage tournament in 1501 (the details preserved in a later copy in the College of Arms, MS M.3), which records the scores for both tilting and running at large. Surviving cheques, usually written on paper, are set out in columns of parallelograms or boxes—those on the left side each showing the name of a Challenger (also know as a Defender or *Tenant*); those on the right showing the Answerers (or *Venants*). Each parallelogram is bisected by a central horizontal line, extending beyond the right side of the box, on which are marked the courses run. Lances broken are represented by vertical strokes crossing through one of the horizontals: top line for a score on the head; middle for the body; and bottom for a foul. Attaints (hits which fail to shatter the lance) are indicated by shorter strokes above the lines.

The majority of surviving cheques are preserved at the College of Arms and include scores for the Field of Cloth of Gold (1520) and other tournaments in Henry VIII's reign. Elizabethan examples include tilts featuring Sir Philip Sidney, Sir Christopher Hatton, Sir Fulke Greville, Robert Devereux, second Earl of Essex, and the Queen's Champion, Sir Henry Lee. One for the Accession Day tournament on 17 November 1596, for example, has Essex challenging all comers and breaking no fewer than ninety-eight lances against his eighteen opponents. No cheques appear to survive after the Elizabethan period, although in the reign of James I there is a tilting list (without the score) for 26 March 1616. The last noteworthy tournament at the English court was for the marriage of Charles I and Henrietta Maria in 1625.

K

KALENDARIUM

The Latin word *kalendarium*, meaning some kind of periodically arranged account book, is applied to medieval manuscript calendars and also to manuals of, for instance, astronomical, astrological, medical, or horticultural texts based on the changing months and seasons of the year. The word is occasionally found used as a formal term for an almanac or a diary. *Kalendarium* appears, for instance, as the heading to the principle manuscript of the celebrated diary of John Evelyn (1620–1706), begun probably in the late 1630s and covering the greater part of his life from 1620 to 1697 (now in the British Library), as well as in the title of his published *Kalendarium hortense: or, the Gard'ners Almanac* (1664).

KING'S REMEMBRANCER

See REMEMBRANCER.

L

LABEL

A label is generally a narrow strip of paper or other material affixed to something and often bearing lettering of some kind. In connection with parchment deeds and the like, however, a label can be a pendent strip or tag at the foot bearing a wax seal. It is in this connection that a satirist could characterize a scrivener as having 'no signe but a few tottering Labells, which are hang'd there to shew their masters desert'. A label might also be a strip of parchment or paper attached or affixed to a document containing supplementary text or, in the case of a will, a codicil. Other types of label include book-labels (*see* BOOK-LABEL) and postal labels (small slips of paper with adhesive backing, such as 'BY AIR MAIL'/ *par avion* stickers).

LACES

The word 'laces' is sometimes used instead of 'cords' in connection with the attachment to certain documents of pendent seals. Laces can also be a feature of some early modern letters, especially those of royal or aristocratic origin, where the document may be tied and secured by means of laces comprising narrow coloured silk ribbons passed through slits in the folded letter and then sealed with wax. Since they were cut in order to open the letter, only the partial remains of such laces affixed by wax to the paper are likely to be present in surviving letters.

LACUNA

A *lacuna* (plural: *lacunae*; the Latin word means 'hole') is a blank space left in a manuscript or other text for a missing word or words. *Lacunae* are most frequently encountered when the scribe has been unable to decipher particular words in his exemplar or when his exemplar is defective. In his *Battle of the Books* (1710), satirizing the classical scholar Richard Bentley, Jonathan

Swift humorously introduces into his own text *lacunae* which are filled with asterisks and signalled in the margin as 'hiatus in MS'.

LAID DOWN

A document, illustration, or any other piece of paper is described as 'laid down', or 'laid-down', when it is pasted or glued on a leaf in a book or album or else on a separate sheet of paper. The item may be pasted in such a way that the verso is rendered inaccessible by the backing sheet; alternatively, the latter may have holes cut into it to allow text on the verso of the document (such as an address, endorsement, or signatures) to show through and be legible (*see also* MOUNT). Some manuscripts comprising a single leaf or bifolium are found mounted in this way when collectors, or even library or archival conservationists, have considered this the best way to preserve them, especially when their condition is fragile.

LAID PAPER

Laid paper, as distinct from wove paper, is paper made in a mould or frame containing wires that leave in the paper narrowly spaced wire-lines (which run the length of the unfolded sheet) and widely spaced chain-lines (which run the width of the unfolded sheet), as well as watermarks. All paper before about 1800 was hand-made and all of it until about 1755 was laid paper. Modern machine-made paper can sometimes simulate laid paper, but it cannot technically be described as such if not hand-made. *Compare* WOVE PAPER.

LAMBREQUINS

See MANTLING.

LAND REGISTRY

See TITLE DEED.

LAST WILL AND TESTAMENT

See WILL AND TESTAMENT.

LATIN

Throughout the medieval and early modern period, Latin, the language originally spoken by the ancient Romans, effectively dominated the areas that once formed part of the Roman Empire. Even with its medieval evolution and regional variations, it was the *lingua franca* of Christendom; the language of church liturgies and sacred texts; the prime language of official, ecclesiastical, and legal documents; and was routinely taught to, and written by, large numbers of educated men (if not women), so that, among other things, scholars could readily communicate with their fellow-scholars of other nations in the commonly understood language. Many also spoke the language, and lectures and disputations in Latin, as well as the staging of plays in Latin, were a normal part of university education. This was despite there being no European consensus about its pronunciation (the philosopher Giordano Bruno, for instance, was mocked for his Italian pronunciation of Latin when he came to lecture at Oxford in 1583). There was, moreover, a flourishing literature of learned discourses, poems, histories, narratives, and other genres written in Latin, in England and elsewhere, much of it confined purely to manuscripts.

A reaction against the use of Latin for English legal and official documents came in the Commonwealth period in the 1650s, when Latin (as well as law-French) was banned in favour of the vernacular understood by everyone. Latin was restored as the official language for legal records with the Restoration in 1660 and not finally abolished until 1733, even though so many precedents of the law, as well as names of writs, remained couched in a language that an ever dwindling number of people was able to understand. Fundamental to so much European culture and history, Latin remains of paramount importance for the deciphering of vast numbers of historical records before that date, as well as for an appreciation of the huge corpus of literature in Latin.

LATITAT

See WRIT OF LATITAT.

LAW REPORTS

See YEAR BOOKS.

LAYOUT

'Layout' is a term chiefly encountered in connection with printing and printed books, but it can equally be applied to manuscripts. The layout is the way the text and ancillary features (such as running heads, illustrations, footnotes, rules, margins, sidenotes, glosses, page numbers, catchwords, etc.) are physically arranged on the page. *Compare* MISE-EN-PAGE.

LEAD POINT

See DRY POINT and PLUMMET.

LEAF

A leaf is a piece of paper or parchment comprising two pages: i.e. the recto, or front side of the leaf, and the verso, or back side. In practice a leaf is formed when a sheet is folded at least once, in which case each half becomes a leaf, whether it remains conjunct with its fellow or cut and separated. In manuscripts, and some early printed books, the leaf is also known as a folio, and leaves are numbered, or foliated, as, for example, 'folio 1 recto, folio 1 verso, folio 2 recto', etc. They are generally cited in abridged form as 'fol. 1r, fol. 2r', etc., or 'f. 1r, f. 2r', etc. Leaves in a book are often loosely referred to as pages, but a page is strictly only one side of a leaf.

LEASE

A lease is a contract, generally (though at common law not necessarily) embodied in a written document, whereby, in return for payment or subject to stipulated rents, one party grants another the possession of land or property for a fixed term while retaining a reversionary interest in the property (*see* Illus. 36). Hence it is also the period of time to which the contract applies, which may vary from a few years or less to the lifetime of the lessee(s), or even on rare occasions to virtual perpetuity, for a nominal period of, say, 4,000 years. The most common type of lease takes the form of an indenture, the half retained by the lessor being known as the 'counterpart lease'.

LEASE AND RELEASE

Lease and release was a common mode of conveyance of freehold property, and therefore the instrument that effected it, from the early seventeenth century, when the practice was legally recognized, until the 1840s. It was designed to keep the conveyance private by avoiding the kind of deed respecting freehold that would have had to be enrolled as a public record in accordance with the Statute of Enrolments (1536). A lease and release involved the conclusion of a bargain and sale whereby someone sold the lease of a property for a specified period, usually one year, and then released the reversion: i.e. negated by deed the lessor's retained interest in the property.

LECTERN

Deriving from a form of the Latin *legere* ('to read'), the term 'lectern' denotes a reading or writing desk, generally characterized by a sloping surface and designed, for the most part, to support large or folio books which cannot easily be hand-held. In church, lecterns are where the choir rest their singing materials or from which readings are delivered to the congregation, the latter type traditionally being elaborately carved in wood or stone, often in the form of an eagle with outstretched wings over a column. Lecterns in scholars' private studies or in scriptoria are frequently depicted in medieval and also in some early modern illustrations of scribes at work, both monastic and secular. Some examples are depicted comprising a sloped writing surface, like a triangular box on a flat desk, above which, attached by a metal swivel, is a second triangular box supporting the scribe's exemplar at or just above his eye level. A rest or support of some kind for the exemplar being copied may well have been a common feature of lecterns and writing desks, as is noted by John Evelyn in his essay 'Of manuscripts' where he refers to the ancient '*Scribs* or *Librarii* hanging' their scrolls 'ouer a convenient frame before their Deskes, perhaps not vnlike what our Scriveners and Lawyers Clearks now vse' (*see* Illus. 22). In the early modern period, lecterns in libraries could also incorporate bookshelves, as well as being commonly situated below bookshelves.

LECTIONARY

Deriving from the Latin *lectio* ('reading' or 'what is read'), the term 'lectionary' means a book containing passages of scripture appointed to be read in a Catholic, Orthodox, or Anglican church; alternatively, it is a list of the passages to be read. Various types of lectionary came in medieval times to be incorporated in the Missal. Examples as late as the sixteenth century can be richly embellished and illuminated.

LEDGER

A ledger, or in older spelling 'lieger', is a register of some kind, usually a substantial manuscript book, originally blank or ruled, and sturdily bound, which is apt to remain in one particular place for reference and entry purposes (*compare* COUCHER). Ledger bindings tend to be characterized by broad leather bands across the spine of the book with criss-cross interlacing, both reinforcing the spine and reducing the chances of the book's slipping on a slanting surface, a type of binding sometimes known as 'stationery binding'. Ledgers may be of folio or large quarto size, but are commonly long and narrow in format. They are usually associated with ecclesiastical, mercantile, estate, administrative, or other professional financial accounts, record- or book-keeping, and often cover extensive periods of time.

LEDGER FORMAT, LEDGER-SIZE

Although ledgers can vary in size, including folio and large quarto formats, their frequently long, narrow shape accounts for the terms 'in ledger format' or 'ledger-size'. A manuscript, of whatever size, may be described as 'in ledger format' when it is made up of sheets folded into gatherings lengthways, i.e. bisected at the shorter side, as opposed to bifolia resulting from sheets folded widthways (*see* Illus. 73). A characteristic ledger-size manuscript is likely to measure in the region of 15 × 5 ½ inches (*c.*38 × 14 cm).

See LIMB.

LEGEND

A legend is an inscription, motto, or caption that accompanies some kind of graphic representation, such as wording set out beneath heraldic coats of arms or on maps, paintings, or coins. Besides its more general meaning, as a myth or supposedly historical story handed down by tradition, a legend in medieval times could also be the same thing as a legendarium: i.e. a book of legends, usually of lives of saints, or of readings used in church containing scriptural passages or extracts from lives of saints.

LEMMA

A term of Greek origin, 'lemma' (plural: lemmata) denotes wording prefixed as a heading, title, or subtitle briefly setting out the argument or explaining the tenor or subject of a composition, tract, or essay. Titles of considerable length, effectively constituting lemmata, are not unusual in early modern discourses and pamplets, both manuscript and printed.

In editing terminology, the lemma is the text chosen by an editor as his or her base or normative text, or else a cue word or phrase quoted from it. Against this text variant readings may be recorded or contrasted in the editor's collations. To save repetition, the lemma is usually represented by a swung dash (~). Thus in collations for a poem by John Donne: 'like an] ~ to ~ B, C; ~ ~ old D' means that the reading in the base text is 'like an'; the reading in the texts designated B and C is 'like to an'; and that in text D is 'like an old'.

LETTER

A letter is a character of the alphabet (*a*, *b*, *c*, etc.). A letter is also one of the most common types of written communication: namely, a manuscript (or, later, typescript) epistle sent by one person to another, generally as a private message, though many are addressed to a larger body of people and intended for a more widespread or public audience. Letters, inscribed on one kind of surface or another, including clay tablets and papyrus, date from ancient times, early letters found in England including Roman examples at Hadrian's Wall. Most surviving letters, however, date from the fifteenth century onwards, a period that coincides with a general increase in literacy.

In the early modern period, when writing paper came in single sheets that tended to be folded as bifolia, the first and, if necessary, second and third pages would normally be used for writing the text and the fourth page for the address. The common procedure for folding the bifolium or leaf would be to fold the top third down and the bottom third up, and then fold the oblong paper about two fifths inwards towards the centre, tucking one side into the 'pocket' formed by the other. A wax seal would then be applied to where the two sides overlapped. This packet would therefore leave the address exposed on the outer side, obverse to the seal, and, when opened (with a knife or by hand), would generally leave portions of the seal at both sides, as well as perhaps a portion of the paper adhering to the seal where torn away. Such features, as well as the fold marks and possible soiling of the address panel where exposed, incidentally indicate that the letter was actually sent, as opposed to one composed or copied and retained by the writer. Some letter-writers were also inclined to write private messages within a triangular area at the bottom right-hand corner of a letter, which was meant to be read and then torn away, although the recipient sometimes left it intact. *See also* ENVELOPE.

Letters may, of course, deal with any number of subjects and serve a wide range of functions, ranging from the expediting of practical, routine, legal, or business matters to personal and intimate communications, written in styles ranging from the highly formal to the casual and conversational. Not surprisingly, apart from those of great philosophical, scientific, and intellectual content written by great thinkers, it is the personal—the more confidential, passionate, dramatic, or amusingly scandalous the better—that tend to engage the historical imagination and throw light on human behaviour. These in turn may range from ardent love letters (such as those of Henry VIII to Anne Boleyn, preserved in the Vatican Library), impassioned pleas for clemency (such as that by the traitor Anthony Babington in 1586, to which Queen Elizabeth remained impervious), poignant farewell letters (by Sir Walter Ralegh to his wife, for instance, on the eve of anticipated execution), letters of assignation (such as one by the Earl of Rochester in the 1670s arranging a tryst with a lady 'at fowr of clock'), or letters by an eighteenth-century London madame (discreetly informing an Earl of the new girls at his service when he visits town), to challenges to duels (one by 'TW' to Thomas Lewis *c.*1680 demands satisfaction 'att 6 of the clock this evening with single rapier' upon pain of being 'posted for a coward'), and other barbed reactions to perceived offences.

The term 'letters', used in the plural form (from the Latin *litteræ*), is also one applied to certain kinds of formal, official, and legal documents, such as letters patent and letters of administration, which are largely named and classified according to their function.

LETTERBOOK

A letterbook, or letter-book, is a manuscript book in which normally copies, or transcripts, of outgoing or incoming letters are entered. Their use is

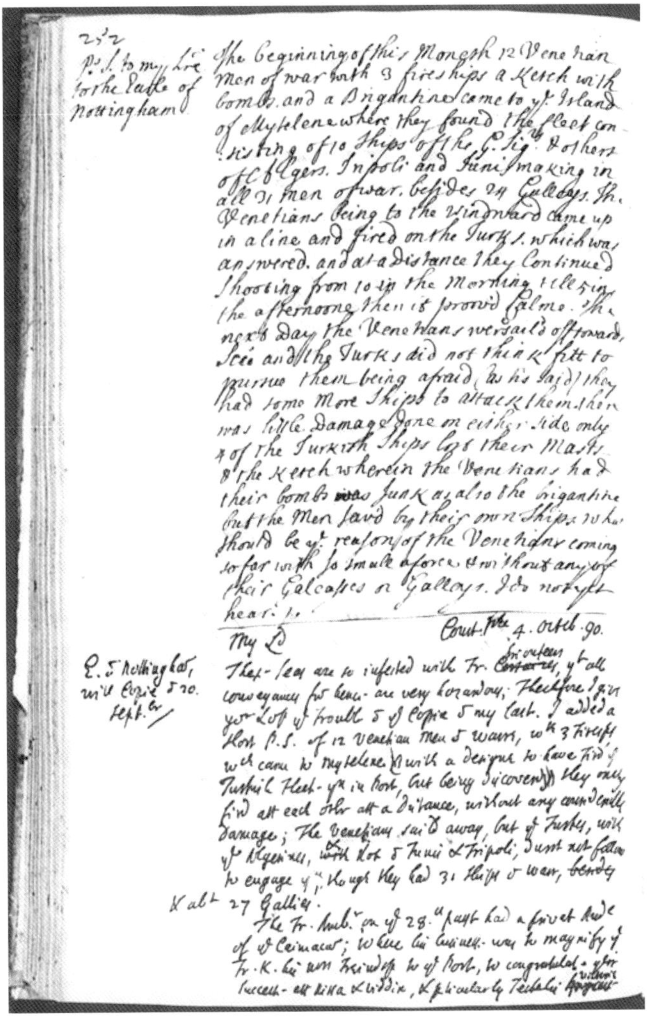

ILLUS. 44 *A page in one of the partly autograph diplomatic letterbooks of Sir William Trumbull, when Ambassador to Constantinople, including a draft letter by him dated 4 October 1690 following a copy of a letter in the hand of a secretary.*

common in government, diplomatic, naval, military, commercial, and other fields, where it is considered useful to have copies of letters, made usually by secretaries, as a retained record (*see* Illus. 44). Letterbooks may also be compilations of letters made for personal reasons, such as letters by a particular writer or group of writers, or as models of epistolary art.

LETTER CARD

A letter card is a type of postal stationery, originally introduced in Belgium in 1882 and officially adopted by the British Post Office in 1892. It is a letter comprising a sheet of stiff paper or card folded over and sealed at the outer edges by perforated strips that can be removed by the recipient in order to read the written contents. The use of letter cards was discontinued in the 1970s.

LETTER OF ATTORNEY

See POWER OF ATTORNEY.

LETTER OF CREDIT

A letter of credit is a type of commercial or business letter used since medieval times to facilitate trade. It was written by one person to another, commonly a banker or merchant, requiring him to give credit or specified goods to the bearer or to a person named therein. The writer undertook to pay any bills drawn by the beneficiary of the credit in accordance with the conditions specified.

LETTER OPENER

'Letter opener' is another term for 'paper knife' or 'paper opener'. Today letter openers can also take the form of desktop automatic machines used in businesses for opening stacks of envelopes at high speed.

LETTERS CLOSE

'Letters close' (Latin: *litterae clausae*) is a plural term often denoting a single document, and means private letters or writs issued by a monarch or Chancery, on a variety of subjects, but for the most part giving orders or instructions to individual royal officials. They are distinguished from letters patent in that they were not 'open' for public inspection but 'closed', being folded and sealed on the outside for the attention of the particular person(s) to whom they were addressed. Such letters and writs, up until the 1540s, were, nevertheless, commonly enrolled in Chancery records. *See* CLOSE ROLLS.

LETTER SHEET

A letter sheet is a type of postal stationery comprising a sheet of writing paper in which is already incorporated a stamp of some kind indicating prepayment of postage or exemption from postal charges. Pioneered as early as 1818 in Sardinia and developed in 1838 in New South Wales, this type of stationery was introduced in Britain in 1840 in the form of the Mulready letter sheet. Designed by William Mulready (1786–1863), it bore around the address portion an elaborate printed design showing Britannia sending forth her messengers to different peoples of the world, with women and children eagerly reading their mail. Widely ridiculed for its pomposity, Mulready's pictorial stationery was replaced a year later by other types of letter sheet and envelope.

LETTERS MISSIVE

Deriving from the Latin *missum* ('something sent'), the term 'letters missive', sometimes applied to a single document, means letters sent by a superior authority, such as a monarch usually under the Privy Seal, conveying a command, permission, or recommendation. In the Church of England they are letters sent by a sovereign nominating the person whom a dean and chapter are to elect as bishop.

LETTERS OF ADMINISTRATION

'Letters of administration' is the legal term for a grant made by a court of probate allowing a person to act as administrator or administratrix of the estate of someone who died intestate (i.e. without leaving a will), or who failed to name an executor, or whose executors refused to administer. The person so appointed is normally the next of kin or someone closely associated with the deceased and will have the same powers as an executor.

LETTERS OF CAPTION

'Letters of caption' is the formal term applied to a letter written by an ecclesiastical dignitary requesting the help of a secular authority in apprehending or bringing to heel a persistent offender of the Church or unrepentant excommunicate.

LETTERS OF COLLATION

'Letters of collation' is the term applied to an official letter of authorization whereby a cleric is admitted to a church or a benefice within a particular bishop's gift by a procedure avoiding the bishop's presenting a clergyman to himself.

LETTERS OF CONFRATERNITY

Since medieval times, letters of confraternity in the Catholic Church are letters or documents relating to persons or institutions elected to confraternity with a religious house, hospital, or community because of their help or support for it. Because letters of confraternity were fairly mass-produced and might bestow upon the recipient benefits, privileges, or spiritual rewards in return for charitable donations, they are sometimes confused with letters of indulgence (*compare* INDULGENCES), although their texts are sometimes less formulaic than indulgences and leave provision for the particular body or individual concerned.

LETTERS OF HORNING

In Scotland, letters of horning were official letters or instructions issued by or on behalf of a monarch under the Signet Seal commanding a law officer to charge a recalcitrant debtor to make payment or perform a particular duty within a specified time under pain of being put to the horn: i.e. declared a rebel or outlaw by an officer's giving three blasts on a horn in a public proclamation. The letters in various burghs were recorded in official Registers of Hornings, some of which are now in the National Archives of Scotland.

LETTERS OF INDULGENCE

See INDULGENCES.

LETTERS OF MANUMISSION

See MANUMISSION.

LETTERS OF MARQUE

Letters of marque are a commission issued in wartime on the authority of the Crown to a private shipowner or commander empowering him to fit out his ship for service as a privateer to attack or capture enemy shipping, the prizes usually to be divided between the shipowner, captain, and crew.

LETTERS OF REVERSION

Reversion in English law is the interest an owner retains in property that is granted, leased, or rented to someone else. Reversion in Scottish law is the right to redeem (usually heritable) property. Letters of reversion in Scotland are the formal instruments made by persons holding other people's property in security for the repayment of debts, whereby they undertake to restore the property to the owner when the debt is settled.

LETTERS OF SAFE-CONDUCT

See SAFE-CONDUCT.

LETTERS OF SLAINS

From medieval times onwards, letters of slains in Scotland were a written statement, made by relatives of someone who had been slain, declaring that they had received an 'assythment' (i.e. indemnification for the loss made to them by the slayer) and could therefore support the offender's application to the Crown for a pardon.

LETTERS PATENT

Letters patent, or Letters Patent (sometimes cited in the Latin form *litteræ patentes*), are official letters or instructions delivered in open rather than sealed form and shown in public as instruments of authorization, as opposed to letters close, which are more private. Those issued by medieval ecclesiastical authorities tended to be couched in formulaic wording beginning *Per hoc praesens publicum instrumentum cunctis pateat evidenter*. The more common secular letters patent, from medieval times onwards, were issued by the Chancery under the Great Seal and addressed in Latin 'To all to whom these presents shall come', concluding 'In witness whereof we have caused these our letters to be made patent...'. Thus they differ in their wording from charters, which have elaborate formulaic addresses to the leaders of society and are always executed in the presence of named witnesses. Engrossed by Chancery scribes on parchment—before 1733 almost invariably in Latin except for occasional entries in English and the compulsory use of English during the Commonwealth period in the 1650s—letters patent were grants by or on behalf of the Crown conferring upon individuals or corporate bodies, such as towns and livery companies, a wide range of special privileges. These included grants of land, titles, offices, pensions, rights (such as to hold markets or fairs), monopolies, pardons, patents for inventions (*see* PATENT), and many other liberties and benefits. Letters patent were enrolled in Chancery on the Patent Rolls. While all letters patent are issued by royal authority, the royal element is sometimes stressed by calling them Royal Letters Patent. *See* ROYAL LETTERS PATENT.

LIBER AMICORUM

A *liber amicorum* (plural: *libri amicorum*; the Latin phrase means 'book of friends') is sometimes also called an *album amicorum* and is a type of album that flourished especially in the sixteenth and seventeenth centuries, originally in Protestant northern Germany, although the fashion spread widely on the continent. *Libri amicorum* were compiled by gentlemen (noblemen, students, lawyers, diplomats, etc.), often young men, who encouraged their friends, hosts, or honourable guests or visitors to write verses, inscriptions, or drawings in them, as well as their signatures, as souvenirs or mementos. In some respects they were forerunners of the autograph album, although *libri amicorum* could sometimes be very much grander productions: written, for instance, on vellum, as well as paper, of varying size, of sometimes considerable length (200 pages or more), leather-bound, and highly decorated or illuminated, with elaborate pen-and-ink or painted illustrations, such as portraits of the contributors and their coats of arms. Famous English people who inscribed *libri amicorum* either on their own travels or for visitors bringing their own albums with them include Charles I (as Prince in 1613, for Sir Thomas Cuming of Scotland); Ben Jonson and Sir Walter Ralegh (for Captain Francis Segar); Jonson again (for the theosopher Joachim Morsius on 1 January 1619/20); Lancelot Andrewes (for Johannes Opsimathes of Moravia in 1616); and John Milton (for Camillus Cardoinus of Naples on 10 June 1639; for Christoph Arnold of Nuremberg on 19/29 November 1651; and, when blind, for Johannes Zollikofer on 26 September 1656).

LIBRARIAN

A librarian is generally a keeper or custodian of a library. The term stems from derivative forms of the Latin *liber* ('book'), although in earlier periods it was closer to the Latin *librarius*, applied to various people who dealt with books, including scribes and booksellers.

LICENCE

As a written document on paper or parchment, a licence is a formal authorization giving permission for someone to do something that would otherwise be prohibited, illegal, or at least restricted. Thus a dramatic licence is a document signed by the Master of Revels or Lord Chamberlain giving an acting company or troupe of entertainers permission to perform (*see* Illus. 45); a licence to travel (or passport) is a written authorization allowing a person to travel abroad, and so on. Other licences issued by civil and ecclesiastical authorities include those allowing someone to sell or trade certain commodities, to open a stall in a market, to act as a letter-carrier, to eat meat in Lent, or to get married.

LICENCE IN MORTMAIN

See LICENCE OF MORTMAIN.

LICENCE OF ALIENATION

A licence of alienation and licence to alienate are both letters patent under the Great Seal whereby the Crown gives consent for one of its tenants-in-chief to alienate land—i.e. transfer the lease, possession, or ownership of the land to someone else—whether by sale, by inheritance, or by some other arrangement. Until the seventeenth century such licences usually incurred a

ILLUS. 45 *A licence for a troupe of acrobats, allowing them to 'exercise Daunceinge on the Roapes, Tumbling, Vaulting and other such like ffeates' with music. It is written on vellum (c.10 ¾ × 11 inches or 28 × 30 cm) in the predominantly secretary hand of an official scribe, with occasional engrossed lettering, and is signed by Sir Henry Herbert, Master of the Revels, 29 August 1631.*

payment, or fine, to the Crown, commonly amounting to a third of the annual value of the land. If the tenant had transferred property without first obtaining a licence, then he would have to pay another fine to secure a pardon of alienation. These licences and pardons are among the letters patent enrolled in Chancery in the Patent Rolls.

LICENCE OF MORTMAIN

A licence of mortmain, or licence in mortmain (the French word means 'dead hand'), issued by the Crown was necessary after 1279 for any lands to be alienated, or conveyed, to the Church or to a college or other corporate body after the death of a vassal or tenant without being forfeit to the Crown under the feudal system of land tenure. The technical procedure involved the vestment of the land in a 'dead hand': i.e. a corporation that neither died nor had heirs. Traces of this legal process survived until as late as 1960.

LICENCE TO ALIENATE

See LICENCE OF ALIENATION.

LICENCE TO MARRY

See MARRIAGE LICENCE.

LICENCE TO PASS BEYOND THE SEAS

Although types of diplomatic passports were issued by officials from medieval times onwards, what is generally known as a licence to pass beyond the seas is a type of English passport issued generally by the monarch, who had a prerogative right to control the movements of his or her subjects overseas. Such licences are most in evidence (at least as recorded in registers in the National Archives at Kew, E 157) from 1573 in the reign of Elizabeth I until 1677 in the reign of Charles II. Usually engrossed on vellum and personally signed by the sovereign, characteristic Elizabethan examples include one issued as early as 25 May 1572, allowing Philip Sidney 'to go out of this *our* Realm of England into the partes of beyond the Seas, and there for his attayning to the knowledge of forrayn Languages to remayn the space of twoo yeeres' (New College, Oxford, MS 328, fol. 40), and one issued in 1593 to William Cooke, permitting him to go abroad for two years 'for his better attayning of languages, learninge, knowledge and experience' (Gloucestershire Record Office, D326/X14). Jacobean and Caroline examples include those granted to soldiers serving in the Low Countries in 1613–33 and to people emigrating to America and other colonies, as well as to merchants and other passengers going abroad for various reasons.

In sixteenth- and seventeenth-century England, before the renewed Licensing Act of 1662 expired in 1695, printers and publishers required a licence to be signed by the official licenser of the press before a book could be legally printed and distributed. The formula authorizing the printing is known as the 'imprimatur' (the Latin word means 'let it be printed'), and this is often reproduced, usually on a separate page, at the beginning of the printed books themselves. A number of original licences do survive, however, in the form of the imprimaturs actually written and signed by licensers on the manuscripts submitted to them for approval. Such examples include manuscript works by Sir John Harington (Richard Bancroft's licence reading 'This Apologye I have pervsed and doe think it may well be printed by Mr Richard Field or any other printer', 29 August 1596, now in the British Library, Add. MS 46368), and Sir Philip Sidney and the Countess of Pembroke (by John Langley, for printing their version of the Psalms in the 1640s, now at Trinity College, Cambridge, MS R. 3.16). In practice, many books and pamphlets were printed without a licence, as enforcement of the Act was very irregular.

LIGATURE

Deriving from a form of the Latin *ligare* ('to bind'), the term 'ligature' in palaeography means a stroke connecting two letters: for instance, the raised curve or loop which may join together *st* or *fl* in early modern scribal manuscripts (*see* Illus. 78). In printing, a ligature may be cast in one piece to combine more than two letters: for instance *ffi*. The term is also sometimes used to denote forms in which two letters are combined in modified shape as a digraph, such as *æ* and *œ*. Also, in the notation of music from about the thirteenth to sixteenth centuries, a ligature was a graphic sign indicating to the performer that two or more consecutive notes of a melody were to be played or sung as a connected phrase.

LIMB

In palaeography, a limb, or leg, is the stroke making a rounded extension to the vertical stem or ascender found in a letter such as *h*. When the extension is closed, as in *b*, it is a lobe or bowl.

LIMN

To 'limn' (the term derived from the Latin *illuminare*, 'to light up') is to paint, usually a coloured portrait, or else, especially in medieval manuscripts, to illuminate or embellish with gold. A limner is therefore one who paints, illustrates, or illuminates manuscripts, as opposed to a scribe who is responsible for the text.

LINE

A line of text is a verbal unit comprising a single row or series of words running across the page. In prose, it may reach the full width of the page or else—if it is at the end of a paragraph, for instance—reach only part-way across. In poetry, a line is the same as a verse. From medieval times onwards, there have been various methods of keeping lines horizontal and regular (*see* RULE), although without ruling, the direction of writing on blank paper can sometimes be erratic. Hence Jonathan Swift's amusing (if unfair) comment on the Lilliputians in Chapter VI of *Gulliver's Travels* (1726):

> But their Manner of Writing is very peculiar; being neither from the Left to the Right, like the *Europeans*; nor from the Right to the Left, like the *Arabians*; nor from up to down, like the *Chinese*; nor from down to up, like the *Cascagians*; but aslant from one Corner of the Paper to the other, like Ladies in *England*.

LINE-FILLER

See FILLER.

LINERS

'Liners' is a term given to the paste-down and free endpaper at each end of a printed or manuscript volume when they are made not of plain paper but of some thicker or better-quality material, such as marbled paper or silk. Liners became fashionable for occasional high-quality bound books, including manuscripts, about the mid-seventeenth century onwards.

LITERARY MANUSCRIPTS

Literary manuscripts are generally understood to be manuscripts bearing texts that may be classified as 'literature', as opposed to musical, legal, scientific, ecclesiastical, or belonging to some other categorization. The definition of 'literature' as currently understood is, however, considerably more liberal than it used to be. Traditionally literature was understood to mean original verbal compositions marked by aesthetic qualities, inventiveness, and imagination, including such genres as poems, plays, novels, and other works of fiction. Distinctions have become increasingly unclear, so that literature may well be considered to include sermons, discourses, political or theological tracts, devotional writings, travel writing, biographies, histories, and other categories of non-fiction, whether marked by traditional literary qualities (fine style, perception, originality, etc.) or not. At its most extreme, literature may be defined as anything written, any verbal construction, any text whatsoever comprising letters. Definitions are further complicated by associated written documents, such as notebooks or commonplace books, which may claim status as literature (especially when they throw light on perhaps early stages of ideas formulated by a writer or thinker) even by more traditional standards.

'Literary manuscripts' perhaps remains a provisionally useful term to distinguish manuscripts bearing texts distinguished primarily for their imaginative or fictive qualities, whatever their subject matter, rather than non-fictional works reporting or discussing real events, experiences, issues, and debates. Nevertheless, there will always be works of technically the latter kind that stretch the boundaries of any categorization because of their extraordinary stylistic or aesthetic qualities: Edward Gibbon's *Decline and Fall of the Roman Empire*, for instance, or T. E. Lawrence's *Seven Pillars of Wisdom*. For examples of literary manuscripts, *see* Illus. 21, 28, 35, 65, and 91.

LITTERA ANTIQUA
See HUMANISTIC SCRIPT.

LITTERA CANCELLARESCA
See CHANCERY HAND.

LIVERY OF SEISIN
See SASINE.

LOBE
In palaeography, a lobe, or bowl, is the closed curved stroke appended to the stem in letters such as *b*, *d*, *p*, and *q*.

LOG
The term 'log-book', usually abbreviated to 'log', denotes a manuscript journal in which are regularly or systematically recorded daily events, most especially one kept on board a ship at sea, with entries usually made by the captain, midshipman, or other officer. Typical entries tend to detail matters such as the navigational course, winds, temperatures, victuals taken on board, other ships and ports encountered, breaches of discipline, punishments inflicted, and other incidents on board ship thought worth recording. Sea-captains were, in fact, obliged to keep such journals, both in the Navy and by commercial shipping companies such as the East India Company. They provided a record

of voyages that, among other things, indicated the ships' seaworthiness in various weather conditions and supplied information on such practical matters as whether the casks of victuals when opened were satisfactory (if they were not, claims could be made against the suppliers). They could then be used as the basis for reports to the Admiralty or company owners.

Logs can take the form of a journal in which a particular officer records his observations while serving on different ships, or else be the log of a particular ship perhaps written by more than one man serving on that ship. Since at least the seventeenth century logs tend to be in folio-size format, neatly but closely drawn up, often in columns (for dates, longitude and latitude position, winds, remarks, etc.), bound in vellum, leather, or other material and often encased in protective canvas. Many logs, particularly in the nineteenth century, are printed commercial stationery, like diaries, in which manuscript entries were made. Numerous logs are also illustrated with pen and ink, pencil, or watercolour drawings of land profiles, ports, ships, scenic views, and other subjects, as well as with maps and diagrams. Such logs were also sometimes compiled from information originally recorded on log-boards (hinged pairs of boards) or log-slates (hinged slates), surviving examples of which are rare.

Some special interest—for both maritime historians and collectors—attaches to whaling logs, which usually date from the nineteenth century, and in which are recorded the details of whaling expeditions in the Atlantic, Pacific, and elsewhere (*see* Illus. 46). The successful kills are usually marked by outline sketches of whales' heads, fins, or tails, and the logs sometimes include more elaborate illustrations showing whale-hunts, as well as other views.

The term 'log' is also applied to other journals such as a naval surgeon's log (detailing the health of a ship's crew, sick lists, and surgical treatments applied) or commercial time-keeping registers (recording the hours worked by employees of a company), as well as aviation logs (*see* Illus. 47). Both the Royal Air Force and commercial airlines have traditionally enforced the keeping of logs by their pilots, principally as a service record, but also for information on how aeroplanes performed.

LONGHAND

Longhand is normal, standard writing in which the words are written in full, as opposed to shorthand.

LOOP

A loop is a curved shape in which the line traced returns to or near its original point of departure leaving an aperture in the middle. In writing, as opposed to

ILLUS. 46 *A whaling log book kept by Robert Newby on the barque* Sir Andrew Hammond *on a whaling voyage in the Atlantic and Pacific Oceans, 1838–41. The opening shows entries for 5–16 October 1838, with sketches of whales' tails in black ink against entries for two of the days to record successful kills.*

printing, the ascenders of letters such as *h* and *l* are often formed as loops, as are the descenders of letters such as *g* and *y*. Medieval and early modern scribes would occasionally accentuate or distort their shapes—for instance, by swinging the return stroke to the left so that the loop is almost triangular—for purely decorative purposes. *See also* CLUBBED and SWASH LETTERING.

LOOSELY INSERTED

'Loosely inserted' is a term generally used by booksellers and cataloguers to characterize leaves or other inserts in a book or manuscript that are loose and unattached, as opposed to tipped-in.

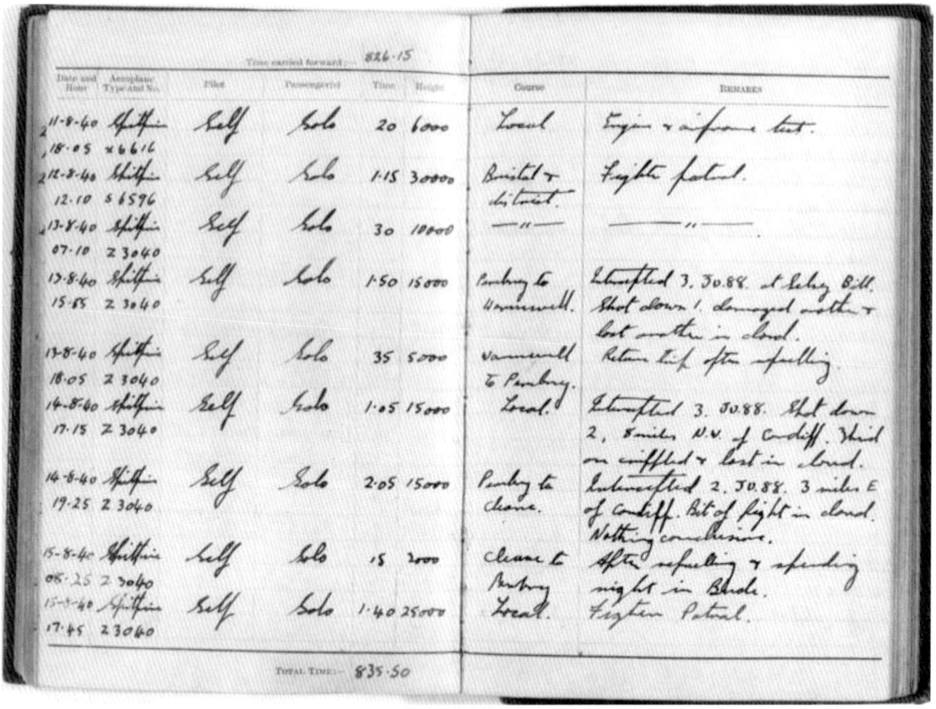

Time carried forward:— 826·15

Date and Hour	Aeroplane Type and No.	Pilot	Passenger(s)	Time	Height	Course	Remarks
11-8-40 18·05	Spitfire X6616	Self	Solo	20	6000	Local	Engine & airframe test.
12-8-40 12·10	Spitfire 56596	Self	Solo	1·15	30000	Bristol & district.	Fighter patrol.
13-8-40 07·10	Spitfire Z3040	Self	Solo	30	10000	—"—	—"—
13-8-40 15·55	Spitfire Z3040	Self	Solo	1·50	15000	Pembrey to [illegible]	Intercepted 3. Ju 88. at Selsey Bill. Shot down 1. damaged another & lost another in cloud.
13-8-40 18·05	Spitfire Z3040	Self	Solo	35	5000	[illegible] to Pembrey.	Return trip after refuelling.
14-8-40 17·15	Spitfire Z3040	Self	Solo	1·05	15000	Local.	Intercepted 3. Ju 88. Shot down 2, 5 miles N.W. of Cardiff. Third one crippled & lost in cloud.
14-8-40 19·25	Spitfire Z3040	Self	Solo	2·05	15000	Pembrey to [illegible].	Intercepted 2. Ju 88. 3 miles E of Cardiff. Bit of fight in cloud. Nothing conclusive.
15-8-40 08·25	Spitfire Z3040	Self	Solo	15	2000	[illegible] to Pembrey	After refuelling & spending night in [illegible].
15-8-40 17·45	Spitfire Z3040	Self	Solo	1·40	25000	Local.	Fighter Patrol.

Total Time:— 835·50

ILLUS. 47 *An opening in the standard-issue partly printed RAF log book of Wing Commander R. R. Stanford-Tuck, showing his autograph entries for 11–15 August 1940 when flying solo a Spitfire in 92 Squadron during the Battle of Britain.*

LORDSHIP OF THE MANOR

See MANORIAL DOCUMENTS.

LOXODROME

Deriving from the Greek *loxos* ('oblique') and *dromos* ('course'), the term 'loxodrome' denotes a feature on a map and is the same thing as a rhumb-line. *See* RHUMB-LINE.

LOZENGE

A lozenge is a rhombus or diamond-shaped ornamental figure, of four equal sides, which features in some heraldic devices, found in manuscripts and other related sources, and also in bookbinding designs.

M

MACRON

When a writer of philological material or transliterations of other languages wishes to represent words phonetically according to pronunciation, the diacritic macron (from the Greek word *makron*, 'long') is a straight horizontal line placed over a vowel to indicate that it is long (for example, over an *a*, as *ā*, pronounced 'ah', as opposed to *a* with a breve, *ă*, as a short vowel). More especially in manuscripts, a macron over a letter in a word signifies the omission of the following letter, hence contributing to an abbreviation: for instance, 'attēd' and 'cō', meaning 'attend' and 'come' respectively (*see* Illus. 1). When a macron is extended over one or more letters as a wavy line it may be called a 'tilde'. *See* TILDE.

MAJUSCULE

A majuscule is a large letter (an upper-case one in typography), the same as a capital, as opposed to a minuscule (*see* Illus. 40 and 65 and *compare* MINUSCULE). In early modern and some yet earlier manuscripts, however—unlike the clear distinctions made in printing—scribes do not always differentiate clearly or consistently between majuscule and minuscule lettering, commonly adopting a freedom of style and range of letter sizes which can include indeterminate, intermediate forms, seemingly neither one nor the other.

MANDAMUS

See WRIT OF MANDAMUS.

MANDATE

Deriving from the Latin *mandatus* ('command'), the term 'mandate' means a letter, especially from a royal or papal authority, giving orders or instructions to someone.

MANICULE

A manicule—also variously known as a 'pointing hand', 'digit', 'fist', 'hand', or 'index'—is a familiar feature in both medieval manuscripts and in manuscripts and printed books of later periods (*see* Illus. 6). Medieval scribes often draw pointing fingers as a decorative extension of a head or animal or some other shape, which, however, sometimes serves to indicate a new paragraph. Early printers adopted a manicule to serve the same purpose in the late fifteenth century. Even more common, especially in the early modern period, is the use of such figures by readers who draw them in the margins, as alternatives to asterisks or trefoils, to point to, signal, or draw attention to particular elements or passages of interest in the text. Their form can sometimes be very whimsical, with hands supplied, for instance, with inordinately long fingers to reach within the text, or else with multiple fingers.

MANIFEST

A manifest, or manifesto, since the sixteenth century is usually a public proclamation of some kind. Alternatively it is a piece of evidence made public to prove or demonstrate something. In a maritime context, since at least the beginning of the eighteenth century, a manifest is a list of a ship's cargo, signed by its master or captain, presented to customs officers. It is also a list of a ship's passengers. The largest surviving collection of such documents is that for the 12 million or so immigrants who passed through Ellis Island, in New York Harbor, between 1892 and 1954. The term is also applied to a list of passengers on an aeroplane.

MANORIAL DOCUMENTS

Manorial documents are records relating to a manor or manors: i.e. to a landed estate, usually in the country, that entails a lordship of a feudal nature. As a unit of estate management or administration, a manor can vary enormously in size, from a few acres to one covering many square miles and several parishes. The lord of the manor, who was not necessarily a nobleman, originally held the estate directly or indirectly from the Crown (being therefore a tenant-in-chief), the inhabitants under his authority including free and unfree tenants and (until the seventeenth century) those bondmen of inferior status bound to their holdings known as villeins (Latin: *villani*, once meaning 'villagers') or serfs (Latin: *servi*, 'slaves'), all of whom paid rent or performed obligatory services for the lord. The better-off free tenant farmers were known as franklins or yeomen, and those tenants who were not free but occupied land from the lord of the manor upon certain conditions were copyholders. The documents arising from manorial administration over the years found in local, county, and national record offices, besides many private family archives, include court rolls (official records of courts baron and courts leet), as well as a variety of manorial charters, rentals, estate accounts, maps, surveys, terriers, stewards' papers, and other land records.

Those records that are judged to be essentially manorial documents, especially court rolls, but excluding title deeds, cannot legally be exported from England or Wales without the permission of the Master of the Rolls. Following the Law of Property Act of 1922 allowing any interested parties access to original manorial rolls, a Manorial Documents Register has been kept since 1926, under the custody since 1959 of the Historical Manuscripts Commission (National Register of Archives), now incorporated in the National Archives at Kew. Manorial documents are also prized in connection with lordships of the manor, titles that can be sold commercially and independently in their own right, usually by certain estate agents. The lordship or seignory itself, which may encompass a few remaining rights relating to fishing, the opening of markets, etc., may be transferred by means of nothing more than a typed legal document, but its prestige is obviously enhanced by access to a healthy dossier of records relating to the manor's boundaries and history and to its previous lords, tenants, and their rights.

MANTLING

In heraldry, mantling, sometimes known by the French term 'lambrequins', is a type of drapery. Mantling is a coloured, often ragged scarf, attached to a helmet, supposedly to keep the sun off. The term is also applied to the robe of estate hanging behind a shield or helmet in certain coats of arms in genealogies (*see* Illus. 18).

MANUAL

Deriving from the Latin *manus* ('hand'), the term 'manual' means any kind of handbook or small book, including a portas and vademecum, designed for ready use and capable of being conveniently carried about for easy reference. Manuscript manuals date from medieval times, when certain kinds of ecclesiastical and liturgical books relating to the administration of the sacraments might be carried for consultation. In a more general and metaphorical use of the term, other types of ready reference books of a more substantial nature can be called 'manuals', such as certain medical books.

MANUALE

As used in the Catholic Church, the Manuale, or *Manuale* or *manual*, is the small handbook—which was circulated in many manuscript copies, with variations—containing the forms of the rituals to be observed by priests in the administration of the sacraments (Baptism, Confirmation, the Eucharist, Penance, Extreme Unction, Order, and Matrimony), in churchings (women's obligatory appearances in church to give thanks for successful childbirth), in burials, and in most of the blessings that priests can give by ordinary or delegated authority. 'Manuale' was the term most commonly used in England from the thirteenth century onwards, but other terms for the same basic book, used chiefly on the continent, include *Rituale, Sacerdotale, Agenda, Institutio Baptizandi, Pastorale, Obsequiale*, and *Sacramentale*. Versions of the Manuale, under different titles and, again, incorporating variant rites and ceremonies (which were subject to a notable papal attempt in 1614 at standardization), were printed in the sixteenth and seventeenth centuries.

MANUMISSION

Since at least the fifteenth century, manumission has been the act or process of releasing someone from bondage or slavery. The term 'letters of manumission', or simply 'manumission', may consequently denote a document or instrument formally authorizing, recognizing, witnessing, or effecting such a release.

MANUSCRIBE

A verbal form of 'manuscript', 'manuscribe' means 'write by hand'. Now obsolete, the term is only occasionally encountered in earlier writers: for instance, in various inscriptions by the scribe Ralph Crane (*fl.* 1589–1632) stating that the manuscript in question had been 'manuscribed' by him or referring to it as his 'Manuscription'.

MANUSCRIPT

Although the term 'manuscript' (Latin: *manu scriptus*) is sometimes used loosely, particularly in modern publishing parlance, to denote any non-print or pre-publication text, such as a typescript or computer print-out, it means a text or document, usually on paper or parchment, literally 'written by hand'. If a document is partly printed, such as certain kinds of forms or certificates, then it is best described as a partly printed document with manuscript insertions. The common abbreviation of 'manuscript' is 'MS', or 'MS', sometimes (but less frequently nowadays) followed by a full stop. This abbreviation is still standard in formal citations of particular manuscripts in libraries: for instance, 'MS Harley 6232' or 'Harley MS 6232'.

MAP

A map, in the most common and technical use of the term, is a detailed representation of some part of the earth's surface, whether of vast areas incorporating continents or of a small local patch of ground, with its various physical and geographical features (*see* Illus. 48). Maps, in a variety of forms and sizes, including mosaics, date back to ancient times, and many were produced in manuscript form, on parchment or paper, in the Middle Ages before they first began to be printed in the second half of the fifteenth century. Both before and after the developments of the great early modern cartographers, maps could be viewed as useful educational and navigational tools and also as visually decorative or aesthetic objects that might be designed for display on walls. For this reason many maps were produced with a variety of embellishments.

Other types of map besides terrestrial representations—the term 'map' being used in a looser sense—include, also since ancient times, maps of the heavens, showing the firmament of stars, sun, moon, and planets, as well as maps showing where particular events, such as military and naval battles, took place. For instance, a map of pen and ink and watercolour drawings, now in the Bodleian Library (MS Eng. misc. c. 13), shows in five sections on a roll the changing dispositions of the English and Scottish forces at the Battle of Pinkie and its aftermath in 1547. For certain types of map, *see also* CHART and PORTOLAN.

MARBLED PAPER

Marbled paper, from which the liners, wrappers, or covering on the boards of some books and manuscripts are formed, is a type of thick, heavily patterned paper produced by a process of exposing paper to a bath of coloured gum or size. The pattern, usually a swirl of colours, results from the stirring or combing of the gum used. Although invented in Japan as early as *c.* AD 800 and developed by the Persians in the fifteenth century, marbled paper came to Europe from the Levant in the early seventeenth century and was being used in England by the 1650s.

MARGIN

Margins are the blank borders surrounding the central block of text on printed or manuscript pages. The four margins may be described as the upper margin (sometimes called the head or top margin), the lower margin (sometimes called the tail or foot margin), the inner margin (next to the gutter in a book and sometimes called the gutter margin), and the outer margin (sometimes called

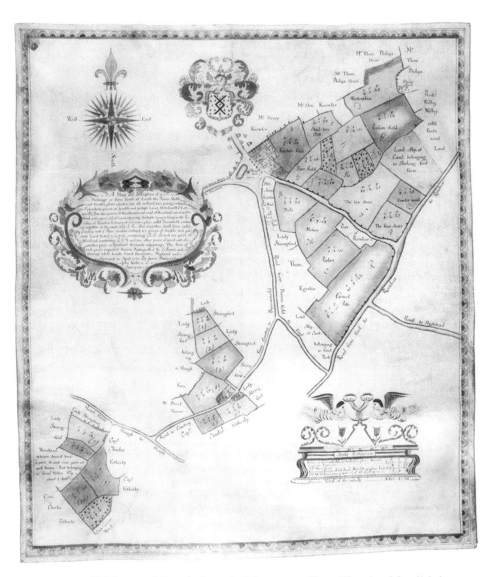

ILLUS. 48 'A Mapp and Description of a Messuage or Farm House', with adjoining buildings and land, near Bloomfield, Kent, being a pen-and-ink, hand-coloured field plan on a membrane of vellum (c.27 × 24 inches or 69 × 61 cm), 'Measured and Surveyed in April 1718 By James Busey and John Wallis Surveyors'. The decorative features include a compass-rose, a coat of arms, a cartouche title, a scale bar embellished with figures of angels and a divider, and an ornate border.

the fore-edge margin). However, it is equally common to find the upper and lower margins distinguished from the other two by being referred to as the upper and lower borders. In many medieval and some sixteenth-century manuscripts, especially illuminated manuscripts, the margins and borders may well be decorated (with foliate or other designs), inhabited (with figures of people or beasts), or historiated (with figures relating to a story). The adjectival form of 'margin', meaning in or relating to the margin, is 'marginal', a term that can also be used figuratively to mean something of peripheral or minor significance.

Other cognates of 'margin' are the obsolescent term 'marginate', meaning to annotate with notes in the margin or else furnish with a margin or border, and the still current term 'marginalia'.

MARGINALIA

'Marginalia', a Latin word meaning 'things in the margin', is a collective term for notes or markings entered by hand in the margins of a book or manuscript by a reader or annotator. Such manuscript insertions, entered neatly or cursorily, formally or casually, may include decorations, diagrams or drawings, glosses, side-notes, markings (such as vertical lines against select passages or trefoils, manicules or pointing hands to draw attention to particular text), corrections of errata or textual emendations, words signposting the subject matter of particular passages or sections, or else brief or detailed comments on the text itself. Marginalia, made by readers of books from medieval times onwards, are common. Some printed books were published with deliberately wide margins, as well as occasionally blank interleaves, in anticipation of annotation by readers: for instance, certain sixteenth-century editions of a standard legal text, Sir Thomas Littleton's *New Tenures*, first published in 1481.

Although sometimes erased or deleted by subsequent irritated owners or librarians, such annotations can throw great light on the responses of contemporary or early readers and on their engagement with the texts, providing valuable sources for the history of readership. When they are particularly perceptive, witty, or revealing in some way, marginalia by particular writers may be prized for their own sake. An outstanding example of this is the large number of surviving books annotated by the poet Samuel Taylor Coleridge (1772–1834), who even had friends lending him books so that he would annotate them and who in fact put the term 'marginalia' into general currency. Other extant books annotated in the margins by well-known persons include examples from the libraries of people as diverse as Archbishop Cranmer (*see* Illus. 49), the controversial Renaissance scholar Gabriel Harvey, the mathematician and astrologer John Dee, the poet and dramatist Ben Jonson (*see* Illus. 51), the parliamentary historian John Rushworth (*see* Illus. 6), and

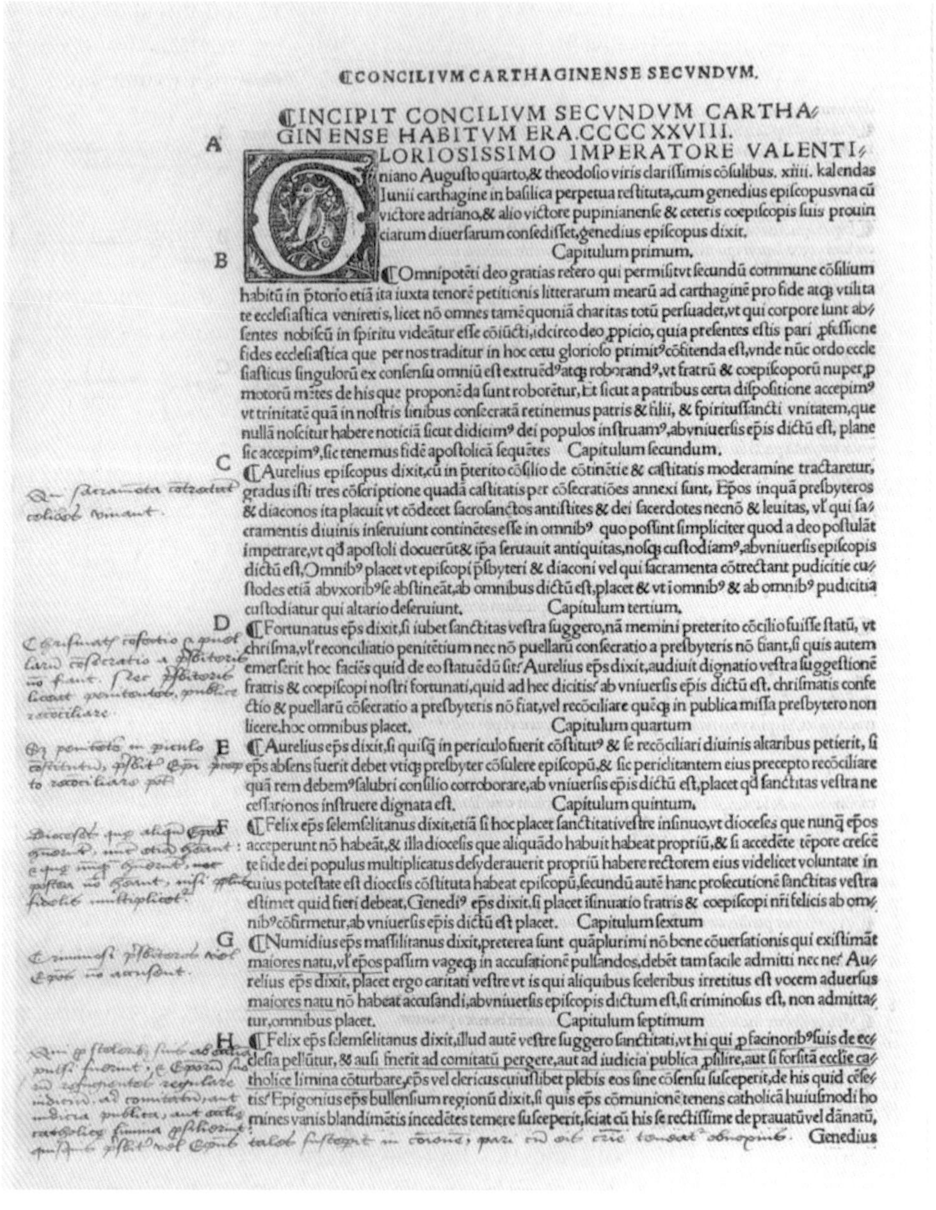

ILLUS. 49 *Autograph marginalia or annotations, in Latin, as well as underlinings, neatly entered by Thomas Cranmer, Archbishop of Canterbury, in his early Tudor secretary hand in one of his theological printed books, a copy of Jacques Merlin's edition of a compendium of early Church Councils* Quatuor conciliorum generalium *(Paris, 1524).*

Dr Johnson's erstwhile friend Hester Lynch Thrale (Mrs Piozzi), who confessed in her diary in 1790 to having 'a Trick of writing in the margins' of her books ('it is not a good Trick', she said, 'but one longs to say something').

MARGINATE

See MARGIN.

MARK

Among the various meanings of the word 'mark', including from medieval times onwards a coin worth 13*s*. 4*d*., a mark is what an illiterate person, or one incapable of writing in full because of illness, inscribes on a document in place of his or her signature: for instance, on a will, deposition, or indenture. It usually takes the form of a cross, *X*, and the name of the person is generally written beside it by the clerk, scrivener, or lawyer responsible for drawing up the document.

MARQUE

See LETTERS OF MARQUE.

MARRIAGE ALLEGATION

A marriage allegation is a written document expressing intention to marry made by the prospective bride or bridegroom or their representative. It records their parish or parishes, their approximate ages, and a declaration that there is no legal impediment to the marriage. Such documents were necessary before a marriage licence could be issued. Allegations were usually retained by the issuing authority; consequently many from the early modern period and earlier survive in local record offices.

MARRIAGE ARTICLES, MARRIAGE CONTRACT

A marriage contract is a legal prenuptial agreement: i.e. a document, deed, or indenture drawn up before a marriage, specifying the terms agreed by both parties, or their families, with respect to financial arrangements, property rights, and future legacies to the children of the marriage. Marriage articles are the particular terms and provisions that are embodied, or intended to be embodied, in a formal marriage contract. The provisions of such documents are usually effected by vesting the settled property in trustees, and the instrument of trust declares the terms of the trusts created. Such written agreements are often drawn up by lawyers or scriveners on parchment, with seals and signatures of the parties concerned, as well as their witnesses. They are found quite commonly among archives of the sixteenth century, especially among those of noble families, where extensive properties, large portions of wealth, and important titles are concerned. *Compare* MARRIAGE SETTLEMENT.

MARRIAGE LICENCE

From the early sixteenth century onwards, a marriage licence was an authorized document that allowed a couple to marry without the customary reading or calling of banns (the public proclamation in church of the impending marriage with time given for anyone to record any known impediment to it) or else to marry in a different parish. Such licences, generally sought to avoid delays or unwanted publicity, could be granted by various ecclesiastical authorities, but were usually issued by or on behalf of the bishop or archdeacon of the diocese in which the marriage was to take place. Most records of marriage licences issued in England and Wales are now preserved at Lambeth Palace, but few of the original licences themselves survive since they would have been shown to, and retained by, the cleric conducting the marriage ceremony and not officially preserved as a matter of course.

MARRIAGE SETTLEMENT

A marriage settlement is a legal prenuptial conveyance of land in tail (i.e. of land descending only to specified descendants of the person concerned), usually vested in trustees, securing property and making financial provisions for the wife and generally for her children. The arrangements involved would be subject to resettlement in each new generation. Such settlements are found quite commonly among archives from the sixteenth to eighteenth century. *Compare* MARRIAGE CONTRACT.

MASONIC DOCUMENTS

Masonic documents are those that relate to the ancient practice of Freemasonry. Freemasons, references to whom date back as early as 1375 in the records of London (although they may well be of much earlier European origin), were stonemasons who formed their own guild, society, or brotherhood, always exclusively confined to men. They expanded from operatives, who were stonemasons by trade, to non-operatives or speculatives, members of other trades, as well as noblemen and gentry who were accepted as honorary members. Although retaining certain trade symbols, such as the Masonic apron, Freemasonry ultimately developed into a society with no specific links to any trade although generally incorporating solidly respectable members of the community drawn largely from the professional and business classes. From medieval times onwards the Freemasons established lodges, premises for regular meetings, ultimately around the world, some of the earliest being in Scotland (where in the late sixteenth century the Freemasons were patronized by James VI) as well as in England. The national Grand Lodge was established in London in 1717. In these lodges secret and elaborate initiation ceremonies took place, but although membership entailed accepting God as the great architect of the universe, Freemasonry was denounced from 1738 onwards by the Roman Catholic Church.

Besides the archives in the Grand Lodge, manuscripts generated by Freemasonry include medieval poems on the subject, the earliest being that in the so-called *Regius* (or Halliwell) Manuscript of *c*. 1390 (British Library, Royal MS 17 A. I); various tracts on Masonic history, and handbooks revealing the constitution and secret proceedings and ceremonies of lodges, which began to proliferate in the eighteenth century. There are also minute books of particular lodges (the earliest known British example being that for Aitchison's Haven Lodge near Edinburgh dating from January 1598 to 1764) and individual certificates of admission. Many celebrated men are believed to have been Freemasons, among them Wolfgang Amadeus Mozart, British writers such as Robert Burns, Anthony Trollope, Rudyard Kipling, and Sir Arthur Conan Doyle, and American presidents including George Washington, Andrew Jackson, Theodore and F. D. Roosevelt, and Harry Truman, as well as many figures in the twentieth-century entertainment industry.

MASTER OF THE ROLLS

Since medieval times, the Master of the Rolls (originally called the Clerk or Curator of the Rolls) was the foremost of the twelve Masters in Chancery. He was the senior clerk who kept the official records or enrolments of documents authenticated (under the Great Seal) in Chancery, such as the Patent Rolls and Close Rolls, and who was also responsible for the appointment of lesser clerks. As his powers increased, he became effectively the Lord Chancellor's deputy, and by the eighteenth century was sitting regularly as a Chancery judge, becoming President of the Court of Appeal in 1875. The office is still in existence and the Master of the Rolls (now a superior appellate judge) is still responsible for the official Chancery records. Among notable holders of the office were Thomas Cromwell (1485?–1540) and Sir Julius Caesar (1558–1636).

MATERIAL TEXT

Material text is a school of modern literary theory that advocates the importance of the physical embodiment of texts (paper, ink, notebooks, tables, almanacs, other writing surfaces) and of the forms taken by texts (annotations, writing exercises, etc.), as well as sometimes the writing instruments used to produce them. It generally analyses and uses that evidence to elaborate wider theories about the culture that those features represent.

MATRICULATION REGISTER

Since the mid-sixteenth century, a matriculation register at a university is one in which are recorded names, usually signed in person, and other details of students when they matriculate (i.e. enrol or are formally admitted as members of the university or college concerned). The matriculand was required to promise to obey university regulations, but, unlike the case with subscription books, no oath was administered. Oaths could not, in any case, be administered to *impubes*, boys aged 14 or under, as some students were.

MEMBRANE

A membrane is a skin of vellum or parchment, often large, rather like an extended sheet of paper, though not of any specified or determinate size. Such membranes are the standard constituents of many, if not most, charters, letters patent, and indentures, as well as court rolls, Pipe Rolls, etc., among other legal and official documents of the medieval and early modern period. When several membranes are involved, whether loosely grouped or else stitched together in some form, they are usually cited by number as 'm. 1', 'm. 2', etc. In a vellum codex, however, the leaves are likely to be cut down and foliated just as if they were paper. Being derived from animal skins, the inner, soft, flesh side of a membrane (i.e. that facing the animal's flesh) is called the 'face' and is the better side for written text. The outer, darker, hair side (i.e. that carrying the animal's hair and often retaining traces of follicles) is the back or dorse, which is less smooth but could still also be used for writing on.

MEMOIR

The term 'memoir' is sometimes used in the early modern period to denote not only a biographical or autobiographical account of someone's life, but also, in a looser sense, any kind of written note, record, or memorandum. In a diplomatic context, a memoir could denote an official report.

MEMORANDA ROLLS

The Memoranda Rolls among the Exchequer Papers in the National Archives at Kew (E 159 and some in E 163) are the officially enrolled records of the King's Remembrancer and (E 368) the Lord Treasurer's Remembrancer. Chiefly written on parchment rolls on a year-by-year basis, those of the twentieth century written in enrolment books, the series is an extensive record of Exchequer business from 1218 to 1994. It includes, among other things, records of proceedings begun by writs chiefly relating to the collection of debts to the Crown arising from seizures and forfeitures, as well as from regular debts and duties.

MEMORANDUM

A memorandum (plural: memoranda; the Latin word means 'to be remembered') is a note recording something to be remembered, whether as a reminder of something to be done or as a record or memento for future reference of something already done. The term can have more specific applications in different contexts: e.g. a financial record of a debt, payment, or other monetary transaction; a legal document embodying the terms of a contract or other agreement; or the formal attestation clause signed by witnesses to a deed (*see* Illus. 93). A memorandum might also be some kind of official summary or plan, or, in diplomacy, a brief account of a situation for use in, or arising from, negotiations. A memorandum book is any kind of book, usually manuscript, in which entries are made recording information to be remembered.

MEMORIAL

'Memorial' is a term used in the early modern period as an alternative to 'memorandum', meaning a note recording something to be remembered. Its use is also recorded in 1588 as meaning the same thing as a day book or waste book, 'a booke where-in a marchaunt discriueth and writeth all his daily businesse' (John Millis, *A Briefe Instruction and Maner how to Keepe Bookes of Accompts*). In addition, a memorial or memorials can be a written memoir or chronicle of events. In a diplomatic context, a memorial may be a document with information or instructions relevant to the matter or negotiations in hand. Also, in a legal context, the term can denote either an abstract of the essential parts of a deed made for purposes of official registration or else a brief prepared by a solicitor for counsel, summarizing the facts of the case and setting out the questions on which counsel's opinion is requested.

METAL POINT

See DRY POINT.

METATHESIS

See SCRIBAL ERRORS.

MIMEOGRAPHED

See FACSIMILE.

MINIATURE

Derived from the Latin *miniare* ('to colour in red'), the term 'miniature', in the context of a manuscript, means an illustration, generally coloured, which is set out on the page as an independent feature, as opposed to being incorporated in decoration or historiation to the borders or lettering. Despite the word's normal connotations of smallness—miniature books, for instance, are 32mo or less in size—miniatures in medieval and sixteenth-century manuscripts may vary in size from small-scale insets to full-page representations. Depicting scenes and figures usually relating to the text, whether religious or secular, miniatures appear in many types of volume. Their attractiveness has led at times to the unfortunate practice whereby manuscripts are broken up so that single pages bearing miniatures might be cut out and mounted separately by collectors (a practice adopted even by as sensitive a connoisseur as John Ruskin) or else sold in this form commercially. When the painted colours are heightened by the addition of gold or silver, the miniature is said to be illuminated.

MINIM

A minim, or minim stroke, is a short vertical and possibly hooked stroke of the pen in writing, most especially in letters such as *i, m, n,* and *u*. Hastily written, connected or unconnected minims, whereby the letters become indistinguishable from one another, are a not uncommon feature of cursive script and an occasional cause of misreading.

MINUSCULE

'Minuscule' is a formal term—used in both palaeography and typography—for a small letter or, in printing, a lower-case letter, as opposed to a capital letter or majuscule (*compare* MAJUSCULE).

MINUTE

A minute is a rough or draft note on something, written for possible elaboration later; or a summary of a transaction or piece of business that has taken place, such as of what was said or agreed in a discussion; or else a memorandum, of a formal or official nature, written as a recommendation or directive on what is to be done. Minutes are generally produced in various government offices, in other official or formal bodies, institutions and societies, and in companies and businesses. A minute book is a volume in which are entered copies of such minutes, most especially proceedings at committee meetings and the like, as a permanent record for reference purposes.

MISBOUND

Leaves or gatherings in a book or codex are said to be 'misbound' if they have been bound in the wrong place, out of sequence, or else upside down or reversed.

MISCELLANY

A miscellany is any kind of volume in which a mixture of literary compositions, of different genres or by different authors, are collected together. In manuscript terms, a miscellany, whether of verse, prose or both, is a compilation incorporating texts written by several authors and generally taken by the compiler(s) from various sources. It is thus distinguished from a manuscript volume of works by, or probably by, only one or two persons. If the compilation is of extracts from works, rather than complete texts, the miscellany might also be described, if not with strict accuracy, as a commonplace book. Those written primarily in verse are poetical or verse miscellanies. Some miscellanies are neatly and formally drawn up, especially when copied from other miscellanies or written by professional scribes by commission, but they may generally be distinguished from anthologies in that the latter tend to be deliberately or formally assembled collections rather than compilations that have, for the most part, evolved, perhaps somewhat randomly, over a period. *Compare* COMMONPLACE BOOK and VERSE MISCELLANY.

MISE-EN-PAGE

Mise-en-page (the French expression means 'putting-on-the-page') is the physical arrangement of the text—e.g. features such as indentation, columns, spaces between paragraphs, etc.—but not the selection of words themselves. Resulting from practical considerations of design and layout, the *mise-en-page* encompasses such elements as illustrations, pagination, running heads, margins, sidenotes, etc., as well as the choice of printing font or style of script, and any decorative features. Although the term is usually found in discussions of printed books, it is just as applicable to manuscripts.

MISSAL

A missal is technically a mass-book: i.e. a book containing the service throughout the year (the texts, including sung chants, spoken prayers, readings, and ceremonial directions) of the Catholic Mass, which is the celebration of the Eucharist or Holy Communion, Christ's sacrifice as prefigured at the Last Supper, by the consecrating and sharing of bread and wine. The word 'mass' itself (Latin: *missa*) apparently derives, from at least the fifth century, from the priest's final versicle dismissing the congregation: *Ite missa est* ('Go, it is dismissed'). The Missal is a kind of amalgamated service book that evolved from, incorporated, or superseded earlier types of liturgical book, notably the sacramentary, gradual, and various lectionaries.

Like books of hours and breviaries, missals are also generally distinguished by the type of liturgy or rites they incorporate: e.g., 'for the use of Sarum' (Salisbury), or 'for the use of Rome' (*see* BOOK OF HOURS). In a looser sense, the term 'missal' was sometimes used to denote any kind of Catholic book of prayers or devotions, especially medieval books of hours and the like, but this usage is now obsolete. Many surviving medieval missals are decorated and illuminated, sometimes richly so. Numerous missals were subsequently printed, both in England and in France for English use, from the late fifteenth century until the Act against Superstitious Books and Images, passed by Edward VI in 1550. By this Act, reinstated after 1558 with the accession of Elizabeth I, missals and other Catholic books, 'written or printed', were—in principle, at any rate—'utterly abolished, extinguished and forbidden for ever to be used or kept in this realm'.

MIXED HAND

Handwriting that combines features of two or more different types of script may be described as a 'mixed hand': e.g. a sixteenth-century hand combining Gothic and humanistic scripts, or a mid-seventeenth-century hand combining letter forms of secretary and italic scripts (*see* Illus. 78).

MONOGRAM

Deriving from the Greek *monos* ('single') and *gramma* ('letter'), the term 'monogram' means a design formed by a combination of two or more alphabetical characters interwoven. A monogram usually embodies the initials of someone's name, such as the form *ER* of Elizabeth, Lady Ralegh (*see* Illus. 86), although some examples incorporate more than initials, such as Narcissus Luttrell's, in which the letters *NARSL* at least can be discerned (*see* Illus. 50). Monograms can sometimes be very elaborate, or ingeniously entangled, so that the letters are not easily recognizable. Such designs, identifying owners, are occasionally found not only on personal stationery, but also in manuscript and printed books, whether inscribed or stamped on a page or on covers, or incorporated in bookplates.

ILLUS. 50 *The book-stamp monogram of the annalist Narcissus Luttrell, combining letters including* NARSL, *with the date '1693' subscribed in his own hand.*

MOROCCO

See BINDING.

MOTTO

Deriving from the Latin *muttum* ('grunt' or 'murmur') and French *mot* ('word'), the term 'motto' in its original usage meant a caption, or legend, usually in Latin, attached to an emblematic design, one which helped to explain the design's symbolic significance: for instance, on the *impresa* of a shield in a chivalric tournament (*see* IMPRESA), or attached to the representation of a coat of arms in a genealogy or armorial. Its purpose was usually either to draw attention to the exploits or ambition of the bearer or to distinguish his family's guiding principle or aspiration.

Personal mottos of comparably noble sentiments were also written by owners in numerous books and manuscripts, especially in the early modern period. Examples of mottos, sometimes derived from biblical or classical sources, used by early modern literary and public figures include John Donne's *Per Rachel ho serito, & non per Lea* (a Spanish version of a line from Petrarch meaning 'I have served Rachel [the contemplative life] not Leah [the active life]'); Ben Jonson's *Tanquam explorator* (a quotation from Seneca meaning 'Only as a scout' [i.e. not necessarily as a convert]: *see* Illus. 51); Lancelot Andrewes's *Et aratrum et ad aram* ('Both to the plough and to the altar'); William Camden's *Jouis omnia plena* (a quotation from Virgil's *Eclogues* meaning 'All things [are] full of Jove [i.e. God]'); George Sandys's *Habere eripitur habuisse nunquam* ('One may be deprived of a possession but not of having possessed it'); John Evelyn's *Omnia explorate: meliora retinete* ('Explore everything: keep the best'); William Browne of Tavistock's *Fortuna non mutat genus* (a quotation from Horace meaning 'Fortune does not

ILLUS. 51 *The title-page of a printed copy of Nathaniel Torporley's* Diclides coelome-
tricæ seu valvæ astronomicæ vniversales *(London, 1602), a treatise about the
computing of astronomical tables, bearing the autograph ownership inscription of
Ben Jonson (*Sum Ben. Jonsoni, *meaning 'I am Ben Jonson's'), partly deleted by a
subsequent owner, and Jonson's autograph motto* Tanquam explorator.

change birth'); Henry Vaughan's *Salus mea ex Agno* ('My salvation [is] through the Lamb [of God]'); and Charles I's *Dum spiro spero* ('While I breathe I hope').

MOUNTED

A piece of material text, illustration, or photograph is mounted when it is affixed to, or laid down on, a sheet of paper or card so that it may be conveniently displayed, in a glazed frame, for instance, or else incorporated in a book or album. If the underlying paper or card mount is cut away so that only an outside border is left to surround and frame the attached text or illustration, it may be described as a 'window mount'. Some valuable books (early Shakespeare quartos, for instance) have been taken apart, their conjugate leaves separated, and the individual leaves mounted in this way, not for the sake of preservation, but to produce volumes that could be bound in uniform size and appearance. Alternatively, a document or illustration may be mounted in a book or album by being attached to a guard. Documents, including maps, are also sometimes described as mounted when they have been reinforced or strengthened by being backed with gauze or linen. *See also* GUARD, LAID DOWN, and SILKED.

MOURNING STATIONERY

Mourning stationery is a feature associated most especially with the Victorian period, not least with Queen Victoria herself, who from 1861 mourned her beloved deceased husband, Prince Albert, for forty years. Mourning stationery for letters, both writing paper and envelopes, was printed with black borders, of varying depths, as a token of bereavement. Black sealing wax, black leather blotters, and jet paperknives were also sometimes used. Such stationery is so frequently encountered, however, that it is not clear whether it always did signify personal mourning, and it may well have become fashionable for general use.

MULREADY POSTAL STATIONERY

See LETTER SHEET.

MUNIMENT

A muniment is a title deed, charter, letters patent, or other document providing evidence of specified rights, privileges, or ownership. A muniment chest is generally a large, sturdy trunk or coffer used particularly for storing such documents. A muniment room, a common feature of great houses on landed estates, usually (but not always) in the basement, dungeon, vault, or strongroom, is a room devoted specifically to the storage of muniments, which may well be kept also in chests of drawers or deed boxes, or else rolled up in tubular containers or stacked or boxed on shelves.

MUSTER ROLLS

'Muster rolls' is a generic term applied to official records of the raising or assembling of local militia in shires. Details are generally given of the men who have presented themselves for inspection, usually by the Lord Lieutenant, and of the arms or equipment they have brought with them, or else of local men who are eligible for military service. The earliest known such return dates from 1297. Documents of this kind are widely scattered in record offices and in private family archives, as well as in the National Archives at Kew (from 1522 onwards) and the British Library. They include a considerable number for times of war or national crisis, among them musters at the time of the Spanish Armada in 1588 and during the Civil War in the 1640s. Muster rolls also exist for most regiments of the regular army from 1760 and for yeomanry and volunteer regiments from 1780 onwards.

N

National Archives

'The National Archives' is the name adopted in 2003–4 for a bureaucratic body administering both the Public Record Office (PRO), which moved to Kew, in south London, in 1997, and the National Register of Archives (NRA). When the decision was made by management executives to re-brand the PRO, it obviously entailed a deliberate obfuscation of the nation whose records are preserved there, perhaps in view of the complicated history of the British Isles, and even of the United Kingdom. The National Archives at Kew (which the re-branding management executives would like to see abbreviated to TNA) contains records primarily of England, but also many relating to Wales, Scotland, and Ireland. Nevertheless, there are separate record offices for these various countries, principalities, provinces, or republics: namely, the National Archives of Scotland (formerly the Scottish Record Office) in Edinburgh; the National Library of Wales in Aberystwyth (whose Department of Manuscripts and Records is the principal Welsh manuscript repository); and the Public Record Office of Northern Ireland in Belfast; as also the National Archives in Dublin (replacing the State Paper Office established in Dublin Castle in 1702 and Public Record Office of Ireland established in the Four Courts in Dublin in 1867). All these repositories preserve series of public records dating back to medieval times, except for that in the Republic of Ireland, since most records preserved in the Public Record Office in Dublin were destroyed by fire in June 1922 during the Irish Civil War. Since so many other countries also have National Archives—such as the National Archives in Washington DC—it now seems necessary to distinguish the British institution as the National Archives at Kew.

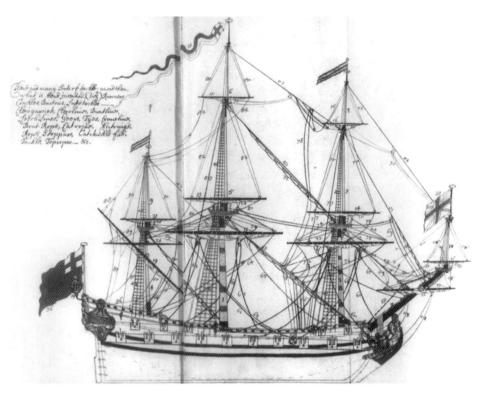

ILLUS. 52 *A page in 'Edward Hilton His Booke 1692', a neatly drawn up compilation of tables, exercises, and diagrams principally relating to navigation. The page is occupied by a coloured drawing of a ship with rigging and tackle systematically numbered for identification, with a summary of the different types of tackle written at the side.*

NATIONAL REGISTER OF ARCHIVES

See HISTORICAL MANUSCRIPTS COMMISSION.

NAVIGATIONAL MANUSCRIPTS

Extant early modern manuscripts relating to maritime matters and cartography, such as portolans and rutters, are complemented by a number of surviving notebooks, as well as more formal volumes and treatises, containing navigational exercises or related materials. They might include entries such as sailing directions in various spheres, instructions on making charts, geographical accounts of various regions, astronomical tabulations, navigational calculations, and other aspects of practical seamanship, as well as geometrical diagrams, maps, and other drawings (*see* Illus. 52). Such manuscripts reflect the great developments in sixteenth- and seventeenth-century navigational theory and practice, in which mathematical principals could help determine the position of ships at sea, as well as new nautical instrumentation and cartographic innovations such as Mercator's projection. Many accounts of voyages of navigation to different parts of the world, left either in manuscript or printed form, have been published since 1846 by the Hakluyt Society. Many naval papers in general have been published since 1893 by the Navy Records Society.

NEAR-CONTEMPORARY

See CONTEMPORARY.

NEUME

Probably deriving from the Greek meaning 'gesture', the term 'neume' means one of a set of signs or graphic symbols used to denote the melody in the notation of plainchant in medieval musical and liturgical manuscripts.

NEWSLETTER

A newsletter is a news report hand-written and sent as a letter to a particular person. Newsletters have flourished from very early times, particularly those written by individuals to distant members of their family or else to business associates to keep them better informed. There are also many written to their patrons by official intelligencers or by political or diplomatic agents abroad. In response to the development of a huge public appetite for news, however, manuscript newsletters flourished as a specifically commercial enterprise in the seventeenth century, more or less concurrently with the rise of gazettes, corantos, and other types of printed newsletters, forerunners of the modern newspaper. Accounts of current public affairs, such as parliamentary debates and court gossip, as well as foreign, commercial, or military developments, were written and then copied out repeatedly, each on a single folded sheet, by professional scribes in a particular office for distribution to individual subscribers around the country (*see* Illus. 53). Pioneers of this type of production were Samuel Pecke, a scrivener with a stall in Westminster Hall in the 1640s, and Captain Edmund Rossingham. The best-known and most influential London-based producer of newsletters, however, was Henry Muddiman (1629–1692), who was awarded a state monopoly in 1660 to print his pro-government newsletters, but who ran for many years a lucrative sideline sending fuller, more informative manuscript newletters, twice a week, to private subscribers who each paid him £5 a year.

Nevertheless, other independent producers flourished who were not under government control, manuscript production being itself a means of evading licensing or censorship. This fact helped to make manuscript news-letters more desirable, as well as more historically valuable objects. Hand-written and ostensibly personalized newsletters may have had a greater cachet for their recipients than impersonal printed news in any case. As early as 1620, for instance, in his court masque *Newes from the New World Discover'd in the Moone*, Ben Jonson has his 'Factor' or agent 'of newes for all the Shieres of England' make an exaggerated but perhaps not entirely fictitious point: 'I would have no newes printed; for when they are printed they leave to bee newes; while they are written, though they be false, they remaine newes still.'

Collections of newsletters of this kind are not common, but some survive in the British Library—such as those produced by Thomas Rugge (1659–72) and by John Starkey and Henry Skipwith (1667–72)—and elsewhere. An especially large collection, of 3,950 newsletters written between 1674 and 1715 to members of the Newdigate family in Warwickshire, is preserved in the Folger Shakespeare Library, Washington DC, and thirty-one newsletters sent to Sir Willoughby Aston from March to December 1672 are in the Osborn Collection at Yale University (b 97).

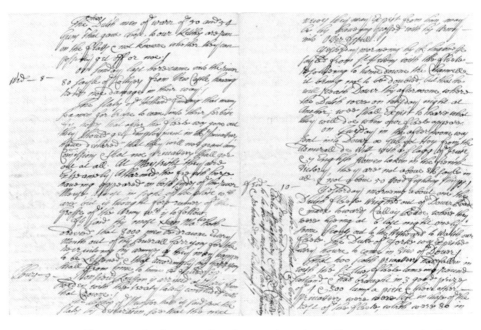

ILLUS. 53 *Two pages of a four-page London newsletter in small quarto format, in the cursive hand of a professional scribe, written partly sideways down the margin to fit the tight format. It gives news of public events, particularly relating to the Dutch and English fleets, on six days during the Third Anglo-Dutch War, 6–11 May 1672.*

New Style

See DATES.

New Year's gift roll

New Year's gift rolls relate to a major annual protocol of the Royal Court which was established well before 1494 and is especially associated with the Tudor period. On the first day of each new year (1 January New Style)—a day of general gift-giving in society at large—courtiers and all the nobility and dignitaries associated with the court or in the monarch's favour were expected to give the sovereign, whether in person or through agents, a suitably expensive or spectacular gift by way of celebration and elite social consolidation. By the same token, the sovereign was expected to give or send them gifts as well. Such gifts might comprise valuable jewellery, gold plate or ornaments, goblets, candied sweetmeats, finely embroidered cushions, handkerchiefs, gloves, slippers, or other items of clothing, writing materials, sumptuously bound books, calligraphic manuscripts (*see* Illus. 54), or other luxury items. They were often chosen for their appropriateness to the character or circumstances of the particular donor or recipient or the relationship between them. This was, moreover, despite the less than ideal bureacratic protocol involved in the gifts' actual presentation, at least by the reign of James I, when the court was thronged with donors and a series of officials and porters had to be paid in order to have a gift delivered.

The New Year's gift rolls are carefully drawn-up official records of these gifts, neatly set out by government scribes, sometimes with pen and ink or coloured decoration, on extremely long rolls of parchment sewn head to foot. They list on one side, in order of social rank and official status, the names of the donors and their gifts, and on the other side the gifts (usually plate) given by the monarch and names of recipients. They were also commonly signed by the sovereign to signify his or her examination and approval. New Year's gift rolls survive for Henry VIII, Mary I, Edward VI, and Elizabeth I (some two dozen for Elizabeth, the greatest number extant), although these are only a fraction of the number originally produced. Now widely dispersed rather than remaining among the Public Records, they are obviously a major source for the history of Royal Court culture and of the various types of artefact produced and valued in the period.

NIB

A nib is the point of a pen, whether of a sharpened quill, always cut at an angle, or the separate steel tip that could be fitted into a pen-holder in the era of steel pens.

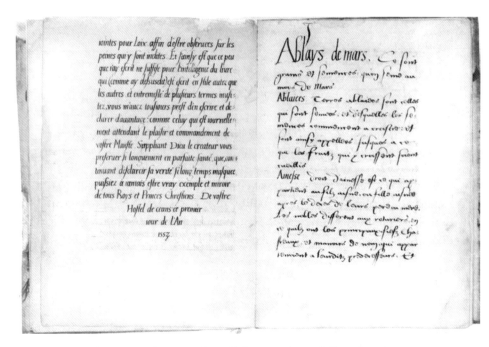

ILLUS. 54 *An autograph manuscript which was written, dedicated, and presented as a New Year's gift to the young Edward VI in 1554 by his tutor and writing master John Bellemain. It is a French glossary, the dedication written in Bellemain's calligraphic italic hand, the main text in his less formal largely secretary hand.*

NONCE VOLUME

See COMPOSITE VOLUME.

NOTARIAL MARKS AND SIGNS

Notarial signs are distinctive patterns or devices written by notaries or scriveners at the end of legal documents in order to help identify or distinguish the handwriting as produced by that particular scribe as a safeguard against forgery. Commonly used in the medieval and to a lesser extent early modern period, especially in Scotland, such personal devices take many forms, ranging from a small loop or knot motif on a plinth to a large, elaborate, intertwined pattern up to several inches long, sometimes incorporating the scribe's motto or even his name. In addition, or instead, the scribe may incorporate what is known as a 'notarial mark' or 'paraph'. The mark is generally a smaller and simpler device, involving a pattern of loops, circles, squares, crosses, stars, interlacing, chequering, or other forms.

The paraph is the same thing except perhaps little more than a concluding flourish. Many examples of these signs or marks are found in the Common Paper of the Scriveners' Company.

NOTARY

The term 'notary' (from the Latin *notarius*: 'clerk' or 'secretary') is sometimes found in the medieval and early modern period loosely applied to any kind of clerk. Nevertheless, the terms 'notary' and 'notary public' relate more specifically to a public office dating back to Roman times. Notaries in Christendom were originally ecclesiastical appointments, made before the Reformation by the Pope and by archbishops as his delegates; subsequently they were appointed (in England) by archbishops or (until 1874) by an officer under an archbishop's authority known as the 'Master of the Faculties'. Their functions might include composing important letters to persons in high office and drawing up complicated legal documents, charters, and marriage contracts, as well as registering other official acts. Notaries, who flourish today much more in the USA than in Britain, remain a narrowly circumscribed branch of the legal profession, within its more traditional secular boundaries, as persons authorized to draw up or attest and certify deeds, contracts, bills, and other formal documents, and to administer oaths and take affidavits. *See also* PROTHONOTARY.

NOTE

A word with many applications, a 'note' is generally conceived in manuscript terms as a brief record or jotting of some kind. It may serve as a reminder, such as notes written for use when giving a speech, or as a memorandum to be more fully developed later, such as drafts for a report or a literary composition. It might also be a brief informal message, such as a note asking an office colleague to return a phone call. In addition, the term is used on occasions to denote a signed receipt or voucher; a written promise to pay a sum of money within a certain period of time; a banknote; a formal diplomatic communication; and a comment written in the margin against a passage in a manuscript or book. The latter, implying a note added to a pre-existing text, is more generally called an 'annotation', while notes at the foot of the page or end of the book are generally called 'footnotes' and 'endnotes' respectively.

NOTEBOOK

A notebook is a book used, or intended to be used, for writing informal jottings or memoranda of some kind (*see* Illus. 62), or else for more formal entries, when, for instance, it is devoted to a particular subject or even used for literary drafts (*see* Illus. 23).

NOVERINT UNIVERSI

The incipit, or opening words, of a common Latin formula used in bonds and some other legal instruments from medieval times onwards was *Noverint universi per presentes*, generally rendered in English legal documents as 'Be it known to all men by these presents'. By the late sixteenth and early seventeenth century, law clerks might be jokingly referred to as 'Noverint men', and a scrivener could be satirized by Wye Saltonstall in 1635 as being 'so impudent in his Art of undoing others, that hee begins with *Noverint universi*, let all men know it'. For various kinds of official grants and warrants, variant English renditions and formulae would run along the lines of 'Know all men by these presents' or 'To all and singular to whom these presents shall come'. By the mid-eighteenth century, legal documents such as bonds, with an English version of this incipit, were produced in printed form with spaces left for the specific details to be entered by hand. *See also* SCIANT PRESENTES.

NUNCUPATIVE

'Nuncupative' is a term applied to a will that was not written down but was expressed by a person by word of mouth before witnesses who could later formally testify to the fact by sworn statements before a court of probate. By a statute of 1678, in force until 1838, it was regulated that for such a will to be valid there had to be at least three witnesses to the wishes expressed by the deceased in his or her last illness and that the wishes so expressed had to be written down within six days of the death.

O

OATH ROLLS

'Oath rolls' is a generic term applied to the enrolled Chancery records kept of the various public oaths of allegiance that various groups of people were obliged to take during the sixteenth to nineteenth centuries. They record names and sometimes other particulars, such as professional status and religion, of those taking often obligatory oaths of loyalty to the Crown and to the Church of England. These records proliferated after the Test Act of 1672, with a notable series of Association Oath Rolls in 1696 (*see* ASSOCIATION OATH ROLLS), and those following the Security and Succession Act of 1701, whereby all officials had to swear an oath of abjuration denying the right of the exiled James II's son to succeed to the throne. Chancery oath rolls for the period from 1673 to 1713 are in the National Archives at Kew (chiefly in C 214, C 215 with other oaths up to 1889, and C 220/9/5–7). So too (in C 215/6 and C 202/44/5) is a series naming officers and men on each ship of the Royal Navy who took the Oath of Allegiance and Supremacy in 1660–1 following the Restoration of Charles II. Further series of oath rolls in Chancery, King's Bench, Exchequer, and Common Pleas include C 184, KB 24, E 3, E 169, CP 10, and PRO 57/5146. These record oaths administered by the Clerk of the Crown, from 1673 to 1985, to lord chancellors, high treasurers, masters of the rolls, masters in Chancery, and a host of other judges, attorneys, commissioners, councillors, and officers of state, as well as those administered in 1709–11 to Protestant refugees (E 169/86).

OBLIGATION

See BOND.

OBLONG

A sheet of paper, leaf, page, book, or manuscript is described as 'oblong' when its breadth is greater than its height. This is a useful term for describing particular rectangular shapes and sizes, where the book or paper is used, or intended to be used, not in an upright position but sideways, as it were: e.g. an oblong quarto or oblong octavo. Many albums, notebooks, and other paper books and stationery items, including music part-books, are designed, sewn, or bound to be used in this form. A complicating factor is when, for example, a notebook is sewn at the edge of one of the short sides and intended to be written along the length of each page, but is actually turned and used in an upright position, with the sewn edge at the top or bottom and the writing running the narrow width of each page. In binding terms, such a book would still qualify as being oblong in physical format although not actually used as such.

OCTAVO

A Latin word meaning 'in eighth' or 'for the eighth time', the term 'octavo' (frequently abbreviated to '8vo') denotes the size of a leaf of paper produced when a standard papermaker's sheet is folded three times: the first fold producing two leaves (four pages) of folio size (being half the sheet), the second four leaves (eight pages) of quarto size (being a quarter of the sheet), and the third eight leaves (sixteen pages) of octavo size (being an eighth of the sheet). The size of an octavo leaf will vary according to the paper manufacturer and trimming by the papermaker or binder, but the average size for the early modern period is approximately 6–8 inches (15.5–20.5 cm) in length and 4–4½ inches (10–11.5 cm) in width. Because of the wires across the width of the papermaker's mould or tray, octavo leaves will have the chain-lines running vertically down the page. A printed or manuscript volume made up of gatherings of such leaves (which will most commonly comprise gatherings sewn in eights: i.e. four pairs of conjugate leaves per gathering, subject to occasional variation) is itself called an 'octavo' as a means of distinguishing it by size and basic format.

Octavo is the commonest size of book, both printed and manuscript, since the early seventeenth century. Manuscripts of octavo size tend to include notebooks, pocket books, some commonplace books, and informal account books, as well as other personal or casual compilations, as opposed to the more formal copying often reserved for paper books in folio or quarto format. For other-sized leaves and volumes, resulting from previous, further, or different folding of each sheet, *see* DUODECIMO, FOLIO, QUARTO, and SEXTODECIMO.

OLD STYLE

See DATES.

OPENING

In bibliography, an opening is the two pages of a book that are visible when it is opened at any point. The page to the left is the verso of a leaf and the page to the right is the recto of the consecutive leaf. In modern printed books, following any preliminaries, the left page is commonly paginated with an even number (from 2 onwards) and the right page with an odd number. Manuscripts, particularly those containing charts or illustrations, are occasionally numbered by openings.

ORDER

An order, as a piece of writing, is a command, instruction, mandate, or injunction directing someone to do something. Depending on the circumstances, it may take the form of a letter, warrant, legal writ, or other document (*see* Illus. 55). In a commercial or banking context, an order is a written and authorized direction to someone to make a payment or else to supply, deliver, or purchase specified goods. An order book is a ledger, register, or other book in which orders are entered or copied as a record: e.g. customers' orders made to a company or business; regimental orders in the army; or naval orders by the Admiralty or a captain on board a ship. In Parliament the order book is the book in which an official record of motions to be submitted to the House of Commons must be entered.

ORDER FOR SIGNALS

As a naval document, an order for signals is one denoting what flags or pennants are to be used by ships in a fleet or squadron and usually how and when they are to be hoisted (*see* Illus. 56). Such orders are usually drawn up, at least in the eighteenth and nineteenth centuries, in a formulaic and tabular fashion on a single page, with the pennants depicted in watercolours, a copy being sent by the commander-in-chief to each ship's captain.

ORDER OF BATTLE

An order of battle is most commonly a type of naval document in which is listed the order in which the ships of a fleet or squadron are expected to sail—i.e. an order of sailing—but specifically in readiness for action. Those best known and preserved relate to the Napoleonic Wars, including orders sent by Lord Nelson, Lord Collingwood, Sir William Cornwallis, and other notable admirals. The orders would be prepared in largely uniform format, in a series of sometimes

... Privy Party, ... to yo[ur] good L[ordshi]ps and the rest. Among other thi[n]gs ... and orderd that vpon the late conference ... confirmed of by his Ma[jes]tie for establishing some fitt course of gouerm[en]t in Ecclesiasticall cause, It was thought conuenyent that some learned and descret persons should be appointed to redress an abuse of dispersing scandalous Bookes, Libelles and Pamphlettes in this Realme ... some haue ben here printed, other brought from beyond the Seas w[i]th great hurt of the subiecte boly co[n]cerning Religion and duty to the State and Superiors ...

...

From the Court at Whitehall ...

1603

Yo[ur] good L[ordshi]ps assured loving friends

Jo: Cant   Ellesmere Canc.   T: Dorset   Lennox   Nottingham

E: Worcester

Suffolke

Devonshire

H. Howard   Ro: Cecyll   W: Knollys   E: Wotton

T. Howard

divided columns on single folio pages or broadsheets, specifying the squadrons and divisions, the names of ships, sometimes the ships' flags or pennants (drawn in watercolours), and the names of their captains and division commanders, with other specific instructions written in a section at the bottom. A neat copy, made by a naval secretary and signed usually by the commander-in-chief himself, would be sent to the captain of every ship. A number of those issued by Nelson to his captains in the days leading up to the Battle of Trafalgar on 21 October 1805 survive in various collections (*see* Illus. 57).

ORDINAL

An ordinal in the Middle Ages was a type of service book containing directions for the order of services, usually for the clergy celebrating the liturgy. In post-Reformation England an ordinal was more specifically a book with the form of service for the ordination of priests and deacons and for the consecration of bishops. The term was also sometimes used to denote any kind of book of rules and regulations.

ORDINANCE

Deriving from the Latin *ordinare* ('to put in order'), the term 'ordinance', in the sense of a text or document, means a decree or command made by a sovereign or other authoritative body, usually to regulate something of general concern or to set out specific rules and regulations imposed. Less legislatively important, permanent, or far-reaching than a statute, an ordinance may, nevertheless, take the form of a public proclamation, whether manuscript or printed.

ORDINARY

The term 'ordinary' has multiple applications in ecclesiastical, legal, and other contexts. As a manuscript in the medieval and early modern period, an ordinary is a book, which may be illuminated, containing the principal texts and order of service in the Catholic Mass. It may also be a devotional manual prescribing rules for leading a virtuous life. In heraldry, an ordinary is a book containing coats of arms classified according to charges: i.e. according to the devices borne on armorial shields.

ILLUS. 55. *An order by the Privy Council for the licensing of the press at the beginning of the reign of James I, commanding the appointment of 'some learned and discreet persons...to redres an abuse of dispersinge scandalous Bookes, Libelles and Pamphlettes in this Realme'. It is written in the secretary hand of an official scribe, and signed by thirteen Privy Councillors including John Whitgift, Archbishop of Canterbury, Lords Ellesmere, Buckhurst, Nottingham, Suffolk, and Devonshire, and Sir Robert Cecil, the day and month of the date left blank, 1603.*

Single and double Pendants

Top sail yard arm

Where hoisted at single & Pendants

Men | When the double Pendants are up & Gulon on board the
they will be hoisted where best seen

Nelson Frigates

Samuel Sutton Esq.
Captain of His Majesty's Ship

The term 'ordinary' is also found used in connection with the staging of miracle plays in Cornwall, where according to Richard Carew (in *The Survey of Cornwall*, 1602), 'the players conne not their parts without booke, but are prompted by one called the Ordinary, who followeth at their back with the booke in his hand, and telleth them softly what they must pronounce aloud'. There is no evidence, however, that bookkeepers or prompters were ever called 'ordinaries' in the professional Elizabethan theatre.

ORDNANCE BOOK

An ordnance book is a ledger or register in which particulars of military stores or supplies are recorded (*see* Illus. 58).

ORIGINAL CHARTER

See CHARTER.

ORIGINAL WRIT

See WRIT.

ORNAMENTATION

See DECORATION.

ORTHOGRAPHY

Deriving from the Greek *ortho* ('correct') and *graphē* ('writing'), 'orthography' is the formal term for spelling or for the subject of spelling as a linguistic study.

OWNERSHIP INSCRIPTION

An ownership inscription in a book or manuscript is one recording the name of the person to whom the item belonged and which may or may not be written in that person's own hand. Thus it is common to find books in the early modern period with inscriptions, usually on title-pages, declaring that this is so-and-so 'his' or 'her book' (or *eius liber* in Latin: *see* Illus. 95), occasionally followed by the price paid for it, or a date, or even the owner's motto (*see* Illus. 51). More elaborate inscriptions may take the form of verses, such as those written by Mary Sidney (*née* Dudley), mother of Sir Philip

ILLUS. 56 *A naval order for signals, for 'Single and double Pendants', set out in grid format, with names of ships, the various pennants painted in watercolours, drawn up by a naval secretary and signed by Lord Nelson ('Nelson & Bronte'). This is the copy sent to Samuel Sutton, Captain of HMS* Amphion, *and was 'Given on board the Victory Off Cadiz', 7 October 1805, two weeks before the Battle of Trafalgar.*

Euryalus	1	Temeraire	Capt. E. Harvey
Phoebe	2	Super	R. G. Keats
	3	Victory	The Commander in Chief / Capt. T. M. Hardy
Sirius	4	Neptune	T. F. Fremantle
Amazon	5		
Entreprise	6	Tigre	Jo. Halliwell
	7	Canopus	Rear adm. Thomas Louis / Capt. F. W. Austen
Aurora	8	Conqueror	Israel Pellew
Termagant	9	Agamemnon	Sir E. Berry Kt.
Ætna	10	Leviathan	H. W. Bayntun
	11	Prince of Wales	Vice adm. Sir R. Calder Bt. / Capt. cummoning
Amphion	12	Ajax	W. Brown
Lively	13	Orion	E. Codrington
Hydra	14	Minotaur	C. J. Mansfield
Niger	15		
Bittern	16	Queen	T. Pender
Thunder	17	Donegal	P. Malcolm
Merlin	18	Spencer	Hon. R. Stopford
Beagle	19		
Weazle	20	Spartiate	Sir F. Laforey Bt.
Unite	1	Prince	Capt. R. Grindall
Chiffonne	2	Mars	G. Duff
	3	Royal Sovereign	Vice adm. Collingwood / Capt. E. Rotheram
Juno	4	Tonnant	C. Tyler
Endymion	5	Belleisle	W. Hargood
Seahorse	6	Bellerophon	Sir T. Cook Kt.
Jalouse	7	Colossus	J. N. Morris
Halcyon	8	Achille	R. King
Martin	9	Polyphemus	R. Redmill
	10	Revenge	R. Moorsom
	11	Britannia	Rear adm. Earl of Northesk Kt. / Capt. C. Bullen
Melpomene	12	Swiftsure	W. G. Rutherford
Naiad	13	Defence	G. Hope
Phoenix	14		
Scrable	15	Kent	
Ambuscade	16	Zealous	Sir T. I. M. Hardy
Pautalus	17		
Nonsuch	18	Thunderer	Wm. Lechmere
Childers	19	Defiance	P. C. Durham
	20	Dreadnought	John Conn

To
The Right Honble. Earl of Northesk
Rear Admiral of the White
&c. &c. &c. Britannia
Command of the Rear squadron

Given onboard the Victory off
Cadiz the 10th day of Octr. 1805

Nelson & Bronte

Sidney, on the front paste-down of a fifteenth-century vellum manuscript of John Lydgate's *The Fall of Princes*:

> This bouk is mine Mary Sidney
> If it [be] fonde before it be lost
> Lett them that finde it of it make no bost
> In seyinge the[y] fonde it before it was lost
> For of souch gayn is liek to come mouche payne 1552
> > Written the 28 daye
> > of November Mary Sidney

Some indications of ownership also take the form of *ex libris* inscriptions. Names alone, perhaps indicating ownership, may be prominently written on title-pages or on versos of title-pages, paste-downs, endpapers, preliminary blanks, or at the beginning or end of the main text. Such inscriptions should be distinguished, however, from random names scribbled into books, down margins, on blank spaces, or elsewhere in the volume, in a random fashion or possibly in childish or semi-literate hands. While such evidence may throw light on provenance—and is sometimes described in library and booksellers' catalogues as 'ownership inscriptions' or 'ownership signatures'—they can sometimes be more accurately defined as juvenile or whimsical jottings or pen trials, possibly even made in imitation of others—the bibliographical equivalent of graffiti.

OXIDATION

Oxidation is the process by which elements react with oxygen to form an oxygen compound. It is relevant to manuscripts in that documents, usually on paper, are occasionally encountered where chemical or biological reactions in the paper and ink—such as when the colour has changed from a black or brown ink to a harsh silver-black or blue, perhaps also bleeding into the paper—are sometimes described as the result of oxidation due to high levels of metallic content in the ink. While oxidation may be a contributing factor, however, it seems more likely that, like damp-staining, these features result primarily from the action of fungus and its metabolites.

ILLUS. 57 *A naval order of battle, listing in columns the names of forty ships of war and thirty-three 'frigates sloops &c^a' in their appointed order (the* Victory *being third in line in the van division), with names of commanders, drawn up by a naval secretary and signed by Lord Nelson ('Nelson & Bronte'). This is the copy sent to the fleet's third in command, Admiral Lord Northesk, on HMS* Britannia. *It is countersigned by Nelson's secretary John Scott, and was 'Given onboard the Victory off Cadiz', 10 October 1805, eleven days before the Battle of Trafalgar (at which both Nelson and Scott were killed).*

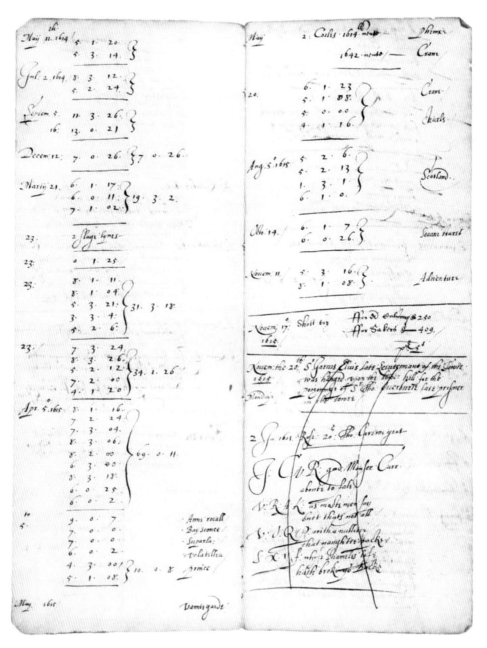

ILLUS. 58 *An opening in an ordnance book, an official ledger in narrow format kept at the Tower of London, the chief arsenal of the realm, 1613–17. It shows entries in the predominantly secretary hand of a professional clerk, dated from 11 May 1614 to 20 November 1615, with accounts relating to provisions for particular ships. At the end, subsequently cancelled by two pen-strokes, is a note on the hanging of Sir Gervase Elwes for the Overbury murder and related satirical verses on Robert Carr, Earl of Somerset.*

P

PACT

See TREATY.

PAGE

A page is one side of a leaf of paper or vellum, whatever the size or format of the manuscript or book. Pagination is consequently the numbering given to manuscripts or books according to their pages (generally cited as 'p. 1', 'pp. 1–2', etc.), as opposed to foliation. Such books or manuscripts may thus be described as paginated rather than foliated.

PAGE PROOF

See PROOF.

PALAEOGRAPHY

Deriving from the Greek *palaiograph* ('ancient writing'), the term 'palaeography', or 'paleography', denotes the study of handwriting and of the history of scripts. It involves such practices as the analysis and description of old manuscripts, the deciphering of texts, the dating and identification of hands and scripts, and recognition of the place of origin of a manuscript and of the scribal practices and conventions represented in it.

PALIMPSEST

Deriving from the Greek *palimpsestos* ('scraped or rubbed away again'), the term 'palimpsest' denotes a writing surface, usually parchment or vellum, that has been used more than once, the earlier writing having been erased or scraped away to allow the surface to be used for a fresh, second or even third, layer of writing. Such manuscripts resulted in the medieval period from the high cost of parchment, which made its reuse or recycling a matter of practical economy. Palimpsests can be very interesting indeed when underlying texts of particular significance are not entirely obliterated and can be discerned with the use of modern technology such as ultra-violet light, digitization, or confocal microscopy: for instance, the previously unknown treatises by the ancient Greek mathematician Archimedes (*c*.287–212 BC), which were discovered in 1906 by the philologist J. L. Heiberg beneath the text of a thirteenth-century parchment prayer book in Istanbul, a palimpsest now on deposit in the Walters Art Museum in Baltimore.

The term 'palimpsest' is also sometimes adopted to describe figuratively a work that has more than one level of meaning or else shifting layers of meaning: e.g. Umberto Ecco's popular novel *The Name of the Rose* (1980), which the author specifically characterizes as 'a palimpsest', or Gore Vidal's 'memoir' *Palimpsest* (1995), so named because of the way 'remembrances are shaped and reshaped with time', with 'many rubbings-out and puttings-in'.

PANEL

A 'panel', the term normally meaning, among other things, a board or flat piece of material, can also, in earlier times, denote a small piece of parchment or roll, most especially that on which a sheriff listed the jurors in a case and which he attached to the relevant writ; alternatively it could be a separate list of jurors. In bookbinding, a panel is generally a compartment formed or enclosed by a frame, or border, on the cover.

PAPAL DOCUMENTS

For types of document issued by the Pope or Papal Chancery, among many other *litteræ ecclesiasticæ*, some relating to England, *see* BRIEF, BULL, DECRETAL, DIMISSORIALS, and ENCYCLICAL.

PAPER

Paper, which was invented in China probably in the second century BC, has been the principal material used as a writing surface since late medieval times. It was introduced to Europeans by the Arabs at least by the ninth century AD, when the earliest Greek manuscripts on paper were produced. The first manufacture of paper in Europe was apparently undertaken by the Moors in Spain by the late eleventh century, although the earliest surviving example of European paper currently recorded is a Sicilian deed dated 1109. The use of paper gradually spread throughout Europe, especially after the invention of printing in the 1450s, not least because of its relative cheapness compared to parchment. Paper was being used in England at least by the early fourteenth century, and paper mills were established there by 1498, although until the eighteenth century most paper used in Britain was imported from France or Italy.

Paper at that time was made by hand principally from rags, originally of wool, cotton, or linen. These were reduced to pulp with water and size, and a measure of the pulp was scooped into a rectangular wooden tray or frame, known as a 'mould', which was then gently shaken to make the fibres fuse together to produce a sheet of paper. Each frame was of a size that a single man could carry and was strung with wires, or bore an inserted screen of wires, which produced chain-lines, wire-marks, and watermarks in the paper. Paper thus manufactured is known as 'laid paper'.

By the mid-eighteenth century a new process of paper-manufacture was invented, producing a smooth paper made on a fine mesh of wires woven together. This type of paper, which predominated from about 1800 onwards, is known as 'wove paper'. As the process of manufacture became more mechanized, so did the demand for paper caused by the increased production of printed books lead to the use of more plentiful and cheaper organic and fibrous materials. These included most notably wood pulp, which was first patented in Germany in 1843. The processing of wood, however, introduced a higher level of acidity into paper, with the result that, before the development of modern acid-free paper, many books of the mid-nineteenth century onwards have turned brown and been apt to crumble away, having a very much shorter life expectancy than the hand-made papers of earlier centuries.

PAPER BOOK

The term 'paper book', occasionally found in early modern records, meant the same thing as 'written book': that is, a manuscript book, or else a book of blank pages designed to be used for writing purposes, as opposed to a printed book. This usage is occasionally encountered in wills, for instance, where a man bequeathes to members of his family his paper books in the hope that his writings therein will be preserved and be of comfort, use, or inspiration to them.

PAPERED SEAL

The term 'papered seal' is sometimes applied to a type of seal, since at least the early modern period, comprising wax overlaid with a small square or rhombus of paper which was then stamped with a hand seal while the wax was still warm, leaving an impression of the seal in relief on the paper (*see* Illus. 42). Perhaps the papered seal most commonly encountered is the Signet Seal, incorporating a royal coat of arms, used for authorizing miscellaneous royal letters and warrants (*see* Illus. 3, 20, and 81). *Compare* WAFER.

PAPERKNIFE

A paperknife (or letter opener or paper opener) is a sharp, pointed knife designed to cut envelopes or open letters that might also be used to cut the pages in unopened books. With their commercialization in the nineteenth and twentieth centuries, paper knives can take sometimes elaborate forms, with handles or blades carved or manufactured, for instance, from fine woods, ivory, silver, mother-of-pearl, or other materials, as well as steel. Paper knives may be distinguished from penknives, which serve other purposes (*compare* PENKNIFE).

PAPER OPENER

See LETTER OPENER and PENKNIFE.

PAPERWEIGHT

A paperweight is a moderately heavy, flat-bottomed object designed principally to hold down papers on a desk to stop them fluttering around or blowing away, although in practice it serves chiefly as a desk or shelf ornament. Developed from about the 1840s onwards and common today as commercially produced souvenirs or *objets d'art* suitable for presents, paperweights are usually no more than hand-sized, embody attractive or colourful views or decorations of some kind, and are most often made of glass, but sometimes of stone, metal, horn, or other material, commonly underlaid with felt.

PARAPH

A paraph is a symbol, such as // or ¶, indicating the beginning of a new paragraph or section in a text. It is also a scribal flourish or device written generally after a signature or at the end of a piece of writing. Paraphs are common enough in early modern literary manuscripts produced by professional scribes, where they tend to take the form of small loops or knots of some kind. When they appear, usually in more elaborate form, in medieval and early modern legal documents, as a partial safeguard against forgery, they may better be distinguished as notarial marks or signs. *See* NOTARIAL MARKS OR SIGNS.

PARCHMENT

'Parchment', a term thought to derive from the town of Pergamena (Bergama in modern western Turkey), which was a notable centre of production in the second century BC, is a pliable writing material that came by the fourth century AD to replace papyrus (made from the stems of papyrus plants) as the dominant type of writing surface before the widespread development of paper by the fifteenth century. Parchment is made from animal skin, often calf or sheep, but also occasionally from goat, pig, deer, or other creature. That made specifically from calfskin, which tends to be of slightly higher quality than most other skins, may technically be called 'vellum'. However, the difficulty of distinguishing one kind of animal grain from another, and the general adoption of the term 'vellum' (especially by bibliographers and bookdealers) to denote any type of parchment, has meant that the terms 'parchment' and 'vellum' have commonly been used interchangeably since at least the early sixteenth century.

The production of parchment involves the splitting, scraping, shaving, de-greasing, and dressing of the skins, the flesh side being the smoother, usually whiter side, best for writing purposes, the hair side being the outer, usually darker side, marked by grain or traces of hair follicles. When parchment was used for codices, the cut skins would usually be arranged so that at each opening the two facing pages would be either flesh side or hair side for the sake of uniformity, not a mixture of the two. Although the quality of parchment varied, it was and remains a relatively expensive material. Its use persisted in the early modern period and afterwards, particularly for deeds, rolls, and other kinds of legal documents and official records that were deemed worth preserving in a material form more durable than paper. It was also used for the more luxurious types of literary manuscript such as calligraphic presentation copies, and, under the name of 'vellum', has commonly been valued as a relatively high-grade binding material for books. *Compare* VELLUM.

PARCHMENT-RUNNER

A parchment-runner is a device for marking out lines on a page at regular intervals and was commercially produced in the eighteenth and nineteenth centuries. It comprised a small brass wheel with steel points or spikes rotating at the end of a narrow metal shaft with a wooden handle. When the wheel was run up the sides of a sheet or membrane it would leave small regularly spaced prick marks or indentations which could guide horizontal ruling for writing purposes. Such devices were associated with scriveners, although advertised as useful 'for solicitors, merchants &c.'. It is not clear whether similar instruments were used for marking or pricking by earlier scribes, instead of penknives, bodkins, or dividers, but it is quite possible.

PARDON

A pardon is a document whereby a person is forgiven or absolved for some offence, by way of mercy or exoneration, or as a remission of payment or punishment, usually granted by a civil or ecclesiastical authority. Typical examples of the former are pardons issued by monarchs, forgiving individuals, for whatever reason, for a variety of misdeeds. These range from the minor infraction of some legal technicality in conveying property to murder and high treason. Such pardons commonly take the form of Royal Letters Patent. Those issued by the Church include late medieval papal indulgences for the remission of sins sold by pardoners (*see* INDULGENCES). Many official pardons issued in England were enrolled in Chancery as a public record on the Patent Rolls.

PARDONER
See INDULGENCES.

PARDON OF ALIENATION
See LICENCE OF ALIENATION.

PARISH REGISTERS
See REGISTER.

PARLIAMENT ROLLS

The Parliament Rolls, also known as *Rotuli Parliamentorum* ('rolls of par-liaments'), are parchment rolls on which are recorded, in the hands of official clerks, particulars of proceedings in Parliament in each session. They are preserved in the National Archives at Kew (an early Exchequer and partly Chancery series of twenty-seven rolls covering the years 1289–1322 in SC 9, and then numerous Chancery rolls from 1327 to the present in C 65). Up until 1534 they record petitions by individuals or by the Commons and the answers received, which formed the basis of Acts of Parliament, as well as details of cases that came before Parliament, particulars of administrative appointments, and occasionally the texts of new statutes. From 1535 on-wards, and particularly from 1629, the information supplied in these rolls became increasingly limited to the public Acts of Parliament themselves.

Supplementary to these rolls in the Chancery records (C 153) is what is known as the 'Vetus Codex' (the Latin *vetus* meaning 'old') or sometimes the 'Black Book of the Tower', which is an early set of transcripts of the Parliament Rolls from 1290 to 1307 and 1320–1, written by various Chancery clerks over a period. The 'Statute Rolls' (C 74) (the Latin *statutum* meaning 'a law') are the Chancery enrolments of notable Acts of Parliament, in their final authorized form, passed between 1277 and 1431 and between 1445 and 1469, with related documents. There is also a collection of miscellaneous Exchequer papers relating to parliamentary proceedings from 1255 to *c.*1625 (E 175).

Deriving from the French *parole* ('word'), the word 'parol' is a legal term normally meaning 'by word of mouth', applied to testimony, statements, pleadings, evidence, and the like that are given orally. The term 'parol writings' is also used to characterize legal documents that are unsealed.

PART

In the theatre, a part, or actor's part—also apparently known, at least in the eighteenth-century theatre, as a 'side'—is the script used and memorized by an actor, which contains those sections of the play relating to the character he or she is performing: i.e. all his or her lines, usually with preceding cue lines (spoken by other actors) so that at each point the actor knows when to speak. In earlier times, such parts would have been entirely manuscript, probably copied out neatly by scribes from the complete theatrical play text, or book.

In his classic *Dramatic Documents* (1931), W. W. Greg records that the earliest known parts that survive (wholly or in fragments) relate to medieval or early modern mystery plays: one, on a parchment roll over 4 feet (1.2 metres) long, for a character or play called 'Dux Moraud' ('Duke Vagabond') dating from the fourteenth century and now in the Bodleian Library (MS Eng. poet. f. 2); another, a volume containing text for the parts of 'third Shepherd', 'third Mary', and 'Cleophas' in a miracle or liturgical play, dating from the fifteenth century and preserved at Shrewsbury School; and yet another, in a narrow paper scroll 4 feet long, for the part of God in a miracle play from Herefordshire c.1570–80 once owned by the Duke of Portland (Greg's photographs of it are in the British Library, Facs. 305). The earliest known surviving part from the professional Elizabethan theatre is for the title-role of Orlando in Robert Greene's play *Orlando Furioso*, a long roll (of which nearly 17 ½ feet, or over 5 metres, about two-thirds of the original, remains) used by the great actor Edward Alleyn c.1591–2. This is now preserved at Dulwich College. Otherwise, probably the earliest known seventeenth-century actor's part is for the character Pragmaticus in Robert Burton's academic Latin play *Philosophaster*, copied in the hand of Thomas Goffe who played the role in the production at Christ Church, Oxford, in February 1618. This part is now preserved in the Harvard Theatre Collection (MS Thr 10.1, fols 48–56).

In music, a part may also be a copy of that portion of the full score that is to be played or sung by an individual musician or vocalist.

PARTBOOK

A partbook, or part-book, is a manuscript or printed music book or songbook in which are entered the musical notation, and words for vocal compositions, for a particular instrument or voice. Among the many surviving examples of music books from medieval times onwards, partbooks date from as early as *c*.1430 but flourished particularly in the sixteenth and seventeenth centuries, when, among other things, many poets' poems and lyrics were set to music. Vocal partbooks, written for the use of different performers, are generally labelled *Tenor*, *Cantus* (soprano), *Altus* (alto), and *Bassus* (bass) respectively. Although a set of as many as ten variously designated partbooks might be produced, a set of four was the most common, the terms *Quintus* and *Sextus* being often applied to any additional fifth or sixth partbook produced, whatever their vocal pitch. Partbooks, most of those in manuscript copied out by professional scribes, are usually oblong in format and capable of being hand-held or rested on music stands during performance. Many Renaissance paintings depicting performances of secular music show partbooks laid open around a table, which may also be laden with fruit or other food. A number of music books, both manuscript (e.g. British Library, Add. MS 31390, *c*.1578) and printed (e.g. John Dowland's *First Book of Aires*, 1597), were also designed so that any opening had four separate parts, each facing a different direction outwards, so that four or more singers or instrumentalists could sit or stand around it and use it at the same time.

PASSPORT

The term 'passport' can be applied to a number of official or diplomatic documents, from medieval times onwards, allowing people to go abroad or else requesting or granting permission for them to be allowed to pass freely in particular countries (i.e. safe-conducts). Those issued in England from about 1570 until the late seventeenth century took the form of a 'licence to pass beyond the seas' and were signed by the sovereign, who retained the prerogative right to control the movement of his or her subjects overseas. From the Restoration period onwards such licences, or passports, could be issued on behalf of the monarch by secretaries of state, although some might still be signed by the sovereign in person. Registers or entry books recording these, in increasing numbers, are preserved in the National Archives at Kew: in SP 44/334–413 (for 1674–1784), FO 366/544 (for 1748–1794), FO 610–611 (for most of 1795 to 1948), and FO 613/2 (for March–May 1915). Although there was some tightening up of regulations after 1846, the majority of travellers going abroad did so without carrying any official documentation, and passports were, in practice, issued chiefly to diplomats and merchants. They did not become compulsory in Britain until the First World War.

Most surviving passports from the late eighteenth century onwards take the form of documents on large sheets of light, thin paper, partly printed

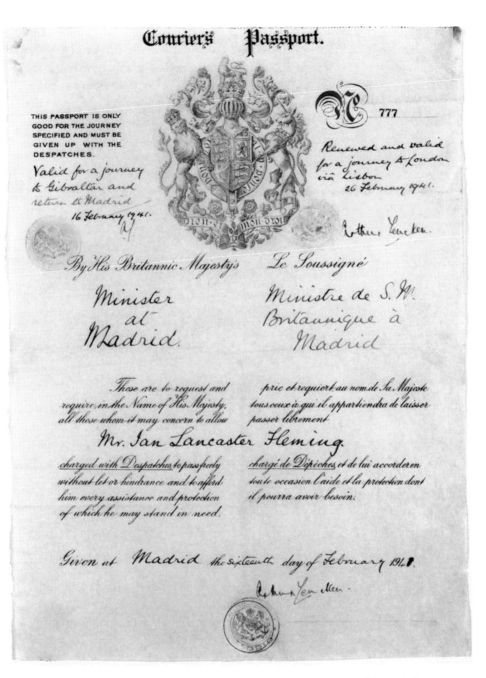

ILLUS. 59 *The Courier's Passport issued to Ian Fleming by the British Minister at Madrid, Arthur F. Yencken, for Fleming's part in the espionage Operation Goldeneye during the Second World War. It is a partly printed large folio-size page in English and French, with manuscript insertions, signed or initialled by Yencken three times and with his official embassy stamps, authorizing a renewal for the third time, 16–26 February 1941.*

with an engrossed heading and appropriate national arms or symbols, and with manuscript insertions providing particulars of the holder. They are almost always signed by the Home Secretary (such as many signed by Lord Palmerston)—although in later years the signature was a facsimile, being part of the printing. They invariably bear subsequent hand-stamps, endorsements, and inscriptions made at the various places stopped en route, which in some respects serve the function of a visa. Also they are often folded within a leather wallet manufactured for that purpose.

The modern type of passport, in the form of a small, largely printed pocket-book, bearing a photograph of the holder, was not introduced until 1921. Other types of passport might be issued by overseas embassies for particular purposes (*see* Illus. 59).

Compare LICENCE TO PASS BEYOND THE SEAS and SAFE-CONDUCT.

PASTE-DOWN

The paste-down in a bound printed or manuscript book is usually that half of the binder's endpaper that is pasted down to the inside of the upper or lower cover. Depending on which end of the book it is, the other half of the endpaper is called either the front (or upper) free endpaper or rear (or lower) free endpaper. Alternatively the paste-down may be a single leaf pasted inside the cover. In medieval and early printed books it might also be of parchment rather than paper and possibly of recycled material (*see* BINDERS' WASTE). A paste-down made of leather—a feature of some relatively modern books, more common in France than in England—is called a 'doublure'.

PASTE-UP

A paste-up is, or can be, a stage in the production of a printed work, such as an auction catalogue, that contains a series of separately numbered texts which have to be arranged to fit the available pages satisfactorily. The process generally involves the cutting up of discrete portions of proof-copy of printed text, including illustrations; arranging them in a suitable order on a series of large sheets (containing printed rules or grids corresponding to the exact size of the pages in the eventual published production), and then pasting them down; deleting or expanding text, by marking or annotating it by hand, where necessary, to make it fit or fill the space available; adding headings, directions to the printer on points of layout, or other features omitted; and renumbering entries and pages where the original sequence in proof has had to be changed. The completed paste-up is then used as model for the production of the final printed version.

The term 'patent', meaning 'open', denotes any document issued for public attention, as opposed to one 'close', meaning 'sealed' or 'private'. It is most often encountered as letters patent, official grants issued by the Chancery conferring a right or privilege of some kind (*see* LETTERS PATENT). In more modern times, however, the most common type of patent is that granting monopoly privileges to an inventor. Such patents, granted to entrepreneurs who applied to have the exclusive right to manufacture their own invention for a specified period, have existed since the sixteenth century, and were regulated notably in 1623 by the Statute of Monopolies, which limited the duration of inventors' patents to fourteen years and made monopolies subject to determination 'according to the common laws of this realm, and not otherwise'. Applications that embodied more precise details and specifications of the inventions, including a huge range of machines, weapons, practical devices, and industrial processes, date from the early eighteenth century. Patents of invention issued by the Chancery and Petty Bag Office were also enrolled, with all their detailed descriptions, as a public record up to 1853, after which the Patent Office was responsible for them. The National Archives at Kew contain enrolments of such patents notably from 1709 to 1848 (C 210 and C 73).

PATENT OF NOBILITY

Patents of nobility are Royal Letters Patent ennobling or raising individuals to the peerage (the ascending order of the English nobility being baron, viscount, earl, marquess, and duke). Such patents, with their formulaic texts traditionally in Latin, are usually engrossed on large membranes of parchment and, depending on the size of the recipient's purse (since the person honoured was responsible for paying for its production), may be lavishly embellished, with an illuminated initial letter portrait of the reigning monarch and the royal arms, with decorated or historiated borders, as well as bearing the pendent Great Seal attached by gold or silver laces (*see* Illus. 76). Some, particularly in the eighteenth century onwards, may also be rolled up and kept in special leather-covered wooden or else metal fitted boxes, shaped to accommodate the large round skippet containing the seal.

Patents of nobility were chiefly granted to men, but there are examples in the early modern period of women elevated to the peerage because of their services to the monarch: for example, Charles II's mistress Lady Castlemaine, created Duchess of Cleveland in 1670 because of 'her own personal virtues', the honour being bestowed when the King wished to end his relationship with her; and Lady Belasyse, created Baroness Belasyse in her own right (*suo jure*) in 1674 by way of compensation for not being allowed to marry the King's brother, James.

For a Spanish type of patent of nobility, known as a *carta executoria de hidalguía, see* GENEALOGY.

PATENT ROLLS

The Patent Rolls in the National Archives at Kew (C 66) are the enrolment, or official registered copies, of letters patent issued by the Chancery from 1201 to the present day, significant interruptions occurring only in the Civil War and Interregnum period. Written chiefly on large membranes of parchment sewn together head to foot, the more modern rolls actually in the form of books, they record not only the grants of office, privileges, rights, pardons, etc. made by the Crown, but also details of innumerable other matters of public interest over the centuries, including accounts of Crown revenues, royal commissions and proclamations, and international treaties.

PATINA

'Patina' (the stress upon the first syllable in pronunciation) is a term occasionally used with reference to pendent seals, especially the Great Seal, attached to charters and letters patent. A patina is the sheen on, or the surface of, objects made of bronze, marble, and other materials, most especially the film or incrustation that may collect over a period of time, through oxidation or other chemical reactions, affecting their colour. Thus a large wax seal may be said to have a brown, or yellow, or black, or red, etc. patina by way of defining its present surface colour, whatever its original colour.

PECIA SYSTEM

The pecia system (the Latin *pecia* meaning 'piece') was a regulated process of manuscript production used chiefly in the thirteenth, fourteenth, and to some extent fifteenth centuries at the universities of Bologna and Paris, and possibly for a time at Oxford and Cambridge. Authorized exemplars of officially approved texts were deposited usually with a stationer, who was a university officer in receipt of certain privileges. From these loaned official exemplars he would make approved copies of his own. He then hired out to students or to other members of the university or to independent scribes numbered 'pieces' (*peciae*) or sections of his copies, normally short quires of four or six leaves—not necessarily taken from a single exemplar of a particular work—by way of instalments, one at a time, for the further copying of particular works. The result was that a particular section might be copied by two or more scribes at more or less the same time. The student or scribe concerned would then have to return the piece to the stationer in order to get from him the next numbered section or instalment (if it was not out to another copyist) for similar copying. This would lead eventually to the copies of the various sections being assembled and bound together to form united transcripts of the complete work which might in turn themselves be copied. Manuscripts produced in this way can be identified by the pecia marks *p* or *pij* written in the margins, as well as by features such as false starts and changes of ink.

This system is to be distinguished from another, much older type of 'assembly line' scribal production, which was still flourishing in the seventeenth century, whereby, to speed things up, a complete exemplar was divided between two or more scribes for simultaneous copying of *different* sections of the text. This process is sometimes known as 'distributive copying'.

The term 'pecia' is also occasionally found in medieval European use to denote a single animal skin, particularly sheepskin, prepared as a single membrane of parchment, which might then be trimmed, folded, and cut to form four folio or eight quarto leaves for writing purposes.

PEDIGREE

See GENEALOGY.

PEN

A pen is any hand-held writing implement used for applying ink to paper, to parchment or, in ancient times, to papyrus. The term, derived from the Latin *penna* meaning 'feather', is generic and covers several different types of implement. The pen may be said to have developed principally from the Roman *calamus*, or split, sharpened reed pen, to the more supple quill cut from a feather, used from about the sixth century onwards, leading to the introduction at the end of the eighteenth century of the steel or metal-tipped pen (although types of metal pens are also recorded from antiquity onwards), until the more modern production of fountain pens, ballpoint pens, fibre- or felt-tipped pens and fineliner pens.

PENCIL

Deriving from the Latin *penicullus* (a 'little tail' or 'little brush'), the term 'pencil' originally denoted a small brush used for painting, a use still recorded as late as the eighteenth century. What became the commonest writing instrument after the pen, the pencil as known today was developed by the early seventeenth century following the discovery near Keswick, Cumberland, in the mid-sixteenth century of large deposits of plumbago, graphite or 'black lead', as it was sometimes called. This type of pure carbon, capable when sawn into narrow rods of tracing a strong black line, would eventually supersede the plummet or lead point used earlier, which could usually trace only a light grey line. Since plumbago easily soiled the fingers and hence the writing surface, it required the use of some kind of binding or holder. The earliest recorded wooden one dates from 1565; others, sometimes known as *porte-crayons*, dating from the seventeenth to nineteenth centuries, were made of steel, brass, or even chased silver. Commercial production of the familiar modern pencils, comprising black lead tightly encased in wood, dates from the late eighteenth century; by 1854 the company of Joseph Banks in Keswick had achieved an output of between 5 and 6 million pencils per annum. Later developments in pencil technology have included pencils made with plastic instead of wood and the familiar propelling pencil (a cylindrical metal or plastic tube with a mechanism for moving a thin length of graphite through a hole in the pointed tip).

PENDENT

The term 'pendent' (from the French *pendant*), used in connection with wax seals, means literally 'hanging' and pertains to any seal affixed to a document by means of a suspended tag or ties—such as a thin strip of parchment or plaited cords or laces—as opposed to wax seals impressed directly on the document itself (*see* Illus. 32, 36, and 40). A document containing a number of pendent seals could be called in the Middle Ages a 'ragman'.

PENKNIFE

A penknife is one of the traditional tools of scribes since at least as early as the medieval period. It is a small knife used principally for cutting or sharpening the nibs of quill pens. It might also sometimes be used for erasing errors by scraping them from the parchment or paper, or, in the absence of other methods, for pricking pages prior to ruling. Early penknives would have a blade with one side flat, the other chamfered. A penknife usually had a rigid handle, of wood or other materials, sometimes with a ring for suspension, or else it was a portable pocket-knife kept in a sheath. By the seventeenth century, if not earlier, the more expensive examples might have decorated handles of ivory, silver, gold, agate, or tortoiseshell. In the numerous illustrations of scribes, especially in the Middle Ages, they are often depicted working with a quill in one hand and a penknife in the other or at their side (see Illus. 79).

By the early nineteenth century the penknife had developed into a narrow jointed blade or blades which closed up within the handle. With the introduction of mechanical quill cutters and of steel-tipped pens, however, penknives had become largely redundant so far as their traditional function was concerned, although the term 'penknife' for any folding pocket-knife has persisted. *Compare* PAPERKNIFE.

PENMAN

A penman in the general sense is anyone who writes or copies texts, whether it be a scribe, clerk, amanuensis, etc. or a writer in the sense of author. The term often has the connotation, however, of one who is skilled in writing: who writes an attractive, even calligraphic script. Penmanship is thus the art of fine writing or calligraphy.

PENNER

A penner is a portable pen-case: i.e. a case or sheath in which to carry pens about. A common accoutrement of scribes, especially itinerant scribes, at least since medieval times, a penner was usually made of horn, leather, or metal. It could also be made of silver or other material, possibly decorated; was sometimes attached to an inkhorn; and was occasionally worn at the girdle. The well-known portrait of Geoffrey Chaucer in the National Portrait Gallery shows him standing and holding in his right hand a small penner.

PENNY BLACK

See UNIFORM PENNY POSTAGE.

PENNY POSTAGE

A penny (*1d.*) was the standard charge per mile for most postal delivery of letters in England from at least the sixteenth century, although the post was variously regulated and subject to higher charges, such as two pence (*2d.*) per mile, in emergencies. A standard penny postage for delivering letters within a wider though still limited area was pioneered in London in 1680 by William Dockwra. Various local penny posts developed in the British Isles in subsequent years, until the Uniform Penny Postage, establishing a single *1d.* rate for delivery anywhere in Britain, was introduced by the Post Office in 1840. *See* UNIFORM PENNY POSTAGE.

PEN PUSHER

The term 'pen pusher', a rather pejorative phrase of nineteenth-century origin, denotes someone whose routine job is confined to sitting at a desk and dealing with unimportant bureaucratic paperwork. Besides providing an alliteration of *p*s, 'pusher' is appropriate in such a context to support the sense of modest effort and energy being applied solely to a pen rather than to significant practical work in the world at large. It is inappropriate in the literal sense, since pens are not generally designed to be pushed, but rather to be drawn or pulled.

PEN REST

A pen rest occurs in a manuscript when the writer or scribe, pausing perhaps absentmindedly, rests his or her pen on the page, making a mark of some kind, but one that is not consciously intended to represent any kind of punctuation. Pen rests are sometimes read, or transcribed, by unsuspecting modern editors as forms of punctuation, such as commas, virgules, or full stops. However, in truth it is not always easy to distinguish between intentional punctuation and accidental pen rests.

The term 'pen rest' may also be used generically to denote any kind of holder in which a pen is placed at rest on a desk or other writing surface. Thus pens might be laid down horizontally in pen trays, or put nib-first into suitably shaped receptacles, or else stood upright nib-uppermost in holes in various types of inkstands, holders, or pen racks. Commercial production of such pen rests flourished particularly in the nineteenth century.

PEN TRIAL

A pen trial, sometimes cited by the Latin term *probatio pennae*, is a piece of scribbling, doodling, or a writing exercise, usually involving only a few words, made by a writer to test his or her freshly trimmed pen or writing style. Such inscriptions are sometimes found in manuscripts or printed books, generally on blank leaves or in margins, entered, perhaps by children, with scant respect for the nature of the book or document to which they happened to have access. In the Middle Ages and later they may well also be the product of scribes, whether actually engaged in testing a pen or else relieving the boredom of a tedious copying task by adding to their transcript unrelated text, doodles, or drawings for their own amusement.

PERFECT

'Perfect' is a term often used by booksellers to describe a printed book that has been checked, collated (usually by comparison with another copy of the same edition) and found to have all the leaves it should have, which are also in the right order. The term is not normally applied to manuscripts, since each manuscript of whatever work has its own character. It may, however, be possible, on various evidence, to check that the text embodied in the manuscript is complete and that the manuscript has its original integrity: i.e. that it does not lack any leaves or portions of leaves that were there originally and evidently intended by the scribe to remain there, excluding leaves deliberately excised because of marred copying. Such examination may not prove the manuscript to be technically 'perfect', but, on the other hand, if the manuscript evidently lacks portions of its text or physical integrity through subsequent mutilation or deterioration, it may properly be described as 'imperfect'. *Compare* IMPERFECT.

PETITION

A petition is a written supplication, entreaty, or application requesting the granting of justice, forgiveness, reparation, a privilege, or reward of some kind. The most commonly encountered petitions are those drawn up on behalf of individuals or corporate bodies, such as guilds and livery companies, and submitted to legislative courts, officials, Parliament, the Privy Council, or the monarch, soliciting a favour, such as recognition or incorporation of their company, or requesting the redress of perceived wrongs or grievances. In the case of petitions submitted by Parliament to the monarch for royal assent, they may relate to proposed measures or changes in the law voted by the House. Some extraordinary petitions could take extraordinary forms: for instance, one by the Company of East India Merchants to the Shah of Persia on 9 April 1660 seeking customs revenues owed to them was elaborately engrossed on a large membrane of vellum with decorated borders containing illuminated coats of arms and images of ships.

For the most part, however, petitions by individuals, at least in the early modern period, were drawn up usually by lawyers, notaries, or scriveners in a standardized form, with a heading incorporating the name of the petitioner, such as 'To the King's Most Excellent Majesty | The Petition of John Smith | humbly sheweth | that . . .', neatly written on a single leaf of paper or, occasionally, parchment (*see* Illus. 60). Often signed by a petitioner referring to himself or herself as 'your orator' (in the sense of one promising to pray for the person petitioned), they were folded to be placed in the hands of the monarch, minister, or other supplicated authority as he walked by. They were confined to a single page so as not to exceed the attention span that could reasonably be expected of the recipient. They were often written in quite small lettering, not only to make the text fit the page but also, perhaps, to denote an appropriate measure of humility by the petitioner. Quantities of such petitions are preserved in the National Archives at Kew, the British Library (many addressed to Charles I, for instance), and, at least in retained copies, in various family archives.

To the Kings most Excellent Ma.ty

The humble petition of Titus Otes

Most humbly Shews That Judgment haueing on Saturday last been entred in your Ma.ts Court of Kings Bench ag.t your petitioner on two indictments of periury assigned in Euidence deliuered aboue six yeares since in Cases of high treason committed ag.t his late Ma.ty of Blessed Memory by Seuerall persons Conuicted attainted and executed for the same: the truth of which Euidence was after Strict and mature examination Solemnly approued by his said late Ma.ty in Councill, the Lords and Comons in Parliam.t assembled, all the Judges of England and Seuerall Juryes. And for that there are Manifest Errors in the Proceedings and Judgments aforesaid ag.t your pet.r

Your petitioner most humbly prayes your Ma.ty warrant to the Lord Keeper of your Great Seale of England to grant your petitioner two writts of Error to the Lord Chief Justice of your Ma.ts said Court of Kings Bench to be directed requiring him to bring before your Ma.ty in Parliam.t at your Parliam.t to be held at Westm.r the 19.th of May instant the Records of the processes and Judgments ag.t your petitioner on both the indictments aforesaid that upon inspection thereof by your Ma.ty in Parliam.t your Ma.ty may Cause to bee further donne what of Right ought to bee done thesame And that in the Meane time Execution of the said Judgments be stayed

And your petitioner shall Euer pray &c

Titus Otes

296

'Philately' (a term coined in the 1860s) denotes the pursuit of postage stamp collecting and also the study of all physical characteristics of stamps, as well as related aspects of postal history and postal stationery, including postal marks, hand-stamps, labels, envelopes, postcards, etc.

PHILLIPPS MANUSCRIPT

A Phillipps Manuscript, or Phillipps MS, usually followed by a number, is a manuscript once owned by the antiquary Sir Thomas Phillipps (1792–1872), who assiduously formed one of the greatest private collections of manuscripts ever recorded. Thus it is a term frequently encountered in descriptions of manuscripts. Comprising manuscripts both ancient and modern, in a wide range of languages and classifications, Phillipps's huge collection was originally housed chiefly at Middle Hill, Broadway, Worcestershire, and then from 1862 at Thirlestaine House, Cheltenham, Gloucestershire. The number cited after 'MS' is that assigned to the manuscript by Phillipps himself in his own privately printed catalogue up to 23,837; after his death numbers up to 26,179 were assigned for probate purposes by Sir Edward Bond, Keeper of Manuscripts at the British Museum. The remaining manuscripts were then numbered up to 38,628 by Phillipps's grandson Thomas Fitzroy Fenwick (d. 1938), although the full count of Phillipps's manuscripts was estimated to be nearer to 60,000. Much of Phillipps's collection was posthumously dispersed in a series of auctions at Sotheby's between 1886 and 1938, and also by private sales. The residue remained in storage until purchased in 1946 by Lionel and Philip Robinson, of William H. Robinson Ltd, Pall Mall, London, who subsequently dispersed it over a period of decades, the last Phillipps sale at Sotheby's, by order of the Robinson Trust, occurring on 13 April 1981. The Robinsons are reputed to have obtained almost as much for individual medieval manuscripts as the estimated £100,000 they had paid for the entire residue collection. A set of the Phillipps catalogues up to MS 38628 annotated with information about the manuscripts' dispersal by the Phillipps scholar A. N. L. Munby (1913–1974), who also published five volumes of *Phillipps Studies* (1951–60), is in the private collection of Martin Schøyen, but bound

ILLUS. 60 *The petition of Titus Oates to James II, 18 May 1685, requesting a writ of error to be granted him so that he might plead his case before Parliament for a remission of the penalties imposed on him for his perjuries in 1678 that had fomented the Popish Plot crisis. The text is laid out in formal petition mode by a professional scribe on a single folio page and signed at the foot by Oates himself.*

photocopies of it are in the British Library and the Bodleian Library, Oxford, as well as at Sotheby's, London.

PHYLACTERY

In the context of art and manuscripts especially of the medieval period, though sometimes later, phylactery is a type of banderole, being a representation of an inscribed or captioned ribbon-like scroll proceeding from a person's mouth, or held by him, usually to indicate his rank or worth (*see* Illus. 65).

PICTOGRAPH

A pictograph, or glyph, is a form of writing in which a word or words are represented by a pictorial symbol: hence pictography is picture-writing. Some of the world's most ancient forms of writing take the form of pictographs, or evolved from pictography, such as Mesopotamian cuneiform, Egyptian hieroglyphics, and the glyphs used by the Mayans of Central America. Types of pictography do survive in the modern world, however, when words are represented in graphic form, such as in road signs or in nineteenth-century rebus letters.

PILOT BOOK

The term 'pilot book', often abbreviated to 'pilot', means an atlas of sea-charts. The term did not apparently gain currency, however, until the publication of John Seller's *The English Pilot* (1671).

PIN

See STYLUS.

PIN-DUST

Technically meaning the fine dust or metal filings produced in the manufacture of pins, 'pin-dust' was also a term sometimes applied in the early modern period to the fine chalky powder known as 'pounce' used to blot ink.

PIPE ROLLS

The Pipe Rolls, originally kept in the Pipe Office and now in the National Archives at Kew (E 372), are the Great Rolls of the Exchequer comprising a record of the monarch's accounts for each financial year. They record audited particulars submitted by sheriffs, stewards, bailiffs, and other agents of the monarch in the shires that were responsible for the royal revenues. They include much other detail of taxation, debts, penalties, and profits from forests and forfeited goods, as well as some Royal Household accounts, such as expenses for troops, ships, and castles. The accounts were entered by Exchequer clerks on both sides of membranes of parchment which were stitched together head to head, Exchequer-style, then rolled up to look rather like a section of drainage pipe: hence the term 'pipe rolls'. They were written in abbreviated Latin until 1733, except for the use of English during the Commonwealth period in the 1650s. The extant series numbers 676 rolls, covering the years 1120–30 and 1155–1833, complete except for gaps in 1216 and 1403.

PLAINTIFF

In a lawsuit, the plaintiff is the person or party making a bill of complaint or initiating the suit, as opposed to the defendant. In a Chancery or other equity suit, both parties might be obliged to provide written answers to interrogatories or statements put to them, although in common law, until 1851, neither party could be asked questions. Before 1833 plaintiffs in real actions (suits in civil law concerning property claims) were called 'demandants'. More recently, under Lord Chief Justice Woolf, the term 'plaintiff' has been replaced by 'claimant'.

PLAITED

Meaning intertwined or braided, and usually used to describe hair, the term 'plaited' is also applicable to the intertwined threads, cords, or laces by which large seals are usually attached to formal documents on parchment such as Royal Letters Patent.

PLAN

A plan is a scheme, design, project, or formulated arrangement for doing or accomplishing something. It can also be a drawing, diagram, or type of map, but is generally distinguished from a map in so far as a plan tends to encompass a somewhat smaller area, such as a plot of land, estate, fields, or district of a town, drawn up on a relatively larger scale and incorporating more minute details. A plan may also be a diagram delineating the arrangement or positioning of walls, rooms, passageways, stairs, landings, etc. of the floor of a building.

PLAT

'Plat' is a Germanic word meaning 'flat'. In 1527 Hans Holbein was paid for painting a plat of a battle scene at Greenwich Palace, which, it has been surmised, suggests a map or aerial view of the subject. The term was also used, at least in the Elizabethan theatre, as synonymous with 'plot'. *See* PLOT.

The plea rolls are official records, or enrolments, of court proceedings for actions brought under the common law from medieval times onwards. Beginning in the time of Richard I in the 1190s, they detail cases heard in the early King's Court and then in other common-law courts up until 1875, although entries became increasingly irregular after the early seventeenth century. From 1234 two distinct series of plea rolls correspond to those for what became the Common Bench (or Common Pleas) on the one hand and the King's Bench on the other, known as *de banco* and *coram rege* rolls respectively. The entries were made by clerks on membranes of parchment stitched together at the top Exchequer-style, each sewn bundle covering a legal term. The numerous plea rolls preserved in the National Archives at Kew for various courts, some including enrolments of deeds and other records, include early series for the courts of Common Pleas (CP 40) and King's Bench (KB 26 and 27) and also for the common-law side of Exchequer (E 32 and E 9). An early collection of plea rolls and Memoranda Rolls for the court of the Mayor of London from 1323 to 1484 is in the London Metropolitan Archives (CLA/024/01/1–102). *See also* BOOK OF ENTRIES.

PLOT

A plot is a plan or scheme, constituting the organizing design that gives a piece of literature such as a play or novel its purpose, structure, or integrity, as well as story-line. A plot may also be an area or messuage of land, a manor, or estate, or else a map, survey, or ground plan thereof. In addition, a plot may be a devious and subversive scheme or conspiracy, as in the Gunpowder Plot of 1605 and so-called Popish Plot of 1678.

In the Elizabethan theatre, a plot (spelt 'plott' or 'plat': see PLAT) denotes specifically a list of characters' entrances and of properties to be made ready for the staging of a particular play. This would help, among other things, to determine how the parts could be allocated and how actors could double up in the various roles. From the evidence of the few surviving examples, the plot would be written in double columns on one side of a broadsheet, measuring approximately 17 × 12½ inches (44 × 32.5 cm), and it would be posted or pinned up backstage for consultation by the prompter, actors, and stage personnel. Four complete examples are known: for the plays *The Dead Man's Fortune*, *The Second Part of The Seven Deadly Sins* (probably by Richard Tarlton: *see* Illus. 61), *Frederick and Basilea*, and *Fortune's Tennis* (three of these are now in the British Library, the second one at Dulwich College). Fragments of plots for *Troilus and Cressida* (probably by Thomas Dekker and Henry Chettle) and *The Battle of Alcazar* (by George Peele) are also in the

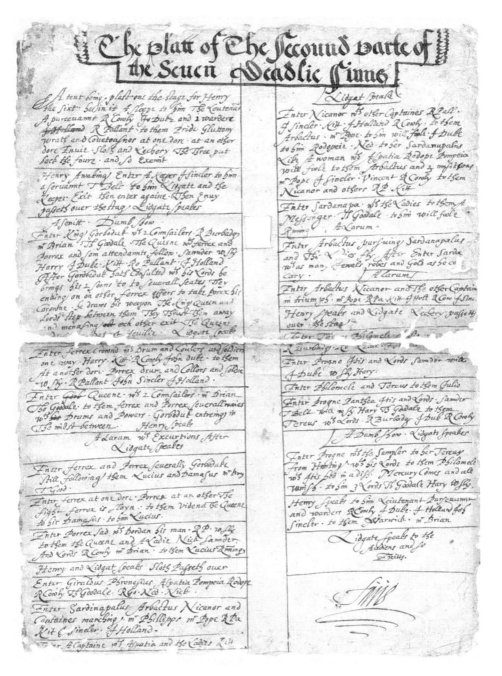

ILLUS. 61 'The platt of The Secound parte of the Seuen Deadlie sinns', a stage plot of c.1590–1591 written in ruled double columns in the italic hand of a scribe on a single sheet of paper, with an oblong hole in the centre where probably posted on a wooden peg, and a finis with spiral flourish at the end.

British Library, and one other, for *The First Part of Tamar Cam*, is known only from a printed transcription made in the eighteenth century. All these plots are reproduced in facsimile in W. W. Greg's *Dramatic Documents from the Elizabethan Playhouses* (1931). In addition, the dramatist Robert Wilson gave the theatrical impresario Philip Henslowe in 1599 a briefly delineated plot of the first act of *The Second Part of Henry Duke of Richmond* in exchange for payment, on the recommendation of the actor Robert Shaa, who said that he had 'heard' and liked the 'booke' (Dulwich College, MS 1, art. 26). Although it is possible that the use of plots of this kind persisted in the theatres before they were closed in 1642, no other extant examples are known and the practice does not seem to have been readopted after the Restoration.

Since it was evidently designed for the practical use of theatre personnel only, this type of plot may be distinguished from any kind of outline or synopsis of the contents or story-line of the play or masque, or from its plot in the literary sense, such as might be written out and given to an audience—for instance, to royal, distinguished, or foreign visitors—for their guidance. The latter is what in Thomas Middleton's *Women Beware Women* (V, ii, 30–1) is called the 'Argument' or 'model / Of what's presented' or, alternatively, a 'device'—as in 'the Deuice of a Maske here, drawne in this paper' in Middleton's *The Puritan* (III, iii, 127–9). It is, nevertheless, a symptom of the looseness and overlapping applications of these terms that even an outline or script of a play used by a spectator might be called the 'plot' in certain circumstances: as in Thomas Kyd's *The Spanish Tragedy* (IV, iv, 9–10, 33–4) where 'the copy of the play... the argument of what we show' given to the King can also be called by him 'the plot'.

PLUMBAGO

Plumbago is a black lead or graphite substance, a form of carbon, used in the manufacture of pencils. Plumbago, whether applied by pencil or as a stick of charcoal material, was also sometimes used instead of ink as dark filling or shading in the decoration of certain kinds of document, such as in occasional initial letter portraits found on Royal Letters Patent (*see* Illus. 38).

PLUMMET

'Plummet' is another term for 'lead point' (*see* DRY POINT).

POCKET-BOOK

A pocket-book is any kind of notebook or small manuscript book made or adapted for conveniently carrying in the pocket, as also subsequently a printed book, such as an almanac, made for similar use (*see* Illus. 62).

ILLUS. 62 *An opening in the pocket-book of Henry Rimborne, a small notebook (c.3½ × 2 inches or 11.5 × 4 cm) which also incorporates a printed almanac for 1658. It shows some of his accounts relating to the Coronation of Charles II, at which he was a yeoman usher, 23 April 1661.*

In addition, the term is applied to a small portable pocket-size case, made of leather or other material, containing compartments for such things as personal papers, bank-notes, bills, receipts, and the like.

POETICAL ALBUM

A poetical album is an album in which are collected manuscript poems. In occasional examples, the poems might be inscribed by the poets themselves for the particular collector: album entries of this kind are known for Byron, Thomas Moore, Coleridge, Longfellow, Wordsworth, Tennyson, Kipling, and John Masefield, among others. More commonly, however, the poems are copied in the album from other sources, generally printed ones, by the collector or by other members of his or her family and friends. They consequently bear witness to literary fashions at certain times or to the favourite poems of a particular family or social circle. Although the practice of compiling manuscript collections of poems, or verse miscellanies, has considerable antiquity, the use of albums in the form of commercially produced stationery products designed for manuscript entries and devoted primarily to verse flourished especially in the nineteenth century. *Compare* VERSE MISCELLANY.

See VERSE MISCELLANY.

POINTING HAND

See MANICULE.

POLAIRE

The Irish Gaelic word *polaire* (pronounced 'pó-la-ra'; plural: *polaireadha*, pronounced 'pó-la-rāā') denotes a type of leather satchel, from about the sixth to the sixteenth century or later, used by Irish monks for carrying books.

PORTAS

Deriving from the French *porter* ('to carry') and *hors* ('outside'), the term 'portas' denoted a small, portable, manuscript breviary, usually written on vellum, which might be carried by a medieval cleric when travelling. From at least the early sixteenth century onwards the term—which had been subject to a variety of different forms and spellings, including 'porthors', 'poortos', 'porter', 'porteus', and 'portehors'—was also applied to small manuals on other particular subjects, such as philosophy.

PORTOLAN

The word 'portolan', also spelt 'portolano' or 'portulan'—terms all deriving from the Latin *portus* ('port' or 'harbour')—means a hand-drawn sailing or navigational sea chart, sometimes called a 'portolan chart', often on vellum, or else a bound collection of such charts, sometimes called a 'portolan atlas'. Portolans delineate routes between ports and outline sea coasts, with their harbours and other features, labelled with their names. The atlas collections might also be cased in protective leather satchel or wallet bindings.

Portolans, which can also be known as 'compass charts' and 'rhumb charts', date from as early as the late thirteenth century and were produced chiefly in parts of Italy, Spain, and Portugal, concentrating mainly on the Mediterranean, but also eventually extending to trade routes worldwide. Bearing latitudinal but not longitudinal markings, they persisted until well into the seventeenth century, although by then they were rendered largely obsolete by the development of new mapping techniques and printed atlases. Designed ostensibly for practical piloting purposes, the more lavish early modern examples made for display are likely to be drawn in different coloured inks, with watercolour wash or shading, and to include not only radiating rhumb-lines or loxodromes, multi-pointed wind-roses or compass-roses, labelling, latitudinal lines, decorated scale bars, roundels, cartouches or banderoles, but also

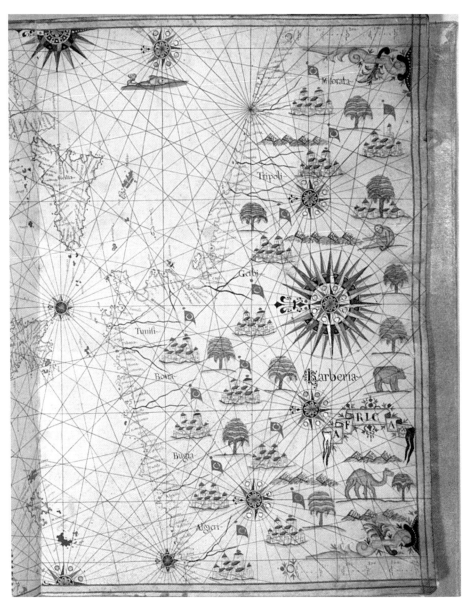

ILLUS. 63 *A portion of one of the coloured manuscript maps on vellum in a large illuminated portolan atlas made in 1635 by the Livorno cartographer Giovanni Battista Cavallini for Ferdinando de' Medici, Grand Duke of Tuscany. The page shows the Barbary Coast from Algeria to Libya, with toponymy, a multi-coloured compass-rose and four half-roses, rhumb-lines in red, a decorated banderole with the caption 'AFRICA', and coloured drawings of trees, towns, flags, hills, a camel, and other animals.*

illuminated armorial devices and topographical vignettes or illustrations of ships, fish, sea-monsters, lighthouses, churches, trees, animals, or other subjects (*see* Illus. 63). *See also* RUTTER.

POST

Besides its modern meanings of 'to mail' or 'send through the post', as also 'to fix to a post' or 'display in a prominent place', the term 'post' in the early modern period, in the context of mercantile book-keeping and accountancy, also meant to copy or transfer an entry from an informal day book, cash book, or waste book into a formal ledger or account book as the official record of a transaction. A posting is therefore the formal record so entered or the act of bringing the formal record up to date.

Post, or large post, is also a size of paper, known by its early post horn watermark, with measurements varying in the eighteenth and nineteenth centuries from 19 × 14 ¾ inches (48.5 × 37.5 cm) to 19 ½ × 15¾ inches (49.75 × 40 cm).

POSTAL MARKS

The generic terms 'postal marks' and 'postmarks' denote a common feature of letters and other documents delivered by post or courier from medieval times onwards. There were various postal services associated with universities, guilds, and other private bodies, as well as the Royal Court. In 1591 a proclamation of Queen Elizabeth prohibited the carriage of letters to and from 'countries beyond the seas' except by messengers authorized by her Master of the Posts. Largely to protect the Postmaster General's revenue, this prohibition and monopoly were extended in 1609 by James I to include inland carriage as well. Various other postal reforms were introduced in succeeding years by Charles I, Oliver Cromwell, and Charles II, generally establishing a centralized Post Office for public use. In each of these services, letters were subject to official marks of one kind or another to record information such as weight, payment, location, or route. Such marks were originally written by hand, but hand-stamps were also used from the Restoration onwards: e.g. the early Bishop marks and Dockwra marks (*see* BISHOP MARK and DOCKWRA MARK). It is not unusual to see urgent letters inscribed on their address panels with instructions to couriers such as 'haste, haste, post haste', 'Hast post hast hast *with* diligence', 'hast post hast for thy lief for thy lief', and the like, the most urgent Elizabethan letters being gallows letters (*see* GALLOWS LETTER and Illus. 29). Some postal instructions could be both insistent and expansive: e.g. 'post of fferybrige I charge you on the Kinges Ma*jes*ties behalf to delyver thes le*tt*res according to ther direcions, vpon payne of yo*ur* allegiance'.

POSTCARD

The familiar type of postal stationery known as a 'postcard', or 'post card', comprising a single small rectangular piece of card or pasteboard, was first issued in Austria in 1869, with England and other countries following suit from 1870 onwards. One side would be in partly printed format for the address to be inscribed; the other side left blank for the sender's message to be written. Picture postcards, in which one side was occupied by a printed illustration (a photographic view of a particular location or some other pictorial image), with the address relegated to half the blank side, developed in the 1880s (after 1894 in England due to postal regulations). Various other types of postcard, including pre-stamped examples and sets issued in concertina-style, have been commercially produced in subsequent years. Those that have tended to be most attractive to postcard collectors date from before the First World War.

POST-MORTEM

See INQUISITION and INQUISITIO POST MORTEM.

POSTSCRIPT

Derived from the Latin *post* ('after') and *scribere* ('to write'), 'postscribe' is an obsolete term occasionally found in early modern usage, meaning to 'write afterwards', as an addition or appendix to a written text or message. The past participle noun form 'postscript' (from the Latin *post scriptum*, 'after what has been written') is, however, still in use, often abbreviated to 'PS', and denotes text subscribed at the end of a letter after the signature. A postscript is hence any addition to a piece of writing containing an afterthought or supplement.

POUNCE

Pounce, sometimes also referred to as 'pin-dust', is a chalky, slightly abrasive powder used by scribes from medieval times until the early nineteenth century principally for two purposes. One was to apply it to the surface of parchment, after it had been first rubbed by a knife or pumice stone, in the parchment's final preparation for writing in order to remove grease and to raise its nap—a process itself known as 'pouncing'. The other was to absorb excess ink on the parchment or paper page after writing, the pounce thus serving as a precursor to blotting paper. Pounce in the earlier period was commonly made from finely ground pumice stone or from pulverized cuttlefish bone, to which was sometimes added the resin gum-sandarac. The type developed later for purely blotting purposes tended to be chalk or else powdered biotite, a magnesium mica. Traces of this metallic, sparkling substance can still occasionally be seen adhering to the dried ink in old manuscripts.

A pounce pot is a container for pounce, perforated at the top so that it could be used to sprinkle the powder on to parchment or on to newly written pages. Pounce pots were usually small turned or rounded pots shaped somewhat like salt cellars but with a concave, or saucer-shaped, top or lid (*see* Illus. 79). Variant forms that came into fashion, particularly in the eighteenth century, included small square-shaped boxes. They were commonly made of wood, brass, pewter, silver, bone, ivory, or other materials, including in later times porcelain and glass. The more expensive types might be heavily decorated or enamelled. Pounce pots were also commonly known as 'sanders', or 'sand-boxes', the term deriving perhaps as much from the occasional gum-sandarac constituent of pounce than from its somewhat sand-like, powdered nature.

POWER OF ATTORNEY

Power of attorney is authority given by one person to another to act on that person's behalf: i.e. to act as his or her agent or legal representative. The authority is conferred in a letter of attorney or a formal deed, an instrument that, as an embodiment of that authority, is commonly itself cited as the power of attorney. Depending on the articles set out in the document, the power granted will generally include authorization for such matters as selling property, handling sums of money, attending to financial arrangements, or making decisions on behalf of the grantor. A common type of power of attorney was known as 'power of attorney to deliver seisin', meaning authority to transfer possession of land. *See also* ATTORNEY.

PRAYER BOOK

A prayer book is a volume of prayers, such as was commonly used in the later Middle Ages for private devotions. Like books of hours and psalters, prayer books could sometimes be elaborately illuminated.

PRECEDENT

See BOOK OF FORMS AND PRECEDENTS.

PRECEPT

Besides its general sense of a rule, maxim, or moral injunction, the term 'precept' can mean specifically a writ issued by a monarch, court, judge, sheriff, or other authority. It could order such things as the attendance of a court, jury, or parliament; the arrest of an offender; the production of a piece of evidence; the holding of an election; or the enactment of other decisions or arrangements. In Scottish law, a precept is a document or instrument conferring a privilege or granting the possession of something.

PRECEPTA RECORDARUM
See RECORDA.

PRECEPT OF SASINE
See SASINE.

PRECIS
Deriving from the French, the term 'precis' means a summary or condensed version of a text. Making a precis was at one time a standard academic exercise to test students' ability to understand the essence or import of certain texts.

PRELIMINARY BLANKS
Preliminary blanks in any kind of volume are blank leaves that are physically integral to the paper stock of the book proper as opposed to endpapers supplied by a binder.

PRENUPTIAL SETTLEMENT
See MARRIAGE SETTLEMENT.

PRESCRIPTION
A prescription is usually a type of written receipt or recipe specifying the ingredients for a medicine, or medical remedy or treatment, intended to cure an ailment and restore health, and is usually (though not necessarily) issued by a doctor or physician. Today a doctor's prescription has the force of authorizing a patient to be issued with the specified medicine by a pharmacist. In earlier times, such instructions would generally be written in a formulaic manner, with Latin terminology, and a system of signs for drams, ounces, and other weights. Prescriptions, which could also be instructions for making cosmetics or other household agents, tended to get passed around and collected or copied into receipt-books in the same way as culinary recipes.

PRESENTATION COPY, PRESENTATION INSCRIPTION
A presentation copy of a book is a book given to someone, usually by the author or publisher and generally incorporating a presentation inscription or a label of some kind signifying the fact. A presentation inscription in a book or manuscript is one specifically written by the donor and recording the gift

THE MINDE OF
THE FRONT.

ILLUS. 64 *The autograph inscription written by Sir Walter Ralegh in a presentation copy of the first edition of his* The History of the World *(1614) given to William Trumbull, English Resident at Brussels. It is inscribed in the upper border of the page containing Ben Jonson's complimentary verses 'The Minde of the Front' facing the title-page.*

of the item. It will usually include the names of both donor and donee, although variants are possible, such as the Latin *Ex dono Authoris*, meaning 'from the gift of the Author' (*see* Illus. 64), or simply 'To' so-and-so or 'From' so-and-so, and it may also incorporate a personal message.

PRESENTATION MANUSCRIPT

A presentation manuscript, from the Middle Ages onwards, is one designed for presentation as a gift to a friend, relative, patron, monarch, or other secular or ecclesiastical dignitary. Some of the most sumptuous illuminated manuscripts in Europe come into this category, occasional examples including notable miniatures depicting in somewhat idealized form the author or scribe making the presentation in person. Many presentation manuscripts of devotional works, political or religious tracts, dissertations, poems, masques, and other types of text were produced in the early modern period, on occasions such as New Year's Day (*see* Illus. 12 and 54) or for special celebrations (*see* Illus. 65). Many were plain copies of texts, but many others were very neat or calligraphic productions, sometimes on vellum, occasionally with illuminated arms or other illustrations, portraits or decorations, and perhaps finely bound in vellum, velvet, or embroidered covers (*see* Illus. 21 and 35).

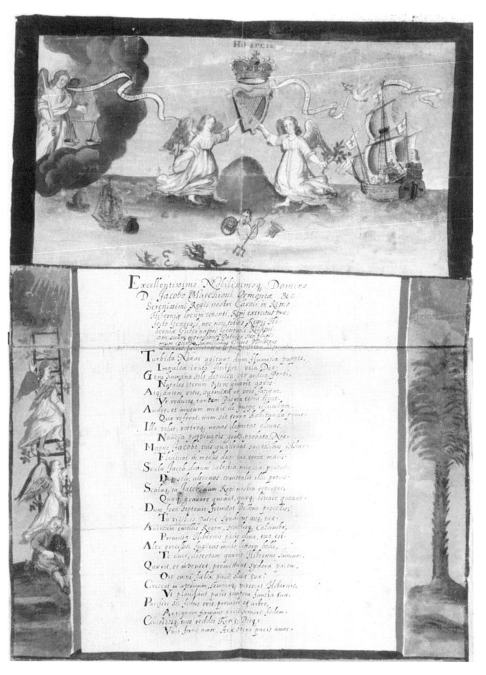

ILLUS. 65 *The presentation manuscript of a celebratory Latin poem in honour of James Butler, Marquess (later Duke) of Ormonde, Lord Lieutenant of Ireland, c.1640s. It is neatly written on a broadsheet, with engrossed initial majuscules, each alternate line indented, the borders embellished with elaborate watercolour scenes and emblematic figures, including Jacob's ladder, a tree, angels bearing the harp of Ireland surmounted by a crown, the Irish Sea, ships and Neptune, and noble sentiments embodied in phylactery.*

PRESENTMENT

A presentment is some kind of formal or official statement, usually of a legal or ecclesiastical nature, made either orally or in the form of a written document. Statements, from medieval times onwards, likely to be termed 'presentments' would include certain formal declarations made by a magistrate, justice of the peace, or constable before a court or other official body; a notification by a jury from their own knowledge of an offence for which an indictment should perhaps ensue; or a report or complaint made by local clerics or churchwardens to a visiting bishop or archdeacon relating to the state of their parish.

PRESENTS

Although the singular term 'present' occasionally appears in legal documents such as in the common formula *Omnibus Christifidelibus ad quos presens scriptum pervenerit* (generally rendered in English documents as 'To all Christian people to whom this present writing shall come'), the plural term 'presents' appears much more frequently, in bonds, certain deeds, letters patent, and other instruments, meaning the present words, statement, letter, writing, or document. The term derives from the French or Anglo-Norman usage in the phrase *par ces presentz* as also from traditional medieval Latin formulae such as *Noverint universi per presentes* ('Be it known to all men by these presents'). In a probate certificate, for instance, the Archbishop of Canterbury does 'by these presents make known to all men...'. Even when 'present' appears in the singular, the plural usage is to some extent reflected in postal instructions written on many early modern address panels where the particular letter is referred to as 'these present'.

PRESS-MARK

The term 'press-mark', or 'pressmark', has nothing to do with the printing press, but derives from the word 'press' meaning a cupboard, especially a large one, perhaps recessed into a wall, with shelves to hold books. A press-mark originally denoted the cupboard where a book was kept, but often in practice also the shelf and even its position along the shelf (thus performing the function of a shelf-mark though not necessarily that of a call number). As used now, a press-mark is a mark, number, lettering, or code inscribed or stamped in a book or manuscript denoting its precise location in a library, whether institutional (such as the British Library) or private (in, for example, a country house). Although press-marks tend to be quite simple— such as Sir Robert Cotton's designations according to the bust of the particular Roman emperor set on each of his presses: e.g. Caligula E. 12—some modern examples (in certain American libraries, for instance) are remarkably unwieldy, serving perhaps as both press-mark and call number and including not only complicated classifications and shelf numbering, but also size of book, binding, name of author, and even date. *Compare* CALL NUMBER and SHELF-MARK.

PRICKING

Pricking is a term applied to one of the methods commonly used by scribes from medieval times onwards for ruling, or drawing straight lines, on pages, whether to mark off margins or borders or for horizontal lines of writing. A sharp-pointed knife, awl, or bodkin would be used to pierce one or more leaves with two or more tiny holes to mark points to be joined up as a guide for subsequent ruling by dry point, lead point, pen, or pencil. Alternatively, it is at least possible that some kind of prototype of the later parchment-runner was sometimes used. *See* PARCHMENT-RUNNER.

PRIMER

See BOOK OF HOURS.

PRINTER'S COPY

Printer's copy is the actual physical manuscript or typescript—or printed text, with manuscript alterations, if this is serving as the basis for a new edition—used by the printer or his compositors for the printing of a particular work. Although extant printer's copy dates from as early as 1467 (St Augustine's *De civitate Dei*, at the Monastery of Santa Scholastica, Subiaco, Italy), relatively few such manuscripts from the early modern period survive, since their rough use in the printing house tended to devalue them as physical objects, and their usefulness once the edition had appeared seemed largely exhausted; therefore the leaves could safely be discarded or put to less noble use. Examples of such manuscripts from later periods are much more common.

Extant printer's copy can generally (though not always) be identified by such features as casting-off marks (*see* CASTING-OFF MARKS), showing page breaks or else where each page of type was estimated to end; numbers, denoting word-counts, page-counts and the like, sometimes in the form of fractions, such as $\frac{10}{B4}$, meaning page 10 and the fourth page of gathering B in the printed edition; marking off, a line or lines drawn to show how far the printer or compositor had reached before a break or interruption; inscribed printing instructions, for the use of italic, bold, type of font, etc.; names of compositors responsible for particular sections; and incidental heavy finger-marks and ink stains, indicating physical handling in the printing shop, as

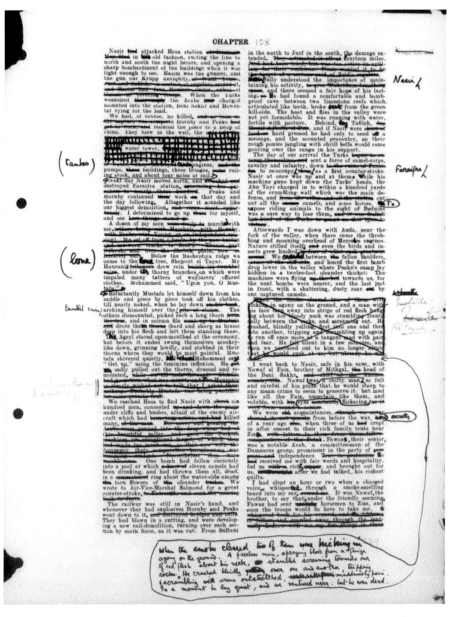

ILLUS. 66 *A page of sheets from the 1922* Oxford edition of T. E. Lawrence's Seven Pillars of Wisdom *with copious revisions in Lawrence's hand, prepared by him as printers' copy for the 1926 Subscribers' edition of the work. A marginal note in pencil on the left is in the hand of Charlotte Shaw, another in-house direction on the right is in another hand, and the page has spindle holes, 1922–4.*

well as other marks and soiling. Among other things, these various calculations and markings reflect the printer's practical aims of determining what text would constitute each forme, so that more than one chase of type could be set by compositors at the same time, as well as establishing the costing of the book and its paper requirements.

Among the most notable surviving examples of the early modern period are original manuscript printer's copy for works, or portions of works, by Sir John Harington (*Orlando Furioso*, 1591, in the British Library, Add. MS 18920), Richard Hooker (*Of the Lawes of Ecclesiasticall Politie*, 1597, in the Bodleian Library, Oxford, MS Add. C. 165), and John Milton (*Paradise Lost*, Book I, 1667, in the Pierpont Morgan Library, New York, MA 307). Extant exempla of printed editions marked up for use as printer's copy include an early edition of a work by Sir Thomas More (now at Yale University, 1f M81 + S529) which was reprinted in William Rastell's folio edition of the collected works in 1557. *See also* Illus. 66.

PRINTER'S MARKS

See PRINTER'S COPY.

PRISONER OF WAR MAGAZINES

Among the documentation produced by British and Allied prisoners of war in both World Wars—including camp registers, paintings, and concert programmes, examples of which are in the Imperial War Museum—are magazines produced by imprisoned servicemen and civilian internees as morale-boosters for circulation, largely clandestine, in their respective camps. In the First World War, there were several such magazines, the best known being those produced in the Ruhleben internment camp situated on a racecourse outside Berlin. A set of these in the Imperial War Museum is bound in the skin of rats killed in the camp.

In the Changi prisoner of war camp, Singapore, between 1942 and 1945, magazines such as *Clink Chronicle*, *Here Today*, and *Exile*, which each ran to several issues, were produced chiefly on an old typewriter with a worn ribbon and paper and ink stolen from the Japanese Administration Office. Charcoal, roots, bark, and leaves were used for further ink and colouring. Each issue, of which there was only one copy, could take up to three months to produce, although the process was speeded up for *Exile*, nine issues of which had appeared by May 1945 in a period of nine months. Their contents included stories, poems, articles, book reviews, and coloured illustrations and drawings. The occasional contributors included the subsequently celebrated cartoonist Ronald Searle.

Prisoners of war are known to have been allowed to send and receive letters from as early as the Napoleonic period. They would be subject to censorship and bear censors' marks accordingly (*see* CENSORS' MARKS). Special stationery for prisoner of war correspondence was first used in the First World War. In the Second World War, some Allied prisoners of war in Germany were allowed to send home as many as two postcards and two letters each month. In the Changi prisoner of war camp run by the Japanese in Singapore in 1942–5, the inmates were allowed to send home a total of five postcards each in that period, most of which took about eight or nine months to arrive. They were allowed to write a maximum of twenty-five words, or else the cards contained pre-typed messages such as 'My health is good/usual/poor', which the prisoner could tick as appropriate.

PRIVY COUNCIL

The Privy Council in England was originally the body of men selected to advise the sovereign and who were authorized to undertake the principal government of the realm under the Royal Prerogative. From medieval times, the King had some form of council, the *Curia Regis*, which was eventually centred at Westminster and which performed legislative, executive, and judicial functions, serving as predecessor to Parliament and the law courts. The Privy Council as such, however, is generally dated from 1540 in the reign of Henry VIII. The administrative work for which it was responsible covered every aspect of national life, including law and order, trade and industry, naval and military policy, and colonial matters. It dealt with the drafting of royal proclamations, the answering of petitions, the issuing of warrants, the writing of committee reports, the authorizing of disbursements from the public purse, and so on.

The Registers of the Privy Council (National Archives, Kew, PC 2), sometimes called the 'Book of Entries', comprise 872 large minute books recording (with occasional gaps) Council proceedings from 1540 to 1978. The entries were made chiefly by Council secretaries, but sometimes bear additions and annotations by Privy Councillors themselves, such as Elizabeth I's principal Secretary of State, Lord Burghley, as well as having very occasional tipped-in related documents, such as signed agreements by contending parties brought before the Council.

The other principal collections of Privy Council records are also in the National Archives at Kew (not only in the PC series but also scattered among Chancery, Privy Seal Office, and State Papers series), some are in the British Library, and many others, such as orders and warrants issued by the Council, are widely dispersed elsewhere (*see* Illus. 55). Many Council warrants are signed by some of the best-known figures in early modern English history, including Cardinal Wolsey, Thomas Cromwell, Robert Dudley, Earl of Leicester, Sir Francis Walsingham, Robert Devereux, Earl of Essex, Sir Robert Cecil, and Sir Francis Bacon.

PRIVY SEAL

See SEAL.

PROBATE

Deriving from the Latin *probatum* ('something tested or proved'), the term 'probate' means the issuing by a lawful court of an official certificate, or the certificate (sometimes called the 'act') itself, declaring in formulaic wording that the will of a deceased person has been proved, or validated as authentic, and that the executor(s) now have the right to administer the person's estate or effects in accordance with the provisions of the will. A probate copy is a registered copy of the will, to which is usually attached the probate certificate, given to the executors to enact, the original will being usually annotated with a copy of the certificate, or attested as proved (*probatum est*), and filed in the court's records. This practice was not consistent, however, and before the seventeenth century it was often the original will that was returned to the executors rather than the copy. A copy of the will and certificate was also usually written into an official register as a public record. Over 300 local ecclesiastical courts in England and Wales were empowered to function as courts of probate, the main court being the Prerogative Court of the Archbishop of Canterbury. This was the probate court for the Southern Province, but had jurisdiction over all England and Wales (for those whose *bona notabilia*, or goods, were worth £50 or more), while the Prerogative Court of the Archbishop of York related to the Northern Province.

The principal register of probate copies of wills from 1384 to 1858 relates mainly to the PCC (Canterbury) and is now in the National Archives at Kew (PROB 11, usually viewed on microfilm and searchable on the internet). Files of related probate documents, or 'exhibits', from 1658 to 1858, are in PROB 31–32, with indexes for the period 1722–c.1900, viewable on microfilm, in PROB 33. Those appertaining to the Northern Province administered by the Exchequer and Prerogative Court of York are more scattered, but the principal collections of surviving northern probate records from c.1321 to 1858 are now in York Minster Library, the Borthwick Institute, York, and the West Yorkshire Archive Service, Leeds. Many other wills, both original and probate copies, are preserved in county record offices or widely dispersed in private collections and muniments.

PROBATUM

The Latin terms *probatum* and *probatum est* mean 'it is tried, tested, or proved'. Among other contexts, one or other of these terms often appears in receipt-books and other culinary and medical manuscripts signifying that someone has tried using the recipe or prescription and that it has proved to be satisfactory.

PROCLAMATION

A proclamation is a formal and public announcement made by the monarch or by some other civil or ecclesiastical authority. Both in the medieval and early modern period, proclamations could take the form of scribal copies issued by, or sent out to, local authorities for display in some public place and for reading aloud, or else, with the invention of printing, as printed texts, usually broadsides (large sheets of paper printed on one side), for similar purposes. Royal proclamations were formally drawn up by the Clerk of the Crown for royal approval and engrossed on parchment before being passed under the Great Seal and their text supplied to the printer.

Such proclamations related to numerous matters of public concern. They included such things as the proclaiming of a new monarch; the introduction or enforcing of new laws, statutes, and taxes; explanations for the raising of armies or for the execution of traitors; declarations of war; steps to stamp out rebellion and to counteract false and seditious rumours; measures to enforce security, to control weapons and firearms, and to ban duelling; the banning of offensive books; the regulation of wages and elimination of abuses; strictures relating to vagabonds, imports and exports, coinage, weights and measures, commodities (such as wool, wine, and cloth), Catholics, and Dissenters; and a variety of other matters.

PROMISSORY NOTE

A promissory note, from at least the end of the seventeenth century, is a written and signed promise, made by one person to another, unconditionally engaging to pay a specified sum of money on demand or at an agreed time. The Promissory Notes Act of 1704 made them negotiable in the same way as bills of exchange. The modern bank cheque is itself a type of promissory note.

PROMPTBOOK

A promptbook, prompt-book, or prompt-copy, is the copy of a play, either manuscript or else printed and marked up by hand, produced for use in the theatre by the bookkeeper or prompter. In the Elizabethan playhouse, the promptbook was called simply 'the book' and was the definitive theatrical text used for the acting of the play in question. This may often have been one and the same thing as the manuscript of the play delivered by the playwright or playwrights, which would also be cited as a 'book' (such as Robert Shaa's contracting with Philip Henslowe in 1603 to deliver 'a booke Called the fower sones of Aymon which booke' to be 'playd by the company'). In his *Dramatic Documents* (1931), W. W. Greg records that some fifteen extant manuscripts of Elizabethan plays show 'reasonably clear signs of use or origin in the playhouse', and the addition of some cues (for entrances, music, thunder, etc.) suggests their possible use, or intended use, by the prompter, although their exact status is not certain. The Elizabethan promptbook evidently contained the exact text of the play, usually after any cuts or changes made by the government censor or licenser, as it was to be spoken by the actors, together with various cues and stage directions.

Extant examples of promptbooks (usually annotated printed texts) from the late seventeenth century show various markings for a series of practical matters to be taken into consideration in the staging, or else for signals to be made by the prompter himself during the performance. These include symbols such as a dot within a circle ($\odot$), an *X* or a hatch mark, #, or a single horizontal line with a row of cross hatches (####) to signify a whistle, bell, or other calls for scene shifts, for actors to get ready to appear, for entrances, or for other effects. Characteristic markings after the Restoration period—by which time the term 'prompter's book' was in use—include those for stage directions, entrances and exits (signalled by abbreviations such as 'PS' [= Prompter's Side] and 'OP' [= Opposite Prompter]), stage 'business', and properties. Examples, from the late eighteenth century onwards can be more detailed and elaborate, incorporating a variety of production details, cues for lighting, music, thunder, opening of trap-doors, etc., as well as stage maps showing the arrangement of scenes, properties, and actors' positions at particular moments in the production, and the ordering of processions and the like (*see* Illus. 67).

Some of these features are shown in the earliest published acting editions, such as [John] *Bell's Edition of Shakespeare's Plays, as they are now Performed at the Theatres Royal in London* (8 volumes, 1774), and indeed almost any printed edition of a play that incorporates promptorial directions can be assumed to have been set from a promptbook. Yet other marked-up 'promptbooks', particularly in the Victorian period, are in truth not so much promptbooks as records of the production, designed as virtually retrospective souvenirs of it (which, however, might still serve as blueprints for provincial or overseas productions). Many of Sir Henry Irving's productions of Shakespeare and

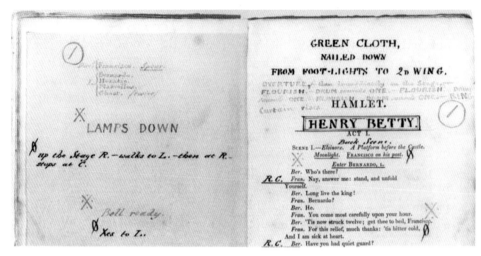

ILLUS. 67 *Part of an opening in a promptbook of Shakespeare's* Hamlet *used by the provincial actor Henry Betty, marked up with directions, signals, and calls for music, curtain, scenery, lighting, entrances, and stage business, c.1844.*

other plays at the Lyceum Theatre in the 1870s–90s, for instance, were commemorated not only by the publication of illustrated booklets, but also by a series of carefully prepared promptbooks compiled by his assistant stage manager, comprising in each case pages of Irving's printed acting edition pasted in an album and subjected to extensive pencil and ink markings, drawings, annotations, additional dialogue, and cast-lists, inscribed in various colours, together with pasted-in illustrations. Modern promptbooks may also include annotated typescripts (*see* Illus. 68).

PROMPTER

The prompter in a theatre is the person who, generally out of sight of the audience, holds and reads the text of the play (or musical score in the case of an opera) during each performance and, among other things, prompts or assists actors (or singers) at moments when they have forgotten their lines (or need musical cues). In the Jacobean theatre the term 'prompter' was evidently used, as is witnessed in Othello's lines 'Were it my cue to fight, I should have known it / Without a prompter' (*Othello*, I, ii, 84–5). The prompter may also, however, have served as the bookkeeper, or book-holder, who had the supremely important responsibility of looking after the company book, the definitive theatrical text used for the performance. *See also* ORDINARY.

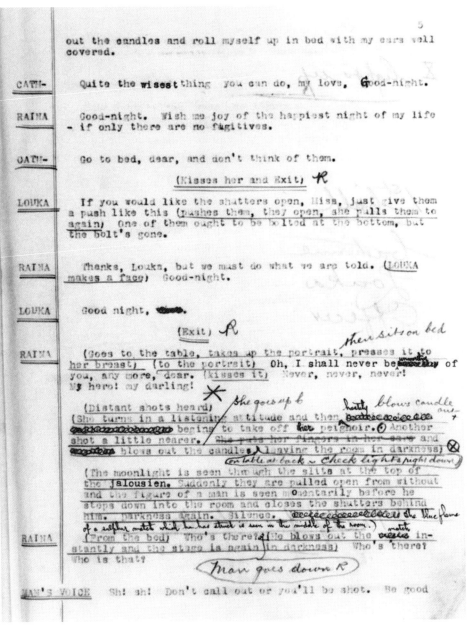

ILLUS. 68 *A page of the working promptbook for the original production of George Bernard Shaw's play* Arms and the Man, *April 1894, being a typescript within paper wrappers produced by a professional London typing agency, extensively marked up in black ink and pencil with revisions to stage directions, stage business, and calls, some in Shaw's minute hand, some in another hand. This is the copy used and retained by the producer and principal actress Florence Farr.*

A proof is a preliminary or trial printed sheet, or set of sheets, of a work, produced by a printer for checking purposes. This facilitates the detection of typographical errors so that corrections and alterations may be made, leading sometimes to the production of further proof-sheets, before the final printing of the edition goes ahead. Proof copy may take the form of long continuous strips or sheets, the lengthy unpaginated versions of which have been known since the nineteenth century as galley proofs (the galley being the printer's tray), or else as page proofs, when the type is set in the form of separate pages.

PROOF CORRECTIONS

Changes written by hand by the author or publisher's proof-reader, chiefly entered in the margins and each keyed in the text by a marker at the site of error, may take the form of proof corrections, rectifying type errors by compositors, or proof revisions, when text is deleted, reworded, or added by the author or others. Revisions can at times be elaborate, involving, for instance, long interlinear interpolations or lengthy paragraphs written in the margins or within bubbles marked for insertion at particular points. Although such proofs may be called 'revised', the term 'proof-corrected' is commonly applied to a proof that has been checked and marked up by the author or in-house reader whatever the nature of the changes made.

Since the earliest days of printing in the 1450s, from which period fragments of proof sheets still survive, there has evolved an extensive series of symbols conventionally used for proof corrections, including such markings as the extended caret (^) to denote where an insertion should go, the peculiar δ to denote a deletion, / to denote the deletion of a character and closing up of the characters either side, underlining to denote changing the type to italic, the step marks (⌐) to denote the start of a new paragraph, and a marginal oblique slash (/) to indicate that the correction is concluded.

Early modern examples of corrected proof sheets—surviving as leaves in bound editions or sometimes as paste-downs, endpapers, or binders' waste, some still in uncut sheets—include several pages in the First Folio of Shakespeare's works (1623), and pages in editions of various dramatic works by Ben Jonson, John Fletcher, George Chapman and Thomas Heywood; John Milton's *Lycidas*; Francis Bacon's *Of the Advancement of Learning*; and Robert Burton's *The Anatomy of Melancholy*. Perhaps the most notable example is a copy of the 1587 edition of Holinshed's *Chronicle*, now in the Huntington Library, which consists almost entirely of proof sheets and contains some 10,000 marginal annotations altering the text.

Since at least the fifteenth century, the term 'prothonotary', or 'protonotary', derived from the title of the holder of a Byzantine court, meant in England a chief clerk or registrar at the central courts. The three prothonotaries at the Court of Common Pleas were the most important clerical officers in the common-law system, responsible for the production each term of vast quantities of judicial writs, legal records, rolls, and files of documentation in Latin. In the King's Bench, the prothonotary was more usually called the Chief Clerk. The Chancery also had a prothonotary, but one of much less importance. In addition, the Papal Curia in the Vatican had protonotaries (spelt without the *h*).

PROTOCOL

Deriving from the Greek *protokollon*, which denoted the first sheet glued to a manuscript or roll explaining its origin, the term 'protocol', used in the context of a document, means a note or record of a transaction or negotiated agreement drawn up and attested as genuine by a notary or public official that forms the basis of a subsequent formal deed or official written or engrossed agreement. A protocol book is a book or register in which copies of such records are entered, usually by or at the behest of the official concerned. More specifically, in a diplomatic context, a protocol is a written record of the negotiated propositions agreed to and signed by the respective parties at a meeting or conference, usually international, forming the basis for a subsequent formal treaty. Alternatively, it is the original draft or minute of some other diplomatic stipulation, declaration, or addendum.

As strictly confidential documents of national interest, most extant English diplomatic protocols, at least for the period 1695–1991, remain in the Public Records (National Archives, Kew, FO 93, and some for the period 1579–1780 are in SP 108), although occasional examples are found in the private and family papers of the ministers concerned. A notable example, preserved for over 300 years in the private archives of Thomas, Lord Clifford of Chudleigh (1630–1673), and his descendants, comprises the drafts and protocols of the Secret Treaty of Dover struck between the representatives of Charles II and Louis XIV in 1670, now in the British Library (Add. MS 65138: *see* Illus. 90).

The term 'protocol' is also sometimes applied to the standard formulae used at the beginning and end of papal bulls, letters patent, and other official and state documents, as distinct from the text relating to the particular matter in hand. These various uses are in addition to the general meaning of the term, denoting prescribed formal etiquette and ceremonial.

See PROTHONOTARY.

PROVENANCE

A potentially important consideration in the evaluation, interest, or importance of any manuscript or old book is its provenance (a French word
meaning 'source' or 'origin'): i.e. evidence of where the item came from, or
what can be established about its original production, its early ownership,
and its history. Evidence might be provided by such features as signatures,
inscriptions and marginalia, identity of handwriting, coats of arms, distinctive binding, bookplates, shelf-marks, loosely inserted notes, or other clues,
as well as collateral evidence such as sales records. Just occasionally an early
owner will obligingly provide virtually all the information needed: for
instance, the inscription in a manuscript of Benjamin Lock's *The Picklock
to Reply,* saying 'This Booke I receaued from M^r [Thomas] Heriot at Sion
howse, Who for many yeares, instructed the Earle of Northumberland in
the Mathematicks when he liued in the tower. A°: 1602. June.6.' (Wellcome
Library, MS 436). On the other hand, a hearsay family tradition about a
manuscript's history, although perhaps plausible, is less than reliable without corroborating evidence.

PSALTER

A psalter (Latin: *psaltarium*) is a book, either manuscript or printed, containing texts of the Psalms (doubtfully attributed to King David) of the Old
Testament, usually in Latin or other translations, often accompanied by
other religious texts and a calendar and prepared for private devotional or
liturgical use. From the early Middle Ages, the Psalms in the Latin version
of the Bible, the Vulgate, provided the groundwork for Christian prayer and
all 150 of them were traditionally recited by monks and priests once every
week, though in different groupings and arrangements. As manuscripts,
they were generally well, if not calligraphically, written, sometimes richly
embellished or illuminated, with images of David with his harp, etc., the
most elaborate examples (such as the fourteenth-century Macclesfield Psalter now in the Fitzwilliam Museum, Cambridge) including hundreds of
little vignettes of grotesque figures, animals, people, and a personification of
Death. The first word of the first Psalm, *Beatus* ('Blessed') in particular
provided an occasion for the illuminator to display his skill by expansively
elaborating the initial *B*.

Most surviving examples are medieval and Catholic, but psalters persisted
in the sixteenth and seventeenth centuries, among adherents of the

Reformed Church. Translating the Psalms indeed became a popular pious exercise among literary-minded public figures, sometimes taking stock of their lives in their later years. Notable English psalters found in manuscript form include those by Sir Philip Sidney and his sister Mary, Countess of Pembroke, Sir John Davies, Sir John Harington, and George Sandys.

A work circulated in manuscript under a name such as 'Tom Tell-Truth' or published under a name like 'Martin Marprelate' is said to be 'pseudonymous' because the name given is not that of the author but a pseudonym, a false name, or *nom de plume*, deliberately adopted to disguise the author's real identity. The term derives from the Greek *pseudos* ('falsehood') and *onoma* ('name'). While many of the celebrated authors who used pseudonyms are now better known by their real names (Charlotte Brontë, for instance, instead of 'Currer Bell'), many others have effectively had their names replaced by their pseudonyms: for instance, Mary Anne Evans ('George Eliot'), Charles Lutwidge Dodgson ('Lewis Carroll'), and Samuel Langhorne Clemens ('Mark Twain').

The word 'publication', meaning in the most literal sense something made public or offered to the public, has traditionally been associated with printed books. Its scope has been extended by modern scholars, notably Harold Love, to include manuscripts, in the sense of 'scribal publication' in the early modern period: i.e. the production and distribution of manuscript copies of literary materials for at least limited public consumption, often by professional scribes on a commercial basis, as in some measure a counterpart to print publication. Thus a text might become 'published' if it became widely known, through whatever medium, as opposed to its being kept restricted within a private sphere. Although it probably remains true that 'published' would denote primarily a text made available in the medium of print—and when a sixteenth-century writer could speak of his collecting 'discourses published or unpublished' he would almost certainly mean 'discourses printed or in manuscript'—the term 'publish' and its cognates were evidently ambiguous and could be of looser or wider application than confinement to the medium of print alone.

Public Record Office

The Public Record Office, commonly abbreviated to PRO, is the celebrated institution which, although still a statutory body entrusted by law with the custody of the State Papers, has been incorporated since 2003 in the bureaucratic institution now known as the National Archives (*see* NATIONAL ARCHIVES). The principal national repository of public records in England, it was established under a statute of 1838 and housed in a large purpose-built edifice in Chancery Lane, London. In 1997, it was re-established in a new building at Kew.

PUBLIC RECORDS

The Public Records in England were defined in the Public Record Act of 1837 as all rolls, records, writs, books, proceedings, decrees, warrants, accounts, papers, and documents whatever of a public nature belonging to Her Majesty the Queen (Queen Victoria). They are therefore the Public Records of the realm, including the State Papers, which date from early medieval times to the present day. Most of those that survive are preserved in the Public Record Office, now at Kew and administered by a department known as the National Archives.

PUMICE

Pumice is a porous lava substance, a pumice stone being a small block of it. Pumice was commonly used from medieval times onwards, both in block form and in pulverized pounce form, in the process of preparing parchment for writing by smoothing it and removing grease and stains. It might occasionally serve in the scraping of old parchment for reuse as a palimpsest. The contemporary mention of pumice stone as being among the standard accoutrements of scriveners in the seventeenth century also suggests that it was commonly used as a form of eraser.

PYE BOOK

The term 'pye book', as used at least by the seventeenth century, means an alphabetical index to rolls and records. In earlier, pre-Reformation times, it was also a book concerning regulations for the celebration of saints' days as affected by the moveable feast of Easter.

QUARTER-BOUND

See BINDING.

QUARTERED

In heraldry, a shield is described as 'quartered' when it is divided into four or more partitions, each containing a coat of arms. Each coat of arms may be different or, alternatively, it may be duplicated in another quarter: for instance, in the arms of Old England the first and fourth quarters are the same (gules, three lions passant gardant in pale, or) and the second and third quarters are the same (azure, three fleurs-de-lis, or).

QUARTO

The term 'quarto' (frequently abbreviated to '4to', sometimes '4°') is a Latin word meaning 'in fourth' or 'for the fourth time', and denotes the size of a leaf of paper produced when a standard papermaker's sheet is folded twice: the first fold producing two leaves (four pages) of folio size (being half the sheet), the second four leaves (eight pages) of quarto size (being a quarter of the sheet). The size of a quarto leaf will vary according to the paper manufacturer and to trimming by the papermaker or binder, but the average size for the early modern period is approximately 7 ½–9 ½ inches (19–24 cm) in length and 6–8 inches (15.5–20.5 cm) in width. Because of the wires across the width of the papermaker's mould or tray, quarto leaves will have the chain-lines running horizontally across the page. A printed or manuscript volume made up of gatherings of such leaves (which will most commonly comprise gatherings sewn in fours: i.e. two pairs of conjugate leaves per gathering, subject to occasional variation) is itself called a 'quarto' as a means of distinguishing it by size and basic format (e.g. the First or Second Quartos of about twenty of Shakespeare's plays). For other-sized leaves and volumes, resulting from previous, further, or different folding of each sheet, *see* DUODECIMO, FOLIO, OCTAVO, and SEXTODECIMO.

The term 'quarto' (or '4to') applied to modern books, of wove paper, can denote a quite different size, usually somewhat larger and more square-shaped than the earlier upright rectangular quarto volumes, and has no connection to the earlier technology of papermakers' trays and the folding of their sheets.

QUATERNION

See QUIRE.

QUATREFOIL

A quatrefoil can be defined as a compound leaf or flower containing four, usually rounded, leaflets or petals radiating from a common centre. It is a figure that occasionally appears in medieval manuscript ornamentation, as also in some heraldic devices and in certain seventeenth-century watermarks, but unlike the trefoil (*compare* TREFOIL), the quatrefoil is found only on rare occasions in readers' marginal annotations in books. A quatrefoil was also incorporated in the signature of Henry VIII, as a flourish following the name 'Henry' in place of the more usual *R* (for *Rex*, meaning 'King'). *See also* Illus. 82.

QUESTIONNAIRE

A questionnaire is a list of questions, usually set out as a form with spaces left for answers by respondents. Such documents may range in nature from government, institutional, commercial, or other general broad-based surveys to investigations by individual researchers into the opinions, tastes, habits, etc. of particular persons. Although the term 'questionnaire' is of relatively modern origin (from *c.*1900), the now virtually obsolete term 'questionary'—which was also sometimes applied in the Church to a catechism or treatise written in the form of questions—dates back to at least the sixteenth century. For instance, a questionary was submitted by the English government to investors (or undertakers) in Ireland on 12 May 1589; the scribal copy containing autograph answers written in the margin by Sir Walter Ralegh is in the National Archives at Kew (SP 63/144/27). Among the modern public figures who regularly responded to types of questionnaire sent to them by journalists was the dramatist George Bernard Shaw.

QUIETUS

A quietus (the Latin word means 'quit' or 'at rest') in the context of the Exchequer is a type of settlement, being an acquittance, discharge, or receipt given by the recipient as evidence of the payment of a debt, or else a formal acknowledgement by a person or institution that an agent's accounts balance and that no more payment is due (the phrase *quietus est* being usually inscribed to mean 'it is settled'). A quietus was commonly given, for instance, to a sheriff or tax-collector at the end of his year of office. A famous literary and metaphorical use of the term occurs in Hamlet's 'To be or not to be' speech when he contemplates making 'his quietus... with a bare bodkin': i.e. settling accounts by stabbing himself to quit or pay back his life, as if he is the debtor.

QUILL

A quill is a pen made from a feather, in which the end is sharpened to a point and slit to allow for the retention and application of ink. Introduced by the sixth century AD, if not earlier, to replace the reed pen, the quill was in common use until superseded by the metal-tipped or steel pen in the nineteenth century. It may therefore claim status as the most dominant writing instrument in the history of literacy. Quills were most generally made from the flight feathers (the first five feathers on each wing) of geese, but could also be made from the feathers of the turkey, swan, duck, crow, occasionally the raven, and even such birds as the pelican and peacock. Contrary to popular belief, and as is clear from numerous depictions of scribes from medieval times onwards, most of the feather was generally cut away to leave little more than the main tube or barrel of the feather for writing purposes. The nib itself was cut at different angles depending on the required thickness of the ink strokes or style or angularity of the script required. To retain sharpness, it would require constant trimming with a penknife or a quill-cutter.

QUIRE

In bibliography, a quire is the same thing as a gathering. The term derives from variants of the French *cahier* and the word 'quaternion' (Latin: *quaterni*), which could also be rendered as 'quair' or 'quaer', denoting a gathering of four sheets (folded to form eight leaves, sixteen pages), which was a common and convenient unit for sewing in medieval times when sheets of parchment or vellum were being used. As the wider use of paper led to thicker gatherings in books, each often comprising more than four folded sheets, the specific association of 'quire' with four was lost and the term was retained simply as a synonym for 'gathering'. 'Quire' as a verb means to arrange sheets in quire or gathering format, as sheets folded and inserted or nested inside one another (therefore quired), as opposed to being arranged

ILLUS. 69 *A quitclaim made by the Quaker leader William Penn certifying receipt from John Goodson of London, surgeon, of £10 for the purchase of 500 acres in Pennsylvania in accordance with their 'Indentures of Bargain Sale and Release', 11 October 1681. The document is drawn up by a law clerk, with flourished engrossed majuscules in the first line. It is signed by Penn ('wm Penn') and bears his seal. It is also signed by three witnesses. It was subsequently docketed and signed as officially recorded by the Quaker Thomas Lloyd, Penn's recently appointed Master of the Rolls in Pennsylvania, on 29 January 1683/4.*

adjacently or sewn together at the hinge as a series of separate bifolia. *See also* GATHERING.

The term 'quire' is also used in the context of paper-manufacturing or stationery to denote a particular quantity of sheets of paper, which served since at least the fifteenth century as a standard unit. A quire of paper produced in France and Italy comprised twenty-five sheets, but a quire of paper produced in England or Holland traditionally comprised twenty-four sheets. *See also* REAM.

QUITCLAIM

A quitclaim is a legally binding document whereby someone makes a formal renunciation of, or release or discharge from, his claim or right to specified property, or else a formal acquittance for payment received. *See* Illus. 69.

R

RAGMAN

See PENDENT.

RAISED BANDS

See SPINE.

RATIFICATION

In diplomacy, ratification is the official confirmation and acceptance by a sovereign, head of state or, most especially, legislative assembly of all the terms of a treaty agreed between the representatives of two or more nations. The formal document or record testifying to such confirmation may itself be called the ratification of a treaty. A number of English examples are preserved in the National Archives at Kew (in SP 108 and FO 94 for the period 1579–1978).

REAM

Since at least as early as the fifteenth century, a ream has been a standard unit in paper-manufacturing and stationery to denote a particular quantity of sheets of paper. Traditionally a ream comprised twenty quires, meaning 480 sheets or, later, 500 sheets, depending on place of manufacture. *See also* QUIRE.

REBACKED

'Rebacked', or 're-backed', is a term used in bibliographical or booksellers' descriptions, meaning that the original spine in the current binding of a book or manuscript volume has been replaced and the joints reinforced. This repair is usually necessitated when the vulnerable joints split and the covers become detached.

A rebus letter (the Latin *rebus* meaning 'with things') is a letter written wholly or partly in the form of pictorial symbols or figurative representations of words rather than in simple language. Although rebuses in general were used in earlier periods—for instance, for family arms and emblems (such as the Harington family arms of a hare sitting with a ring in its mouth on a barrel or ton)—rebus letters, many of them highly decorative or colourful, flourished especially in the nineteenth century and were produced as a playful diversion, particularly for younger recipients. Writers who occasionally enjoyed writing such letters include notably Charles Lutwidge Dodgson ('Lewis Carroll'), who could write to the young Alice Liddell a letter with, for instance, a drawing or picture of an eye for the word 'I', of a letter (epistle) for the word 'letter', of a deer for the word 'dear', of a figure '2' for the word 'to', and so on. Thus, while many of the drawings in rebus letters might be literal representations (pictures of a house for 'house', trees for 'trees', etc.), some of the symbols used might involve the sounds of words, representing a kind of homophonic transcription.

REBUTTAL

See REJOINDER.

RECEIPT

A receipt, sometimes called more formally a 'bill of receipt' or 'ticket of receipt', is generally a brief written document, usually signed, acknowledging that payment for something has been received, or else that goods have been taken into possession or custody (*see* Illus. 70). The document therefore constitutes evidence retained by the payer or consignor showing that the payment or consignment has been made. The Receipt was also a department of the Exchequer, which kept records of payments.

In addition 'receipt' is another term for 'recipe', meaning a statement of the ingredients and required method of preparation for making a culinary dish or beverage; alternatively, it might be a prescription for a medical remedy to cure an ailment or restore health, or else one for cosmetics, for charms, or for some other household agent. In many cases a book of receipts, or receipt-book, is the same thing as a recipe-book, but might also contain, or even principally comprise, medical prescriptions. *See* Illus. 71 and 72.

RECENSION

A recension is a distinct or revised version of a text, resulting from a careful and critical overhaul of that text. In textual criticism and editing, recension

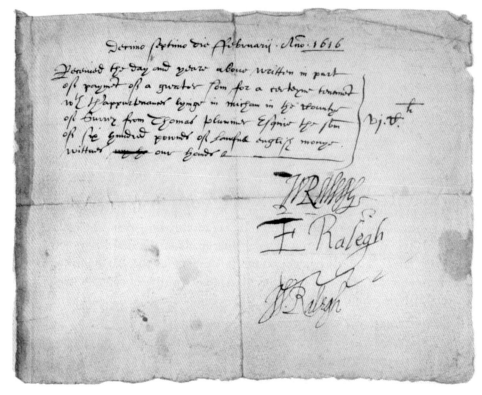

ILLUS. 70 *A receipt, in a secretary hand, for 'vi.C.^{li}' (£600) as part-payment for the manor of Mitcham, Surrey, sold to Thomas Plummer, MP, by Lady Ralegh (in order to help finance her husband's last expedition to Guiana following his release from the Tower). It is signed by Sir Walter Ralegh, Elizabeth (née Throckmorton), Lady Ralegh, and their son Walter (who was subsequently killed on the expedition), 17 February 1616/17.*

is also the attempt to reconstruct, from all the evidence of relevant surviving manuscript or printed texts, the earliest recoverable form of the original text, or archetype, that lies behind them.

RECIPE

'Recipe' is the more widely used modern term for what was once commonly called a 'receipt', but meaning specifically a culinary receipt rather than a medical prescription. A recipe-book is similarly a volume or compilation devoted largely to culinary receipts, although in practice medical prescriptions usually get collected along with them. Manuscript recipe-books—forerunners of modern cookbooks—survive in considerable numbers from the fourteenth century onwards. Up until the mid or late seventeenth century, they seem to have been largely written by men (who were the cooks in great houses), but from at least the early eighteenth century they were predominantly by women. They are frequently written in various hands by different members of a family, sometimes over more than one generation. Individual recipes can be found subscribed with the name of the person from whom the compiler acquired it, occasionally with the annotation *probatum est*, meaning 'it has been tried' (i.e. proved successful). Recipe-books most frequently show wear, tear, or staining because of direct use in the kitchen, although some were kept as rather grand, neatly written, clean, and well-preserved volumes intended for posterity (*see* Illus. 71 and 72).

RECIPIENT

A recipient, in a manuscript context, is the receiver or person who received the letter or document sent to him or her. It is usually the person to whom the letter or document is addressed and who may, therefore, be the one responsible for any docketing or annotations that may appear on the letter, such as details of when it was received and who sent it, or even a subscribed draft reply.

RECITAL

In a deed, a recital is a preliminary statement or summary (beginning 'Whereas...') explaining the *raison d'être* and purpose of the document.

RECOGNIZANCE

Since the Middle Ages, a recognizance, or recognisance, was a kind of bond and obligation, except that it did not require a seal, but was acknowledged before a court or magistrate and formally recorded. The document obliged the person concerned (the cognizor or conuser, who was said to 'take recognizance') to perform some action (such as to keep the peace, repay a debt, or not leave the vicinity) under specified conditions. A sum of money or other surety might be stipulated that would be forfeited if what was promised was not successfully performed.

RECORD

A record, in general usage, is any kind of document or any piece of information or testimony preserved in writing, one which might be consulted, cited, and used as evidence in historical or other arguments. A record office is a repository of such documents, whether national, county, or local, depending on the type of office concerned.

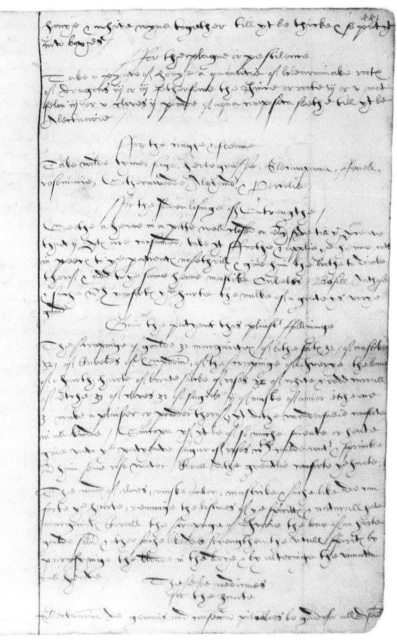

ILLUS. 71 *A page in a large quarto manuscript receipt book, written in the north of England in a (male) secretary hand c.1590, showing a series of medical prescriptions or treatments relating to 'the plague or pestilence', 'the coughe & fleame' (phlegm), 'the soden losinge of Strengthe', a 'plaist^r' (plaster), and 'medicines for the harte'.*

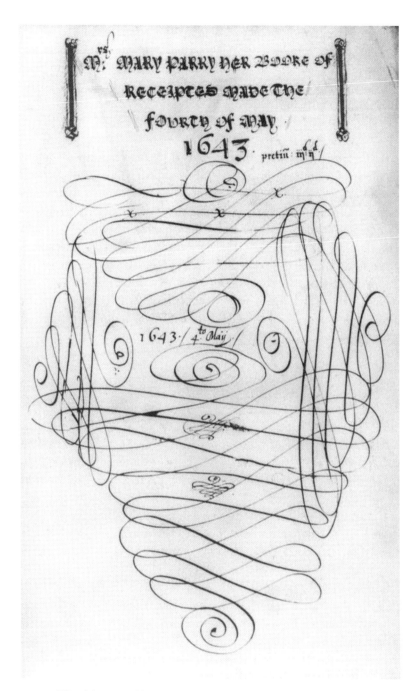

ILLUS. 72 *The title-page of 'M^{rs}: Mary Parry her Booke of Receaptes made the Fourth of May 1643', decorated with a series of spiral flourishes.*

In legal usage, the term 'record' is applied more specifically to an official written account or minute of proceedings in a case, one that a superior court might order to be brought up from an inferior court as evidence and that was enrolled on parchment in a court of record. A record had special evidentiary value, higher than that of a deed, and could not be controverted.

The term *recorda* (the Medieval Latin word means 'records') is sometimes applied to state administrative and legal records in general, but particularly to certain classes of records of proceedings in inferior courts that were sent to, and enrolled in, the Exchequer after the latter's issue of certain writs. Considerable numbers of these, from the time of Edward III (early fourteenth century) onwards are preserved in the National Archives at Kew (such as in the E 143 and E 156 series). Series are also preserved there relating to the King's Bench, such as KB 145, dating from 1324 to 1688. Some subsidiary files in this series are known as *precepta recordarum* (the Latin meaning 'rules, orders, or commands of records'). Subsequent files up to 1984 are in KB 16.

See COMMON RECOVERY.

The recto side of a leaf or folio, as opposed to the verso, is the front side, often abbreviated to *r* (fol. 1r, fol. 2r, etc.). It corresponds to the right-hand page, bearing an uneven page number (1, 3, 5, etc.), in a paginated book when laid open. An alternative form of abbreviation for rectos is *a* (fol. 1a, fol. 2a, etc.), although this system is now becoming obsolete, partly because confusion arises when an intermediate leaf between, say, 1 and 2 might be numbered fol. 1a.

Recusant Rolls

A recusant (the original French term means 'one who refuses') was someone, whether Catholic or Protestant Dissenter, who refused to conform to the rites of the Church of England and failed to attend services in his or her local parish church. Recusants thereby fell foul of the 1559 Act of Uniformity, which established a fine of 12*d.* for each absence on a Sunday or Holy Day. This fine was increased to £20 a month in 1581 (although collected only sporadically and selectively in practice). The penalties for non-attendance continued to increase over the years, including the forfeiture of goods and property of religiously and politically active families. Priests who celebrated Mass were subject to the death penalty from 1563 onwards, and a considerable number of Catholic missionaries were indeed executed in the reigns of Queen Elizabeth and James I. The Recusant Rolls in the National Archives at Kew (E 376, a duplicate series in E 377) are annual lists drawn up in the Exchequer based on returns by county sheriffs giving particulars of the fines and forfeitures imposed on named recusants in each county, with sometimes descriptions of their lands, for most years from 1592 to 1691. Recusant accounts for the period 1581–91 are included in the eleven rolls for that period among the Pipe Rolls (E 372).

RED TAPE

Since the eighteenth century, red (or pink) tape was commonly used to tie together folders of official correspondence or other papers on particular topics in government administration and later in the Civil Service and other public and bureaucratic institutions. In consequence, 'red tape' ultimately became a somewhat pejorative term signifying cumbersome, excessive, finicky, time-consuming, and generally unnecessary adherence to bureaucratic regulations, procedures, and protocols.

REGISTER

A register is any kind of manuscript volume in which entries are made in a regular and systematic manner as a formal or official record. Registers normally have relatively short entries, their contents looking like extended lists, although other examples may contain longer accounts of proceedings, etc. Among the many types of registers relating to ecclesiastical, legal, commercial, and other civil matters, found chiefly in national and local record offices, are, for instance, archbishops' and bishops' registers (relating to official episcopal business); parish registers (recording baptisms, marriages, and burials in each parish: *see* Illus. 73); registers of sequestration (recording the confiscation of estates of Royalist delinquents by Parliament in the 1640s and 1650s); electoral registers (listing names of people entitled to vote in particular areas); registers of writs (*see* REGISTRUM BREVIUM); and the Registers of the Privy Council (*see* PRIVY COUNCIL).

In bibliography, the term is also applied to a table at the end of a printed book showing the order in which the quires are to be bound up and, sometimes, where plates are to be inserted.

REGISTER OF CONVOCATION AND CONGREGATION
See GRACE BOOKS.

ILLUS. 73 *A page in the register of St Giles' Cathedral, Edinburgh, in a narrow vellum-bound ledger format (c.9 × 3¼ inches or 23 × 8 cm), which altogether covers the period 1672–84. It shows entries from 11 May to 21 September 1673 made by a clerk recording twelve marriages, including two involving a 'Writter' (clerk or notary), and the entries were afterwards scored through with oblique pen-strokes or slashes.*

Deriving from the Latin *registrarius* (an officer of the court or one who keeps records), the term 'registrar' means someone who keeps a register in an official capacity: hence an official recorder in an ecclesiastical, legal, academic, or other civil institution. In medieval times, the term was commonly rendered as 'registrer', and from *c*.1580 to the end of the eighteenth century in certain legal contexts as 'register'. At some universities the term 'registrary' is used: for instance, at Cambridge, where today the Registrary is officially described as Head of the Unified Administrative Service and Secretary to the University Council.

REGISTRAR GENERAL

See CENSUS.

REGISTRUM BREVIUM

Manuscript collections were made of the forms of original writs in law, by way of formularies compiled for the guidance of Chancery clerks, and one or more versions recorded about 1227 became known as the 'Register of Writs', or *Registrum Brevium*. Such collections, which varied in content, but were of fundamental importance in the development of the law, were among the commonest species of medieval English legal manuscripts (*see* BOOK OF FORMS AND PRECEDENTS). A version of the Register was printed as *Registrum omnium brevium* ('The register of all writs') by William Rastell in 1531.

REJOINDER

As a legal document in a bill court (such as Chancery, Star Chamber, or the equity side of Exchequer), a rejoinder is a written reply by a defendant to the plaintiff's replication in response to the defendant's answer to the plaintiff's bill of complaint. In a common-law court all these pleadings were originally made orally, although recorded in writing. If further responses by the two parties ensue, that by the plaintiff to the defendant's rejoinder is known as a 'surrejoinder', one by the defendant to this is known as a 'rebuttal' or 'rebutter', and one by the plaintiff to this is known as a 'surrebuttal' or 'surrebutter'. For the full sequence of responses and counter-responses by the two parties, *see* ANSWER.

RELEASE

As a document, a release is generally a written discharge from an obligation: e.g. a receipt for payment of a debt or a formal acquittance drawn up and granted when the terms of some agreement have been fulfilled. More specifically in English law, a release is a deed conveying a reversion to the tenant in possession of particular property. *See* LETTERS OF REVERSION.

REMEMBRANCER

The term 'remembrancer' occurs in different contexts. Deriving from the sense of one who records things so that they will be remembered, the term was applied to certain officials, both in local and central government. From the thirteenth century, the Lord Treasurer's Remembrancer was the principal clerical officer in the Exchequer of Receipt side of the Exchequer, who was responsible for dealing with Crown revenues, auditing, and debt-collecting. The Memoranda Rolls for the Lord Treasurer's Remembrancer from 1217 to 1837 are in the National Archives at Kew (E 368).

The King's (or Queen's) Remembrancer—an office still in existence—was originally the principal clerical officer in the Exchequer of Pleas side of the Exchequer who dealt with Crown business and also lawsuits by debtors and accountants. He attended sittings at the Court of Exchequer and eventually supervised the collection of debts due to the sovereign. He was later custodian of the Great Seal of Exchequer, the seal of office of the Chancellor of the Exchequer, and performed (and still does) various ceremonial duties. Enrolments of this office from the mid-twelfth century to 1994 are in the National Archives at Kew (E 159 and some in E 163 series): *see* MEMORANDA ROLLS.

A Remembrancer for the Corporation of the City of London, from the sixteenth century onwards, was the official who represented the Corporation before parliamentary committees and at Council and Treasury boards.

'Remembrancer' is also a term sometimes applied to any kind of manuscript memorandum book or register in which particulars are entered for the record. Hence it is sometimes used in titles of printed books in which details of some subject are set out so as to be remembered. Books from the 1620s onwards containing the word 'remembrancer' in their titles (*Davids Remembrancer, Britaines Remembrancer, Londons Remembrancer, Englands Remembrancer,* etc.) are legion.

REMOVAL ORDER

See SETTLEMENT CERTIFICATE.

RENTAL, RENT-ROLL

A rental is a type of manuscript ledger or register, as is a rent-roll, that derives its name from its original form as a parchment roll, but may in fact be a manuscript book. Its purpose is to list a person's lands and properties and the rents paid on each of them by specified tenants, by way of keeping account of the landowner's income from leased estate. Rentals abound in old family and estate archives, in record offices, and in private muniments.

REPLICATION

As a legal document in a bill court (such as Chancery, Star Chamber, or the equity side of Exchequer), a replication is a written reply made by the plaintiff in response to the defendant's answer to the plaintiff's bill of complaint. In a common-law court all these pleadings were originally made orally, although recorded in writing. For the full sequence of responses and counter-responses by the two parties, *see* ANSWER.

REPORT

A report is an account of something, usually a formal written statement setting out the results of an investigation into some matter, or else setting out facts or opinions on the condition, progress, or success of something: e.g. a school report on a pupil or the result of an inquiry into a delayed building project. The term therefore applies to the document embodying that account.

REPOSITORY

In the context of books and manuscripts, a repository is any building where books and manuscripts are kept, such as libraries and record offices. Although the term may apply to any of the great libraries and record offices, as well as possibly buildings used for this purpose by private collectors, it may also imply that this is where the items repose, meaning that it is where they rest on deposit, possibly on a temporary basis, and are not necessarily owned by the institution or permanently housed there.

RESERVOIR PEN

See FOUNTAIN PEN.

RÉSUMÉ

Adopted from the French, the term 'résumé' means a summary, synopsis, or brief report, conveying the main or essential points of information about a particular matter.

RETURN

'Return' is a term applied to several kinds of document, in different contexts, from medieval times onwards. As well as once meaning simply a reply (to a letter, dispatch, or demand), a return can be a report written by a sheriff in response to a writ sent to him by a court, or as an endorsement on it, in which he explains how far he has been able to carry out the court's instructions. It may be a report by a returning officer, also in response to a writ, concerning the election of Members of Parliament. Alternatively, it may be any kind of official report in which numbers or statistics are set out in connection with a particular subject: for instance, an ordnance return detailing supplies in store.

In a military or naval context, a return is a report incorporating a count of the dead and wounded after a battle or campaign, one that may take the form of a straightforward list or tally or else be an official detailed breakdown drawn up perhaps in a series of columns. *See* Illus. 74.

REVERSE

The reverse or back side of a leaf in a book or manuscript is the verso, as opposed to the recto. A manuscript volume may also be said to be reversed, or written from the reverse end, when it is used from both ends: i.e. the writer(s) or compiler(s) write entries in the volume not only from the front proceeding towards the back but also turn the volume around and use it from the back end proceeding towards the front (so whichever way the volume is held the writing at the other end will be upside down). This practice is fairly common with notebooks, commonplace books, and the like. It may occur because a new owner of the manuscript wished to make a fresh start or personal use of it by using blank leaves at the end, or else because the original compiler(s) wished to distinguish a species of text or subject matter as different from that represented in the initial entries at the other end.

REVERSION

See LETTERS OF REVERSION.

REVISION

Deriving from a form of the Latin *revidere* ('to look at again'), the term 'revision' denotes an alteration that constitutes a textual innovation introduced by the author, such as deliberate verbal deletion, addition, insertion, or rephrasing. Revisions may occur at any stage of authorial composition, usually in the draft stage, but also sometimes in a fair copy, or else in a

ILLUS. 74 *A 'Return of Services performed by the Indians of Colonel Guy Johnson's Department. of the Killed. wounded &ca & damages done to the Rebels from the beginning of the Year 1780. to the end of 1781'. It is set out in tabulated or grid format on a large sheet of paper by an official clerk on the Loyalist side during the American War of Independence and gives details of numerous skirmishes.*

Return of services performed by the Indians of Colonel Guy Johnson's Department of the [Indian] Affairs &c of damage done to the Rebels from the beginning of the Year 1780 to the end of 1781.

manuscript to which the author later returns to produce a new or revised version of the work (*see* Illus. 8, 13, 23, 28, 68, and 90). A scribe or editor cannot technically make revisions in someone else's work, but only emendations, sophistications, or an adaptation. The term may also be distinguished from 'correction', denoting the rectification of a purely mechanical error such as the unintentional omission of a word or a misspelling.

REVOCATION

Deriving from the Latin *revocare* ('to rescind or call back'), the term 'revocation' denotes a deed, or a clause in a deed, cancelling or revoking some previous deed.

RHUMB-LINE

A rhumb-line or rhumb, also known as a 'loxodrome', is an oblique line drawn on a sea chart, portolan, or map. It is usually one in a series of lines radiating from a central point and often intersecting with lines radiating from other points, each central point frequently set within a compass- or wind-rose (*see* Illus. 63). Rhumb-lines thus represent directions of the compass for winds and serve to guide pilots in setting navigational courses between ports and harbours. A 'rhumb-chart' is another term for a 'portolan'.

RIBBON

Ribbons, or laces—narrow strips of fine material such as silk—feature in manuscripts as occasional ties to letters or books.

ROLL

A roll is a document written usually on parchment, each membrane of which is stitched to the next, either head to foot (Chancery-style) or head to head (Exchequer-style), to form either a long continuous scroll or else a series of membranes stacked on top of each other and sewn at the upper edge, that can be rolled up into cylindrical shape. Rolls of various kinds, bearing text that can be unrolled and read either vertically or horizontally, date back to ancient times and were gradually replaced in the early medieval period by codices. The use of rolls persisted for administrative purposes, however. Extant series of rolls are generally official records of legal and financial matters of state importance, but also include local manorial rolls (*see* Illus. 19).

Certain heraldic rolls produced to celebrate notable events can be strikingly spectacular: for instance, the Great Tournament Roll of Westminster at the College of Arms, which comprises thirty-six membranes of vellum, altogether 59 feet 6 inches in length and 14¾ inches wide (over 18 metres × 37.5 cm). It bears painted representations in procession form of all the participants in the tournament of 12–13 February 1511 celebrating the birth of (the short-lived) Prince Henry to Henry VIII and Katherine of Aragon.

Some other manuscripts take the form of rolls, whether on parchment or paper, for convenient storage because of their size, such as long genealogies, estate maps, or certain alchemical manuscripts. With various kinds of documents, especially official and manorial ones, however, the traditional term 'roll' may persist even when the roll form has been abandoned: for instance, a rent roll may actually be written in a manuscript book; an electoral roll may be some kind of typescript; and rolls of honour and rolls of service (following the First World War, for instance) may be formal calligraphic and illuminated manuscripts or printed books. As with other classes of manuscripts, rolls are usually known by the specific types of information they record: for instance, subsidy rolls and hearth tax rolls, which document different kinds of tax payments. In common legal usage today the term 'roll' can mean the bundle of plea rolls for a law term.

For some particular types of roll or Rolls, *see* ASSOCIATION OATH ROLLS, BEAD-ROLL, CHANCERY, CHARTER ROLLS, CLOSE ROLLS, COMPOTUS ROLLS, CONFIRMATION ROLLS, CONTROLMENT ROLLS, COURT ROLL, ESSOIN ROLLS, EXCHEQUER, FINE ROLLS, MEMORANDA ROLLS, MUSTER ROLLS, NEW YEAR'S GIFT ROLL, OATH ROLLS, PARLIAMENT ROLLS, PATENT ROLLS, PIPE ROLLS, PLEA ROLLS, RECUSANT ROLLS, and TITHE ROLL.

ROLLER

A roller is a rounded length of wood or other material, or a spindle-shaped small pole like a culinary rolling pin, around which a roll could be wrapped or folded (*see* Illus. 75). Dating from ancient times, and used in various cultures, including Judaic and Christian, rollers could sometimes be elaborately shaped, with varied tapering. Especially important examples, such as those bearing scrolls used in liturgies, could be carved in more precious materials such as ivory.

ROLL OF ENTRIES

See CONTROLMENT ROLLS.

ROMAN SCRIPT

See ITALIC SCRIPT.

RONEOED

See FACSIMILE.

ILLUS. 75 *A figure depicted near the end of a 12½-foot (3.81-metre) alchemical scroll of 1624, carrying a very elongated and pointed roller bearing a scroll.*

Ropework is a type of scribal, as well as embroidery or textile, decoration characterized by patterns of twisted braid or plaits.

ROTA

See BULL.

ROTULET

'Rotulet' is a term occasionally used to denote a small roll, including a rolled up single membrane of parchment.

ROTULI PARLIAMENTORUM

See PARLIAMENT ROLLS.

ROTULUS

Rotulus (plural: *rotuli*) is the Latin form, occasionally used in official records, of 'roll'. The official responsible in each county or shire for the collection and preservation of public legal documents was known as the *Custos Rotulorum* ('Keeper of the Rolls').

ROUNDED HAND

Rounded hand is any handwriting or script, from early medieval times onwards, in which the letter forms tend to be curved or have a rotundity of appearance, as opposed, for instance, to square-shaped or compressed lettering. What is sometimes called 'rounded hand' is the mixed hand that came to predominate in England by the mid-seventeenth century when secretary script tended to merge with features of italic script.

ROUNDEL

A roundel, being a small drawn circle, ring, or disc in various colours, is a common feature of manuscript genealogies or pedigrees, and usually contains lettering (*see* Illus. 30). The gold variety is called a 'bezant'. Roundels also occasionally appear as decorative features in the form of circular vines and the like in medieval manuscripts. In early modern manuscripts, roundels of a kind may even be encountered in the form of linked bubbles embodying text in notebooks or drafts where, for instance, someone may be working through the points of an argument by setting it out diagramatically: e.g. George Puttenham's draft summary of his dealings with his brother-in-law in 1578 'drawn owte in tables' in the National Archives at Kew (SP 12/127/31).

Royal Commission on Historical Manuscripts
See HISTORICAL MANUSCRIPTS COMMISSION.

Royal Household accounts

Royal Household accounts are detailed records of the expenses involved in maintaining the Royal Household, as opposed to other offices of the realm. They are usually found neatly and systematically drawn up by official scribes in formal books, with ruled columns, similar to establishment books (*see* ESTABLISHMENT BOOK), or else they may themselves be incorporated in establishment books. The relevant offices, including secretaries, the revels, court musicians, players, chapel personnel, the wardrobe, the kitchen, the jewel house, archers and hunting officers, are customarily listed with their annual or periodic fees or salaries. *See* Illus. 25.

Royal Household accounts may also be found collected as separate warrants, receipts, and other documents, or else set out in separate ledgers, where many more details of disbursements are given. For instance, a series of account books, rolls, and related papers kept by Queen Henrietta Maria's Treasurer, Sir Richard Wyn, now in the National Library of Wales (Wynnstay MSS 161–186), record the Queen's revenues and also payments made on her behalf from 1629 to 1642 to innumerable pensioners, including maids of honour, the designers and writers of masques Inigo Jones, Ben Jonson, and Walter Montagu, the court dwarf Jeffrey Hudson, and various musicians and painters, as well as expenses for jewellery and for routine supplies such as ink and paper. Some of these books are signed by the Queen in various places to signify her approving the accuracy of the accounts.

Royal Letters Patent

Letters patent and Royal Letters Patent are basically one and the same thing, since both are authorized by the sovereign. Letters patent are often termed 'Royal', however, when, as is usually the case, they are not only specifically issued in the name of the sovereign, rather than by the Privy Council or other bodies, but their royal authority seems to be in some respects highlighted. They may also allege the monarch's personal involvement (*teste rege* or *teste me ipso*). Although earlier examples were relatively modest in format, by the early modern period such patents, usually bestowing high offices or privileges, are often engrossed on large membranes of parchment, sometimes filling two or more stitched together. Expensively produced examples might not only have the name of the monarch at the beginning heavily engrossed, but also be embellished with decorated or

ILLUS. 76 *Royal Letters Patent of George I, a patent of nobility elevating to the Irish peerage Trevor Hill as Baron Hill of Kilwarlin and Viscount Hillsborough, the text in Latin, with an illuminated initial letter portrait of the King, the upper border and margins adorned with heraldic emblems, coats of arms, and other devices, on two membranes of vellum, 21 August 1717.*

historiated borders. The most distinctive royal feature of all would be if the patent bore an initial letter portrait of the monarch limned in pen and ink (*see* Illus. 37 and 38) or, most expensively, coloured or illuminated. *See* INITIAL LETTER PORTRAIT and Illus. 76.

From at least the seventeenth century onwards, and possibly earlier, valued patents of this kind were commonly kept by their owners in fitted boxes. By the late seventeenth or early eighteenth century, such boxes were usually wooden with decorated paper lining, often covered in leather, and sometimes embellished with floral or other devices or figures tooled in gilt. Up to a yard (91.5 cm) long, these boxes were often slightly T-shaped, the horizontal top accommodating the rolled-up scroll, the circular compartment beneath accommodating the pendent impression in wax of the Great Seal, usually in its skippet. Since 1914 some Royal Letters Patent have been issued on paper and bear wafer seals.

RUBRIC

Deriving from the Latin *rubricare* ('to colour red'), the term 'rubric', in the context of a book or manuscript, means a heading, to a chapter or section, written or printed in red ink. A book or manuscript is said to be 'rubricated' when not only headings but also initial capitals, paragraph marks, or occasional words are written or painted in red. The scribe responsible for rubricating could be called a 'rubricator'. There are even examples of manuscripts (such as a copy of Valerius Maximus, *c*.1475, at Chatsworth House) which still contain a list of instructions to the rubricator as to the precise elements in the text that were to be rubricated.

In earlier liturgical books, the term was also applied to directions for the conduct of divine service and to a calendar of saints' days.

The term 'rubric' is now generally used to denote preliminary matter, such as an introductory note, explanation, or instruction, that is not part of the principal text, whether it appears in red or not.

RULE

A rule is a straight line drawn on paper or parchment, usually today with the help of a ruler. Thus ruled lines on a page are regularly spaced horizontal lines drawn as a guide for even writing, and a ruled margin or ruled border is a margin or border at the side, top, or bottom of a page marked off by a drawn vertical or horizontal line (*see* Illus. 12, 21, 25, 30, 35, and 87). Ruling in manuscripts from medieval times onwards, including the ruling of columns or the framing or boxing-off of portions of text, could be done in a variety of ways and with different writing implements and materials, including dry point (in the early medieval period), lead point (from the eleventh century), and ink (from the thirteenth century onwards). Lines could be regularized by the use of pricking (possibly through patterns, a technique used by painters), by sometimes elaborate frames, grids, or templates, some with wires, laid over or pressed into the page (for columns, etc.), or, just occasionally, by ink-soaked string stretched down the page (which, at least in the early modern period, usually leaves a rather fuzzy impression). Rules in ink might be in any colour, but, unless the same ink as the main text is used, they seem to be most commonly in red.

RUNNING HEAD

A running head or running title is a headline or short title repeated continuously at the top of each page, or each alternate page, of a book. Such headlines usually comprise the title of the work, or an abbreviated version of it, or else the heading, in some form, of the section or chapter of the work. These terms are usually applied to printed books, but running heads and running titles can be found in manuscript bibles and treatises at least as early as the late eleventh century and certainly up to the early modern period.

RUTTER

The term 'ruttier', commonly rendered as 'rutter', was adopted in England from the French *routier de la mer* at the beginning of the fifteenth century, although it is often applied to a certain type of book, whether manuscript or printed, from before or after that date. A rutter may be simply a book of sea-charts, the same thing as a portolan atlas (*see* PORTOLAN). More commonly, however, the term denotes a maritime guidebook with directions for sailing between ports on trade routes, information about tides, and other navigational particulars.

S

Σ

See SIGMA.

SACRAMENT CERTIFICATE

Following the Test Act of 1672, directed against Catholic recusants, all persons appointed to public office, civil and military, were compelled not only to take the Oath of Allegiance to the monarch as 'the only supreme governor of this realm' with supreme authority in 'all spiritual and ecclesiastical things' as well, but also to receive regularly Holy Communion in the Church of England. A Sacrament certificate (the term derived from the Latin *sacramentum*, 'a consecrating' or 'surety'), signed by the minister, churchwarden, and two witnesses, testifying to the person's having received the sacrament of the Lord's Supper in the Anglican Church, had to be produced and delivered at quarter sessions (quarterly meetings of the Justices of Peace in each county). Although the regulations governing such certificates varied in different reigns, and fewer were issued as the eighteenth century wore on, the law requiring them was not repealed until 1828, before the Catholic Emancipation Act of 1829 came into effect. Most of the extant certificates are preserved among the quarter sessions papers in county record offices or among various court records in the National Archives at Kew.

SACRAMENT TOKEN BOOKS

Since at least the fifteenth century until the Civil War, in accordance with laws compelling attendance at church and the receiving of the Sacrament, or Holy Communion, it was a practice in many parishes to use tokens both to record the fact and to acquire income for the church. Churchwardens, who, at least by Elizabethan times, went around from house to house for this purpose, gave tokens to parishioners, who were expected to give a penny or halfpenny for them. The tokens would then be handed back to the church

354

when the person attended Communion service. The records of this practice kept by churchwardens are known as 'Sacrament token books' or simply 'token books'. Those for Southwark, for instance, preserved in the London Metropolitan Archives, date from 1578 to 1640, and record details of householders, the number of possible communicants in each family, and other information about them.

SAFE-CONDUCT

A safe-conduct, sometimes called 'letters of safe-conduct', is a type of passport whereby a monarch or other authority in a host country grants to a particular person, usually a foreigner, the privilege of being able to make a journey in specified territory under that authority's jurisdiction without fear of arrest or molestation or having his or her goods seized so long as the traveller complies with whatever conditions are imposed. Those granted by English monarchs were usually passed under the Great Seal and enrolled in Chancery.

Alternatively, from medieval times onwards, what could be called a safe-conduct might take the form of an official document identifying the bearer and requesting anyone in foreign territory to grant him free passage. Thus, in 1394, for instance, Edward III's son, John of Gaunt, drew up a Latin open letter on vellum under his seal requesting free passage for Niccolò da Lucca whom he was sending to Italy, Germany, and elsewhere as his envoy to undertake certain negotiations (British Library, Additional Charter 7487). Such safe-conducts could take various forms, whether written on vellum or paper, and were usually signed or sealed by the authority concerned. Some from the early eighteenth onwards were printed with spaces left for the relevant details to be inserted by hand.

Safe-conducts might also be requested on behalf of, or awarded to, subjects passing through enemy lines in a time of war. One signed in 1777 by the American General Horatio Gates during the American War of Independence, for instance, effected the release and safe passage of his British prisoner Major John Dyke Acland and his wife, Lady Harriet Acland, after she had personally crossed enemy lines to tend to her badly wounded husband.

SALUTATION

Deriving from the Latin *salutatio* ('greeting'), the term 'salutation' means a greeting, usually of a somewhat formal kind, as in a charter or in a military salute. The formulaic wording of a writ from the monarch to a sheriff, for instance, bore the word *salutem* in the first line. The term 'salutation' may be applied to the conventional modern greeting at the beginning of letters, 'Dear...' or 'My dear...', which became standardized by the eighteenth century. Earlier forms of salutation were more varied, although still incorporating very respectful addresses to the recipient ('Right Worshipful', 'My Lord', 'Sir', etc.). Some fairly standardized forms were adopted for a range of official communications, such as royal letters beginning 'Right trusty and wellbeloved, we greet you well' or Privy Council letters beginning 'After our very hearty commendations' and the like. To reduce the formality and to personalize the salutation when a modern letter is typed, it is not uncommon to see writers changing the wording or adding the salutation in full by hand—an occasional feature of Winston Churchill's letters, for example.

SAMIZDAT

Derived from the Russian *sam* ('self') and *izdatelstvo* ('publishing'), the term 'samizdat' is modern, in use since *c*.1966. It denotes the clandestine or underground circulation of articles or books, expressing dissident political views, in the form of carbon-copy typescripts or copies run off duplicating machines or photocopiers, without the knowledge or approval of the authorities. In a more extreme form, it is a modern equivalent of the circulation of sometimes subversive political tracts in the early modern period by means of unlicensed printing and scribal manuscripts.

SAMMELBAND

The German word *Sammelband* (plural: *Sammelbände*) is sometimes used to denote a composite volume of two or more works, whether printed, manuscript, or both, bound together.

SAND-BOX, SANDER

See POUNCE POT.

SAND TRAY

What is sometimes called either a 'sand tray' or 'sand table' is, or was, a long tray, *c*.6 inches × 5 feet (15 × 1.5 metres), raised on legs like a trestle, containing sand in which children might be taught to trace letters, figures, etc. It can come complete with an eraser: a board with a handle that can be dragged from one end to the other to level the sand. A fine Victorian example can be found in Dennington church, Suffolk. Types of smaller sand trays, or sand tray play sets, are still marketed for children to draw and write in today.

SASINE

In Scotland, an instrument of sasine (i.e. the English 'seisin', similarly pronounced as 'say-zin'), sometimes loosely referred to as simply a 'sasine', is a deed prepared by a notary conveying or establishing possession of feudal land or property. It specifically testifies that the traditional public ceremony for the transference of property (the handing over of symbols of the land such as a clod of earth or twigs) has been properly conducted in the presence of at least two male witnesses. In early feudal times, this ceremony ensued upon a precept of sasine, a separate deed in which a laird or other superior ordered his bailie, or bailiff, to allow the property to be conveyed to a vassal. Records of sasines in various burghs exist from medieval times onwards. From the sixteenth century to the present day, but more generally from 1617 onwards, instruments of sasine have been entered as a public record of land possession in the General Register of Sasines, a vast series of volumes now in the National Archives of Scotland. This register makes it possible, at least in theory, to trace the history of ownership of every house in Scotland from 1617 onwards.

SATCHEL BINDING

See WALLET.

SCALE BAR

On maps and portolans, the scale bar is a horizontal strip or rectangular box containing a line in graduated divisions with measurements denoting the scale of the map: i.e. how many miles, kilometres, or nautical leagues are represented by the given lengths. Scale bars on some maps can be elaborately decorated or else incorporate explanatory text (*see* Illus. 48).

SCALLOPED

Derived from 'scallop', the round-shaped shellfish, the term 'scalloped' is used to describe parchment indentures or chirographs that have been cut so that they have at the top a wavy edge, of an undulating pattern akin to a series of segments of circles, either concave or convex (*see* Illus. 36). This was formed, at least in original practice, when a single membrane was cut in two halves (or into three or four parts), forming the indenture or chirograph and its counterpart(s), which could be matched together as a perfect fit if any dispute about their authenticity arose.

SCHEDULE

Used widely in modern times to mean a 'timetable', the term 'schedule' is also traditionally applied to other types of document. Most notably, a

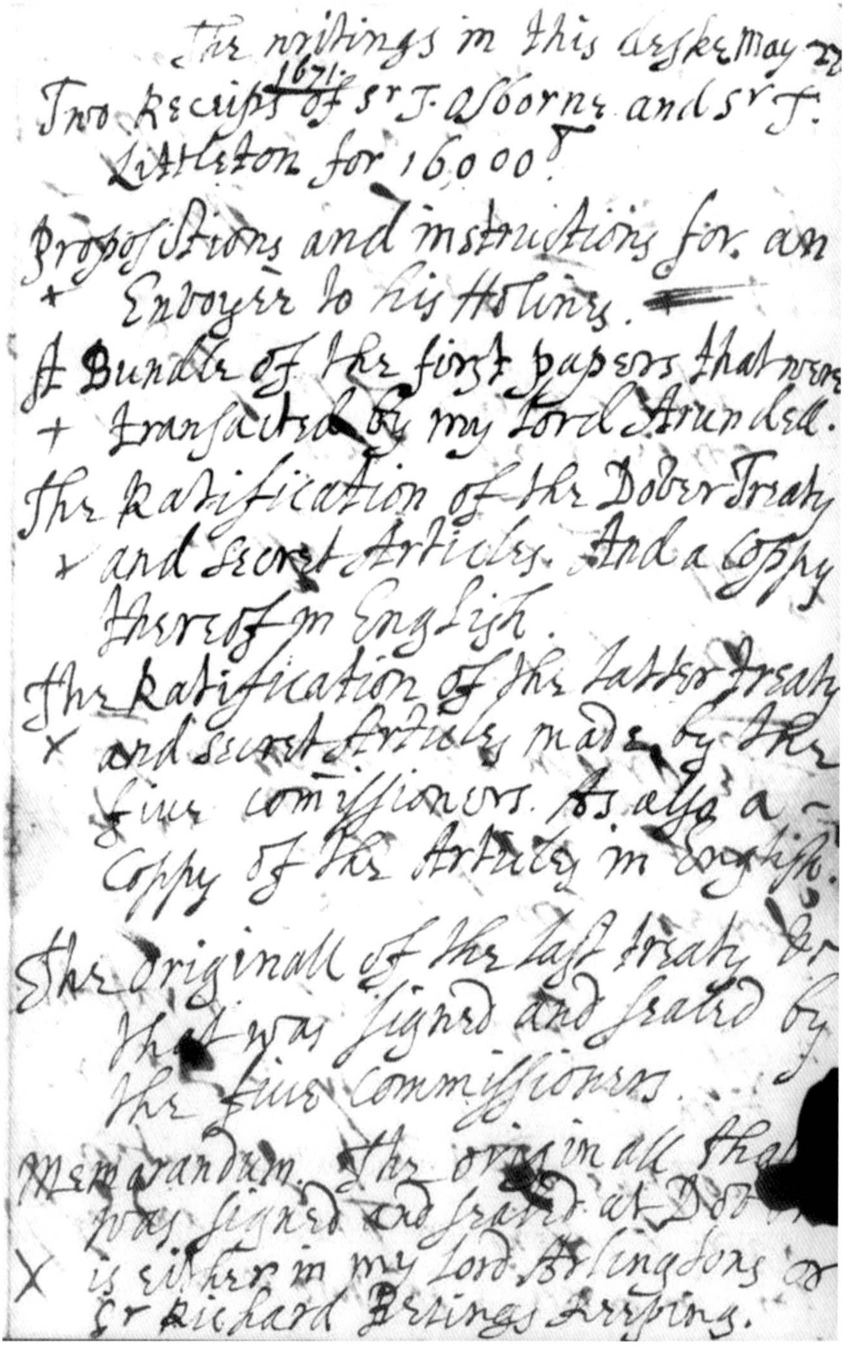

The writings in this deske May 27
1671
Two Receipts of Sr J. Osborne and Sr J.
Littleton for 16,000ℓ

Propositions and instructions for an
+ Endoyer to his Holines.

A Bundle of the first papers that were
+ Transacted by my Lord Arundell.

The Ratification of the Dover Treaty
+ and Secret Articles. And a Coppy
thereof in English.

The Ratification of the latter Treaty
× and secret Articles made by the
five commissioners. As also a
Coppy of the Articles in English.

The Originall of the last treaty
that was signed and sealed by
the five Commissioners.

Memorandum. The originall that
was signed and sealed at Dover
× is either in my Lord Arlingtons or
Sr Richard Billings keeping.

ILLUS. 77 *An autograph schedule by Thomas, Lord Clifford of Chudleigh, of 'The writings in this deske May 27 1671'. The list includes the Secret Treaty of Dover papers.*

358

schedule is a parchment or paper sheet appended to a will or other legal document in which are detailed supplementary relevant particulars, such as a list or inventory of the person's goods and chattels, the fixtures in a lease, or a codicil to the will. A schedule is also a list of documents, such as a list of family muniments, or a list of the documents relevant to a particular legal case or other matter. *See* Illus. 77.

SCIANT PRESENTES

The incipit, or opening words, of a common Latin formula used in bonds and other legal instruments from medieval times onwards was *Sciant presentes et futuri quod...* (sometimes abbreviated to *Sciant prsent & futur qd...*), meaning 'Know those present and future that...'. *See also* NOVERINT UNIVERSI.

SCORE CHEQUE

See JOUSTING CHEQUE.

SCRAPBOOK

A scrapbook, or scrap-book, is a book or album of blank leaves designed or used for the affixing of separate pieces of paper or card containing printed or manuscript texts and designs. It differs from manuscript compilations, such as commonplace books, not only in the nature of its contents, but also because the entries are pasted-in rather than being inscribed by hand. Scrapbooks, as commercially produced products, designed primarily for young people and sold by stationers, flourished especially in the nineteenth century. Characteristic examples contain such things as coloured paper cut-outs and illustrations, depicting flowers, birds, waterfalls, castles, windmills, etc., as well as newspaper and magazine cuttings, silhouettes, valentine cards, cartoons, crests cut from letters and envelopes, programmes, menus, printed jokes and riddles, and other souvenirs and ephemera, as well as pressed flowers and leaves. Many of these contents could take the form of 'scraps', taken from ready-made sheets of coloured designs and illustrations produced and sold by stationers for specific use in these albums, including such things as toy theatre sheets. Scrapbooks can vary considerably in size: although most are no more than about 18 inches (36 cm) in length, some exceptionally large examples can measure a yard or metre or more.

The term 'scrapbook' can also be used in a metaphorical sense in titles of books, implying a miscellaneous or casual hodge-podge of information, presented without any formal overall structure or arrangement.

Errors made by scribes in the copying of manuscript texts take many forms, most of them familiar to those who engage in any kind of transcription work. The identification of such errors, and of the types of error they exemplify, may not only help editors to establish the textual readings that lie behind them, but also to establish the habits of particular scribes by which their work may be assessed. Copying mistakes, in any period, occur when scribes are subject to failing concentration, wandering attention, tiredness, or plain carelessness. They may occur when, for instance, a scribe carries in his head too many words, resulting in his losing some of them (ellipsis), or writing down other, similar sounding words (homophones, such as 'bow' and 'bough'). He may unintentionally repeat words or even whole lines, jumble up letters within a word, copy incorrectly when his exemplar contains unfamiliar or foreign words, including proper names (a common occasion for faulty copying), or when he makes misguided attempts to clarify words or passages in his exemplar that he does not understand. Alternatively, errors may accrue when scribes' exemplars are defective, not entirely legible, have confusing abbreviations, or are marked by other textual features open to misinterpretation. Scribes might also feel obliged to supply themselves the missing words in lacunae.

The recognition of unclear or complicating factors in an exemplar is sometimes deliberately signalled by a scribe. In medieval manuscripts, for instance, words may be written with a row of dots beneath, indicating cancellation or expunction, but without further change so as not to spoil a neatly written page. Alternatively, the mistake may be written or explained in the margins—even, on occasions, proudly proclaimed by being encased in a frame to show that the text has been checked for accuracy. Even more common are instances when one word is written over another. This may reproduce a revision in the scribe's exemplar—the word superscribed being a preferred substitute for the word underneath, which, however, is left undeleted—or else may reflect the scribe's uncertainty as to what is the correct reading, or even, perhaps, represent his deliberate addition of a reading found in another exemplar.

Some characteristic and generally recognized types of scribal error (the technical terms for some of which are Greek) include:

anticipation: when a scribe carries in his head several words, but starts conflating them, writing letters or words that come next before he has finished writing the first one (e.g. 'put putting' instead of 'but putting');

dittography: the unintentional repetition of words or of letters in a word;

eyeskip (*homoioteleuton*): when a scribe moves back to the wrong point in his exemplar after his eye has wandered, commonly when the last word copied occurs again lower down on the page and he mistakenly jumps to that point, omitting the intervening words;

homoioarchon: the confusion of two words in close proximity that have the same beginning;

metathesis: the inversion or misplacing of letters within a word;

transposition: when words are copied in the wrong order.

Such errors can, of course, also sometimes characterize typographical script produced on typewriters or computer keyboards. Here attention to the particular keyboard or type of keyboard used may help to elucidate garbled text (when, for instance, adjacent letters have been accidentally hit).

SCRIBBLE

To scribble is to write hastily, roughly, carelessly, and slovenly, and scribbling is writing so characterized. Examples encountered in various periods include rapidly written notes and jottings of various kinds, generally entered as personal memoranda not intended for reading by other people, and scrawled inscriptions and defacements, usually (but not always) by children, in books and manuscripts.

SCRIBBLER

A scribbler is someone who scribbles or is responsible for a particular piece of scribbling. Since at least as early as the sixteenth century, the term has also been a pejorative one denoting an inferior, incompetent author.

SCRIBE

Deriving from the Latin *scriba*, the term 'scribe' denotes a person responsible for the writing of a manuscript text. The term is commonly used to denote a professional clerk or copyist, in the sense of one who is a reasonably accomplished penman, whose employment it is to write or copy out documents, and who is likely to be attached, possibly as part of a team, to some kind of office or institution (ecclesiastical, royal, legal, academic, commercial, etc.), or else employed in the shop of a stationer or scrivener (*see* Illus. 22 and 79). The term may, however, just as readily be applied to amateurs, such as a member of someone's family, household, or social circle who makes copies of that person's writings, or to anyone else who copies out a text for whatever reason.

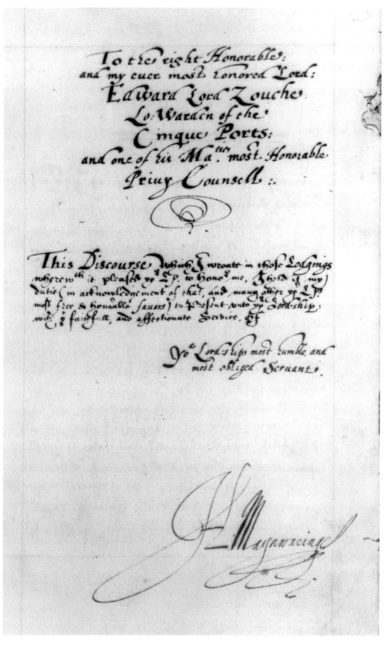

ILLUS. 78 *The dedication of a lengthy naval treatise,* The Sea-Man's Dictionary *by Sir Henry Mainwaring, in a formal copy made by the professional scribe Ralph Crane and signed by Mainwaring himself, c.1620s. Crane's characteristic mixed secretary and italic hand is marked by such features as accentuated ascenders, a ligature on the* st, *and a small spiral flourish.*

Since early medieval times, most scribes—including the Writers of the Court Letter, Writers of the Text Letter, and all the clerks of Chancery, Exchequer, and of other courts and government departments, as well as all the monks responsible for so many religious books—would appear to have been male, although the evidence is not altogether clear. There were certainly nuns engaged in scribal work on the continent. Scholars have speculated that there may have been a medieval tradition of nuns copying books in England, but at present there is only one undisputed example of a manuscript so written. It is a twelfth-century volume of sermons and treatises now in the Bodleian Library (MS Bodley 451), and associated with St Mary's Abbey, Winchester. In the colophon, the anonymous scribe refers to herself as a *scriptrix* (as opposed to a male *scriptor*). By the early modern period, however, there are many examples of writings copied by female scribes, including nuns. Notably industrious copyists among English Benedictine nuns, for instance, include the four daughters of Elizabeth, Lady Falkland (1586–1639), at Our Lady of Consolation in Cambrai, whose manuscripts are now widely dispersed in French and British local and ecclesiastical archives, and also Dame Barbara Constable, many of whose transcripts of religious texts at Cambrai between 1638 and 1681 are now at Ampleforth College.

There is also a difference between Britain and the continent in the amount of information that scribes give about themselves. Although English scribes do occasionally identify themselves in their colophons (as also professional notaries and sometimes scriveners with notarial marks), they are less forthcoming than their continental counterparts. A commonplace book written by the monk Romain Lenon at Chartres *c*.1500, for instance, is signed by him no fewer than seventeen times. Johannes Trithemius, author of *De laude scriptorum* ('In praise of scribes') in 1492, approved of monastic scribes subscribing their names to their manuscripts as an encouragement to others to imitate their example. He may not, however, have approved of the scribe Antoine Vincent, who signed a manuscript in 1447 and added the comment *Pro scripto pena detur una pulchra et amorosa puella* ('As a penance for your writing, may you be given a beautiful and amorous girl'). Even then, elements of personalization, whereby scribes specifically draw attention to their own work, are more often made anonymously. Such comments may take the form of, for instance, an opening pious invocation like *Oret voce pia nobis Virgo Maria—Dirige scribentis spiritus alme manus* ('May the Virgin Mary with a pious voice pray for us—Kind spirit guide the hands of the writer'), or else something more mundane like the sigh of relief in the explicit *Tam longum tandem finisti penna laborem* ('Such a long task, pen, you have at last finished').

By the early modern period, although plenty of writers and commonplace-book compilers, as well as the writing masters (including the calligrapher Esther Inglis), identified themselves, most professional scribes and copyists, responsible for the distribution of current manuscript tracts, lampoons, and other literary materials, did not. A notable exception is Ralph Crane (*fl.* 1589–1632), who, among other things, was commissioned by the King's Company of players in 1618–25 to copy plays by Shakespeare and other dramatists and who himself wrote poems. *See* Illus. 78.

SCRIMSHAW

Scrimshaw is a type of nautical artefact, or handicraft, which was produced by sailors, especially in the nineteenth century. It comprises, most commonly, carvings on whalebone, whale teeth, or seal tusks, sometimes on shells, ivory, or other materials, produced during long voyages. Such carvings, which can sometimes be very detailed, elaborate, and intricate, tend to include depictions of ships, mermaids, women, and other figures, scenes, and seascapes, with occasional verbal inscriptions recording the name of the carver, his ship, some nautical verse, or other wording or captions. Although often carved on materials derived from what are now officially protected species, such as the sperm whale, scrimshaw is highly prized by collectors, one of whom was President John F. Kennedy.

SCRIP

The term 'scrip' in the early modern period could denote a small piece of paper, usually with writing on it, or else just a scrap of writing. In a commercial context, probably as an abbreviation of 'subscription receipt', a scrip was a receipt for a portion of a loan. More specifically, a scrip, or 'subscription certificate', later denoted a provisional commercial document, issued by a company or lending body, entitling the holder to specified shares in a joint-stock undertaking—provisional because it would be replaced, usually in instalments, by the shares, debentures, or bonds that it represented. In a looser sense the word 'scrip' might also be used to mean any share certificate.

SCRIPOPHILY

Deriving from the Latin *scriptum* ('something written') and Greek *philia* ('love'), the term 'scripophily' is of modern coinage and denotes the collecting of bonds and shares or stock certificates of financial institutions and commercial companies, including banks, insurance, electricity, mines, oil, railways, and other businesses, as well as governments and special areas such as the US Confederacy in the 1860s. Such documents, partly printed or engraved, sometimes in elaborately decorated form, were given to investors as material evidence of their ownership of capital and are usually signed by directors of the issuing body, sometimes also by the investors themselves (those signed by famous American financiers such as J. P. Morgan and John D. Rockefeller are especially valued by collectors). Commercial bonds and shares, originally hand-written, were issued and traded in Italy from medieval times onwards, and elsewhere in Europe particularly from the seventeenth century onwards. However, the great majority of share certificates that survive and tend to be collected today, and to which the term 'scripophily' chiefly applies, date from *c.*1800 onwards.

SCRIPT

In a general sense, the term 'script', derived from the Latin *scriptum* ('something written'), means any kind of writing or piece of writing by hand. In palaeography, the term denotes more specifically an identifiable type or system of writing, with all its distinctive forms and characteristics, usually belonging to a particular historical period or location (Carolingian, humanistic, court, secretary, italic, etc.). The script in this sense is therefore the basic style or model adopted by a scribe or which he has in mind when he writes. This is as opposed to the hand, which is the specific example of that writing on a document, one that will bear a generic resemblance to the writing of other scribes adopting the same mode, but that might also bear the personal idiosyncrasies and distinguishing features of the particular writer as an individual. This distinction is, however, often blurred by the common use of 'script' and 'hand' as synonymous.

In common modern usage, a script may also be the text used in a performance of some kind, whether written, typed, or printed, such as the script for a play, film, television or radio broadcast.

SCRIPTOR

See BUREAU and SCRIBE.

SCRIPTORIUM

A scriptorium (plural: scriptoria; the Latin word means a 'writing room'), may be a room or premises where the physical process of writing or copying by one or more persons takes place or else it can be a team of scribes, not necessarily working in the same room. Scriptoria in the Middle Ages included groups of monks (or possibly nuns) in monasteries and abbeys, copying and sometimes illuminating religious and scholarly texts, and also teams of scribes in other ecclesiastical, government, and court establishments where documentation of an official nature was produced. Moreover, secular scriptoria flourished at universities and under the commercial direction (if not necessarily on the premises) of independent urban stationers, who produced a stream of manuscripts—legal, literary, academic, and religious, including books of hours—for ready sale or on commission. Given the number of neatly copied manuscripts that survive, with the same series of hands sometimes appearing over and over again, especially between the 1620s and 1640s and the 1670s and 1690s, professional scriptoria of some kind would also appear to have flourished in London and possibly elsewhere in the early modern period, despite the invention of printing. While, from medieval times onwards, illustrations showing individual scribes at work are quite common, the graphic depiction of any room or premises where two or more scribes are working at the same time is very rare. For one continental example, *see* Illus. 79.

ILLUS. 79 *A woodcut in a German edition of Petrarch (1559, first printed in 1532) showing a scriptorium, being a German stationer's or scrivener's shop with three scribes working on sloped desks or at the counter, while the proprietor, also engaged in writing, attends to a customer. Other features illustrated include books and documents filed against walls by the use of straps or belts, as well as quills, two pairs of scissors, one possibly a divider, an hourglass, a penknife, and one or more pounce pots.*

Derived from the Latin *scriptura* ('writing'), the term 'scripture', or 'scriptures', was sometimes applied to writings in general, but since medieval times has normally been reserved to denote the texts of the Old and New Testaments of the Bible.

SCRIVENER

Deriving from the Old French *escrivain* ('writer', 'clerk'), the term 'scrivener' is sometimes loosely applied to any kind of clerk (for instance, 'Adam, his owne scriveyn', depicted by Chaucer with good-humoured exasperation because of his careless copying). The term denotes specifically, however, a member of a profession of considerable antiquity, which ultimately incorporated a range of practitioners and functionaries—from medieval Writers of the Court Letter (legal documents), as opposed to Writers of the Text Letter (literary manuscripts), to early modern entrepreneurs and financial brokers, precursors of the modern stockbroker and banker. Well before the sixteenth and seventeenth centuries, when they seem especially to have flourished, scriveners performed certain of the basic functions of notaries and attorneys, such as conveying property and drawing up and witnessing wills, petitions, depositions, and other writings. They eventually also engaged in brokering and moneylending. They were sufficiently respectable and powerful by 1373 to establish in London their own Scriveners' Company—although it seems likely that many subsequent freelance scriveners flourished without any connection with this City livery company. Nevertheless, the social and religious stigma associated with usury, coupled with their reputation for sharp practice in a period of great expansion in credit transactions, not to mention their alleged relative ignorance of Latin and the finer points of law, made scriveners a popular target for satirical treatment in poems, pamphlets, and on the stage ('A Scrivener is a Christian Canniball that devoures men alive' is a not untypical characterization). The result is that by the eighteenth century the profession declined in favour of that of the more qualified lawyers and solicitors.

Many scriveners evidently began life as humble clerks or copyists and may even have functioned as such for much of the time. In an official complaint made in 1395 about scriveners opening on Sundays and Holy Days, for instance, the scrivener is described as one who 'keeps shop, or holds his stall open...and writes and pursues his craft openly...and hangs outside many documents and various writings'. In a fictitious dialogue published in 1683, a banker recalls how 'some few years past' a young scrivener could 'take a half-Shop, and furnish it with a Ream of Paper, half a score pair of Indentures, 100 of Quills; a Bottle of Ink; a Pumice-Stone; a Pen-Knife, and . . . four Labels on a Poll at the Shop-window', where he would 'Engross a pair of Leases, write now and then' some kind of bond, 'and sometimes a Love-Letter for a Servant-Maid, or so'. Scriveners should be distinguished from other kinds of scribe, however, by reason of their specifically scrivening functions: i.e. their legal and moneylending activities. Nevertheless, some practitioners could be called both 'scriveners' and 'notaries'—for instance, Humphrey Dyson (d. 1632/3), who officially described himself as a public notary but was repeatedly referred to by his contemporaries as a scrivener. It is not clear whether this was because he was qualified to perform both jobs or because of some contemporary blurring of the terms 'scrivener' and 'notary' as if synonymous. Many scriveners—or at least the most successful, some of whom (such as Sir Robert Clayton, 1629–1707) became very rich—are likely to have been employers of scribes rather than scribes themselves.

Although most scriveners were men, there was also the very occasional practising female scrivener, at least by the late sixteenth century. An example is Margaret Spitlehouse (née Legge), daughter of a Bury St Edmunds scrivener, who worked as one herself part-time between 1583 and 1596, despite bearing eleven children. Thirteen wills drawn up by her were discovered and recorded by John Craig in 1991.

SCRIVENERS' COMPANY

The Scriveners' Company, properly called The Worshipful Company of Scriveners, was founded in London as a self-governing corporate body of Writers of the Court Letter (scribes who wrote legal documents as opposed to literary texts) in 1373, although their attempts to regulate their profession date back at least to 1357. The Company was incorporated, with a new constitution, by a royal charter of James I in 1617. Although after a period of expansion its power gradually waned in the eighteenth century with the rise of solicitors, this City livery company still functions today with jurisdiction over London public notaries. It has occupied various premises over the years, the main Scriveners' Hall (formerly Bacon House) in Noble Street, near the church of St Mary Staining, being occupied from 1631 until destroyed by the Great Fire in 1666 (it was afterwards rebuilt, but sold to the Coach-Makers' Company in 1703).

The Company arms, granted in 1634 by Richard St George, Clarenceux King of Arms, feature an eagle with outspread wings holding in his mouth a penner and inkhorn standing upon a book, with the motto *Scribite scientes*

('Write, ye learned men'). At some later stage the motto *Litera scripta manet* ('The written word abides') was also adopted, but was subsequently abandoned.

Although in its heyday an influential body, governing perhaps a core establishment of London professional scriveners, the Company did not include among its members many practising scriveners whose names are known from other records. Its traditional concern with the production of almost exclusively legal and financial documents also effectively excluded nearly all scribes whose hands are found in late medieval and early modern literary manuscripts. An interesting feature of its membership, however, is that it very occasionally admitted women—at least from 1665, when Elizabeth Billingsley was apprenticed to James Windus and his wife, Anne, as was Lucy Saunderson the following year. *See also* COMMON PAPER OF THE SCRIVENERS' COMPANY.

SCRIVENER'S PALSY

The term 'scrivener's palsy' was apparently coined in the nineteenth century to denote writer's cramp. The modern equivalent is the condition generally known as repetitive strain injury (RSI), characterized by the painful seizing up of muscles in hands, wrists, and forearms, which, since the early 1980s, has been seen as an occasional occupational hazard of people who work continually on computer keyboards. Although there are earlier cases of typists suffering from this affliction (such as the novelist Henry James), there is curiously little evidence to suggest that writer's cramp of any severity afflicted monastic or secular scribes in earlier periods, although presumably they must have been occasionally susceptible to it.

SCROLL

Deriving from the Old French *escroe* or *escroue*, the term 'scroll' generally means a roll of parchment or paper (or papyrus in earlier times) containing writing (*see* Illus. 4, 18, and 75). The scroll was the predominant form in which lengthy text was preserved before the development of the codex. It is not accidental that in modern computer terminology someone may be said to 'scroll through' a continuous file on-screen since in this respect an electronic text is closer to the scroll than to the codex or book. From at least the sixteenth century, the term 'scroll' has also sometimes been used to denote a letter or other piece of writing, especially in Scotland (and *see* the variant forms ESCROW and SCROW). Scrolls may, in addition, appear in representations as sheets of paper with the ends rolled up, in heraldic coats of arms, banderoles, cartouches, and other ornaments.

SCROLLWORK

Scrollwork is embellishment or ornamentation characterized by a scroll motif. Alternatively, it is a form of decoration in the manner of a scroll, such as shields with curled borders or ribbon-like appendages (*see* Illus. 38). From medieval times onwards, types of decorative scrollwork can sometimes be found in manuscripts, as well as in watermarks, maps, stained glass, woodwork, brocade, metalwork, furniture, and stringed musical instruments.

SCROW

'Scrow', or as a diminutive form 'scrowet', is an obsolete form of the word 'scroll'. In use from at least the thirteenth to the seventeenth century, especially in Scotland, the term might also denote writings, or even a particular kind of writing such as a list or schedule. There was an office of Clerk of the Scrow (*Rotulorum Clericus*) meaning Clerk of the Rolls or Clerk of the Register. *Compare* ESCROW.

SCRUTOIRE

See BUREAU.

SEA CHART

See CHART and PORTOLAN.

SEAL

From ancient times onwards, the principal means of authenticating a piece of writing was not by signing it, but rather by affixing to it, or impressing upon it, a seal, the design of which signified the authorizing person or office concerned. Cylindrical seals were rolled across clay tablets as long ago as the fourth millenium BC in Mesopotamia (the present Iraq). Types of seal in both clay and wax were used by the Romans; lead or metal seals, called *bullae*, were adopted by the early popes; but the most popular material for seals, which had largely prevailed in Europe by as early as the eighth century, was wax. Charters, deeds, and other formal, legal, or official writings issued by statesmen, churchmen, nobles, judges, corporations, guilds, other institutions, and even ordinary people for land transactions, as well as sovereigns and potentates, were validated chiefly by virtue of a process whereby coloured molten wax was dropped on to the parchment document and pressed with a suitably designed hand-stamp or die to leave in the wax a particular impression (*see* Illus. 36 and 69). Some medieval parchment documents were slit horizontally to leave a tongue free at the right side to which the seal was attached, but this method soon became obsolete. When the seal was attached to the face of a document by being pressed through a cross-shaped incision (+) and then flattened at the back, as was often the case before the eleventh century, the seal can be described as 'en placard'.

Alternatively, for large seals, the wax was poured into a shaped matrix of metal, ivory, wood, or jet and removed when the wax had cooled and hardened. The wax seal would then be attached to the document through slits by means of cords, strips of parchment, or ribbons, which had presumably transected the matrix when the impression was cast. Pendent seals would often be awarded some measure of protection by being kept in bags of parchment, linen, canvas, or even silk-lined leather, those for certain royal seals being known as 'burses'. Sturdier containers of wood or metal usually for large seals are known as 'skippets'. The commonly used material for seals was beeswax, mixed with a one-third portion of resin. Since seals of this substance have proved to be fragile and easily broken (many medieval and later seals exist only in fragments, even when kept in bags), many seals from the sixteenth century onwards were made of shellac, which gives them a somewhat hard, glossy character. More modern seals have tended to be made of even more durable cellulose acetate plastic.

The various types of seal that have developed over the centuries are legion, their size, shape, and even colour depending on the function they performed. Ranging in size from about half an inch (1.4 cm) to 6 inches (15.5 cm) in diameter, most seals are circular in shape, although some ecclesiastical seals are oval or shield-shaped, and some triangular examples are known. Royal seals, since the eleventh century, are headed in importance by the Great Seal (*see* Illus. 32, 33a, and 33b), followed by a host of official seals of smaller size, including the Signet Seal (a smaller, usually papered seal impressed directly on the document, kept by the monarch's secretary or by the Signet Office: *see* Illus. 81); Privy Seal (an intermediate one kept usually by the Lord Privy Seal and which could be used to authorize the attaching of the Great Seal to a royal charter or grant); and even a variant Privy Signet Seal (*see* Illus. 20); as well as those of the various courts of Chancery, Exchequer, King's Bench, Common Pleas, etc., besides one for the Duchy of Lancaster. The more important posts in a government are thus conferred by the Crown by delivery of the seals of office and surrendered by delivering up those seals.

The term 'seal' is one that has always been applied, somewhat ambiguously, both to the wax impression and to the matrix, die, stamp, or device that produced it. Developments of the latter from at least early modern times onwards include so-called ring seals (personal devices attached to rings worn on the finger and impressed into warm wax when sealing letters, etc.), desk seals (fixed to wooden or other handles, as personal or official hand-stamps), and fob seals (engraved seals suspended from chains worn over waistcoats, like fob watches, particularly fashionable in the eighteenth and early nineteenth centuries).

Impressions of seals, usually applied by mechanical means, or else embossed imitation seals, have persisted in modern times usually in the form of discs of red plastic or paper affixed to documents such as share certificates. This is more in a spirit of impressive-seeming tradition than because of any authenticating function they might perform. For some particular types of seal, *see* FOB SEAL, GREAT SEAL, PAPERED SEAL, and WAFER SEAL, and *see also* BURSE, COURSE OF THE SEALS and SKIPPET.

SEAL-TEAR

A seal-tear, or seal tear, is the tear in a letter resulting from its having been roughly opened when sealed. Before the introduction or common use of envelopes, letters were usually folded, with the address written on the exposed panel on the outer leaf, and then sealed with wax to hold the folding in place. When the recipient opened it, unless carefully slicing it with a knife, part of the page bearing the seal (or part of the seal) would almost invariably tear away, leaving a small strip of paper still attached to the seal. Since this was normal, many letter-writers, at least by the early nineteenth century, left a space in their text where it could be anticipated that the seal would leave a hole in the letter when opened.

SECRETAIRE

See BUREAU.

SECRETARIAL

The term 'secretarial' means of or pertaining to the work of a secretary. It is not to be confused with the adjectival use of the term 'secretary' applied to a particular type of script or handwriting.

SECRETARIAT

Although derived from the Latin *secretarium* denoting the office of a secretary, the term 'secretariat' was coined possibly no earlier than the nineteenth century. It denotes an office or room where a secretary or group of secretaries conduct their business. Such offices might be attached to private households and estates, the Royal Court, government departments, episcopal palaces, universities, or various other premises where secretaries work. The term is also collectively applied to the team or series of secretaries who worked, whether at the same time or consecutively, for a particular person: thus historians may refer, for instance, to the secretariat of the Earl of Leicester or of the Earl of Essex in the Elizabethan period.

SECRETARY

Derived from the Latin *secretarius* and etymologically linked to the word *secretum* ('secret'), the term 'secretary' denotes someone employed to conduct correspondence, to write or copy documents, and to handle other paperwork and related business, often for an individual person, whether in an office or department of some kind or in a private household. The connotation of secrecy applies in the sense that the secretary is a species of clerk entrusted with private matters and expected to maintain strict confidentiality. The traditional importance of the latter is attested by instances such as when the Roman Emperor Augustus had a secretary's legs broken for revealing to others the contents of a letter, or when in 1578 Sir Philip Sidney threatened to 'thruste' his 'Dagger' into his father's secretary, Edmund Molyneux, if he ever read any of Sidney's letters to his father without their consent ('And truste to it, for I speake it in earnest ... ').

Depending on the nature and level of employment, the secretary, male or, only in more recent times, female, might be expected to write or transcribe documents or make written entries in person or else have subordinate clerks do the actual writing. Secretaries might also specialize in particular types of writing or languages. Henry VII had a Latin Secretary, Petrus Carmelianus, for instance, who was one of the earliest people to use italic script in England, and Queen Mary I was attended by Roger Ascham in that employment, while John Milton later served the Commonwealth government as Secretary for Foreign Tongues (i.e. Latin). Yet another poet, Edmund Spenser, served from 1580 to 1582 as Secretary to Lord Grey, Lord Deputy of Ireland.

As an office of intrinsic responsibility, the position of secretary is one long adopted for the designation of senior ranks of government and other corporate bodies in general, including such offices as that of Secretary of State or the Secretary of a guild, society, company, or institution. The traditional recognition of the importance of secretaries (in all senses, but most especially because of their heavy responsibility in keeping confidences) is attested by privately circulated Elizabethan and Jacobean manuscript tracts such as *A Treatise of the Office of a Councellor and Principall Secretarie to her Majestie* by the Clerk of the Privy Council Robert Beale (1541–1601), the anonymous *Il secretarie qualificate* of 1606 (Folger Shakespeare Library,

MS Add. 622), and *The State of a Secretaries Place with the Perill* attributed to Sir Robert Cecil, Earl of Salisbury (1563–1612). The second of these describes a secretary as, for instance, 'no other then a keeper, his brest no other then a Prison, to which his *Maste*rs secretts are com*m*itted', while the third compares the solemn 'counsells' between a Prince and his Secretary to 'the mutuall affection of twoe louers vndiscouered to theire frinds'.

For other uses of the term 'secretary', *see* BUREAU and SECRETARY SCRIPT.

SECRETARY SCRIPT

Secretary script, or secretary hand (the word 'secretary' sometimes written as 'Secretary'), is the type of writing that was most commonly used for everyday business in England in the fifteenth, sixteenth, and seventeenth centuries. A generic hand, which evolved from an Italian notarial script and was probably imported into England from France, secretary was in use in England as a documentary script by *c*.1370, established as a formal book-hand by *c*.1380, and was the dominant English script, widely (though not altogether) replacing Anglicana, by *c*.1440. Secretary was the most common type of writing used by men (but very rarely by women), whether as a cursive hand or in a set hand for formal engrossing (by law clerks, for instance). Its use persisted despite occasional hurdles, such as when the Court of Common Pleas ruled in 1588 that it was illegal for a sheriff to return a writ in secretary hand, because when worn it would be illegible.

Secretary lettering seems peculiar by comparison with modern writing, those characters perhaps not immediately recognizable to readers today including particularly the secretary forms of *a, c, e,* g, *h, k, p, r, s, v,* and *x*. With the advent of italic script from Italy by the sixteenth century, which is much closer to modern writing, secretary script became gradually modified, evolving by the mid-seventeenth century into a transitional mixed or rounded hand. Although some secretary letter-forms (such as the inverted *e*) did persist for a while in the eighteenth century, this type of hand was all but obsolete, for most practical purposes, by *c*.1700. For examples of secretary hand, *see* Illus. 3, 7, 11, 25, 26, 28, 36, 41, 49, 55, 70, 71, 81, 82, 87, and 91.

SEISIN

In English feudal land law from medieval times onwards, seisin is the legally justified possession of land by someone who actually occupies and uses it, that person being described as 'seised' of the land. Barring clear evidence to the contrary, seisin, which originally meant being accepted as tenant by a lord of the manor, came to be commonly regarded as prima facie evidence of ownership. 'Livery of Seisin' (meaning 'delivery of possession') is the term used for the act of putting someone in possession of land, especially by means of a traditional ceremony involving the handing over of symbols of the land, such as a clod of earth or twigs, in the presence of witnesses. This ceremony eventually became redundant, and by the sixteenth century a deed of bargain and sale recording the transaction concerned was deemed sufficient evidence of lawful possession. *See also* SASINE.

SEMI-SUBSTANTIVE

See SUBSTANTIVES.

SEPARATE

The modern term 'separate' denotes a manuscript or printed text produced or issued as a physically independent unit, rather than being part of a larger entity or book: e.g. a Restoration lampoon written or printed on a single leaf or bifolium and circulated in this form, or a modern offprint of a published article.

SERIF

In palaeography, the term 'serif' (possibly derived from the Middle Dutch *screve*, a 'finishing-off stroke') denotes a short cross-stroke—a decorative horizontal or curved extension, often amounting only to a flick of a quill—projecting or trailing from the stem at either the head or foot of a letter, such as is found in the seventeenth century, for instance, in some written forms of *g*, *h*, *p*, *r*, and *q* (*see* Illus. 2). Various types of serif, of differing thickness and direction, are also found in medieval scripts, as well as in certain typographical fonts.

SERJEANT-AT-LAW

From the fourteenth century onwards, serjeants-at-law (the term derived from the Latin *servientes ad legem*, 'servants at law') were a superior type of pleader or barrister, functioning principally in the Court of Common Pleas, and traditionally constituting the highest order of counsel at the English Bar. Over the years they even had their own London inns, each known as Serjeants' Inn, situated variously in Holborn, Fleet Street, and Chancery Lane. Their pre-eminent position was challenged in the seventeenth century by the rise of the King's Counsel, officers whose equal status, if not effective precedence, was confirmed by Charles II in 1670. Nevertheless, despite their decline, serjeants continued to flourish in some degree and to enjoy certain limited privileges, including up to at least 1873 their exclusive right to appoint judges in the superior courts.

In the post-medieval period they traditionally wore a gown and scarlet hood and also a coif, a small white silk or linen cap fastened under the chin surmounted by a black skullcap, for which reason serjeants were also known as the Order of the Coif. Various eminent serjeants-at-law were distinguished writers, legal and otherwise, among them the Elizabethan poet Sir John Davies (1569–1626) and the author and dramatist Sir Thomas Noon Talfourd (1795–1854).

SET HAND

'Set hand' is an evaluative term used to denote a hand where the letters are carefully formed, with the pen generally lifted between strokes (as opposed to 'cursive hand' and 'free hand'). From the twelfth to the sixteenth century, each of the English government departments and central law courts at Westminster had their own set hand, a formal and regular script designed to maintain maximum uniformity for more important documents such as letters patent and official enrolments (but not writs). *Compare* FREE HAND.

SETTLEMENT CERTIFICATE

In the early modern period, a settlement certificate, or, more technically, an Indemnity Certificate of Settlement, was one issued by local churchwardens or overseers of the poor to a person living in a particular parish, establishing his or her right to do so and to claim relief under the Poor Law. It might also allow him or her to move to another parish where the authorities there might permit residence on a temporary basis on condition that the person would not be a burden on the parish. There were various statutes and Acts of Parliament from medieval times onwards relating to poor people, including the Poor Relief Act of 1601, but it was an Act of 1697 that authorized local authorities to issue settlement certificates if they wished. Even so, the local authorities still had the right to make a removal order to move poor persons and their dependants back to their parish of origin, although only after carrying out an obligatory formal examination. Documents relating to such matters up to the Settlement Act of 1834, including settlement certificates, settlement examinations, and removal orders, can be found in various parish archives and in those of quarter sessions (quarterly meetings of the Justices of Peace of each county, where appeals against removal orders were sometimes heard), now preserved in local and county record offices.

SEWING

Sewing, or stitching with thread, vertically down the inside fold at the centre of each gathering and into adjoining quires, is the traditional means by which folded sheets and gatherings have been fastened together to form books and booklets, whether bound or unbound, printed or manuscript. When the gatherings of very thin pamphlets are stitched sideways rather than sewn down the fold, they are said to be 'stabbed'. Besides simple ties through one or more holes punched through the paper, alternative forms of holding pages or gatherings together in modern times include paper fasteners, stapling, and spiral or ring binders.

SEXTODECIMO

The term 'sextodecimo' (a Latin word meaning 'in sixteenth' or 'for the sixteenth time'), frequently rendered as 'sixteenmo' and usually abbreviated to '16mo', denotes the size of a leaf of paper produced when a standard papermaker's sheet is folded four times: the first fold producing two leaves (four pages) of folio size, the second four leaves (eight pages) of quarto size (being a quarter of the sheet), the third eight leaves (sixteen pages) of octavo size (being an eighth of the sheet), and the fourth sixteen leaves (thirty-two pages) of sextodecimo size (being a sixteenth of the sheet). The size of a sextodecimo leaf will vary according to the paper manufacturer and to trimming by the papermaker or binder, but the average size for the early modern period is very approximately 3½–4 inches (9–10.25 cm) in length and 2 inches (5 cm) or so in width. Because of the wires across the width of the papermaker's mould or tray, sextodecimo leaves will have the chain-lines running horizontally across the page. A printed or manuscript volume made up of gatherings of such leaves (which will most commonly comprise gatherings sewn in sixteens: i.e. eight pairs of conjugate leaves per gathering, subject to occasional variation) is itself called a 'sextodecimo' or 'sixteenmo' as a means of distinguishing it by size and basic format. For different-sized leaves and volumes, resulting from previous, further or different folding of each sheet, *see* DUODECIMO, FOLIO, OCTAVO, and QUARTO.

Sextodecimo is the smallest size of paper or volume generally found in early modern books and manuscripts, and was used for small pocket-books, notebooks, and the like. In principle, however, the papermaker's sheet can be folded yet more times, or in different ways, to produce a vigesimo-quarto (24mo: forty-eight pages), or a trigesimo-secundo (32mo: sixty-four pages), and very small books of this kind, specifically produced as 'miniatures', are encountered occasionally.

The *s fermé* (the word *fermé* in French means 'closed'), also known in French as a *fermesse*, is an intersected or slashed capital letter *S*, somewhat like the italic dollar sign *$*. It is occasionally found, either singly or in a sequence (*$ $ $ $*), in sixteenth- and seventeenth-century manuscripts, notably poetical texts, to indicate a pause or division in the text or a conclusion to it. It is also sometimes found written on the address leaves of early modern letters, especially by women, possibly as a mark of affection.

SHAFT

In palaeography, a shaft is a single upright stroke, such as the stem in *k* or *t*.

SHEET

A sheet is a single piece of paper, generally a quite large one, which may be folded one or more times to produce a series of leaves and pages. The principal sheet relevant to bibliographers is that which, subject to subsequent trimming, is produced by the papermaker from a mould or tray, and which is then folded to produce the basic book units of folio, quarto, octavo, etc. leaves assembled in quires. Any conjugate pair of leaves, of whatever size, having been folded and cut, then itself constitutes a sheet in so far as it is a single piece of paper. *See* FOLIO.

SHELF-MARK

A shelf-mark, or shelfmark, in a book or manuscript in a library is, specifically, a press-mark that denotes not only the cupboard, or press, in which a book is located, but also the shelf within the cupboard, and possibly also the position of the book on that shelf. In practice, what is commonly called a press-mark usually incorporates what is in effect a shelf-mark. The shelf-mark in a library book can be still operative, accurately designating where the book is now located, but many books and manuscripts also have inscribed in them, usually inside the upper cover, old shelf-marks left by former owners. These provide occasionally useful evidence of provenance. *Compare* CALL NUMBER and PRESS-MARK.

SHORTHAND

Shorthand is a system of writing at speed by means of abbreviations, signs, or symbols, and is therefore the opposite of longhand, the normal mode of writing a text in full. Shorthand, of one type or another, dates back to the ancient Greeks, but what has always been regarded as the first modern

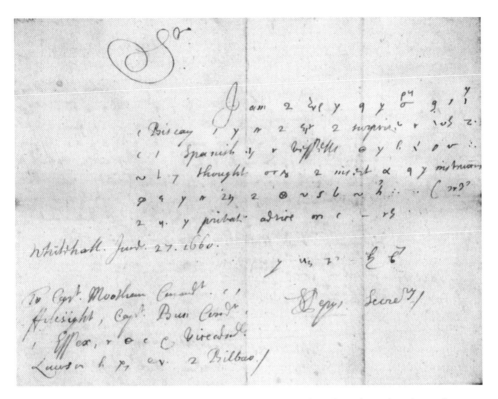

ILLUS. 80 *Samuel Pepys's autograph retained copy signed, written in alternating longhand and shorthand (according to Thomas Shelton's stenographic system), of a naval letter, giving instructions to Captains Mootham and Bun and to Vice-Admiral Lawson on convoys to the Bay of Biscay, 27 June 1660.*

system of shorthand was invented by Timothy Bright, MD, and expounded in his book *Characterie, an Arte of Shorte, Swifte and Secrete Writing by Character* (1588), for which he was granted a fifteen-year patent by Elizabeth I. Bright's system, based partly on the alphabet and partly on arbitrary signs, was, however, superseded within fourteen years—not by the ideas for 'swift writing' set forth by the writing master Peter Bales in *The Writing Schoolemaster* (1590), but by the system invented by John Willis in 1602. *See* STENOGRAPHY and Illus. 80.

SHOULDER-NOTE

A shoulder-note is a side-note, in a printed or manuscript book, that is positioned in the outer margin at the top corner of the page.

The Latin for 'thus' or 'so' and usually rendered in italic and in parentheses or square brackets, the word *sic* is commonly used in transcriptions to follow a word that appears to be misspelt or misused, but which is quoted exactly as it appears in the original source. The *sic* therefore indicates that the word is rendered deliberately in this form, that it is really how it appears in the original, and is not a mistake or misprint in the present transcription.

SIDE

See PART.

SIDE-NOTE

In a printed or manuscript book, a side-note is a note in the (generally outer) margin, usually positioned against the text to which it refers. Side-notes may perform various functions, including sign-posting the subject of particular passages or sections for ready reference, commenting on the text, or glossing certain words in the text. Marginal comments are generally described as side-notes when they form part of the original printed or manuscript production. If they are manuscript additions made by subsequent readers they constitute marginal annotations or marginalia.

SIGLA

Sigla (singular: siglum) are abbreviations for words. Comprising particular letters, or other marks or characters, sigla proliferated in medieval Latin documents, and many examples are still a common feature of texts (for example, 'p.' for 'page', 'f.' for 'folio', '&' for 'and').

The term is most usually encountered, however, in scholarly editions of works, produced both before and after the invention of printing, where each text or textual witness is represented in abbreviated form in the textual footnotes, appendices, discussions, collations, or stemmata, by letters or numbers: e.g. single (A, B, C, etc.), multiple (Ba, Ca, etc.), or combined (such as 'F1', 'F2', for 'First Folio', 'Second Folio'). In modern editing, the sigla for manuscripts can become quite lengthy and unwieldy when they attempt to condense information about both location and call number within a collection (such as 'Bla27' for 'British Library Additional Manuscript 272045'). Attempts to establish one universally recognized system of sigla have been mooted (notably by Harold Love), in place of the present practice where each editor draws up his or her own sigla for a particular edition, but such standardization has yet to find common acceptance.

The capital form of the sigma *Σ*, the Greek letter for *S*, is a conventional symbol used in textual collations in scholarly editions. In a detailed listing of the variant readings, where each variant is followed by the sigla representing those texts in which it appears, the symbol *Σ* means that the reading appears in all the remaining significant texts.

SIGNAL BOOK

A signal book is a naval book containing hundreds of systematically drawn up recognized signals made principally by means of ships' flags or pennants, and also with sail formations, set out with accompanying instructions and drawings. Illustrations of ships in sail will show, for instance, the respective flags and indicate formations, such as 'To Tack', 'For the Fleet to Wear and bring too on the other Tack', 'To bring too on the Starboard Tack', 'For the Blew Squadron to tack and gain the Wind of the Enemy', and so on. The first major British co-ordination of flag signals was made in 1673 by James, Duke of York (later James II). The first printed signal book was published between 1714 and 1717, in pocket-book form, by Jonathan Greenwood. Other versions appeared later, notably in 1776 and 1790, as signal systems were developed by Admiral Lord Howe and others.

In the absence of a centralized standard printed version, however, numerous manuscript books of signals were produced by and for naval officers incorporating the signal codes currently in use, many of them drawn up by the admiral commanding a particular fleet. Most extant examples are octavo-size leather-bound pocket-books, the flags all hand-coloured, often with additional instructions and notes made by the owner. Some examples also contain additional drawings and watercolours. Signal books of a larger and official nature are sometimes signed by the Commissioners of the Admiralty. Various written instructions to the fleet sent by admirals, such as Lord Nelson, detailing sailing tactics to be employed as they approach the enemy, make reference to specific pages of the current signal book used by that fleet and sometimes transmit alterations to it. The commander-in-chief might also occasionally call for his officers' signal books to be examined for consistency.

SIGNATORY

A signatory, or in older parlance a signator (both terms deriving from the Latin *signatorius*, 'relating to sealing'), is the person who personally signs, or makes his mark in, a document. These are more formal alternatives to the older term 'signer'. *See* SIGNER.

Derived from the Latin *signatum* ('something marked or signed') and also *signatura* ('the matrix of a seal'), the term 'signature' since at least the late sixteenth century means a person's own name, whether rendered in full or only with initials or in abbreviated form, written in his or her own hand. As a representation in some manner of a person's distinct character or identity, the signature has commonly been valued, whether as a means of authenticating royal, official, ecclesiastical, legal, or financial documents, or, in more modern times, as a collectable item by so-called 'autograph hunters'. While in earlier times stress was laid on the authentication of a document (i.e. visible confirmation that it was written or issued with the approval of the person in whose name it appears) by the use of distinctive seals, signatures also came to be used by way of reinforcement, eventually becoming the predominent token of authenticity. Popes would sign documents from at least the eleventh century onwards, the first English king to sign in person being Richard II in 1386.

The official term for an actual royal signature (or document containing it) is 'sign manual', although from at least Henry VIII onwards some monarchs avoided the labour of signing routine warrants by having hand-stamps of their signatures made which secretaries could apply to documents in their stead (these can usually be distinguished by the slight fuzziness of the impression, differing from the flow of a signature when drawn by a continuous movement of the pen: *see* Illus. 81). Needless to say, signatures can vary hugely in style, from a short wavy line or jagged scribble to the progressively grand, carefully drawn and highly decorated signature of Elizabeth I, for instance, which would eventually extend several inches (*see* Illus. 41 and 82). On the other hand, it is quite common to encounter routine indentures and other legal documents, including depositions and wills, that are signed with a mark, usually a cross, *X*, indicating either that the signatory was illiterate or else (in wills) too ill to sign in person. In that case, his or her name would usually be written at the side by a scrivener or lawyer for identification purposes, or else simply 'signed' by the scribe on that person's behalf. Noblemen's secretaries were sometimes entrusted to write and sign in their masters' names as well. For examples of signatures by various people, *see* Illus. 1, 10, 12, 16, 20, 26, 36, 40, 42, 45, 55, 56, 57, 59, 60, 78, and 93.

The term 'signed' is also sometimes used loosely, and somewhat confusingly, to mean that the printed or manuscript text in question bears the name of the author, or an ascription, even if it is not a signature inscribed by the author in person.

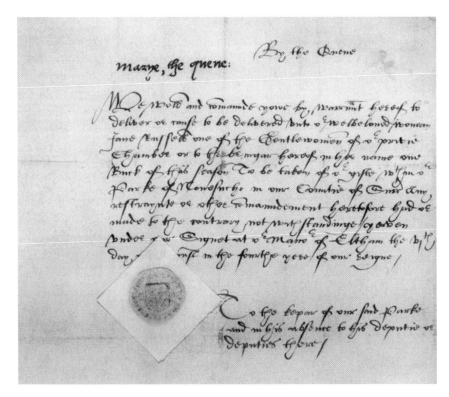

ILLUS. 81 *A letter issued by Queen Mary I, ordering 'one Buck of this season' to be delivered from Nonesuch Park to one of her ladies-in-waiting, written in the secretary hand of an official scribe, with a hand-stamped 'signature' ('Marye, the quene:') and papered Signet Seal, 6 August 1556.*

In a bibliographical context, a signature is a symbol identifying a particular gathering or leaf within the gathering, used to help the scribes, or binders, or compositors to put them in the right sequence. Gatherings are generally distinguished by one or more alphabetical letters (A, B, C, etc., AA, BB, CC, etc.) and leaves by the occasional addition of numbers (A2, AA2, etc.). A particular page might thus be cited as, for example, sig. BB2^{r} or sig. CC3^{v}.

SIGNER

The term 'signer' has been used since at least the early seventeenth century and denotes the individual who personally signs a document. It is the same thing as a signatory. Perhaps the most famous signers, known by that term, are the fifty-six men who signed the American Declaration of Independence on 4 July 1776. *See* SIGNATORY.

SIGNET

Deriving from the Latin *signatum* ('something marked' or 'signed'), the term 'signet' means a small seal, usually fixed into a finger-ring, or signet-ring, used to stamp an impression in hot wax. The term 'signet' is hence used also to signify the hard wax impression itself and, on occasions, even a document bearing such an impression.

SIGNET SEAL

See PAPERED SEAL and SEAL.

SIGN MANUAL

Since the fourteenth century 'sign manual' has been the formal or official term for the signature of a sovereign, inscribed by him or her in person, or for the document bearing such a signature. The name was usually followed by an *R* to denote *Rex* (King) or *Regina* (Queen), although certain queens, such as Mary I and Anne Boleyn, signed themselves more fully with their names followed by 'the Quene'. Queen Victoria and her successors, from 1876, added to their *R* the letter *I* for *Imperatrix* (Empress [of India]) or *Imperator* (Emperor [of India]). The sign manual was distinct from a document signed on the sovereign's behalf by a secretary or with a hand-stamped signature (*see* Illus. 41 and 82). A sign manual was the first step in the process leading to the production of a document bearing the Great Seal (*see* COURSE OF THE SEALS). Besides freshly drawn-up warrants, a sign manual might also take the form of a petition to the monarch that he or she signed in approval for the appropriate officials to put into effect.

SILKED

Documents or manuscript leaves can be described as 'silked' when they have been subject to conservation work by being coated or encased with a pasted-down gauze or transparent, filmy, silk-like fabric. Although intended to reinforce and preserve leaves of paper that might have become worn, torn, and fragile, silking also makes the writing beneath look slightly fuzzy and imprecise and the fabric may be prone to discoloration over a period. Sheets so treated are, moreover, liable to become inflexible and to stick to each other. Although not as bad a treatment as some nineteenth- and early twentieth-century conservation treatments (such as the thick sealed perspex windows that encase each disjunct leaf of the *Booke of Sir Thomas Moore* in the British Library), silking is a mode of manuscript conservation now generally discredited. *Compare* MOUNT.

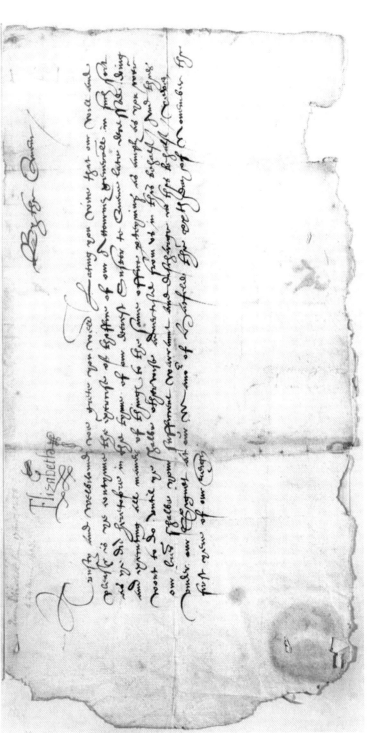

ILLUS. 82 *A royal warrant issued by Queen Elizabeth I under her Signet Seal (now lacking) three days after her accession, confirming the position of Sir Edward Saunders as Attorney-General, 20 November 1558. It is written in the secretary hand (with prominent spurred a) of an official scribe, and bears the sign manual ('Elizabeth') inscribed in the new Queen's as yet modestly small italic script with calligraphic flourishes akin to the quatrefoil used by her father Henry VIII, but without the terminal R signifying Regina (Queen).*

'Singleton' is a term sometimes applied to a single leaf, one that is independent, not conjugate with another.

SKETCH-BOOK

A sketch-book is a book of blank leaves of drawing paper designed to be used for artistic sketching and drawing purposes, or which has been so used. The term may also be applied to any other kind of notebook used for literary or musical 'sketches': i.e. rough or preliminary drafts, outlines, or designs. Sketch-books of the artistic variety have been in use since the Middle Ages, but seem to have flourished particularly in the late eighteenth and nineteenth centuries, not least when ladies and gentlemen, as well as scholars of various kinds, went on continental tours and felt obliged to record in graphic form the scenes, landscapes, buildings, paintings, and sculptures that they saw. *See* Illus. 83.

ILLUS. 83 *A pen-and-ink and wash sketch of the valley of Baalbeck in Lebanon in the octavo sketchbook kept by the botanist Joseph Dalton Hooker to record his scientific expedition to Syria and Palestine, 3 October 1860.*

ILLUS. 84 *The chased copper-lidded skippet with silver-thread and silk tassels attached by purple silk and silver-thread cords to a formal instrument of diplomatic appointment issued by Queen Victoria, 2 November 1899. The skippet contains (not seen here) an impression in red wax of the Great Seal of Victoria.*

SKIPPET

A 'skippet', the term being a diminutive form of 'skip', meaning a 'little box or basket', is a round box or container designed as a protective case to fit around a large wax seal pendent from an official document, usually a letters patent on parchment. Sturdier substitutes for the parchment, linen, canvas, or silk-lined leather bags in which seals were sewn in earlier times, skippets were originally made of wood, sometimes subsequently of bone or ivory, and, most commonly in later periods, of black-japanned or sometimes gilt tin. Exceptionally grand and expensive examples, attached to particularly distinguished patents of nobility, instruments of important diplomatic appointments, grants of arms, and the like, can be of elaborately chased silver or gold. *See* Illus. 84.

SLAINS

See LETTERS OF SLAINS.

SLAVERY RECORDS

A disturbing, but highly revealing, category of historical documents is that relating to the practice of slavery. Although servitude was, in principle, prohibited in England as early as 1102 (though not effectively abolished in England and Wales until 1772), it flourished in the British colonies, and elsewhere, especially from the sixteenth to nineteenth centuries (the Arab slave trade had meanwhile flourished from at least the eighth century onwards). Many maritime, commercial, conveyancing, and even military and political records in numerous archives touch on aspects of the slave trade. Among those occasionally encountered are lists and inventories of slaves connected to deeds and accounts for particular sugar and tobacco plantations in the West Indies. These usually give the slaves' names and other details such as age, type of employment ('servants', 'hoing', 'weeding', etc.), state of health, and the price paid for them or at which they were valued, as well as the names of mothers (but not fathers) of newborn babies. They sometimes also have comments on slaves' behaviour, their punishment for misdemeanours, or their cause of death. For example, records for Antigua c.1768 include entries such as: 'Cumberland a Negroe that had lik'd to have kill'd the white Overseer & likewise a Negroe Wench', 'Quashy... a Young fellow... confin'd in the Stocks in the boiling House from whence he broke loose, & in endavoring to make his escape thro' the roof therof... broke his neck', 'a fine sensible Creole Negroe, but of a very passionate turbulent disposition' who was hanged for murder, and 'an able Negroe & distiller, but a very great rogue'. Details of the transportation of slaves are sometimes also recorded in ships' logs. *See* Illus. 85.

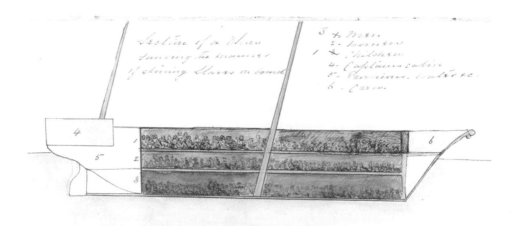

ILLUS. 85 *A captioned watercolour drawing of a 'Section of a Dhow showing the manner of stowing Slaves on board', the children on the uppermost level, women on the second level, and men on the lowest level. This appears in a log book compiled by F. A. S. Fauwell on HMS* Duke of Wellington *and* Forte, *sailing to and from India and Ceylon, 1869–72.*

SLIPCASE

A slipcase is a fitted box designed to contain and protect a book or set of books, having one side open to allow the spine(s) of the book(s) to be visible. Slipcases are of relatively modern origin.

SLOPE

See WRITING SLOPE.

SOLANDER BOX

A solander box is a type of hinged box made in the form of a book for enclosing and preserving prints, plates, maps, and manuscripts, as well as books. It was invented, initially to store botanical specimens, by Dr Daniel Charles Solander (1736–1782), who was a pupil of the Swedish botanist Carolus Linnaeus (1707–1778) and became Keeper of Printed Books at the British Museum as well as a Fellow of the Royal Society. Today's solander boxes, used by archivists, curators, and collectors, tend to be boxes custom-made and fitted to the specific printed or manuscript item(s) contained. They are made of state-of-the-art acid-free materials (paper, boxboard, plywood, buckram, polythene) in the interests of conservation.

SOLICITOR

A solicitor is a type of lawyer qualified to conduct certain kinds of legal proceedings for clients, subject to differing functions and restrictions over the years. Originally, in the fifteenth century, solicitors were legal or business agents who 'solicited causes' by acting as advisers to clients and could instruct attorneys on their behalf. They came to specialize in equity matters and were allowed to practise in some courts, although not in the superior courts where attorneys had the privilege of representation. Solicitors rose in eminence as a distinct profession in the seventeenth and eighteenth centuries. However, since they conducted much of the same routine legal work as any other kind of lawyer, or qualified practitioner of the law, including conveying property, drafting wills and settlements, administering trusts and the like, they have virtually become synonymous with 'lawyers' as general practitioners, except in one respect. At least until recently, they have generally maintained their distinction from barristers, who, since the fifteenth century, have been qualified to act as clients' counsel in the superior courts and to speak as advocates on their behalf. *Compare* ATTORNEY and BARRISTER.

SOPHISTICATED

The term 'sophisticated' in everyday life denotes someone smooth, cultured, suave, well mannered, charming, and the like, or something fashionable and of high quality. In a bibliographical, textual, or editorial context, it has a more pejorative connotation. 'Sophistication' here (the term closer to the Medieval Latin *sophisticare*, 'to adulterate or corrupt') implies some degree of intervention or complication in the normal state of things. Thus a book that is described as 'sophisticated' is one that has been doctored, disguised, or faked in some way, such as having been rebound with leaves, gatherings, or a dust-jacket taken from other copies or editions of the book, or even from facsimiles, to look as if it is all a genuine original edition. A text is described by editors as 'sophisticated' if it shows evidence of interference or contamination, such as might be found in a manuscript by a scribe who has made his own unauthorized changes to the text or else, even with the best intentions, has complicated his copy by combining readings from two or more different exemplars or textual traditions. Textual sophistication may be distinguished from corruption in that the former is a deliberate process, intended in some sense to give a false impression, rather than the result of accident or carelessness.

SOUNDING

The measurement of the depth of water in the sea, especially along coasts, ascertained by dropping a line weighted usually with lead, is known as a 'sounding' or 'soundings'. Such soundings are often found recorded as entries in logs or on maps.

SPELLING

Spelling, or orthography, is one of the most salient features of any old manuscript, since writers and scribes may use a variety of different forms. It is not unusual, particularly in the early modern period, to encounter words, including proper names, spelt in two or more different ways even in the same document. This is because English spelling did not tend to become standardized until the mid-eighteenth century, particularly with the publication of the greatly influential dictionary of Samuel Johnson (first printed in 1755, reaching a fourth edition by 1773). Even professional scribes could vary their spellings, sometimes luxuriating in a profusion of otiose or double letters (*e*s, *l*s, *s*s, *t*s, etc.), possibly enjoying an element of capriciousness and relishing both variety and indeterminacy rather than mechanical regularity and consistency. This element could also extend to particular lettering—alternating, often at random, three different graphic forms of the letter *e*, for instance—as well as their frequent casual or deliberate failure to distinguish clearly between majuscule and minuscule lettering, even for proper names or for the beginning of lines of verse.

It is also quite common to find personal letters written more or less phonetically, usually by men of limited education or by women, including ladies of superior rank (*see* Illus. 2). Thus, for example, Lady Ralegh writes words in a form that largely expresses how they sounded to her (*see* Illus. 86):

> Your kinnes and me ladis conteneweth to the end: and euer wich must and douth bind me to aknooleg hit foreuer:: for my sicke esstat I wryt to you:– the mannar ther of befor: I contenew euen so stell: yet haue I such help: as I may: but I will now bi: your ladis medsen:...tell your fathar bether:: I asur you trewly I neuer desiared: nor neuer wolde desiar my lebbarti: with out the good likekeng: ne aduising of sur: W R:...

Such examples of phonetic or semi-phonetic spelling can throw light on contemporary pronunciation and even on particular writers' accents. Spelling may also, in any case, indicate the regional origin of particular manuscripts, especially in the medieval period.

SPINDLE-HOLE

A feature of modern office management, spindle-holes are small round holes left by a small mechanical punching device in letters or documents, usually in the top corner or left margin, so they can be filed in ring binders. *Compare* STAB-HOLE.

SPINE

The spine of a bound volume, printed or manuscript, is the narrow back of the book—enclosing the edge where the book is sewn together—which, at least from the sixteenth century onwards, has normally (though not always) faced outwards when standing on a shelf. It is therefore distinct from the lower cover, which might be thought of as the back of the volume when it is lying flat on a table. Since about the twelfth century, spines on codices and books have developed from flat surfaces, to ones with raised bands (horizontal ridges for the sewing bands or cords), and, since the early sixteenth century, to rounded glued spines and other types. Since the sixteenth century, spines have also been commonly lettered with the name of the author or title of the book (but *see* FORE-EDGE LETTERING).

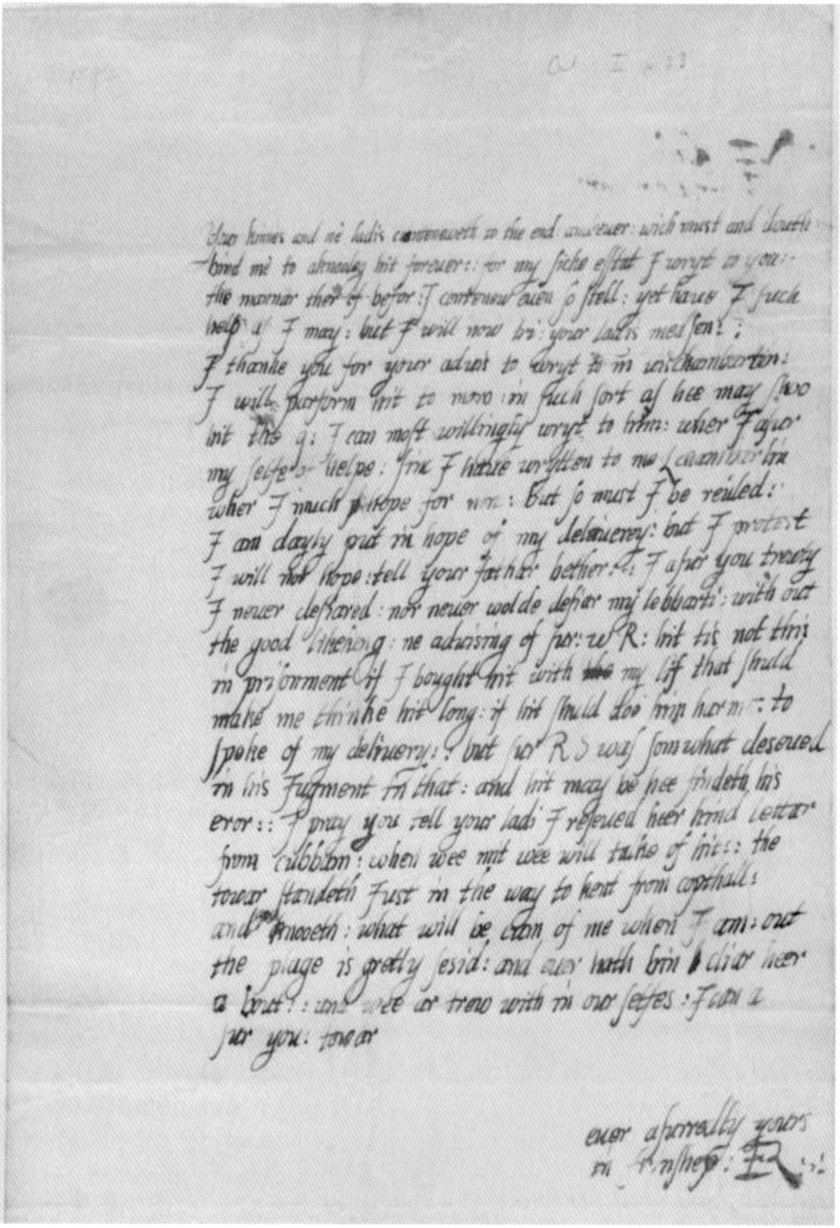

ILLUS. 86 *An autograph letter signed with her initials ('ER') in the form of a monogram by Elizabeth (née Throckmorton), Lady Ralegh, to Sir Moyle Finch, concerning her imprisonment in the Tower after her clandestine marriage to Sir Walter Ralegh, between August and December 1592. It is written in her italic script with virtually phonetic spelling.*

Spines are often torn at the top because of tugging fingers, whereas, at least whenever possible, books should only be removed from shelves by grasping the covers from both sides.

SPIRAL FLOURISH

A fairly common feature in early modern manuscripts, a spiral flourish is a decorative inscription that takes the form of a continuous, curved, winding line like a tapering swirl. It is likely to be a scribe's concluding vertical flourish to mark the end of a text, but might also appear as a decoration, sometimes upside down or horizontal, to titles or headings. *See* Illus. 72, 78, and 95.

SPONGE PAPER

See CARBON COPY.

SPRAYWORK

'Spraywork' is a generic term for a type of decoration, normally delicately executed, in medieval and very occasionally early modern manuscripts, involving elaboration in the border, often of an initial letter, characterized by feathering, foliation, or a diffusion of other patterns or motifs. The term is not to be confused with strapwork. *Compare* STRAPWORK.

SPURRED

In palaeography, a letter is described as 'spurred' when it is written to form a somewhat spiked shape, with a sharply accentuated extension (*see* Illus. 82). The term is notably applied to a certain formation of the letter *a* in secretary script: e.g. in discussions of Shakespeare's handwriting as represented by his few known signatures.

STABBED

A small book, pamphlet, or magazine is said to be 'stabbed', as distinct from 'sewn', when the gatherings are stitched through sideways rather than vertically down the centre of the folds. For this form of fastening, which has been used on occasions at least since the sixteenth century, a series of small holes is first stabbed through the leaves, with an awl, bodkin, or needle, before the thread is passed through.

STAB-HOLE

Some letters or other documents bear stab-holes because they were pierced when filed on string or, in more recent times, on desk-top spikes. Such holes are usually small, with no paper-loss, unlike spindle-holes where small roundels of paper have been punched out.

STAINING

Besides damp-staining and dust-staining, manuscripts may be subject to various other types of staining. Common ones are bacterial or fungal corrosion or discolouring through exposure to heat or the elements. The writers of manuscripts might themselves be responsible for some stains, such as spilt ink or traces of substances consumed while writing. The addiction to coffee of the French novelist Honoré de Balzac (1799–1850), for instance, led to rings left by cups of coffee on his manuscripts. It is possible that similar brown rings on the British Library manuscript of *Confessions of an English Opium-Eater* (1821) by the essayist Thomas De Quincey (1785–1859) were left by glasses of laudanum, a liquid form of opium. On some of Handel's manuscripts in the British Library, including *Zadok the Priest*, are purple rings suggesting contact with a wine or port decanter. No doubt more than one other author or composer has splashed or knocked over glasses of alcoholic drinks on his or her manuscripts. Other substances that have contaminated, or been impregnated in, manuscripts on occasions include tobacco smoke, cigarette ash, spots of candle wax left by writers or readers working by candle light, paw marks left by domestic animals, and even, in one instance, radium, exposure to which led to the death of the physicist Marie Curie (1867–1934) and is reported to have left her papers radioactive. *See also* FINGERPRINT.

STAMP

A stamp may be either: (a) an adhesive or gummed postage stamp, generally affixed to letters or their envelopes, of a kind introduced to the world in 1840 with the Penny Black; or (b) a mark, device, number, text, or signature printed or impressed upon a paper surface or other kind of document by means of a mechanical instrument (*see* Illus. 81); or (c) the instrument itself used for making such impressions, most commonly a hand-stamp.

STAMP ALBUM

Stamp albums are albums designed to accommodate collections of postage stamps and related items such as first-day covers. The first commercially produced stamp album was manufactured by the Lallier company in France in 1862. The most popular type of album in England was that first published in 1872 by the successful postage stamp dealer Stanley Gibbons (1840–1913). Since then such albums have taken many forms, including loose-leaf or ring binders, with different printed headings to guide the arrangement of the collection, or with patterns of squares to help the collector mount the stamps in neat alignment. They have no particular relevance to manuscript artefacts except in so far as they share with autograph albums the privilege of being one of the two universally best-known types of album.

STAMP DUTY

Stamp duty was introduced in Britain in 1694 as a type of taxation on paper and vellum, ostensibly for a four-year period while the country was at war with France, although it remained in force indefinitely. Its imposition is most evident in the number of indentures and other legal and official documents relating to conveyances and financial transactions from then onwards that have affixed to them at the side small labels of embossed blue paper in evidence that stamp duty had been paid.

STANDISH

From at least the fifteenth century, 'standish' was the common term for an inkstand, although the word was sometimes also used to denote simply an inkpot.

STATE PAPER OFFICE

See STATE PAPERS.

STATE PAPERS

The State Papers are those documents among the Public Records comprising principally the records of the various secretaries of state, from the thirteenth century onwards, that were eventually organized by the State Paper Office. (They are to be distinguished from other government records, such as Chancery, Exchequer papers, etc., which were originally kept in separate offices.) The State Papers include letters, writs, documents, rolls, and records relating to the various branches of government, including correspondence between monarchs and their officials, diplomats, and foreign rulers on matters of state.

A Clerk of the Papers of State was apparently first appointed at Whitehall *c.*1578 in the reign of Elizabeth I, although the details of the appointment are unclear. The first overseer of the State Papers on an informal basis may possibly have been the Privy Councillor Dr Thomas Wilson (1523/4–1581). Under James I, Dr Wilson's nephew Sir Thomas Wilson (*c.*1560–1629), was appointed Keeper of the Records in conjunction with Levinus Monk, and later Ambrose Randall, inheriting, in Wilson's own words, 'all the buisnes, w^{ch}: had bin left' by his predecessors from 1522 to 1590 'Mixte into 20 seuerall cubords, according to their years and tymes' and of which he 'made a booke of particuler Registers'. In accordance with a plan he drew up on 29 July 1610 (or 1618), Wilson was responsible for a thorough reorganization of the State Papers. Although struggling against inadequate accommodation, under-staffing, and underfunding in 'this poore and painfull office wherin', he said, he served the King, he established a system of categorization of the State Papers, according to the countries concerned, with subdivisions according to subject, such as law, church, military, economy, crime, etc., as well as rules whereby the papers of deceased secretaries of state should be retained, and he was a zealous pursuer and recoverer of state papers that had been dispersed. He thereby laid at least a notional foundation for future developments in the ordering and preservation of the State Papers, despite all the subsequent inefficiency, personal retention of state papers by secre-taries of state such as Cecil and Winwood, and the disruptions caused by the Whitehall fire of 1619 and the Civil War of the 1640s.

Today the State Papers represent perhaps the single most important collection in the Public Record Office, now incorporated in the National Archives at Kew (SP series). They cover the period from 1231 to *c.*1888, but chiefly that from Henry VIII to 1782.

They are divided principally into:

State Papers Domestic (classified largely by reign: thus SP 10 for Edward VI, SP 11 for Mary I, SP 12 for Elizabeth I, and so on);

State Papers Ireland (from 1395 to 1784 in SP 53–58, 60–64);

State Papers Foreign (the general series from 1547 to 1577 classified as SP 68–70, others from 1544 to 1871, largely classified by country, or town such as Rome, Venice, and Simancas, chiefly in SP 71, 75–86, 88–110);

State Papers Colonial (CO series, including America).

Most of those from the early sixteenth to the late eighteenth century are recorded, usually in summarized form, in over 200 printed *Calendars*, published from the 1850s onwards after the State Papers came under the control of the Master of the Rolls. Not all state papers are preserved there, however, in view of the earlier dispersal, and many are in major libraries such as the British Library and Lambeth Palace, or else among the family papers of great private estates, most notably those of James I's Secretary of State Sir Robert Cecil at Hatfield House.

Nor is the definition of 'State Papers' clear-cut, since many records categorized as Chancery or Exchequer papers, for instance, might just as readily be called 'State Papers'. The definition of State Papers as official papers generated by a minister's employment by the state and therefore the property of the state is still disputed. Sir Winston Churchill, for instance, refused to relinquish to the nation his huge archive kept at Chartwell, which he insisted was privately owned. (The bulk of it, not already donated by Lady Churchill, was purchased by the nation with National Lottery money in 1995 and is preserved at Churchill College, Cambridge.)

STATIONER

The term 'stationer' (Medieval Latin: *stationarius*) originally denoted a type of tradesman who acted as middleman between universities and the producers of books. On a purely commercial basis, stationers organized or facilitated the commissioning of approved books, their copying and distribution, their binding or repair, and the supplying of relevant materials to craftsmen. The term simultaneously denoted independent booksellers who were 'stationary': that is, those who had fixed stalls or shops as distinct from itinerant vendors (*see* Illus. 79). Stationers of this type are recorded in the thirteenth and fourteenth centuries in such locations as Oxford and Cambridge, and in London, where by the sixteenth century their principal locations were in the vicinity of High Cross in Cheapside and in St Paul's Churchyard. By the mid-seventeenth century, and especially since the eighteenth century, stationers became largely distinct from booksellers, even though still selling some books, by concentrating more on the purveying of miscellaneous writing materials and 'stationery'.

STATIONERS' COMPANY, STATIONERS' REGISTER

The Stationers' Company, properly the Worshipful Company of Stationers and Newspaper Makers, is a City livery company that has a distinguished history pertaining to the publishing and selling in the British Isles of books and other printed materials. However, the company originated before the invention of printing, when in 1403 Writers of the Text Letter and manuscript limners and illuminators petitioned the Lord Mayor of London to form a guild or trading company with suitable wardens to oversee the affairs of each craft. Its first royal charter was granted by Queen Mary I in 1557, after which, for the next four centuries, until 1911, and subject to government licensing, censorship, and other changing regulations, the Company was the principal body officially empowered to control printing and copyright, enforce trading monopolies, and regulate the book trade.

The Company is housed in Stationers' Hall, London EC4, on a site it has occupied since 1606, the Hall having been rebuilt in the 1670s after the

Great Fire of London. Its extensive historic records are still preserved there. They include most notably the Stationers' Register, begun in 1557 as a record of printers' or publishers' right to print specific works. It incorporates details of every book or edition they claimed as their property, whether actually published or not.

STATIONERY

Stationery is commercially manufactured writing materials. These include notepaper or letter-paper, which might be either standard and mass-produced or else personalized with printed or embossed address, crest, or heading, as well as envelopes and related appurtenances, such as leather-framed blotters, rulers, penholders, and even pens and pencils, sold by stationers. Although stationery of this kind was developed in the eighteenth century, occasional earlier prototypes of personalized stationery can be found. For instance, after 1588 the papermaker John Spilman produced special paper for Queen Elizabeth bearing royal watermarks: one a crowned *ER* cipher, the other her arms within the Garter.

STATIONERY BINDING

See LEDGER.

STATUTE BOOK

Statutes (Latin *statuta*) are laws made by the legislative body of a state or of a civil or ecclesiastical institution. A statute book, or book of statutes, is therefore one embodying such laws. Books of statutes relating to the state, which were privately compiled, all varied from one another, some even containing spurious legislation. This was because the wording of many statutes was written by judges or clerks and, despite occasional copying from Parliament Rolls, there was no single definitive text or source available. Such books, which survive by the hundred, are perhaps the most common type of English legal manuscript of the Middle Ages. With the printing of statutes from the 1480s onwards, the production of manuscript copies declined rapidly.

Examples relating to other bodies can be elaborately engrossed, decorated and even sometimes illuminated to signify their importance: for instance, the statutes of certain chapels, colleges, and guilds or livery companies.

STATUTE ROLLS

See PARLIAMENT ROLLS.

STEEL PEN

The use of various types of metal pens is recorded from ancient times, with notable developments occurring from at least the mid-sixteenth century onwards. However, what is most generally known as the steel pen, or metal-tipped pen bearing a metallic nib, was developed in the late eighteenth and early nineteenth centuries. When technical problems were overcome, such as the requisite flexibility of the steel and the need to use less acidic ink to eliminate the possibility of rust or corrosion, this new type of pen was being commercially manufactured in Sheffield, Birmingham, and elsewhere by the 1800s, had gained sufficient popularity to be mass-produced and mass-marketed by 1833, and effectively superseded the quill.

STEM

In palaeography, the stem is the main, vertical stroke in letters such as *b, h, l, p, r, t,* and *y.* The stem is more specifically described as an 'ascender' if it is upright and rises above the baseline of writing (as in *b, h, l*) and a 'descender' if it hangs below the line (as in *p, y*).

STEMMA

Derived from a Greek and Latin word meaning 'garland' (generally placed on an ancestral image, hence meaning 'ancestry' or a 'pedigree'), the term 'stemma' (plural: stemmata) denotes a genealogy or family tree. It is most commonly used in the context of editing or textual criticism, where an attempt is made to reconstruct the chain of descent or lineage of a work that exists in several texts or versions, whether manuscript or printed. Such an attempt is to trace the pattern, sequence, or order of transmission and the relationships between the extant texts, as well as those postulated but no longer in existence, establishing which text is copied or derived from which and, if possible, which one is the earliest. The relationships are generally represented in the form of a diagram, with alphabetical letters or sigla representing the texts. A relatively simple example is shown in the figure:

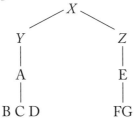

This means that, from available evidence, the editor or textual critic has deduced that the original but no longer extant archetype X was subject to two separate traditions of copying, represented by the hypothetical texts Y and Z, each characterized by certain readings; the extant text A being copied from Y, and E from Z. Texts B, C, and D are each copied from text A, and F and G from E.

Such stemmata can become very much more complicated when large numbers of manuscript copies are available; when the work exists in more than one version, or was perhaps copied several times at different stages of the author's composition or revision of it; when there is evidence of the former existence of intermediary, but no longer extant texts (or links in the chain); and when some texts show signs of contamination or conflation, incorporating readings from more than one textual tradition. *See also* TRANSMISSION.

STENOGRAPHY

Derived from the Greek *stenos* ('narrow') and *graphē* ('writing'), the term 'stenography' means the art of writing in shorthand (and *see* SHORT-HAND). The term came into general use following the publication of John Willis's *The Art of Stenographie* (1602), which expounded an original shorthand system based wholly on the alphabet. This proved to be so useful and influential that it superseded the earlier, less practical systems of Timothy Bright (1588) and John Bales (1590) and was the basis for subsequent developments. Since then, various systems of stenography have been devised. Among them is that expounded as *Tachygraphy* (1638) by Thomas Shelton—the one used by Samuel Pepys for his celebrated *Diary* in 1660–9 (*see* Illus. 80), as well as by the Parliamentarian John Rushworth. Highly influential systems were later developed by Samuel Taylor in 1786, based on a consonantal alphabet of nineteen letters, and by Sir Isaac Pitman in 1837, a phonetic system based on sounds called 'phonography'.

A 'stenographer', a term that seems not to have come into general use before the early nineteenth century, is a writer of shorthand. The term 'stenograph', in the same period, might mean, as a verb, to write in shorthand or, as a noun, a report written in shorthand. Later in the century, a stenograph was also a kind of typewriter that could mechanically reproduce shorthand writing.

STET

The Latin *stet* means 'let it stand' and is a standard term used in printers' proof-correcting. Written in the margin of a proof sheet, it signifies a change of mind by the proof-reader and means 'ignore the correction made here and let the text stay as it was'. 'Stet' may also sometimes be indicated in proof corrections by dots underneath a word.

STITCHING

See SEWING.

STRAPWORK

Strapwork is a type of scribal decoration found most often in late medieval and early modern manuscripts, including some deeds and letters patent (*see* Illus. 37, 38, and 95). It takes the form of an embellishment to the initial letter of the text, comprising patterns of parallel strips or ribbon-like bands of ink or occasionally plumbago criss-crossing each other perpendicularly and usually extending into the border. Such patterning is also sometimes called 'trelliswork'. When the straps or ribbons seem to be interwoven, as in some medieval manuscript decoration, it may be called 'interlacing' or 'interlace'. The term 'strapwork' should not be confused with 'spraywork'. *Compare* SPRAYWORK.

STRIKE

As a term used in relation to postal matters, a 'strike' means a particular impression or example of a hand-stamp: i.e. the date stamp or other stamped postal mark on a specific letter or envelope, with all its peculiar characteristics, such as whether it is a fine or poor impression, clear or faint, etc.

STROKE

In palaeography, a stroke is a line in the formation of a letter made by a single movement of the hand without change of direction. Thus, a scribe might write the letter *l* in a single stroke if it were a continuous loop back to the point of origin or in two strokes if he inscribed the vertical ascender and then doubled back upon himself. Various qualified types of stroke include headstroke, for, say, the cross-stroke (or cross-bar) on a *T* or *t*, and otiose stroke, for a superfluous flick of the pen trailing a letter, usually at the end of a word, which is not an intrinsic part of the letter. Strokes can also be distinguished as downstrokes, which tend to be inscribed with some pressure and are therefore quite thick, and upstrokes, which tend to be inscribed with less pressure and are thinner.

STUB

A stub in a printed or manuscript volume, bound or unbound, is what was once a leaf, conjugate with another, which for some reason has been cut down to a narrow strip alongside the gutter. This may have been done before or after the gatherings were sewn. For instance, a belated addition of a single leaf might be sewn or glued in with a stub acting as an overlap (like a guard); alternatively a scribe might have marred his copy and therefore deliberately cut away the page, leaving only a narrow inner margin, or stub, in order to continue afresh on the next leaf. Occasional manuscript volumes, such as notebooks or commonplace books, are encountered where a considerable number of leaves have been cut down to stubs, either because blank leaves have been deliberately excised for other uses or because the written texts on them were extracted for independent circulation or for reasons of censorship. In printed books a stub might also remain when a cancelland has been removed and a cancel affixed in its place. *Compare* GUARD.

STYLUS

A stylus is perhaps the earliest known writing instrument, dating from at least 3500 BC in Mesopotamia. It was a broad-headed, pointed, or sharpened stick, generally of wood, metal, or bone, used for impressing characters or, with the sharp edge, pictographs on clay or wax tablets. Those styluses with triangular heads could, when heated, also be used to smooth the wax on tablets for reuse. The stylus was the precursor of the reed pen.

In the early modern period, styluses of silver, brass, copper, or other metal, sometimes called 'pins', were associated with the use of tables.

SUBSCRIBE

Derived from the Latin *subscribere*, the term 'subscribe' means to 'write underneath' or 'write below', being the opposite of 'superscribe'. In this literal sense, subscriptions most frequently occur as additions at the end of texts such as letters, when the writer adds some (often formulaic) wording such as 'Yours sincerely' followed by a signature. Since subscribing one's signature to a document could mean approving or supporting the nature or import of that document, the term 'subscribe to' could also come to signify supporting financially a cause or undertaking. Thus, the term 'subscription' was also used from the seventeenth century onwards to mean support given to particular publishing enterprises, a book published by subscription being one at least partly financed by subscribers who had signed an agreement to buy copies of the book at a certain rate in advance. *See* Illus. 10 and 42.

SUBSCRIPTION BOOK

In universities and colleges, a subscription book or register is one signed by persons subscribing to oaths, notably the Thirty-Nine Articles of the Church of England, the use of the Book of Common Prayer, or, later, to being a bona fide member of the Church of England. Such oaths were required, at least at Cambridge, of those students graduating BD (Bachelor of Divinity) and DD (Doctor of Divinity) from 1613 onwards and of those graduating BA (Bachelor of Arts) and MA (Master of Arts) from 1617 onwards. Specific volumes bear the signatures of those subscribing to the Act of Uniformity, to the oaths instituted under William and Mary, and to other oaths. The Oxford subscription books date from 1581. Such books may bear interesting or rare signatures of, for instance, well-known writers: e.g. John Milton at Cambridge in 1629 and 1632, the dramatist Thomas Middleton at Oxford in 1598, and the poet Thomas Randolph at Cambridge in 1628 and 1631. *Compare* MATRICULATION REGISTER.

SUBSIGN

To subsign a document is to subscribe, or write beneath the text, one's signature. A subsignation is the signature thereby produced, the term sometimes implying that the document has also been sealed.

SUBSTANTIVES

The substantives, or substantive elements, of a written or printed text are what editors judge to be its essential, verbal constituents, as distinct from the incidentals such as punctuation, spelling, and capitalization (*compare* INCI-DENTALS). The term 'semi-substantive', however, was used by the bibliographer Fredson Bowers to distinguish incidentals that on certain occasions affect meaning as much as substantives. An example of this would be the commas in the sentence 'The cat, which is black, is mine', as distinct from 'The cat which is black is mine': the first meaning that 'the cat is mine and it is, incidentally, black'; the second meaning that 'it is the black cat (as distinct from cats of different colour) that is mine'. The words 'which is black' in the last instance constitute technically a restrictive clause (though this would be clearer if the word 'that' were used here instead of 'which'); the commas in the former instance distinguish those words as being a non-restrictive clause.

SUMMARY

A summary is an abstract, digest, epitome, precis, or synopsis of a text.

SUMPTUOUS

'Sumptuous' is a term favoured by booksellers to describe extremely expensive, elaborate, and luxurious bindings that exhibit exemplary displays of craftsmanship. Such bindings are characterized by features such as high-quality leathers (coloured morocco, etc.) and fine tooling (in gilt perhaps, with decorative elements such as painted floral inlays, lozenges, volutes, corner-pieces, dentelles, and other emblems and motifs), by well-reputed master binders. Books—chiefly printed, sometimes manuscript—were bound in such style in the early modern period either as presentation copies for distinguished patrons or else by wealthy owners and collectors themselves. Sumptuously bound books of this period can fetch thousands of pounds as collectors' items today. (A fine collection was assembled, for instance, by the late John Paul Getty for his Worseley Library.)

SUPERSCRIPT

Derived from the Latin *superscribere*, the term 'superscribe' means literally to 'write above' or 'write over': i.e. the opposite of 'subscribe' (*compare* SUB-SCRIBE). A superscription may be a name or text inscribed on the upper part of a document, or even the address written on the outside of a letter. Superscript lettering within a text is that written at a raised level, such as appears in many abbreviations: the *r* in 'M^r' or the *e* in 'y^e', for instance. Alternatively, it may be used for a supralineal insertion: such as the word 'he' as it appears in 'and so ^{he} went'. Such raised lettering or text may itself be termed 'superscription'.

SUPPLICAT

Since at least the mid-sixteenth century, a supplicat (written in its Latin form as *supplicat*, meaning literally 'he entreats') is a formal petition for a degree or for incorporation in a university. It might be written and perhaps signed in the hand of the student concerned, but was more often written in the hand of a college official or butler on that person's behalf.

SUPPORTERS

In heraldry, supporters are the figures, such as rampant lions or other creatures, that stand holding the sides of a nobleman's armorial shield in an achievement (*see* ACHIEVEMENT).

SUPRALINEAL

Meaning 'over the line', the term 'supralineal' is applied to a manuscript correction, revision, or addition inserted above a line in a manuscript or printed text, such insertions usually being marked by a caret (*see* Illus. 8). If the insertion occurs between two lines of text it may equally be called 'interlineal'.

SURREBUTTAL

See REJOINDER.

SURREJOINDER

See REJOINDER.

SURRENDER

A surrender is the legal process, usually embodied in an instrument of enactment, whereby a tenant gives up rights in a property to a reversioner (the owner who retains his interest in the property). It is therefore the opposite of a release (*compare* RELEASE).

In a different context, the term 'surrender document' might also apply to a wartime instrument of surrender whereby the representatives of a military force, nation, or regime formally admit defeat and, possibly under certain conditions, surrender to their opponents. An example of an unconditional surrender is the one-page typed document (now in the Imperial War Museum) signed by the German Delegation and Field-Marshal Montgomery on Lüneberg Heath on 4 May 1945, whereby the German forces in most of northern Europe formally capitulated to the Allies.

SURVEY

As a document, a survey is a formal written description of something based on a detailed overall inspection or examination. It usually entails a description and mapping of geographical features of some part of the earth's surface, most commonly the examination of a tract of land or an estate, usually for legal or accounting purposes, to ascertain its nature, boundaries, tenure, buildings, condition, and value. From medieval times onwards, a survey has usually taken the form of a manuscript book, sometimes calligraphically set out and incorporating maps and drawings (*see* Illus. 87). Examples appear in numerous estate archives, in local record offices, and in private muniments. The most famous survey of all is the Domesday Book in the National Archives at Kew (E 31), a great general assessment of landed property in England commissioned in 1086 by William the Conqueror. Although actually comprising two manuscript books, this King's Book (*liber regis*) had acquired its name Domesday by the 1170s as being analogous to the final account at the Last Judgement.

SUSPENSION

See ABBREVIATION.

The Dungion

The Postron

Warkes Toune

Twede Water

The circumferaunce of the castell of

ILLUS. 87 *A page in a large formal survey of the Baronries of Wark, Wooler, and elsewhere in Northumberland, commissioned by or for Sir Thomas Grey (d. 1589), c.1570. The page incorporates a watercolour representation of Wark Castle and town, and the neat professional secretary script is set out within ruled margins with an embellished and coloured initial letter and engrossed lettering in the first line.*

SWASH LETTERING

In palaeography, the early modern word 'swash', connoting vigour, boldness, and swaggering (as in 'swashbuckling'), is sometimes applied to lettering written in exaggerated form, characterized, for instance, by heavily accentuated loops or swirls on descenders or by other vigorous curves and flourishes, including the long *s*.

SWIB

A term of very recent coinage (by the literary scholar Ernst Honigmann), 'swib' is a useful abbreviation, being an acronym of 'single word in brackets', 'single' here also including two words joined by a hyphen or apostrophe: e.g. '(spaniel-like)' and '(I'faith)'. This is a recurring feature in certain early modern dramatic texts, including Shakespeare and manuscripts by the scribe Ralph Crane who was working in the 1620s.

SWUNG DASH

A swung dash is a tilde-shaped flourish (~) sometimes used by scribes as a line-filler or by editors to represent the lemma (*see* LEMMA).

SYLLABUS

Derived from Greek and originally denoting a parchment label, the term 'syllabus', at least from the seventeenth-century onwards, means a brief preliminary table, synopsis, or outline of the contents of a discourse or treatise. In a Catholic ecclesiastical context, a syllabus is specifically a tabulated summary of errors and false doctrines condemned by the Pope. In general modern usage, a syllabus is a summary of, or agenda for, an academic course or series of lectures.

SYNAERESIS

Synaeresis (the Greek word means 'seizing together') is a fairly common feature of early modern written documents, including those of an official nature. It is the contraction of what would normally be written as two vowels, and pronounced as two syllables, into a single vowel or diphthong, pronounced as a single syllable: e.g. when 'the end' is written as 'thend'.

SYNOPSIS

A synopsis (the Greek word means 'general view') is, at least since the early seventeenth century, a brief summary, or tabulated set of headings, encapsulating in concise form the essential elements or nature of a subject or literary work, to give an overall view of it.

T

TABLE BOOK

See TABLES.

TABLE OF CONTENTS

A table of contents is a common feature of printed books in the early modern period, and was sometimes adopted for manuscript volumes as well. It is a list of the contents of the volume, set out in the correct sequential order with page or item numbers, usually located near the beginning of the volume, although occasionally added at the end. Such lists can sometimes be added by subsequent owners, when, for instance, the volume is a composite collection of pamphlets bound together later. A table of contents is to be distinguished from an index, which provides a quite separate and usually more detailed alphabetical key to the contents of the book. *Compare* INDEX.

TABLES

Derived from the Latin *tabula* (plural: *tabulae*), the terms 'tables' and 'writing tables' are often used as synonyms of 'tablet' or 'tablets', being some kind of stiff writing surface, treated so that the writing is easily erasable and the surface can effectively be used over and over again. They were evidently subject to inscription not by pens, but by styluses. The term 'table book' is also used frequently in the early modern period and is probably synonymous with 'tables' except that it implies a writing medium in a book or codex format, or possibly a hinged pair of tables (for there are many references to tables coming in pairs), as distinct from a single wooden tablet. Even so, these often interchangeable terms, also complicated by the occasional incorporation of blank tables in printed almanacs, evidently denoted a variety of types and forms, made of different materials and with varying uses.

Commercially produced writing tables cum almanacs in England date from c.1577 and surviving examples are relatively uncommon. A characteristic one (now at the University of Illinois) is the *Writing Tables with a Kalender for xxiiii Yeeres* printed in London by James Roberts for Edward White in 1598 and containing a series of yellow waxy pages within a goat-skin wallet binding. It includes the specific instructions:

> To make cleane your Tables, when they are written on, Take a little peece of a Spunge, or a Linnen cloath, being cleane without any soyle: wet it in water, and wring it hard, & wipe that you haue wryten very lightly, and it will out, and within one quarter of an howre, you may wryte in the same place agayne: put not your leaues together, whilst they be very wet with wyping.

The materials used for such reusable surfaces would seem to have included ass's skin, stiff paper or card varnished or coated with wax, or else with a kind of plaster made of gesso mixed with glue and linseed oil, or else bitumen, as well as parchment, which the French physician Sir Theodore Turquet de Mayerne is reported to have used for his table book after applying to the leaves a resinous compound that could be readily washed. The binding of such items could be as plain or as expensively luxurious as any other kind of book, and it might sometimes incorporate its own stylus, or pin, which could be pulled out and used for writing on the spot.

Other contemporary references suggest types of small (perhaps octavo or sextodecimo) pocket books for ephemeral jottings, such as the 'table-book' with 'the names of several places where he was to go' that was found in a dead man's pocket and shown to Samuel Pepys on 10 May 1667. Alternatively they might be somewhat more elaborate sketchbooks, such as the 'Table-Book of Pictures' drawn by Anne King praised by the poet Jasper Mayne and which he urged should be 'clasped' shut to stop her 'fair pictures' of 'sprightly dames' from escaping. There are also numerous well-known references to tables and table books in Shakespeare, where the general sense is that their surface bears impressions rather than normal inscriptions applied with ink; that they are portable; that they record ephemeral memoranda (as distinct from engraved monuments); and that the text is essentially erasable ('And therefore will he wipe his tables clean, And keep no tell-tale to his memory': *Henry IV, Part II*, IV, i).

It may be added that table books bear no relation to any kind of book designed or inclined to be left lying around on household or office reception furniture for casual browsing, such as modern so-called 'coffee-table books'. *See also* TABLET.

TABLET

The term 'tablet', the diminutive form of the word 'table', traditionally denotes a flat slab of some kind, usually of stone or metal, bearing, or intended to bear, a carved or engraved inscription, such as a memorial fixed to a wall. It is a term also applied, however, to writing surfaces involving small, flat, slab-like boards, or slate, or else sheets of stiff paper or card, which may sometimes be hinged as a diptych. From antiquity to more modern times, a tablet might be made of wood or occasionally ivory and, if not prepared for the application of ink, was likely to be coated with wax, or with other suitable materials, such as gesso mixed with glue and linseed oil and perhaps powdered white lead or else black bitumen, to receive impressions made by a soft-metal stylus. Tablets were generally used for informal purposes, like notebooks, or for teaching. Some were made with handles like horn books, some attached to belts like girdle books, yet others strung together at one end with leather thongs so they could open up somewhat like fans, or else they might be incorporated in a leather case or binding rather like a codex. The term 'tablet' persists in modern times to denote any flat, slab-like writing unit, such as a file pad. *See also* TABLES.

TABLE-TALK

'Table-talk' is a term commonly used in the sixteenth and seventeenth centuries to denote gossip, anecdotes, and familiar conversation enjoyed largely at the dinner table. Such informal social discourse, especially when involving a well-known person or raconteur and when reported by someone present, also became a minor literary genre, one that tended to circulate in manuscript form. A notable example is the *Table-Talk* of the legal historian and scholar John Selden (1584–1654), which was not published until 1689, but of which innumerable manuscript copies were made more than half a century earlier. Another, not so widely circulated, is the table-talk of the author and diplomat Sir Henry Wotton (1568–1639) as recorded by his secretary William Parkhurst, and what is also effectively table-talk is the celebrated record by William Drummond of the conversations he had with the bibulous dramatist Ben Jonson when Jonson visited him in Scotland in 1619. Other manuscript collections of anecdotes and miscellaneous gossip, reporting memorable, witty, characteristic, or entertaining things said by well-known people, include John Aubrey's 'Brief Lives' (in the Bodleian Library) and a quarto notebook by Sir Francis Fane (Shakespeare Birthplace Trust Record Office, E 93/2).

TACK

The term 'tack' is occasionally encountered in connection with legal documents and means a tenure or tenancy, usually leasehold, of land, a farm, a tenement, or other property. In parliamentary usage, it is a measure tacked on to a bill with which it has no intrinsic relation.

TAG

'Tag' is a term sometimes applied to the pendent strip, or label, at the bottom of a parchment deed bearing a wax seal. In literary usage, a tag is a brief addition or appendage to a text, such as a neat quip or moral by way of conclusion.

TALLY

Derived from the Latin *talea*, the term 'tally', or 'tally stick', from at least the twelfth century onwards, was a type of stick or rod, usually of hazel-wood and squared, bearing written details on the smooth sides recording the amount involved in a debt or payment and with notches incised at one side to indicate the totals. The stick was cleft lengthways across the notches, and the debtor and creditor each retained one half as legal proof of the transaction. One part (usually the larger of the two sections) kept by the creditor was called the 'stock'—the origin of the modern term for a financial certificate—and the other section, kept by the debtor, was called the 'counterfoil' or 'counter-stock'. Up until 1826, tallies were especially employed by the Royal Exchequer as official receipts for payments of taxes or loans to the sovereign, and the counter-stocks were kept, often strung together, in storage bags. After periodic auditing, it was customary to destroy them. It was the burning of a huge number of old tallies that led to the destruction by fire of the old Houses of Parliament in 1834 (a scene witnessed by the collector Sir Thomas Phillipps, who tried to save what documents—if not tallies—he could). Some tallies are still preserved, however, among the Exchequer papers in the National Archives at Kew (in E 402/347, for example).

The term 'tally' also has a more general application as a score, reckoning, account, or the like. Some Exchequer tallies may therefore also take the form of narrow strips of parchment a foot or so long recording such things as fines paid to the sovereign with respect to land conveyances. In addition, the term 'tally' is sometimes applied to a piece of wood or card marking a space on a library shelf where a book has been temporarily removed.

TATTOO

Tattoos are a form of body decoration in which more or less permanent designs on the skin of men or women are produced by a process involving the puncturing of the skin with sharp instruments and the insertion of pigments. A feature of various cultures since ancient times, tattoos reached perhaps their most elaborate form as a type of indigenous art among the Polynesians encountered by Captain Cook in the eighteenth century. Each of the Maori chiefs in New Zealand, for instance, had his face covered with an intricate, arabesque design, peculiar to that individual. For this reason tattoos were subsequently used as a type of signature on at least one occasion when land deeds were drawn up by European settlers. In the large indenture on parchment drawn up by William Charles Wentworth in 1840, by which he attempted (unsuccessfully, as it proved) to purchase the South Island of New Zealand from the Maoris, the document was signed by eight Maori chiefs in the sense that a European scribe wrote down their names against token impressions of seals in red wax and then carefully reproduced in pencil, and in their presence, the distinctive facial tattoo (or *moko*) of each chief consenting to the agreement. This laborious method of authorization was not, however, used for the all-encompassing Treaty of Waitangi in the same year, whereby an eventual total of 512 Maori chiefs conceded total sovereignty over all their land to Queen Victoria.

TELEGRAM

Derived from the Greek *tēle* ('far away') and a form of *graphē* ('writing'), and dating from the mid-nineteenth century, the term 'telegram' means a message, dispatch, or communication sent electronically by telegraph. Telegrams are usually partly printed forms in which space is left for the message to be written by or on behalf of the sender and, when received, by the operator, unless, alternatively, the message is printed off by a receiving instrument. *See* Illus. 88.

TEMP.

A word often encountered in descriptions of records and documents is *temp.* followed by the abbreviated name in Latin of a monarch. It is an abbreviation of the Latin word *tempore*, meaning 'in the time of'. Thus '*temp.* Hen[rici] VII' means 'in the time of Henry VII' (i.e. during his reign from 22 August 1485 to 21 April 1509); '*temp.* Eliz[abethae]' means 'in the time of Elizabeth I' (i.e. during her reign from 17 November 1558 to 24 March 1603), and so on.

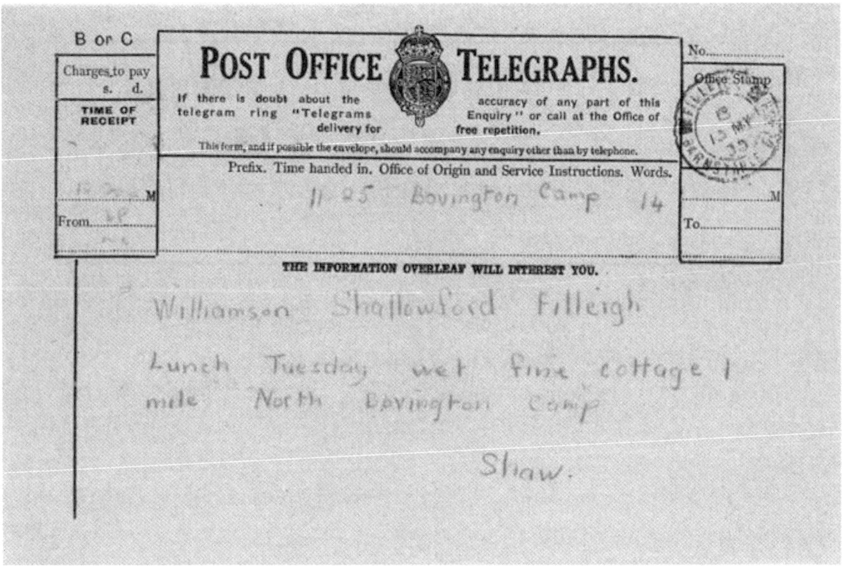

B or C

Charges to pay s. d.

TIME OF RECEIPT

From

POST OFFICE TELEGRAPHS.

If there is doubt about the accuracy of any part of this telegram ring "Telegrams Enquiry" or call at the Office of delivery for free repetition.

This form, and if possible the envelope, should accompany any enquiry other than by telephone.

No.

Office Stamp

Prefix. Time handed in. Office of Origin and Service Instructions. Words.

11 25 Bovington Camp 14

To

THE INFORMATION OVERLEAF WILL INTEREST YOU.

Williamson Shallowford Filleigh

Lunch Tuesday wet fine cottage 1 mile North Bovington Camp

Shaw.

ILLUS. 88 *The last telegram sent by T. E. Lawrence ('of Arabia'), under his adopted RAF name of Shaw. This is the message as received and written on a printed form by a Devon Post Office operator, with a date stamp, and delivered to Henry Williamson, 13 May 1935. Arranging a meeting for the following day, it was sent from Bovington Camp a mile from Lawrence's Dorset cottage of Clouds Hill, on the return journey to which he had his fatal motorcycle accident.*

TERMINUS A QUO, TERMINUS AD QUEM

See DATES.

TERRIER

Deriving from the Latin *terra* ('land'), the term 'terrier' means a document or register in which is described a landed property, whether of a lord or landowner or of his tenants within the manor. It may specify the site or whereabouts of the property, its size or acreage, its boundaries, its tenants and their rents, and the holders of adjacent lands, as well as, in earlier feudal times, its vassals. For one type of terrier, *see* GLEBE TERRIER.

TESTAMENT

See WILL AND TESTAMENT.

TESTATOR, TESTATRIX

A 'testator' (a Latin term) is a person who makes a will, or who has died leaving a will, as distinct from someone who has died intestate, without leaving a will. If the person is a woman, the formal term generally used is 'testatrix'.

The term 'testator' was very occasionally used in the early modern period to denote a witness: i.e. one who testifies to the truth or authenticity of something, such as a signatory witnessing an indenture.

TESTE

The Latin term *teste* ('in witness') is traditionally the initial word in the final clause of a royal writ naming the person who authorizes the affixing of the royal seal; hence it denotes the clause itself. The document may then be described as 'tested' by that authority.

In a more general sense, a *teste* or teste can denote the clause(s) identifying a witness (*testis*) or witnesses (*testes*), as well as usually the date, in any kind of deed or charter.

TESTIMONIAL

Since at least as early as the late sixteenth century, the term 'testimonial' (Latin: *testimonium*, 'evidence' or 'proof') has been used in the context of a written document to denote a letter or certificate that constitutes a reference or recommendation: i.e. one bearing witness to someone's character, ability, or qualifications.

TEXT

Derived from the Latin *textum* ('something woven'), which is also related to the words 'textile' and 'texture', the term 'text' means the wording of any piece of writing, manuscript or printed. In a specifically literary context, it denotes the original or main body of wording or verbal structure that constitutes a book or manuscript, or any part of it, excluding subsidiary additions such as preliminaries, notes, and appendices.

TEXT HAND

See COURT HAND.

TEXTUAL COMMUNITY

A term of recent coinage, a 'textual community' means a place or social circle where manuscript texts are or were produced, read, and circulated by and for a certain group of people. Medieval examples include monasteries, convents, and abbeys where there was a scriptorium producing copies of religious texts for restricted communal use. Other examples, extending into the early modern period, include certain households, usually aristocratic or gentrified, where manuscripts were written for a limited circle of family and friends; universities and colleges, where groups of students produced, copied, and exchanged texts of various kinds; the Inns of Court in London, where similar literary activity flourished; and the Royal Court itself, where much literature over the years was written, collected, or passed about among courtiers and ladies-in-waiting, as well as by secretaries of state and other ministers and their staff. Such communities might not necessarily be confined to one place or geographical area, however. They might comprise a widely dispersed, albeit notionally circumscribed, network of communicants, such as that of the poet Katherine Philips (1632–1664), whose circle of friends and literary correspondents was scattered throughout England, Wales, and Ireland. *See also* COTERIE.

TEXTUAL CRITICISM

Textual criticism is a branch of scholarship devoted to the study and analysis of texts, whether extant in printed or in manuscript form. The study involves close scrutiny of every aspect of a text, both its substantive and incidental constituents, as well as its physical embodiment. It also entails detailed collation of the different copies, exempla, or versions of a work in order to understand or reconstruct the process of transmission. While textual criticism is a study in itself, independent of other considerations, it is, in practice, often linked to the requirements of editing in that it may help to determine the accuracy, trustworthiness, or authenticity of different texts; the nature of different readings (whether corruptions due to copyists' carelessness or misunderstanding, deliberate scribal emendations, or genuine authorial revisions); the authorship of the work (based on stylistic analysis, for instance, if there is evidence of multiple authorship or additions by others); and, possibly, identification of the text that is the earliest or nearest to the author, thereby producing the evidence whereby an editor may restore the text as closely as possible to its original form, free from obtrusive errors and unwarranted alterations and interpolations. *See also* BIBLIOGRAPHY.

THONGS

Thongs, meaning cords or ties made of narrow strips of soft hide, or tawed (white) or tanned leather, are occasionally the means whereby bundles of parchment deeds have been kept attached or strung together. Thongs are also narrow strips of leather commonly used in bookbinding before the late sixteenth century, when they were gradually replaced by cords.

Ties are usually ribbons, of coloured silk or other material, sometimes thongs of soft leather, fixed into the sides or outer edges of books and intended to be tied in a bow so as to keep the vellum or leather covers closed in an attempt to prevent them from warping. Ties, or traces of them, such as slits cut into the covers where the ties were once set, are a fairly common feature of manuscript volumes from medieval times onwards and of printed books up to about the mid-seventeenth century. Ties of silk or other material were also sometimes used to enclose and keep early modern folded letters in place, either instead of seals or supplementary to seals. Seals sometimes remain on the folded outer leaf of a letter attached to portions of ties that were otherwise cut away when the letter was opened by its recipient.

TILDE

A tilde (a Spanish word, pronounced 'til-day') is the diacritic mark ~ , a short wavy line found in Spanish words above the letter *n* when the sound *ny* is signified (as in *mañana*). In early modern English script, what is effectively a tilde in all but name was commonly written by scribes over individual or sequential letters simply as a flourished variant of, and performing the same function as, a macron, signifying an abbreviation: for example, 'comĩssion' for 'commission', 'lr̃es' for 'lettres' (letters), 'eccliãl' for 'ecclesiastical', and so on. Alternatively, a series of swung dashes or flourishes in tilde form may sometimes be written by a scribe for decorative effect or as fillers to close up an otherwise blank space in or following a line of text. *Compare* SWUNG DASH.

TIPPED-IN

In modern bibliographical and booksellers' parlance, the term 'tipped-in' is applied to a leaf or leaves that have been inserted in a sewn book or manuscript and are attached to it, usually by means of glue at the inner edge, sometimes on guards. Such leaves may thus be distinguished from those unattached or loosely inserted.

TITHE ROLL

A tithe roll, or tithe book, is a manuscript register recording payments of tithes and related arrangements and apportionments in a particular parish, tithes being the 10 per cent of income or farming produce that every parishioner since feudal times was expected to contribute to the parish rector (but not to a vicar). This tax was levied both by the Catholic Church and by the subsequent Church of England, although it was resented by nonconformists and repudiated by Quakers. Tithe books, mostly dating from the seventeenth to the nineteenth century—as well as related papers such as tithe maps and tithe awards (i.e. after the Tithe Commutation Act of 1836, schedules incorporating commissioners' valuation and payment decisions in each parish)—are preserved chiefly in county record offices and in the National Archives at Kew.

TITLE DEED

As a legal term since about 1421, 'title' denotes legal right to property, whether as lord, or as reversioner, or as tenant in possession. Although it has taken various forms over the centuries, and the nature of the ownership and rights concerned have varied considerably, a title deed is a conveyance whereby rights to property, or real estate, are legally transferred from one party to another and which constitutes formal evidence of title. Generally written in Latin up to 1733 (except for the Commonwealth period in the 1650s), and in English thereafter, title deeds passed at common law with the land itself and were not treated as independent private property. Although the system of registration of title, centred on the Land Registry in London, was adopted in 1862, it was still deemed necessary, at least until the 1920s, for owners to retain all deeds relating to the history of their property, even if it were over a period of centuries, in support of their title to it. This accounts for why so many thousands of title deeds, from medieval times onwards, are preserved in so many old family and other archives deposited in record and estate offices, as well as in private muniments.

Many such deeds summarize the history of the property in repetitious formulae, even if their antecedents, the original earlier deeds, no longer survive. For this reason, title deeds—many of which also include descriptive details and even plans of the property concerned—are a major source of information for local historians, even if the sheer quantity of surviving examples generally gives them little commercial value and does nothing to halt their widespread dispersal. For their part, modern property-owners who have acquired property within the past thirty years have no legal compunction to preserve related deeds dating any further back, since no claims to owner-ship by anyone else dating back any further have legal validity.

TITLE-PAGE

The title of a literary work of any kind is its main title, as distinct from other headings or sub-headings that the work might contain, and also as opposed to the colophon, which in earlier times might appear at the end of a work to

ILLUS. 89 *Autograph draft by the radical parliamentarian and regicide Henry Marten of a title-page for his unfinished tract* The Rights of y[e] PEOPLE of England, *written for intended publication, 1647.*

serve the function of a title. The title may also mean specifically the title-page, or title-leaf, at or near the beginning of a volume. Here a full page is devoted to announcing the title and perhaps subtitle of the work, with other related information such as author (and usually also publisher, printer, place and date of publication, in printed books), before other preliminaries (such as a preface). Title-pages, as distinct from occasional titles set out prominently as headings on the first page of the main text, are not entirely unknown in medieval manuscripts, although their rare appearances are usually on the verso of the leaf facing the first page of text, rather than on the recto as later.

To all intents and purposes, however, the title-page as known today was an innovation gradually introduced by early European printers, from about

1463 onwards (from about 1490 in England). They eventually replaced the medieval colophon and also served as commercial advertisements for the book (booksellers and stationers would hang them up as such). Whereas the publishers of incunables originally imitated manuscripts, some of their innovations—including title-pages—began to be imitated in turn by scribes in the production of manuscripts. Thus title-pages appear in many early modern manuscripts, often in centred and flourished form, occasionally even quite elaborately embellished, to conform to new standards. *See* Illus. 72 and 89.

TOKEN BOOKS

See SACRAMENT TOKEN BOOKS.

TOP COPY

See CARBON COPY.

TOPONYMY

Derived from the Greek *topos* ('place') and *onoma* ('name'), the term 'toponymy' means place names, or else denotes the study of place names. Among other things, it is a modern collective term applied to the labelling of towns, ports, harbours, lighthouses, etc. in portolans and maps. *See* Illus. 63.

TRADITION

A textual tradition is a particular line of descent in the transmission of a text. *See* STEMMA.

TRANSCRIPT

Derived from the past participle of the Latin *transcribere* ('to write over or across'), the term 'transcript' means a copy or duplicate of a text, whether written by hand, typed, printed, or otherwise produced, and is the physical item itself. A transcription is a transcribed text—i.e. the verbal structure embodied in a transcript—or else the general process of copying, as distinct from a specific physical artefact. The two terms are often, though incorrectly, used interchangeably.

TRANSLITERATE

To transliterate is to replace the alphabetical characters of one language with those of another, representing as closely as possible the same sounds, a transliteration being the rendition thus produced. So, for instance,

Βιαθανατοσ, the Greek title of John Donne's thesis on suicide, is transliterated by contemporary scribes as *Biathanatos*. A transliteration may thus be distinguished from a translation, which entails a replacement of words in one language by different words in another that have the same meaning.

TRANSMISSION

In the context of textual criticism and editing, 'transmission' (a term derived from a form of the Latin *transmittere*, 'to send over or across') is the process by which a text is conveyed, or transmitted, from one party to another, or from one form to another, or else the series of such conveyances to which a text might be subject. An example of transmission would be if, say, an author's text were dictated to an amanuensis, or copied directly from the author's holograph by a scribe, and the amanuensis's or scribe's copy were then used as the exemplar for one or more further copies, each of which was in turn used as exemplar for yet further copies, which were themselves copied, and so on. If such a process can be traced, with perhaps the drawing-up of a stemma (*see* STEMMA), it might establish what happened to the text at each stage of its journey—how it might have been subject to scribal errors, interference, emendation, adaptation, etc.—and even perhaps throw light on the probable nature of the original text if that no longer survives.

TRANSPOSITION

See SCRIBAL ERRORS.

TREATY

The term 'treaty' may be applied to a private agreement, but more commonly denotes an international agreement, drawn up in a formal document on vellum or paper and signed by the relevant heads of state or their appointed ministers, representatives, or negotiators. The text, usually based on a preliminary draft or protocol, will set out, clause by clause, mutually accepted rights, obligations, and undertakings by the states or parties concerned (*see* Illus. 90). In modern times treaties may also be subject to ratification by the Crown or Parliament or equivalent national legislative bodies, such as the Senate in the USA, where they must either be accepted in full or else rejected and cannot at that stage be amended or ratified in part or conditionally if they are to be put in force.

Since 'treaty' is a generic term, different treaties may be known under different titles denoting various types of agreement. They include:

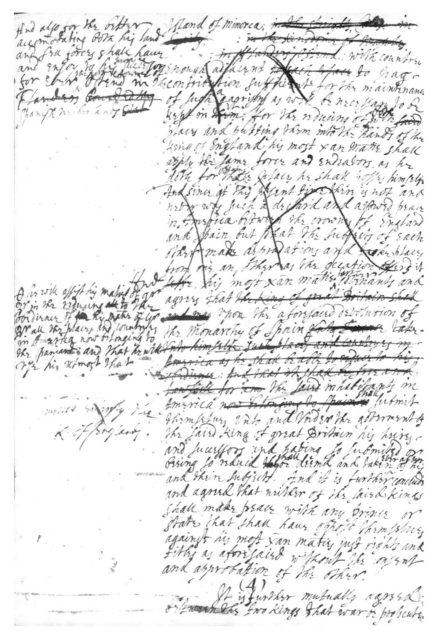

ILLUS. 90 *A page of the autograph draft by Thomas, Lord Clifford of Chudleigh, of the protocol for the Secret Treaty of Dover struck between Charles II and Louis XIV, 1670. It shows heavily revised text for propositions respecting the 'devolution of the Monarchy of Spain' and the bringing of 'all the places and countries in America now belonging to the Spaniard' under the government of the King of Great Britain.*

421

concordat (e.g. the French Concordat of 1801 between Napoleon and Pope Pius VII for the re-establishment of the Roman Catholic Church in France);

convention (e.g. the controversial Convention of Cintra in 1808 for the evacuation of Napoleon's army from Portugal);

pact (e.g. the secret Nazi–Soviet, or Molotov–Ribbentrop, non-aggression Pact of 1939);

charter (e.g. the Charter of the United Nations established by 185 states in 1945);

accords (e.g. the Geneva Accords struck between the Palestinians and Israelis in 2003).

Medieval and early modern treaties concluded by monarchs might also take the form of Royal Letters Patent under the Great Seal, confirming or renewing all the agreed terms, that would be exchanged between the two parties. Some treaties might be drawn up in quite spectacular fashion: for instance, that establishing 'perpetual peace' between England and France on 18 August 1527, which is illuminated and bears a heavy seal of gold (National Archives at Kew, E 30/1109). Large numbers of other treaties, or official transcripts and Chancery enrolments of them, with related papers, from c.1200 to 1780, are preserved in the National Archives under various classifications (including C 64, C 76, SP 103, and SP 108).

TREFOIL

Derived from the Latin *tri* ('three') and *folium* ('leaf'), the term 'trefoil' means a trifoliate leaf: i.e. a leaf, such as a clover, comprising three rounded sections. Apart from being a form that occasionally occurs in earlier manuscript ornamentation and in heraldry, the trefoil is a fairly standard figure drawn by readers in the margins of both manuscript and printed books in the early modern period to draw attention to particular sentences or passages of interest. In this respect it serves as a widespread substitute for, or alternative to, a manicule or pointing hand (*see* MANICULE). Perhaps the largest collection of books containing this mark is in the Folger Shakespeare Library, Washington DC, among the W. T. Smedley collection of some 2,000 books assembled before 1912 by one W. M. Safford. He was under the illusion that because certain markings, notably the trefoil, were used by Sir Francis Bacon in one of his autograph notebooks, then all books found with similar markings could be identified as his.

See STRAPWORK.

TRENCHERS

In the medieval and early modern periods, wooden plates known as 'trenchers', in royal or noble households, could be occasional sites not only for hand-painted decorations, but also for inscribed verses, homilies, biblical quotations, or witty epigrams, for the entertainment of dinner guests. They were usually thin and small in size, either round or square, and the text was inscribed either directly on the wood or else on paper discs pasted to them. The text was generally relegated to the border or else to the underside, to be turned over and read, possibly aloud, after the sweetmeats on the topside had been consumed. Examples of such trenchers dating from the Elizabethan and Jacobean periods include a set (part of which is now in the Victoria and Albert Museum) of originally a dozen trenchers with *Verses given to the Lord Treasurer upon Newyeares Day, c.*1605, by the poet Sir John Davies.

TRICK

In heraldry, a trick is a pen-and-ink outline of a coat of arms. The term usually occurs when arms in a heraldic manuscript are described as 'drawn in trick', meaning sketched in pen and ink, as distinct from being painted or emblazoned in their proper colours (*see* Illus. 5). A trick may incorporate letters to represent the various tinctures or colours of the original arms— perhaps *G* for 'Gules' (red), *S* for 'Sable' (black), *V* for 'Vert' (green), and so on—and with numerals to denote the number of objects involved (such as a feather and '3' to denote three feathers). The term may also be used as a verb: as, for instance, in a reference to arms 'tricked in the margin'.

TYPESCRIPT

The term 'typescript'—sometimes abbreviated in a bibliographical or publishing context to 'TS', 'Ts' or 'ts'—means a page, or series of pages, of text produced by the use of a typewriter (*see* Illus. 68). In the literary world, typescripts might be produced by the author himself, using his own fingers, or else by a secretary or typist, who might be typing from the author's manuscript or from an earlier revised typescript or else directly from dictation (as, for instance, was Henry James's preferred method of composition from the 1890s onwards, having abandoned the attempt to type himself because of repetitive strain injury). What is generally believed to be the first novel submitted to a publisher in typescript form is Mark Twain's *The Adventures of Tom Sawyer* (published 1876).

Typescripts would generally be produced in duplicate, with the top copy directly facing the back of the typing ribbon serving as the main, clearest copy, and one or more carbon copies produced by sheets of black or blue carbon paper underneath, each overlaying another sheet of paper, providing serviceable though less clean impressions (*see* Illus. 13). Typewriters could also be used, if wished, to produce text on a continuous scroll, although this method was not widely used. If the text were typed on to a stencil, or subject to some mechanical process, whereby further copies could be run off in facsimile form, the resultant copy might still be described as a typescript, though one categorized by the duplication process used (*see* FACSIMILE).

In its loosest sense, the term 'typescript' is still sometimes used to denote any material text composed of machine-made 'type'-style lettering, including electronic computer print-outs, as distinct from handwritten copy or traditional printing from inked type.

TYPEWRITER

The typewriter is a writing machine by means of which alphabetical characters may be printed at considerable speed with the use of a keyboard. Prototypes date back at least to 1714, when Henry Mill was granted a patent for a design by Queen Anne. A series of developments by other European and American inventors after 1784 led to the first modern efficient typewriter patented in 1868 by Christopher Latham Sholes and subsequently mass-produced in the 1870s by the gunmakers E. Remington and Sons. A successful portable version was not produced until 1909. An electronic version was patented by Thomas Edison as early as 1871, although not developed until much later, before being superseded by the electronic word processor and today's personal computer. Well-known writers who used typewriters, most of which are still preserved in their houses or museums, include Henry James, Rudyard Kipling, George Bernard Shaw, T. E. Lawrence, P. G. Wodehouse, and Ian Fleming.

The term 'typewriter' in the late nineteenth century could also denote a typist, the person who used the machine.

U

UNBOUND

An unbound book or booklet, whether printed or manuscript, sewn or otherwise, is one that has never been bound. The term 'unbound' may be distinguished from 'disbound', which means that it was once sewn and bound, but that the binding has now been removed.

UNDERLINING

Underlining, <u>like this</u>, is a standard feature in proof-correcting, indicating to the printer that the words underlined should be printed in italics, *like this*. Underlining is also quite common in books, where readers have underlined particular lines or passages of interest to them for future reference, as an alternative to vertical lines in the margin or other markings. Promptbooks and actors' copies of plays may also have underlining, to highlight cue lines, stage directions, or particular parts. No doubt there are many other instances where underlining is used to draw attention to particular elements in texts. In manuscripts, there are examples of underlining used by scribes in previous centuries, but they are relatively rare, their preferred modes of highlighting particular words being rubrication, engrossing, or the use of majuscules.

UNEDITING

The school of unediting in modern textual criticism and editing theory is a reaction to what is perceived to be a long-standing tradition of editorial interference with certain early modern texts, one that is felt to obscure and needlessly complicate the view of the evidence. This approach has arisen especially with regard to the texts of Shakespeare, which have been subject to an exceptionally large number of editions over the years and where editors have felt obliged to impose their own views on the text. Scholars who wish to unedit these texts are interested in exposing, or peeling away the layers of, all such editorial intervention and, instead, confronting the texts in their earliest known material forms, whether printed or manuscript, and studying them in minute detail, including the incidentals of punctuation, spelling, etc., as well as layout. Their view is that, even when these texts contain evident errors, the errors may be authorial or (if scribal, compositorial, etc.) may illuminate the work by throwing light on how it has been misunderstood or mis-transmitted. As a scholarly exercise or investigation, such scrutiny arguably leads to a focus on physical evidence that is usually banished from the abstract debates of editors, encourages a fresh perception of details otherwise overlooked, and leads to an understanding of what is perceived to be institutional distortion. It should be added that this is hardly an approach that is likely, in practice, to be applied to all literary texts, which are generally edited with the prime intention of making them accessible to modern readers.

UNFINISHED

The adjective 'unfinished' applied to a work or text denotes one that the author did not complete or which he or she abandoned. *Compare* IMPERFECT and INCOMPLETE.

UNIFORM PENNY POSTAGE

The system of postal delivery known as Uniform Penny Postage came into operation in Britain on 10 January 1840. By this system, the Post Office charged a single uniform rate of 1*d.* for any letter weighing no more than half an ounce to be delivered from and to anywhere in Britain, regardless of distance. This was, in fact, a revolutionary and highly consequential development, having been established by the postal reformer Rowland Hill (1795–1879) after a prolonged and bitter struggle in the face of considerable opposition. Hill's colleague Sir Henry Cole declared, 'It will be the glory of England for all time that she was the first country to adopt this ray of light.' To facilitate the process, four months later the world's first adhesive postage stamp, the Penny Black, was introduced (*see* Illus. 24), being first officially used on 6 May 1840, the same day also seeing the introduction of the Two-Penny Blue stamp for letters weighing up to one full ounce. The basic rate of 1*d.* per half ounce irrespective of distance within Britain lasted until 1918.

UNTITLED

A literary work that has been given no title, or else a text that bears no title in a particular copy, may be described as 'untitled'. It may lack a title because it was never given one by the author or because the title has simply been omitted by the copyist. If the copy in question has no title, but there is reason to believe that it once did, because what may have been a title-page is now missing, the work or text is generally described as 'lacking title'. In such instances, the title should be distinguished from any heading that appears on the first page: for example, 'Chapter 1: Of the Knowledge of God' clearly relates to only part of the work, not the whole.

UTERINE

See VELLUM.

UTRUM IN ALTERUM ABITURUM ERAT?

A question in Latin, meaning literally 'Which of the two will have departed into the other?', *Utrum in alterum abiturum erat?* is an oft-cited maxim, which gained particular currency in early modern studies of scriptural and classical texts (the question was asked, for instance, by Erasmus in his critical commentaries on the Gospels). Roughly paraphrased as 'Of two readings, which is more likely to have been transformed into the other?', the maxim embodies a traditionally basic principle of textual criticism and arises from the common view that certain kinds of scribal alteration will tend to occur because of scribes' basic tendency to simplify difficult readings encountered in their exemplars. *Compare* DIFFICILIOR LECTIO POTIOR.

V

VADEMECUM

A vademecum (the Latin word means 'go with me') is a portable manual or handbook. Carried about for ready use, perhaps suspended from a belt, a vademecum in the Middle Ages might well consist of leaves folded in a concertina-like format and containing a calendar, almanac, or medical information for easy consultation by someone such as a physician. Later examples tended to be pocket notebooks or reference books.

VARIANT

In textual criticism, editing, and the associated process of collation, a variant, or variant reading, is a reading in one or more manuscript or printed texts that is different from the one in the particular text under scrutiny or being used as an editor's copy-text (the latter is generally cited in an editor's textual apparatus as the lemma and the variants identified with sigla: *see* LEMMA and SIGLA). Alternatively, all the different readings in the various witnesses at a particular point in a text may be classed as variants, because they differ from one another. Thus, for instance, in three texts that have respectively the readings 'the man patted the dog', 'the man patted the poodle', and 'the man patted the spaniel', the variants, or variant textual readings, are 'dog', 'poodle', and 'spaniel'; alternatively, if an editor's copy-text has, say, the word 'dog', then the variants are 'poodle' and 'spaniel'. It is even possible to find variants in a single text: e.g. when a scribe, perhaps not sure of a reading or because he is consulting more than one exemplar, writes one word above another in his copy, or else in a printed book where the author or printer has spotted errors or alternative readings which he lists separately as *errata*.

In bibliographical parlance, 'variant' as an adjective is also used to describe a copy of a printed edition of a book that exhibits features (elements of the text, illustrations, binding, etc.) different from other exempla of that edition.

Deriving from the Latin for 'calf', the term 'vellum' technically denotes a writing or binding material made from calfskin, although, in practice, the word is used as a synonym of 'parchment'. 'Vellum' is certainly the favoured term of bibliophiles and booksellers, regardless of fine distinctions as to whether the material is actually from a calf or from some other animal. However, vellum is quite distinct from calf, which entails a different treatment of calfskin resulting in a brown colour and leathery or (for reversed calf) suede texture, as distinct from the normal smooth white or yellow texture of vellum. A vellum binding may comprise stiff boards covered with vellum or else 'limp vellum', which is a soft vellum not backed or reinforced. The type of vellum sometimes known as 'uterine vellum' and used for very high-grade books is an especially fine, white, smooth and silky material. The term derives from its supposedly being made in medieval times from aborted or newly born calves, kids, or lambs, although it is most commonly applied to a certain quality of skin rather than to its origin. *Compare* PARCHMENT.

VERBATIM ET LITERATIM

A Latin phrase, *verbatim et literatim* means 'word for word and letter for letter': i.e. written as a literal or diplomatic transcription, copied or quoted from some text exactly and precisely as the original, without any corrections, changes, or editing whatsoever.

VERSE MISCELLANY

A verse miscellany, or poetical miscellany, is, as a manuscript, a compilation of predominantly verse texts, or extracts from verse texts, by different authors and usually gleaned from different sources. Verse miscellanies in England seem to have flourished among the literate classes especially in the sixteenth and seventeenth centuries, and to some extent in the eighteenth and nineteenth centuries. Besides containing poems by some of the greatest poets of the age, whose works were largely confined to circulation in manuscript form, these miscellanies bear witness to a great contemporary appetite for poetry, as well as to various literary and reading coteries, or textual communities, based at locations such as the Royal Court, particular country houses, various university colleges, the Inns of Court, and certain ecclesiastical and parliamentary environments. Their compilers include authors, scholars, and antiquaries, as well as politicians, lawyers, clergymen, merchants, students, and other private individuals. Verse miscellanies may be compiled in paper books of different sizes, the most formal usually in folio volumes; written neatly or cursorily, in one or more hands, depending on their owners, and their texts copied either from manuscript separates of single poems or linked groups of poems or else selectively from other people's collections that got passed around.

Well-known examples of extant Tudor verse miscellanies include the Arundel Harington Manuscript (at Arundel Castle), with poems by Henry, Earl of Surrey, Sir Thomas Wyatt, Sir Philip Sidney, Sir John Harington, Sir Walter Ralegh, and others; the Devonshire Manuscript (British Library, Add. MS 17492) and the Blage Manuscript (at Trinity College, Dublin, MS 160), both also with poems by Wyatt, etc. Even greater numbers of seventeenth-century examples exist. These range from Jacobean and early Caroline verse miscellanies with poems by John Donne, Ben Jonson, Richard Corbett, Thomas Carew, and their contemporaries (*see* Illus. 91) to the innumerable, often commercially produced manuscript volumes of 'Poems upon Affairs of State'—with frequently scandalous political lampoons by wits such as John Wilmot, Earl of Rochester—that flourished in the reign of Charles II and his successors, from the 1670s to the early 1700s. Notable Scottish verse miscellanies, many of which gather together poems of medieval as well as early modern origin, include such examples as the Bannatyne and Asloan Manuscripts (National Library of Scotland, MSS Adv. 1. 1.6 and 16500) and the Maitland Folio and Quarto Manuscripts (Pepys Library, Magdalene College, Cambridge, MSS 2553 and 1408).

Verse miscellanies are sometimes also described as 'poetical commonplace books', which is not a strictly accurate term unless they are systematically arranged under subject headings. Something of the academic commonplace-book habits of compilation do, however, persist in many early modern miscellanies, even when compiled primarily for entertainment rather than for educational reasons. Common instances are when the compiler is minded to give poems fresh, non-authorial titles, sometimes in Latin and with erudite or classical associations, highlighting the general theme that the poem illustrates: 'In commendation of declining beauty', for example, or *Laus Musicae* ('The Praise of Music'), or *Dirae* ('The Furies').

VERSION

A version is a particular state or form of a text or work that may be distinguished as a separate entity. Thus an author may write one or more early versions, later versions, expanded versions, abridged versions, and so on, each complete in itself, as well as versions adapted by the author or by someone else for another genre, such as a stage or screen version of a novel. Examples of works that exist in different versions include Sir Thomas

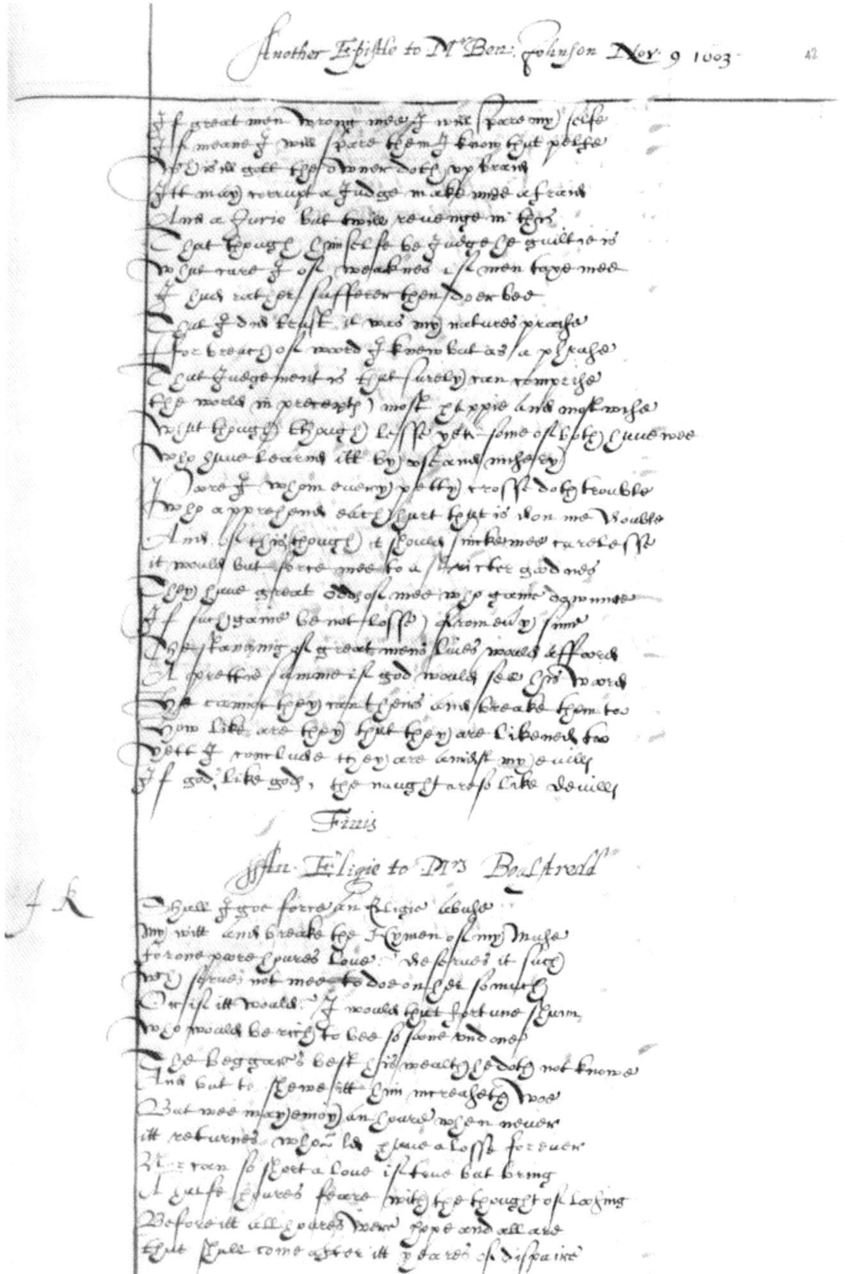
Another Epistle to Mr Ben: Johnson Nov. 9 1603

Finis

An Elegie to Mrs Boulstred

ILLUS. 91 *A page in a verse miscellany (known as the First Dalhousie Manuscript) of sixty-seven folio leaves containing copies of ninety-six poems entered in an accomplished secretary hand, including verses by John Donne, Sir Henry Wotton, Francis Beaumont, Sir John Harington, Sir Walter Ralegh, and others,* c.1620s. *This page contains poems by Sir John Roe dated 1602–3, the first concluding with a formal 'Finis'.*

Malory's *Morte d'Arthur*, William Langland's *Piers Plowman*, and Shakespeare's *King Lear*. A version of a work is not the same thing as a draft, which is a particular type of manuscript or typescript characterized by its status in the composition of the work and, generally, its incompleteness. There may, indeed, be more than one extant draft of a version (*see* DRAFT).

VERSO

The verso side of a leaf or folio, as opposed to the recto, is the back or reverse side, often abbreviated to *v* (e.g fol. 2v). It corresponds to the left-hand page, with an even page number (2, 4, 6, etc.), in a paginated book when laid open. An alternative form of abbreviation for verso is *b* (fol. 1b, fol. 2b, etc.). This system is becoming obsolete, however, partly because confusion arises when intermediate leaves between, say, 1 and 2 might be numbered fol. 1a, fol. 1b, etc.

VESTRY DOCUMENTS

'Vestry documents' is a generic term denoting the records, including minute books of meetings and account books of churchwardens, overseers of the poor, and other local officials, kept by the vestry. The vestry was the governing body of a parish, deriving its name from the room in the church where meetings took place. This body effectively exercised responsibility for local government in the sixteenth and seventeenth centuries following the decline of the feudal manor courts system. Vestry documents are preserved in many local record offices, their prime holders in London being the Guildhall Library, London Metropolitan Archives, and City of Westminster Archives Centre. *See also* CHURCHWARDENS' ACCOUNTS.

VETUS CODEX

See PARLIAMENT ROLLS.

VIGNETTE

Adopted from French, the word 'vignette' denotes a small illustration or ornamental design which is normally part of a blank sheet or of one bearing text, but which is not enclosed within a frame or border, being set only against a blank space on the page. Vignettes may appear in manuscripts, such as letters, notebooks, or travel journals, but otherwise appear in printed books usually at the beginning or end of a chapter. Vignettes may also be printed on formal stationery, whether as decoration or for advertising purposes, such as engravings on some bookplates and cartes-de-visite (*see* Illus. 14), or the views heading much nineteenth- and twentieth-century hotel notepaper.

VIIS ET MODIS

A *viis et modis* (the Latin term means 'by ways and means') is a summons to appear in court which, if the person summoned could not be found by any ways or means, was affixed to his or her doorway. Such a document was often exhibited in court to testify that the summons had been served.

VIRGULE

A common feature of medieval and some early modern manuscripts, a virgule is usually an oblique line or forward-sloping slash (/) being a punctuation mark signifying some kind of pause or break, the equivalent of a comma. The double virgule (//) was a type of paraph and was also used as a full stop. An alternative form of virgule is an upright line (|) sometimes used, following Greek and Latin models, to mark off the caesura (the break within a metrical foot near the middle of the line) in a verse.

VISA

Derived from the Latin meaning 'things seen', the term 'visa', since the nineteenth century, denotes a type of passport, or else a stamped or written entry in a passport, authorizing entry into a particular country.

VISITATION

A visitation is a formal visit of inspection made by a civil or ecclesiastical authority to examine the state of affairs in a particular place.

Ecclesiastical visitations in the Middle Ages and early modern period were made periodically by archdeacons to their archdeaconries and by bishops to their dioceses (technically every one and three years respectively), resulting in a flurry of paperwork before, during, and after the event. A Citation Mandate was sent to each incumbent to be read out in church, summoning all church officials (including churchwardens, parish clerks, schoolmasters, surgeons, and midwives) to appear at a particular time and place, and Visitation Articles were also issued listing the subjects of inquiry. The Visitor would bring with him his Register, Call Book, and Fees Book, in which to record attendances, absences, and fees collected. The clergy would bring their Letters of Orders and related documents proving their clerical credentials. Some of the lay people would bring their licences to practise their craft. Some of the clergy and churchwardens would bring their Presentments, answering the Visitation Articles and reporting on the state of the parish and parishioners' behaviour since the previous visitation. Following the visitation, the Visitor would issue injunctions formally setting out his orders for improvements and, when necessary, imposing penances. Other books would be kept as registers or reference copies of various of these documents and to record the decisions and actions relating to them.

In a heraldic context, between 1530 and 1686 a visitation was an official and periodic visit made by a King of Arms or other deputized herald to a particular area or county in order to examine and enroll the arms and pedigrees of the most prominent families there. Hence the term also denotes the ensuing detailed, systematic, and sometimes lengthy report produced by him or his associates at the College of Arms, or a manuscript copy of it. Notable examples are the county visitations produced by such prominent heralds and antiquaries as William Harvey (Suffolk, 1561), William Camden (Rutland and Warwickshire, 1618–19), Sir Henry St George (Cornwall, Devon, and Wiltshire, 1620–3), and Sir William Dugdale (Derbyshire, Nottinghamshire, etc., 1662–4). These visitations were confined to manuscripts, with limited circulation in their own time, but since the nineteenth century a number have been published, particularly by the Harleian Society. They provide a valuable and frequently unique source of information for local historians, as well as genealogists, although their accuracy is far from reliable when the visiting officials record matters beyond living memory.

VISITING CARD

See CARTE-DE-VISITE.

VISITORS' BOOK

A visitors' book is an album in which visitors to a household, company, guild, factory, exhibition, ship, conference, embassy, institution, or other kind of venue are, or have been, encouraged to sign their names to record their visit. Such books may also be called 'guest books', perhaps especially when the visitors stay or lodge in the house overnight or for a period. Usually accompanied by dates or other comments and inscriptions, they are retained by the host as a souvenir or record of attendance. Visitors' books have been popular in prominent households etc. from the early nineteenth century onwards, and stationers have published blank-leaf albums, with sometimes sturdy or fine leather bindings, designed specifically for this use. It could be a matter of pride to the host if the signatories included celebrated or distinguished persons. Besides throwing light on particular social circles, associated with certain families or great estates, for instance, such books can have some historical interest, or be occasionally valued by collectors in the same way as autograph albums.

VOLVELLE

Derived from a form of the Latin *volvere* ('to turn'), the term 'volvelle' means a kind of revolving wheel sometimes found affixed to pages within certain kinds of medieval manuscripts and early modern manuscript and printed books. Made of one or more concentric movable circles of parchment or paper, with markings yielding variable and usually computational information when the wheels and perhaps particulars on the underlying page are aligned with each other, they are generally of an astronomical or astrological nature, or else devoted to mathematical, geometrical, or navigational matters.

VOUCHER

Etymologically related to the words 'avouch' and 'vouch for', the term 'voucher' denotes a document that attests the correctness of a monetary transaction or of financial accounts, such as a receipt recording the delivery of goods, payments, etc. The archives of family estates are often full of such records, the vouchers being retained as material evidence for accurate account-keeping and fiscal management.

In a lawsuit, a voucher to warranty is one calling on someone else to warrant or vouch for the title in dispute.

W

WADSET

In Scotland from the late Middle Ages onwards, a wadset was a type of conveyance whereby land was transferred to someone to satisfy a debt or obligation, but with the provision that the land was recoverable when the debt was paid off by other means.

WAFER

As a substitute for wax, a wafer, or wafer-seal, is a small disk or medallion of flour mixed with white of egg, gum, gelatine, and colouring matter, which when moistened and applied to paper can be used for sealing folded letters or envelopes. Produced by stationers and especially popular in the late eighteenth and early nineteenth centuries, wafers of this kind usually bore engraved intaglios of classical or other figures in white against a blue or other coloured background. Adhesive paper wafers of various kinds, in disk or butterfly tab form, are still commercially manufactured today (although not used on deeds). As a mode of sealing, wafers date on the continent from at least the early modern period. A monopoly patent for manufacturing such items in England was granted to Matthew Cox in 1635. *Compare* PAPERED SEAL.

WALLET

'Wallet' is a term sometimes used to describe a type of binding in which the back cover of a book, usually of limp vellum or leather, is extended to enclose the fore-edge and to fasten into a slot, buckle, or metal clasp in the front cover. Various kinds of printed books, such as almanacs, can sometimes have wallet bindings, but so also, since medieval times, can manuscript devotional books, notebooks, pocket vademecums, and the like. Bindings of this kind, when the cover is designed to be extended and wrapped around, perhaps with a strap, may sometimes also be called 'satchel bindings'. *See also* HOLSTER BOOK.

WARRANT

'Warrant' is a term applied to various types of written document, including vouchers and receipts. Most commonly, however, a warrant is a document issued by some authority, such as the monarch, Privy Council, or other court, administrative, or judicial body, or by bodies within government administration to one another, conferring on a person some particular authority, or else empowering him to perform a specific act or task, such as make a payment, arrest someone, or conduct a search. *See* Illus. 26 and 82.

WASH

In painting, wash is a thin coat of watercolour paint, or a light watercolour background or filling, which may be applied to a pen and ink drawing. This is a feature often found in illustrated manuscripts, including *libri amicorum*, albums, travel journals, sketchbooks, and sometimes logs.

WASTE BOOK

In commercial or business usage, a waste book, or waste-book, is a manuscript account book in which financial transactions, chiefly payments and receipts, are recorded in a rough or cursory manner just as they occur, with the intention of their being copied or posted more neatly in a more formal account book afterwards. Sir Francis Bacon refers to his keeping certain kinds of commonplace books in similar fashion, 'like a Marchant's wast booke where to enter all maner of remembrance of matter...*without* any maner of restraint', entries that might selectively be recopied in formal 'title bookes' later on. Examples of scriveners' waste books of 1610–17 in the National Archives at Kew (WARD 9/271 and 9/351) take the form of either a large folio volume or else long, narrow ledgers. *See also* DAY BOOKS.

WATCH-BILL

In a naval context, a watch-bill is a formal list of the petty officers, seamen, and marines of a ship of war, which includes details of each man's station and the watch he was appointed to: i.e. when he was on watch or sentinel duty. The watch was traditionally the principal method of organizing work at sea, the procedure involving half the crew taking over every four hours from the other half.

WATERMARK

A watermark is the device or design impressed into a sheet of paper as a result of the manufacturing process. In early papermaking, wires in the tray or mould were twisted into various shapes, the paper produced being thinner where the fibres touched the wires, leaving a design which was visible when the paper was held up to the light. Although certain types of design (such as pillars or posts, bunches of grapes, Strasbourg lilies, and pots and urns: *see* Illus. 92) are so common as to be virtually indistinguishable, watermarks were originally used as trade marks, and many found in early modern paper can denote, or be associated with, particular manufacturers, as well as with particular places and dates. Certain watermarks, such as a foolscap or post horn, were also used to distinguish particular paper sizes. The range of watermark designs in hand-made paper is vast, ranging from simple lettering or geometrical shapes, through figures such as animals, birds, flowers, insects, horns, and croziers, to elaborate beehives, scrollwork, and coats of arms.

In the seventeenth century, papermakers also introduced countermarks, which are smaller additional devices usually set in the half of the sheet opposite to the watermark (*see* COUNTERMARK). In most books and manuscripts, the watermark generally appears in the centre of a folio leaf, in the centre of the inner margin of a quarto leaf, at the top of the inner margin of an octavo leaf, at the top corner of the outer margin of a sextodecimo leaf, and distributed to one or other of the margins in a duodecimo leaf. Although principally associated with laid paper, watermarks were also often incorporated in wove paper, where in early nineteenth-century examples, for instance, the name of the manufacturer and exact year of manufacture are often clearly visible. Modern machine-made paper, especially that used for stationery, may well incorporate similar features.

WATER-STAINING

See DAMP-STAINING.

WAX

The familiar substance we call wax was originally derived from beeswax, was then more commonly a mixture of beeswax with other substances, and later tended to be made from lac or shellac, derived from the incrustations produced by insects on certain trees. Wax is the substance used for the seals attached to legal and official documents since early medieval times, and it sometimes also provided the waxy coating on reusable writing tablets.

ILLUS. 92 *A characteristic urn or pot watermark, of which there were many variants, in early- to mid-seventeenth-century paper.*

WHALING LOG

See LOG.

WILL AND TESTAMENT

A will is a document in which a person (the testator or testatrix) formally declares his or her intention and wishes as to the disposal of his or her property or other desired measures to be taken after his or her death. It may be holograph—i.e. written out entirely in the hand of the testator—or else, much more commonly, written as a formal document by a lawyer, scrivener, notary, or legal clerk on the testator's behalf, and signed by the testator. Often it may also be countersigned by witnesses to the signing. It is not unusual for wills to be signed on behalf of the testator by the lawyer or legal scribe, especially when the testator is on his or her deathbed or too ill to sign in person (hence a mark in such circumstances is not necessarily evidence of the testator's illiteracy), and for it to remain legally valid. A will may be written on either parchment or paper. If drawn up by a lawyer or other professional agent, its text is likely, from medieval times onwards, to be phrased largely in prescribed legal terms and formulae, including phrases such as 'being of sound mind', and with the testator's initial bequest of his or her soul to God and expression of confidence in ultimate resurrection and salvation, or the like. Until 1837, when it became law that wills could be made only by persons aged 21 years or more, they could be made by any male over the age of 14 and any female over the age of 12. Also, until 1882, a married woman could make a will only with the consent of her husband. A person may make more than one will in his or her lifetime, the last superseding all others and being the one put into effect after death. If a person's will or declared intention in such matters is not actually written down, but declared orally to witnesses who will testify to the same, it is said to be nuncupative. If a person leaves no will at all, or one unclear in its intentions, he or she is said to be, or to have died, intestate.

A will and a testament are basically the same thing, except that in earlier times a will tended to be instructions to the testator's trustees for the disposal of real property (there was no direct disposal by will of freehold property except by local custom or through a trust until the Statute of Wills in 1540), while a testament set out the testator's wishes with regard to personal effects and chattels. These might include matters such as legacies to a local church, to charities, or to the poor, the appointment of executors, and instructions as to where his or her body should be buried. The two terms have remained linked, tautologically, in the phrase 'last will and testament'.

Many thousands of wills, from medieval times onwards, survive. Original wills (or copies) retained by the Prerogative Court of Canterbury—the principal probate court in the realm—from 1485 to 1858, are preserved in the National Archives at Kew (chiefly in the PROB 10 series). Many others are in county or other local record offices, among privately owned family papers, or in lawyers' offices (where they are not normally available for inspection without the permission of the families concerned). Although they exist in such huge numbers, are relatively common, and, for the most part, of little commercial value as collectors' items, wills can be among the most useful documentary sources for historians, genealogists, and biographers, as well as, in some cases, providing a rare or unique example of the handwriting or signature of a particular person. Perhaps the most famous original English will in existence is that of William Shakespeare (PROB 1/4, dated 25 March 1616). *See also* PROBATE.

WIND-HEAD

In cartography, a wind-head is a traditional decorative feature, being a graphic depiction of a human head from whose mouth a wind is blown.

WIND-ROSE

In cartography, a wind-rose is basically the same thing as a compass-rose, the numbers of winds marked varying from eight to thirty-two. *See* COMPASS-ROSE.

See MOUNT.

WIRE-LINES

In laid paper, wire-lines are the light, close-set parallel lines, just visible when held up to the light, that run perpendicular to the more pronounced chain-lines (*compare* CHAIN-LINES). They are left in the paper by the wire mesh running the length of the papermaker's tray or mould.

WITNESS

A witness is someone who attests, or gives evidence or testimony to, the truth or facts of something. Thus a witness to a deed, will, or other legal document is a person who signs it to testify or affirm having observed the transaction in question take place, to confirm that the document has actually been signed by the parties concerned, and therefore to validate and authenticate the document. The signing, or countersigning, by the witness is itself termed 'witnessing', a document so signed being 'witnessed'. Witnesses' signatures on wills, deeds, etc. are usually subscribed at the foot of the text or else entered as endorsements on the verso. *See* Illus. 93.

WORKING MANUSCRIPT

'Working manuscript' is a modern term sometimes used to denote a manuscript work or text that is still in progress: i.e. a draft, not yet finished by the author or ready for outside viewing, or alternatively one left or abandoned in that state (*see* Illus. 23 and 28). The term 'working' is also applicable to other types of text that are seen as being used and added to, such as certain promptbooks (*see* Illus. 68).

WORMHOLE

Besides bacteria and fungus, there are many living organisms that prey upon books and manuscripts. A not uncommon sight is volumes that have been gnawed at some time for food by mice or rats, and their bodies have even been found in attics wrapped in leaves of old manuscripts which have served as their shrouds. No predator is more common, however, than book-worms—maggots or larvae of various species, often laid in books as eggs—which eat their way through paper leaving narrow, elongated holes across leaves or through whole books.

Though universally reviled by librarians and book collectors, book-worms are, however, very occasionally useful in that the holes they leave

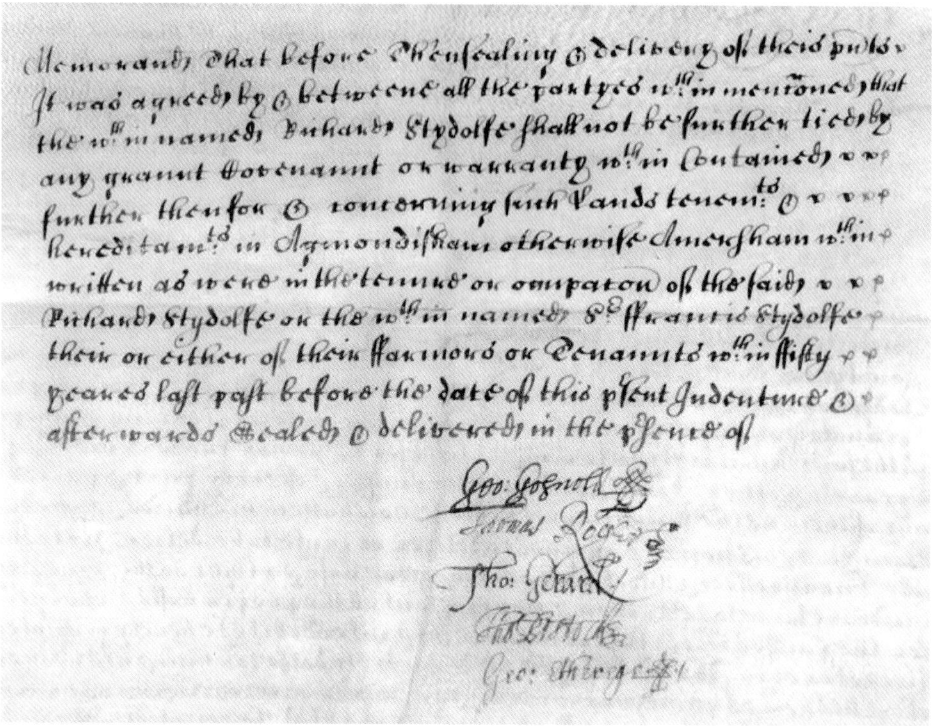

Memorandum that before thensealing & delivery of theis pnts
It was agreed by & betweene all the partyes wthin mentioned that
the wthin named Richard Stydolfe shall not be further tied by
any graunt Covenant or warranty wthin conteined
further then for & concerning such Lands tenemts &
hereditamts in Agmondisham otherwise Amersham wthin
written as were in the tenure or occupation of the said
Richard Stydolfe or the wthin named Sr ffrancis Stydolfe
their or either of their ffarmors or Tenants wthin fifty
yeares last past before the date of this pnt Indenture &
afterwards Sealed & delivered in the presence of

Geo: Gosnold
Tho: Gerard
Geo: Etherege

ILLUS. 93 *The formal 'memorandum', or attestation clause, on the back of a vellum indenture for the sale of a manor in Amersham, Buckinghamshire, 1 November 1657. It was written by a law clerk and bears the signatures of five witnesses, including the 21-year-old future playwright George Etherege, who was then apprenticed as an articled clerk to the attorney George Gosnold in Beaconsfield.*

can provide clues as to the composition of an unpaginated book or quire that has since been broken up in some way. The leaves may perhaps be re-assembled in the correct order by aligning the wormholes in them, or else the wormhole may show which leaf was once adjacent to, or conjugate with, another. Such a feature has been used as material evidence, for instance, in arguments for the authenticity of the long-disputed Vinland Map (now at Yale University, MS 350A), which purports to date from the mid-fifteenth century and to prove that the Vikings discovered America before Columbus. The pattern of wormholes shows that the map was once bound with two other contemporary manuscripts whose authenticity is not in doubt.

See SCRIVENERS' COMPANY.

WOVE PAPER

Wove paper is smooth paper made on a fine mesh or screen of wires woven together, as distinct from laid paper, which is hand-made and bears chain-lines and wire-lines. The process of making wove paper was invented in 1756, being first manufactured by James Whatman (1702–1759). The first printed book to use it, at least for some of its pages, was John Baskerville's 1757 edition of Virgil's *Bucolica, Georgica et Aeneis*. From about 1800 onwards, this type of paper predominated. Some modern wove paper can be mistaken for laid paper in so far as it may bear what seem to be chain-lines and wire-lines, but are so only by virtue of artificial imitation. *Compare* LAID PAPER.

WRAPPER

A wrapper is a book cover made of paper or, with earlier manuscript volumes, of parchment, as distinct from the usual binding of boards, cloth, leather, etc. Wrappers—plain, lettered, or pictorial—have traditionally served as covers on relatively thin or ephemeral printed publications, such as pamphlets and magazines, but are also found on earlier manuscript separates, usually formed of stiff grey paper or the like. A wrapper is usually sewn, glued, or otherwise attached, therefore forming an integral part of the book or pamphlet.

The term is sometimes also applied to a sheet of paper of some kind loosely wrapped around the pamphlet as a protection. In this case, it is more properly a dust-wrapper. In a postal context, a wrapper is a sheet or strip of paper enclosing a letter or packet for delivery.

WRAPPING PAPER

Wrapping paper, used to wrap around food or other things, is a common household item. In earlier times, it could take the form of any kind of ephemeral paper material that happened to come to hand, so that wrapping paper can sometimes prove more interesting. Although not as rich a source of discoveries as binders' waste (*see* BINDERS' WASTE), paper used centuries ago to wrap bundles of documents in particular archives have yielded literary manuscripts such as the Melbourne fragment of a Jacobean tragedy (*see* Illus. 28) and, elsewhere, a complete text of William Cartwright's Oxford play *The Royal Slave* (1636).

Since medieval times, a writ was a written order or warrant issued in the name of the sovereign. Following receipt of a complaint by a plaintiff, an original writ (authorized writ originating an action), known in Latin as a *breve*, was issued in the monarch's name by the Chancery and generally addressed to a sheriff. Written in Latin on thin strips of parchment and usually sealed in wax with the tip of the Great Seal, early examples of writs in general, for which suitors would always be charged a fee, also technically included letters patent (for public commissions) and letters close (sealed instructions to individuals). They could serve a variety of purposes, but their principal function was to allow access to the process of justice as a prerequisite to litigation at one of the superior courts at Westminster.

Some types of writ made in the form of executive commands, associated especially with reviews by the superior courts of cases and procedures in inferior courts, were known as 'prerogative writs'. Another species of original writ, commanding a sheriff to do something to restore a plaintiff's right, was called a 'praecipe writ' (the Latin *præcipe* meaning 'command', or *præcipimus*, 'we command'). What were called 'judicial writs' could also be issued to sheriffs by King's courts, under their own seal, after they had acquired jurisdiction over the particular matter when the original writ was returned to them by the sheriff. The official clerk responsible for filing original writs in the Common Pleas was known as the Keeper of the Writs or *Custos Brevium*. Because of their fundamental importance in this regard, and not least because, in any subsequent litigation, writs had to be followed to the letter and within fixed procedural frameworks, manuscript collections were made of the forms of Chancery writs to be used as models, one or more versions recorded about 1227 being known as the 'Register of Writs' (*see* REGISTRUM BREVIUM). In more modern times, until 1980, writs were still being issued in the name of the sovereign, ordering particular things to be done, but the term 'writ' is no longer in use, being replaced by what is now called a 'claim form'.

Until steps were taken by 1833 to create a uniformity of writ, numerous species of writ developed over the centuries, each defining a particular action. Each was generally known by Latin words incorporated in its particular Latin formulaic opening. A few examples are:

Writ of attachment: for the arrest of a person or seizing of property.

Writ of certiorari (the Latin meaning 'to be informed'): issued by a superior court, notably the King's Bench, ordering another court, usually inferior, to supply information on a case by way of certification or so that the proceedings in a case might be taken over by the superior court.

Writ of covenant: alleging breach of a covenant by one party to it.

Writ of elegit (the Latin meaning 'he has chosen'): ordering the seizure of a moiety (half) of a debtor's land and all his goods, except for oxen and beasts of the plough, towards satisfying a creditor until the debt was paid off. The seizure was extended to all the debtor's land in 1838.

Writ of exigent or exigend (the Latin *exigere* meaning 'to demand' or 'call on'): commanding a sheriff to summon a defendant indicted of felony, who had failed to appear in court, to deliver himself up upon pain of outlawry or forfeiture of his goods, the exaction concerned being the proclamation in the county court calling for the defendant to come in.

Writ of fieri facias (the Latin meaning 'may you cause to be made' and usually abbreviated to 'fi.fa.'): ordering the seizure of chattels so that money could be raised from someone against whom a court judgment had been made.

Writ of habeas corpus ad subjiciendum (the Latin meaning 'may you have the body brought forth'): a prerogative writ issued originally by the King's Bench and other courts, ordering a gaoler to produce a prisoner in person and explain the cause of his detention so that the court might decide whether it was justified or not. This reflected what has traditionally been viewed as a basic principle of natural justice, a freeman's right dating back to early medieval times, being a safeguard against illegal or arbitrary imprisonment.

Writ of latitat (the Latin meaning 'he is in hiding'): issued by the King's Bench since the fifteenth century ordering the arrest and bringing to court of a defendant supposedly 'lurking' in a county outside Middlesex; abolished in 1832.

Writ of mandamus (the Latin meaning 'we command'): a prerogative writ issued by the King's Bench since the early seventeenth century principally as a means of protecting those deprived of public office by borough or city authorities; used more widely in the twentieth century to compel possibly dilatory public officers or courts to perform their statutory duties or exercise their proper jurisdiction in some matter.

Writ of mittimus (the Latin meaning 'we send'): sending a record or summary thereof from one court to another; also sometimes one commanding a gaoler to receive or keep in safe custody someone who was to answer to a criminal charge.

Writ of præmunire (the Latin meaning 'to fortify or protect in front', but confused with the medieval Latin *præmonere*, to 'warn', 'admonish'): originally instructing a sheriff to order someone to appear in court to answer for contempt, but subsequently applied to the prosecution of a wide range of offences, particularly those prompting protection of royal rights of jurisdiction. Notable examples include præmunires issued by Richard II and Henry VIII prohibiting certain practices enjoined or supported by the Pope that were felt to impinge on the monarch's interests.

Writ of prohibition (the Latin *prohibere* meaning 'to forbid'): a prerogative writ halting proceedings in a court on the grounds that the case does not properly belong to it.

Writ of subpœna (the Latin *subpœna* meaning 'under penalty'): a *subpœna ad respondendum* was in medieval times a writ issued by the Chancery ordering a defendant to appear and answer charges to a bill of complaint. More generally later, a subpœna is one commanding someone to appear in court, subject to penalty for failure to comply, to give evidence or testimony on oath. A *subpœna ad testificandum* ('under penalty to exhibit') might be issued when the recipient was required to give evidence, and a *subpœna duces tecum* ('under penalty you should bring with you') when the recipient was required to bring to court relevant documents for examination.

Writ of summons: commanding an appearance in court or else summoning a peer to attend parliament.

Writ of supersedeas (the Latin meaning 'you shall desist'): halting particular legal proceedings previously authorized, or suspending the powers of an officer.

Writ of venire facias (the Latin meaning 'cause to come'): summoning a jury.

WRITER

A writer, as commonly understood today, is an author or anyone who writes anything in the sense of producing an original verbal composition. Before the nineteenth century, the term 'writer' would have denoted more specifically a professional clerk who was employed in office work, to make copies or written records or entries of some kind. In Scotland, 'writer' might also mean a Writer to the Signet (known by the initials 'W. S.'): i.e. a member of the oldest and leading Scottish society of solicitors.

For medieval and early modern Writers of the Court Letter and Writers of the Text Letter, *see* SCRIVENER.

WRITING

Writing in general is the practice of creating text by virtue of the formation of words: hence the text so produced, in whatever form it may take. 'Writing' may denote more specifically text produced by hand with the use of pen, pencil, or other hand-held implement on a writing surface, as distinct from lettering produced by a mechanical process such as printing, typewriting, or electronic reproduction.

Although various types of portable writing cases and holders developed from medieval times onwards, the writing box as a piece of furniture dates principally from the sixteenth century and became particularly fashionable in the eighteenth and nineteenth centuries. Writing boxes took the form of a relatively shallow polished wooden box, sometimes with lined compartments and a brass handle and lock, with a sloping lid to provide a writing surface. Some early writing boxes could, by contrast, be very much more elaborate and gilded: e.g. one probably made by Henry VIII's limner Lucas Hornebolte, c.1525–7 (now in the Victoria and Albert Museum). Such boxes would be capable of being set down on a flat table, or else perhaps rested on the lap when travelling.

The typical early nineteenth-century type would be covered in morocco or other leather and contain interior trays or compartments for holding pens, inkwells, paper, wax, and other writing materials. Well-known writers who used writing boxes, some of which are still preserved, include Jane Austen (who nearly lost one, containing all her 'worldly wealth, £7', when she accidentally left it in a chaise in 1798), the Brontë sisters, and Charles Dickens (*see* Illus. 94). Writing boxes used by Lord Nelson and his mistress Lady Hamilton are also preserved.

ILLUS. 94 *A travelling writing box owned by Charles Dickens, made of fruitwood, the top flaps opening to reveal an angled leather-covered writing slope, with compartments for pens, inkwells, etc.*

Derived from the Latin *manus* ('hand'), the term 'manual' means a handbook compiled or kept for ready reference. A writing manual is specifically one setting out forms and examples of handwriting, usually in different styles or scripts, as models of good or beautiful writing. Often with accompanying practical instructions, on how to cut or hold a pen, etc., such manuals were intended for guidance or imitation. They bear witness to a considerable demand for practical help in the formation of handwriting, and possibly for some measure of standardization, as an aid both to education and to social advancement. Some manuals, whether by writing masters or amateurs, are effectively a series of proudly executed calligraphic exercises (*see* Illus. 95). They are found in both printed and manuscript form from the sixteenth century onwards. What was effectively the first printed writing manual was Sigismondo Fanti's *Theorica et pratica* (Venice, 1514), the first in England being John de Beau Chesne and John Baildon's *A Booke Containing Divers Sortes of Hands* (1570).

ILLUS. 95 *A page in a manuscript writing manual of 1684, an oblong octavo book comprising a series of alphabetically arranged calligraphic exercises, bearing the ownership inscriptions 'A Coppy, Book Written, by me, Tho, Nickallson, ffeb, 21. anno, Domini,* MDCLXXXIV' *and 'Nathaniell Wells eius liber; Anno. Aprill, 14, 1684'. This page illustrates the letter* C, *which is an engrossed and decorated initial letter to a moralistic text, incorporating heavily inked strapwork and a depiction of Adam and Eve with the Serpent in the Tree of Knowledge, with other foliate motifs, decorative borders, and a spiral flourish.*

A writing master, especially in the early modern period, was an expert and usually professional penman, capable of producing highly accomplished calligraphic writing in various styles and of giving instructions in the art of fine writing to others. Some early writing masters, in sixteenth-century Italy, were attached to the Papal Chancery; others were attached to royal courts, such as the appropriately named Jean Belmain, who instructed the young Edward VI and his sister the future Elizabeth I (*see* Illus. 54), or Martin Billingsley, who instructed the future Charles I. Writing masters flourished far more widely in society at large, however, and there were even public contests in the profession: e.g. that in London in 1595, before a crowd of nearly a hundred onlookers and five judges between Peter Bales and Daniel Johnston for the prize of a golden pen (Bales won). Neither was instruction in writing the exclusive preserve of men. Besides the remarkable work of the calligrapher Esther Inglis (*see* Illus. 12), calligraphic exercise books can be found, for instance, by Sarah Cole in 1685 and Mary Serjant in 1688, each of whom describes herself as 'Scholler' (pupil) to Elizabeth Bean or Beane, '*Mistre*ss in the Art of Writing and Arithmetick' (Folger Shakespeare Library, MS V. b. 292, and Yale University, Osborn MS fb 98).

WRITING SLOPE

A writing slope, sometimes called simply a 'slope', is a type of portable writing box, only smaller, thinner, more delicate, and lacking interior compartments. Such slopes, made of wood, were commonly used by ladies for private correspondence. In a more general sense, various types of furniture, such as certain bureaux and chests of drawers, might be said to incorporate a writing slope in the form of a possibly hinged writing surface that could be pulled down or opened up for writing on. Various types of sloping surfaces, resting on desks or tables and used for reading or writing purposes, are shown in illustrations of scribes and writers from medieval times onwards, and may also be described as writing slopes.

WRITING TABLE

See DESK.

WRITING TABLES

See TABLES.

See TABLET.

WRITTEN

When texts, books, or documents are described in the early modern period as 'written', it means simply written by hand as opposed to printed. Some wills, for instance (such as that of the Suffolk draper Thomas Fella in 1639), specify bequests of 'written bookes' of the testator's 'owne writing' and distinguish between 'bookes and written bookes'.

Y

YEAR BOOKS

In a legal context, what are known generically as 'Year Books' are compilations of law reports, being accounts of procedural matters in actual common law cases, highlighting the judges' and counsel's debates and formulation of the points at issue, although not the decisions or reasons for judgments. Made probably by clerks or law students, who exchanged notes, and originally written in Anglo-French, they served as guides for subsequent pleaders and were subject over the years to extensive recopying in manuscript form. These compilations, which from the 1290s were arranged by law terms, flourished from about the mid-thirteenth century onwards. Printed Year Books flourished from *c*.1481 until *c*.1545 (for 1535).

Select Bibliography

I am, inevitably of course, indebted to the *Oxford English Dictionary* for guidance on many terms cited here. I have also picked up information from a host of other printed sources, in addition to what I have gleaned from my own work on manuscripts over a period of three decades. Consequently, no attempt is made here to give a comprehensive record of every publication in any way consulted for, or relevant to, the present dictionary. The following is offered only as a small selective list of some of the publications that might be useful to readers wishing to explore further particular subjects and their terminology or wishing to find facsimile examples of certain types of manuscript.

Alchemy
Lyndy Abraham, *A Dictionary of Alchemical Imagery* (Cambridge, 1998; repr. 2001)
Almanacs
Bernard Capp, *English Almanacs 1500–1800* (Ithaca, NY, 1979)
Archives
Christopher Kitching, *Archives: The Very Essence of our Heritage* (Chichester, 1996)
Autograph albums and *libri amicorum*
M. A. E. Nickson, *Early Autograph Albums in the British Museum* (British Museum, London, 1970)
Baga de Secretis
L. W. Vernon Harcourt, 'The Baga de Secretis', *English Historical Review*, 23 (1908), pp. 508–29
Bibliography and textual criticism
Fredson Bowers, *Bibliography and Textual Criticism* (Oxford, 1964)
John Carter, *ABC for Book Collectors* (1952), 8th edn rev. Nicolas Barker (London, 2004)
Philip Gaskell, *A New Introduction to Bibliography* (Oxford, 1972)

Geoffrey Ashall Glaister, *Encyclopedia of the Book* (1996), 2nd edn with introduction
  by Donald Farren (New Castle, DE, and London, 2001)
Ronald B. McKerrow, *An Introduction to Bibliography for Literary Students* (Oxford,
  1927; repr. 1972)

Binding
Jane Greenfield, *ABC of Bookbinding* (New Castle, DE, and Nottingham, 2002)

Cartes-de-visite
F. C. Schang, *Visiting Cards of Celebrities*, 2nd edn (Paris, 1973)

Collectors
Seymour De Ricci, *English Collectors of Books & Manuscripts (1530–1930) and their
  Marks of Ownership* (New York, 1930; repr. 1969)

Commonplace books
Peter Beal, 'Notions in Garrison: The Seventeenth-Century Commonplace Book',
  in *New Ways of Looking at Old Texts*, ed. W. Speed Hill (Binghamton, NY, 1993),
  pp. 131–47
Earl Havens, *Commonplace Books: A History of Manuscripts and Printed Books from
  Antiquity to the Twentieth Century* (Yale University, New Haven, CT, 2001)
Ann Moss, *Printed Commonplace-Books and the Structuring of Renaissance Thought*
  (Oxford, 1996)

Conservation
Jane Greenfield, *The Care of Fine Books* (Guilford, CT, 1988)

Cursitor
Christopher Kitching, 'The Cursitors' Office (1573–1813) and the Corporation of the
  Cursitors of Chancery', *Journal of the Society of Archivists*, 7, no. 2 (October 1982),
  pp. 78–84

Dates
C. R. Cheney, *A Handbook of Dates for Students of British History* (1945), rev. Michael
  Jones (Cambridge, 2000)

Diplomacy
Peter Barber, *Diplomacy: The World of the Honest Spy* (British Library, 1979)

Drama and theatre
W. W. Greg, *Dramatic Documents from the Elizabethan Playhouses: Stage Plots,
  Actors' Parts, Prompt Books*, 2 vols (Oxford, 1931)
Grace Ioppolo, *Dramatists and their Manuscripts in the Age of Shakespeare, Jonson,
  Middleton and Heywood: Authorship, Authority and the Playhouse* (Abingdon and
  New York, 2006)
Edward A Langhans, *Restoration Promptbooks* (Carbondale and Edwardsville, IL,
  1981)
Edward A. Langhans, *Eighteenth Century British and Irish Promptbooks: A Descrip-
  tive Bibliography* (London and New York, 1988)

Charles H. Shattuck, *The Shakespeare Promptbooks: A Descriptive Catalogue* (Urbana and London, 1965) [and see also his 'The Shakespeare Promptbooks: First Supplement', *Theatre Notebook*, 24, no. 1 (October 1969 – July 1970), pp. 5–17]

Joel Trapido, Edward A. Langhans, James R. Brandon, and June V. Gibson (eds), *An International Dictionary of Theatre Language* (Westport, CT, and London, 1985)

Editing manuscripts

P. D. A. Harvey, *Editing Historical Records* (British Library, London, 2001)

Michael Hunter, *Editing Early Modern Texts: An Introduction to Principles and Practice* (Basingstoke and New York, 2007)

Footnote

Anthony Grafton, *The Footnote: A Curious History* (Cambridge, MA, 1997)

Forgery

Alfred Hiatt, *The Making of Medieval Forgeries: False Documents in Fifteenth-Century England* (London and Toronto, 2004)

Genealogy

Terrick V. H. FitzHugh, *The Dictionary of Genealogy* (1985), 5th edn rev. Susan Lumas (London, 1998)

Graffiti

Juliet Fleming, *Graffiti and the Writing Arts of Early Modern England* (London, 2001)

Handwriting and palaeography

W. S. B. Buck, *Examples of Handwriting 1550–1650* (1965)

Giles E. Dawson and Laetitia Kennedy-Skipton, *Elizabethan Handwriting 1500–1650: A Manual* (New York, 1966)

Alfred Fairbank and Bruce Dickins, *The Italic Hand in Tudor Cambridge* (London, 1962)

A. J. Fairbank and R. W. Hunt, *Humanistic Script of the Fifteenth and Sixteenth Centuries* (1960; repr. Oxford, 1993)

Hilary Jenkinson, *The Later Court Hands in England from the Fifteenth to the Seventeenth Century*, 2 vols (Cambridge, 1927)

Jean F. Preston and Laetitia Yeandle, *English Handwriting 1400–1650: An Introductory Manual* (Binghamton, NY, 1992)

Heather Wolfe, *"The Pen's Excellencie"* (Folger Shakespeare Library, Washington DC, 2002)

Heraldry

Thomas Woodcock and John Martin Robinson, *The Oxford Guide to Heraldry* (Oxford, 1988)

C. E. Wright, *English Heraldic Manuscripts in the British Library* (British Museum, London, 1973)

Historical documents

Elizabeth Hallam and Andrew Prescott (eds), *The British Inheritance: A Treasury of Historic Documents* (British Library and Public Record Office, London, 1999)

Andrew Prescott, *English Historical Documents* (British Library, London, 1988)

Vincent Wilson Jr, *The Book of Great American Documents*, 3rd edn (Brookeville, MD, 1998)

Illuminated manuscripts

Michelle P. Brown, *Understanding Illuminated Manuscripts: A Guide to Technical Terms* (London, 1994)

Indulgences and letters of confraternity

R. N. Swanson, 'Letters of Confraternity and Indulgences in Late Medieval England', *Archives*, 25, no. 1 (April 2000), pp. 40–57

Jousting and imprese

Sydney Anglo, 'Archives of the English Tournament: Score Cheques and Lists', *Journal of the Society of Archivists*, 2 (1960–4), pp. 153–62

Alan R. Young, *The English Tournament Imprese* (New York, 1988)

Latin

Janet Morris, *A Latin Glossary for Family and Local Historians* (Birmingham, 1989; repr. 1990)

Law

J. H. Baker, *An Introduction to English Legal History*, 4th edn (London, 2002)

Elizabeth A. Martin (ed.), *A Dictionary of Law*, 5th edn (Oxford, 2003)

David M. Walker, *The Oxford Companion to Law* (Oxford, 1980)

Letters and letterbooks

A. R. Braunmuller, *A Seventeenth-Century Letter-Book: A Facsimile Edition of Folger MS. V. a. 321* (Newark, DE, London, and Toronto, 1983)

Pedro Corrêa do Lago, *True to the Letter: 800 Years of Remarkable Correspondence, Documents and Autographs* (London, 2004)

A. N. L. Munby, *The Cult of the Autograph Letter in England* (London, 1962)

Alan Stewart and Heather Wolfe, *Letterwriting in Renaissance England* (Folger Shakespeare Library, Washington, DC, 2004)

Peter C. Sutton, *et al.*, *Love Letters: Dutch Genre Paintings in the Age of Vermeer* (Bruce Museum, Greenwich, CT, and National Gallery of Ireland, Dublin, 2003)

Literary manuscripts

P. J. Croft, *Autograph Poetry in the English Language: Facsimiles of Original Manuscripts from the Fourteenth to the Twentieth Century*, 2 vols (London, 1973)

Chris Fletcher, *1000 Years of English Literature: A Treasury of Literary Manuscripts* (British Library, London, [2000])

Desmond Flower and A. N. L. Munby, *English Poetical Autographs* (London, etc., 1938)

W. W. Greg, *et al.*, *English Literary Autographs, 1550–1650*, 3 vols (Oxford, 1925–32)

Hilton Kelliher and Sally Brown, *English Literary Manuscripts* (British Library, London, 1986)

Anthony G. Petti, *English Literary Hands from Chaucer to Dryden* (London, 1977)

Manicule

William H. Sherman, *Toward a History of the Manicule* (posted on the internet March 2005)

Manorial papers and muniments

Joy Bristow, *The Local Historian's Glossary of Words and Terms* (1990), 3rd edn (Newbury, 2001)

F. G. Emmison, *How to Read Local Archives 1550–1700* (London, 1973; repr. 1988)

Marginalia and printers' markings

H. J. Jackson, *Marginalia: Readers Writing in Books* (New Haven, CT, 2001)

J. K. Moore, *Primary Materials Relating to Copy and Print in English Books of the Sixteenth and Seventeenth Centuries* (Oxford, 1992)

Roger E. Stoddard, *Marks in Books, Illustrated and Explained* (Cambridge, MA, 1985)

Notaries and scriveners

C. W. Brooks, R. H. Helmholz, and P. G. Stein, *Notaries Public in England since the Reformation* (London, 1991)

John Craig, 'Margaret Spitlehouse, Female Scrivener', *Local Population Studies*, 46 (1991), pp. 54–7

Francis W. Steer, *Scriveners' Company Common Paper 1357–1628 with a Continuation to 1678* (London, 1968)

Francis W. Steer, *A History of the Worshipful Company of Scriveners of London* (London and Chichester, 1973)

Pencil

Henry Petroski, *The Pencil: A History of Design and Circumstance* (New York, 1992)

Philately and postal history

Philip Beal, *A History of the Post in England from the Romans to the Stuarts* (Aldershot, 1998)

James Mackay, *Philatelic Terms Illustrated* (London and Ringwood, 2003)

Provenance

David Pearson, *Provenance Research in Book History: A Handbook* (London, 1994; repr. 1998)

Public records

Guide to the Contents of the Public Record Office, 3 vols (London, 1963–8)

R. B. Wernham, 'The Public Records in the Sixteenth and Seventeenth Centuries', in *English Historical Scholarship in the Sixteenth and Seventeenth Centuries*, ed. Levi Fox (London, 1956), pp. 11–30

An extensive series of Browsing Leaflets and Research Guides to numerous subjects and categories of Public Records are also posted on the National Archives internet website (www.nationalarchives.gov.uk)

Scribes and scribal publication

Peter Beal, *In Praise of Scribes: Manuscripts and their Makers in Seventeenth-Century England* (Oxford, 1998)

Harold Love, *Scribal Publication in Seventeenth-Century England* (Oxford, 1993)

P. R. Robinson, 'A Twelfth-Century *Scriptrix* from Nunnaminster', in *Of the Making of Books: Medieval Manuscripts, their Scribes and Readers: Essays Presented to M. B. Parkes*, ed. P. R. Robinson and Rivkah Zim (Aldershot, *c*.1997), pp. 73–93

H. R. Woudhuysen, *Sir Philip Sidney and the Circulation of Manuscripts 1558–1640* (Oxford, 1996)

Scrimshaw
Charles R. Meyer, *Whaling and the Art of Scrimshaw* (New York, 1976)

Signal books
Barrie Kent, *Signal: A History of Signalling in the Royal Navy* (Clanfield, [1993])

Tables
Peter Stallybrass, Roger Chartier, J. Franklin Mowery, and Heather Wolfe, 'Hamlet's Tables and the Technologies of Writing in Renaissance England', *Shakespeare Quarterly*, 55, no. 4 (Winter 2004), pp. 379–419

Textual communities and coteries
Claude J. Summers and Ted-Larry Pebworth (eds), *Literary Circles and Cultural Communities in Renaissance England* (Columbia, MO, [2000])

Title deeds
Julian Cornwall, *Reading Old Title Deeds* (1994), 2nd edn (Birmingham, 1997)

Verse miscellanies
Mary Hobbs, *Early Seventeenth-Century Verse Miscellany Manuscripts* (Aldershot, 1992)

Watermarks
C. M. Briquet, *Les Filigranes: The New Briquet*. Jubilee edn, ed. Allan Stevenson, 4 vols (Amsterdam, 1968)

Edward Heawood, *Watermarks Mainly of the 17th and 18th Centuries* (Hilversum, 1950; repr. 1969)

Daniel W. Mosser, Michael Saffle, and Ernest W. Sullivan II (eds), *Puzzles in Paper: Concepts in Historical Watermarks* (British Library, London, 2000)

Writing implements
Michael Finlay, *Western Writing Implements in the Age of the Quill Pen* (Carlisle, 1990)

Joyce Irene Whalley, *Writing Implements & Accessories from the Roman Stylus to the Typewriter* (Newton Abbot and London, 1975; repr. 1980)

Writing manuals (printed)
Ambrose Heal, *The English Writing-Masters and their Copy-Books 1570–1800* (Hildesheim, 1962)